Contemporary Environmental Politics

This new collection presents an overview of the key themes found in contemporary green political thought, especially the industrialized nations.

Bringing together *Environmental Politics'* leading articles since the early 1990s, this new book charts a fascinating period in which environmental politics developed from a marginal position in society and the academy, to its current place in the intellectual mainstream.

Subdivided into clear sections on political theory, social movements, political economy and policy questions, and assisted by a contextualising introduction, this volume focuses on a set of major themes:

- the character of green political theory;
- relationships with other political traditions and theories;
- origins and dynamics of contemporary environmental politics;
- differences, similarities and tensions between the North and South;
- the relationship of environmentalism to market economics and ecological modernisation;
- environmental aspects of distributive justice at the local, national and global levels;
- the roles, value and valuing of nature in green theory and institutional practice.

As a compilation, this book is unique. It delivers a snapshot of a whole variety of issues in the field and is therefore suited to teaching purposes, especially at postgraduate level. In addition, as each section is chronologically arranged, an evolution of related ideas can be clearly seen and appreciated, which builds an excellent understanding of the field of environmental politics.

Piers H.G. Stephens is Assistant Professor in environmental philosophy at Lyman Briggs School, Michigan State University, USA.

John Barry is Acting Director at the Institute of Governance, Public Policy and Social Research, Queen's University Belfast, UK.

Andrew Dobson is Professor and Research Coordinator at the Open University, UK.

Environmental Politics/Routledge Research in Environmental Politics

Edited by Matthew Paterson
University of Ottawa

Graham Smith
University of Southampton

Over recent years environmental politics has moved from a peripheral interest to a central concern within the discipline of politics. This series aims to reinforce this trend through the publication of books that investigate the nature of contemporary environmental politics and show the centrality of environmental politics to the study of politics per se. The series understands politics in a broad sense, and books will focus on mainstream issues such as the policy process and new social movements as well as emerging areas such as cultural politics and political economy. Books in the series will analyse contemporary political practices with regards to the environment and/or explore possible future directions for the 'greening' of contemporary politics. The series will be of interest not only to academics and students working in the environmental field but will also demand to be read within the broader discipline.

The series consists of two strands:

Environmental Politics addresses the needs of students and teachers, and the titles will be published in paperback and hardback. Titles include:

Global Warming and Global Politics
Matthew Paterson

Politics and the Environment
James Connelly and Graham Smith

International Relations Theory and Ecological Thought
Towards synthesis
Eric Laferrière and Peter Stoett

Planning Sustainability
Edited by Michael Kenny and James Meadowcroft

Deliberative Democracy and the Environment
Graham Smith

EU Enlargement and the Environment
Institutional change and environmental policy in Central and Eastern Europe
Edited by JoAnn Carmin and Stacy D. VanDeveer

Routledge Research in Environmental Politics presents innovative new research intended for high-level specialist readership. These titles are published in hardback only and include:

1 **The Emergence of Ecological Modernisation**
Integrating the environment and the economy?
Stephen C. Young

2 **Ideas and Actions in the Green Movement**
Brian Doherty

3 **Russia and the West**
Environmental cooperation and conflict
Geir Hønneland

4 **Global Warming and East Asia**
The domestic and international politics of climate change
Edited by Paul G. Harris

5 **Europe, Globalization and Sustainable Development**
Edited by John Barry, Brian Baxter and Richard Dunphy

6 **The Politics of GM Food**
A comparative study of the UK, USA and EU
Dave Toke

7 **Environmental Policy in Europe**
The Europeanization of national environmental policy
Edited by Andrew Jordan and Duncan Liefferink

8 **A Theory of Ecological Justice**
Brian Baxter

9 **Security and Climate Change**
International relations and the limits of realism
Mark J. Lacy

10 **The Environment and International Politics**
International fisheries, Heidegger and social method
Hakan Seckinelgin

11 **Postmodern Climate Change**
Leigh Glover

12 **Contemporary Environmental Politics**
From margins to mainstream
Edited by Piers H.G. Stephens with John Barry and Andrew Dobson

Contemporary Environmental Politics

From margins to mainstream

Edited by
Piers H.G. Stephens
with John Barry and Andrew Dobson

Routledge
Taylor & Francis Group

LONDON AND NEW YORK

First published 2006
by Routledge
2 Park Square, Milton Park, Abingdon, Oxon OX14 4RN

Simultaneously published in the USA and Canada
by Routledge
270 Madison Ave, New York, NY 10016

Routledge is an imprint of the Taylor & Francis Group, an informa business

© 2006 Piers H.G. Stephens with John Barry and Andrew Dobson for
selection and editorial matter; individual contributors, their contributions

Typeset in Times New Roman by
Newgen Imaging Systems (P) Ltd, Chennai, India
Printed and bound in Great Britain by
Biddles Ltd, King's Lynn

British Library Cataloguing in Publication Data
A catalogue record for this book is available from the British Library

Library of Congress Cataloging in Publication Data
A catalog record for this book has been requested

ISBN10: 0–415–39155–5
ISBN13: 978–0–415–39155–9

Contents

List of figures   ix
List of tables   xi
Notes on contributors   xiii
Preface by the series editors   xvii
Acknowledgements   xix

1 **Introduction**   1

PART I
Theory   9

2 **The high ground is green**   11
   ROBERT E. GOODIN

3 **Social ecology and 'the man question'**   18
   ARIEL SALLEH

4 **Green liberalisms: nature, agency and the good**   32
   PIERS H.G. STEPHENS

5 **Habermas and green political thought: two roads converging**   52
   ROBERT J. BRULLE

PART II
Green movements   71

6 **Why did New Zealand and Tasmania spawn the
   world's first green parties?**   73
   STEPHEN L. RAINBOW

7 **Environmentalism and the global divide**   94
   ERIC LAFERRIÈRE

8 **Strategies of resistance at the Pollok Free State
   road protest camp**   114
   BEN SEEL

PART III
Green political economy   143

9 **Free market environmentalism: friend or foe?**   145
   ROBYN ECKERSLEY

10 **Public choice, institutional economics,
    environmental goods**   160
    JOHN O'NEILL

11 **Ecological modernisation, Ecological modernities**   179
    PETER CHRISTOFF

PART IV
Policy   201

12 **Power, politics and environmental inequality: a
    theoretical and empirical analysis of the process of
    'peripheralisation'**   203
    ANDREW BLOWERS AND PIETER LEROY

13 **The Global Environment Facility in its
    North–South context**   231
    JOYEETA GUPTA

14 **Explaining national variations of air pollution levels:
    political institutions and their impact on
    environmental policy-making**   254
    MARKUS M.L. CREPAZ

15 **Citizens' juries and valuing the environment: a proposal**   276
    HUGH WARD

    Index   297

Figures

9.1   Orientational axes of green economics vs free
market environmentalism   152
12.1   Location of brickworks in the Oxford Clay belt
at the beginning of the 1980s   213
12.2   Location of Tessenderlo   216
12.3   Radioactive waste sites in the United Kingdom   221
13.1   Walls within walls   233

Tables

11.1	Types of ecological modernisation	191
14.1	Country specific, per capita man-made emissions of traditional air pollutants (dependent variables) in 1980 and 1990–91 for eighteen industrialised democracies	265
14.2	Political dominance, energy consumption per capita, GDP per capita, growth of GDP per capita in per cent for eighteen countries in 1980 and 1990 (independent variables)	266
14.3	Multiple regression estimates (ols with heteroskedasticity consistent standard errors) for pooled cross-sectional/time series panel analysis	267
14.4	Multiple regression estimates (ols with heteroskedasticity consistent standard errors) for pooled cross-section/time series panel analysis	267

Contributors

Andrew Blowers OBE is Professor of Social Sciences (Planning) at the Open University, UK. He has written several books on planning and political issues including *The Limits of Power*, *Something in the Air*, *The International Politics of Radioactive Waste* and *Planning for a Sustainable Environment*. For the Open University he has co-edited the three-volume series on *Environmental Policy in an International Context* and three volumes in the series *Environment: Change, Contest and Response*. For three decades he was a leading county councillor in Bedfordshire specialising in environmental and planning matters. He has been prominent in environmental policy making as a member of the Radioactive Waste Management Advisory Committee (1991–2004) and the Committee on Radioactive Waste Management (since 2003) and as an independent director of Nirex, the radioactive waste disposal company. In 2000 he was awarded the OBE for services to environmental protection.

Robert J. Brulle is an Associate Professor of Sociology and Environmental Science at Drexel University in Philadelphia, Pennsylvania. His research focuses on the US environmental movement, critical theory and public participation in environmental policy making. He is the author of several articles in these areas and is the author of *Agency, Democracy and the Environment: The U.S. Environmental Movement from a Critical Theory Perspective* (MIT Press, 2000). He has also taught at Goethe University in Frankfurt, Germany, at the University of Uppsala, Uppsala, Sweden and George Mason University in Fairfax, VA. He received his PhD in sociology from George Washington University in 1995.

Peter Christoff is coordinator of Environmental Studies in the School of Anthropology, Geography and Environmental Studies at the University of Melbourne. He has published widely with an emphasis on Australian environmental politics and policy, and strategic planning for ecologically sustainable development. He is also on the Board of Greenpeace (Australia-Pacific) and the Executive of the Australian Conservation Foundation.

Markus M.L. Crepaz received his PhD in Political Science at the University of California, San Diego, an MA degree in Political Science at Bowling Green

State University and his undergraduate degree at the University of Salzburg Austria. He explores the impact of institutional designs on a host of political and economic outcomes, such as income inequality, economic growth, public spending, longevity and environmental outcomes. More specifically, he argues that some institutional configurations (collective veto points) enable state capacity while other configurations (competitive veto points) restrict state capacity. His current research project investigates the distributional conse-quences of attitudes on the welfare state in comparative perspective. His research has been published in the major comparative and European Politics journals.

Robyn Eckersley is a senior lecturer in the Department of Political Science at the University of Melbourne, specialising in environmental political theory and policy. Her major publications include *Environmentalism and Political Theory: Toward an Ecocentric Approach* (SUNY Press, 1992); *Markets, the State and the Environment: Towards Integration* (Macmillan, 1995) (as editor) and *The Green State: Rethinking Democracy and Sovereignty* (MIT Press, 2004); *The State and the Global Ecological Crisis* (MIT Press, 2005) (edited with John Barry). She is currently working on *Political Theory and the Environment*, CUP (edited with Andrew Dobson), forthcoming in 2006.

Robert E. Goodin is Professor of Social and Political Theory and of Philosophy, Research School of Social Sciences, Australian National University. He is founding editor of *The Journal of Political Philosophy* and author of, most recently, *Reflective Democracy* (OUP, 2003). He specialises in political theory and public policy, especially the philosophy and politics of the welfare state and of the environment.

Joyeeta Gupta is a Professor on Climate Change Law and Policy at the Institute of Environmental Studies at the Vrije Universiteit Amsterdam and she holds a part time position as Professor in Policy and Law of Water Resources and the Environment at the UNESCO-IHE Institute for Water Education in Delft, NL. Joyeeta Gupta has published extensively in the area of environmental governance, climate change and North–South relations. She is Editor-in-Chief of *International Environmental Agreements: Politics, Law and Economics*, is on the editorial board of a few other journals and is a member of several national and international scientific steering committees.

Eric Laferrière is co-author of *International Relations Theory and Ecological Thought* (Routledge, 1999). Foundations for the book were laid in his EP arti-cle (1994) and a subsequent one in *Millennium: Journal of International Studies* (1996), where the ecological strengths and weaknesses of international relations theories were first explored. He has argued for a philosophical and critical opening of IR theory, as a means to assert related values of peace, sustainability and community in a modern context. He teaches Modern Philosophy, Political Theory and Environmental Ethics at John Abbott College in Montreal, CA.

Pieter LeRoy is Professor of Political Sciences of the Environment at the University of Nijmegen, the Netherlands. He has published on the societal and political aspects of environmental conflicts (nuclear power, the location of industries and infrastructures, the siting of waste facilities, etc.), on the strategies of the environmental movement and on environmental policies. His recent research focuses on the emergence of new environmental policy arrangements in the context of shifts in governance (www.kun.nl/milieubeleid/staf/leroy). He also has a professorship at Antwerp University, Belgium, where he coordinates a research consortium on environmental policies (www.uia.ac.be/mbw). He is a member of various advisory boards in Belgium and the Netherlands. Over the last decade he chaired the steering committee of the Flemish 'state of the environment' report.

John O'Neill is Professor of Philosophy at Lancaster University. He has written widely on the philosophy of economics, environmental philosophy, political theory, ethics and the philosophy of science. He is the author of *The Market: Ethics, Knowledge and Politics* (Routledge, 1998) and *Ecology, Policy and Politics: Human Well-Being and the Natural World* (Routledge, 1993) and co-editor (with Tim Hayward) of *Justice, Property and the Environment: Social and Legal Perspectives* (Ashgate, 1997) and (with Ian Bateman and Kerry Turner) of *Environmental Ethics and Philosophy* (Edward Elgar, 2001). He has also written reports on environmental valuation for the European Parliament and the European Commission.

Stephen L. Rainbow has moved away from academic life since 1994. He has worked as a senior manager at the NZ Historic Places Trust, the Auckland City Council, and is now the Director of Urban Strategy at Wellington City Council, where the practical application of sustainability principles is a key priority. He completed three terms as New Zealand's first 'green' city councillor and was subsequently involved with the establishment of the 'Bluegreens'; this is a green movement associated latterly with the National (conservative) party, largely because of its views about the interdependence of successful economic and environmental outcomes.

Ariel Salleh is a sociologist of knowledge with experience in water politics and science for people projects. She taught the first Australian ecofeminist course at University of New South Wales in 1983 and was Adjunct Professor in Environmental Education at New York University in 1992. She is now Associate Professor in Social Ecology at the University of Western Sydney. Salleh has many published articles and one book, *Ecofeminism as Politics* (Zed Books, 1997). She serves on the Boards of *Organization & Environment*; *Capitalism, Nature, Socialism*; the Australian Government's Gene Technology Ethics Committee and ISA Research Committee, Environment and Society.

Ben Seel has moved on from higher education since 1996. After working on a Transformation of Environmental Activism project at the University of Kent he moved on to the Kendal Project, Patterns of the Sacred at Lancaster

University until 2002. He currently studies and teaches Buddhism at Manjushri Kadampa Meditation Centre in Conishead Priory, Cumbria.

Piers H.G. Stephens is a features editor (Books, Film, Music and Other Media Reviews) and Utopian and Futures Co-editor of the journal *Organization and Environment* (http://www.coba.usf.edu/jermier/journal.htm). He attained his PhD in environmental philosophy at the University of Manchester, UK, in 1997, and now works in the USA as Assistant Professor in environmental philosophy at the Lyman Briggs School of Science, Michigan State University. He has co-edited two books, *Perspectives on the Environment 2* (Avebury, 1995) and *Environmental Futures* (Macmillan, 1999), and contributed articles and reviews to various journals, including *Environmental Politics*, *Organization and Environment, Environmental Values, Ecotheology* and *Capitalism, Nature, Socialism.*

Hugh Ward's current research focuses on the effects of a nation's overall position in the network of international environmental regimes affects its performance on sustainability indicators. His longer-term research interest is on whether is it possible to construct a case for central planning and state ownership as important institutions in a sustainable society against criticisms mounted by green theorists on the basis of the Soviet experience.

Preface by the series editors

It is a pleasure for us to be writing the preface for this collection of essays as we believe that it marks another important stage in the development and maturity of environmental politics as a discipline.

Since its conception, the journal *Environmental Politics* has played a significant role in establishing environmental politics as a legitimate and significant area of study, quickly becoming the primary location for publishing academic articles in the discipline. This collection of essays, chosen by Piers, John and Andy from the first ten volumes of *Environmental Politics*, not only provides a useful overview of contemporary work in this area but is also representative of the high standard of material published by the journal. One of its strengths is its commitment to diversity – both in terms of subject matter and approach – and this is reinforced in this collection by the inclusion of articles on green political theory, movements, political economy and policy. It is hard to believe that the journal is now in its second decade – it certainly ages us!

The publication of this volume also allows us to reinforce the links between the journal and the Routledge Environmental Politics series in which this collection appears. Just as the journal continues to publish significant articles in the discipline, we believe that this series has become a well-established location for publishing accessible yet challenging book-length analyses of contemporary environmental politics. The journal *Environmental Politics* recently became part of the Routledge fold and we are pleased that we have reached agreement that special editions of the journal also will now appear in this series, thus increasing the potential readership and hence the impact of what is often ground-breaking research. We hope that this will prove to be a fruitful relationship for the environmental politics community.

Finally, we would like to pay a special tribute to Stephen Young who (with the entrepreneurial Michael Waller) was responsible for launching both the journal and this series of books back in the 1990s. He played a crucial role in establishing the discipline and, along with the editors of the journal *Environmental Politics*, we are proud to count him as a friend, thank him for all his hard work over the years and wish him a long and happy retirement.

Matthew Paterson
Graham Smith

Acknowledgements

Parts of this book have also appeared in the following articles published in the Routledge journal *Environmental Politics*:

Andrew Blowers and Pieter LeRoy (1994), 'Power, Politics and Environmental Inequality', *Environmental Politics*, Vol. 3, No. 2, pp. 197–228.

Robert J. Brulle (2002), 'Habermas and Green Political Thought: Two Roads Converging', Vol. 11, No. 4, *Environmental Politics*, Vol. 11, No. 4, pp. 1–20.

Peter Christoff (1996), 'Ecological Modernisation, Ecological Modernities' *Environmental Politics* Vol. 5, No. 3, pp. 476–500.

Markus M.L. Crepaz (1995), 'Explaining National variations of Air Pollution Levels: Political Institutions and their Impact on Environmental Policymaking', *Environmental Politics*, Vol. 4, No. 3, pp. 391–414.

Robyn Eckersley (1993), 'Free Market Environmentalism: Friend or Foe?' *Environmental Politics*, Vol. 2, No. 1, pp. 1–19.

Robert E. Goodin (1992), 'The High Ground is Green', *Environmental Politics*, Vol. 1, No. 1, pp. 1–8.

Joyeeta Gupta (1995), 'The Global Environmental Facility in its North-South Context', *Environmental Politics*, Vol. 4, No. 1, pp. 19–43.

Eric Laferrière (1994), 'Environmentalism and the Global Divide', *Environmental Politics*, Vol. 3, No. 1, pp. 91–113.

John O'Neill (1995), 'Public Choice, Institutional Economics, Environmental Goods' *Environmental Politics*, Vol. 4, No. 2, pp. 197–218.

Stephen Rainbow (1992), 'Why Did New Zealand and Tasmania Spawn the World's First Green Parties?' *Environmental Politics* Vol. 1, No. 3, pp. 321–46.

Ariel Salleh (1996), 'Social Ecology and the "Man Question"', *Environmental Politics*, Vol. 5, pp. 258–75.

Ben Seel (1997), 'Strategies of Resistance at the Pollok Free State Road Protest Camp', *Environmental Politics*, Vol. 6, No. 4, pp. 108–39.

Piers H.G. Stephens (2001), 'Green Liberalisms: Nature, Agency and the Good', *Environmental Politics*, Vol. 10, No. 3, pp. 1–22.

Hugh Ward (1999), 'Citizens' Juries and Valuing the Environment: A Proposal', *Environmental Politics*, Vol. 8, No. 2, pp. 75–96.

1 Introduction

If you can face the prospect of no more public games
Purchase a freehold house in the country. What it will cost you
Is no more than you pay in annual rent for some shabby
And ill-lit garret here...
Learn to enjoy hoeing, work and plant your allotment
Till a hundred vegetarians could feast off its produce.
It's quite an achievement, even out in the backwoods,
To have made yourself master of – well, say one lizard, even.
Insomnia causes more deaths among Roman invalids
Than any other factor (the most common *complaints*, of course,
Are heartburn and ulcers, brought on by over-eating.)
How much sleep, I ask you, can one get in lodgings here?'[1]

Thus wrote the Roman poet Juvenal in his Third Satire, *Against the Life of the City*, in approximately AD 110. There is nothing especially new about dramatic moral contrasts validating the simple virtues of nature's realm against the corrupting characteristics of the urban condition, and such notions can be found amongst antecedents as varied as the Sophists, the Stoics, the popular medieval ballads of sylvan liberty, various agrarian styles of republicanism and, of course, the Romantics. But though all these traditions may be tapped into by modern greens, the rise of a *politics* explicitly and self-consciously centred upon the moral importance of non-human nature is a recent phenomenon, a product of the distinctive problems and possibilities of modern society, and as the editors of this volume know well, as recently as a decade ago many academics regarded this novelty, green politics, as a passing fad.

It was against this background, with the fall of the Berlin Wall and a series of successes for European green parties as recent memories, that the journal *Environmental Politics* was born. It rapidly became the leading European journal in the field, focusing largely on green issues and politics in the developed countries of the North, and in the years since the journal's founding, the supposed fad has not only come to stay but matured into a rigorous, stimulating field of intellectual enquiry and discussion.

Accordingly, this compilation volume seeks in part to chart this progression by offering the reader a selection of the key published papers published in

Environmental Politics, from Robert Goodin's welcoming introduction to the very first issue right through to the current interfaces of green politics with the theoretical ideas of major figures like Jurgen Habermas and the practical 'risk society' issues raised by air pollution policies and citizens' jury valuations. In making our selections, we have operated on several core criteria. First, we have selected those articles which have shown most prescience and influence in shaping the development of environmental politics within the time frame: Robyn Eckersley's paper on free market environmentalism, for instance, sets out a series of key objections that have informed most objections to the creed ever since, whilst Eric Laferrière's work on international environmental tensions clearly anticipated the types of battle line and flashpoints that have since evolved in the debate over the nature, virtues and vices of globalisation. Other contributions, such as Ben Seel's, have earned their place through capturing a particular political moment and distilling durable broader lessons from it or else carve out a distinctive niche in the development of the field through their unusual focus and/or their centrality for understanding the generation and motivation of environmental concerns, as with the papers of Robert Goodin and Stephen Rainbow. Second, we have attempted to cover a broad range, so that readers may gain a view not only of the evolution of the field but also a snapshot of the current state of play, and so another strand of selection policy touches upon the future, with papers such as those by Ariel Salleh and Hugh Ward pointing to debates that are ongoing and central to the field as it now stands. Third, we have attempted to ensure the presence of a diversity of significant voices to cover a range of concerns, and as part of this strategy, a self-denying ordinance was deployed: work by members of the journal's editorial board was deliberately excluded from consideration, thus minimising the dangers of personal hobby horses being ridden in the selection process.

This leads us to questions of themes and structure. We have chosen to split the book into four parts, giving representative samples of the best work in the areas of green political theory, of green movements and organisational studies, green political economy and in analyses of policy issues. In compiling and organising the collection, we have tried to balance the requirements of diversity, looking at the breadth of green concerns, with those of evolutionary coherence, giving some impression of how the field has developed from its novel, radical and intellectually marginal origins into an important area of mainstream politics and study. We believe the combination now present represents the best of what *Environmental Politics* has produced, chosen under optimal conditions to capture the development and diversity of the field.

Part I: Theory

Since political theory is the area that provides the defining spinal structuring to such developments, we begin the book with this part. A feel for the general *raison d'etre* of the journal in its earliest days can be gleaned from Robert E. Goodin's opening paper, the first ever to be published in *Environmental Politics*, which not only contextualises the global nature of green politics' concerns but also advances an argument for the validity and promise of green political theory as a help in advancing ecological improvement and as a guide to political strategy. Goodin here outlines a set of claims that have been associated with his name ever since and have endured in green thought, arguing for the essential logical coherence of the bundle of values that he sees as properly unifying green political parties and for the need both to stress these in political praxis and to distinguish them from the extraneous lifestyle-orientated baggage often associated with them. In doing so, he advances a position that tacitly stresses the uniqueness of the green political vision and the possibility of its attaining success precisely by being true to what he sees as its particular core values.[2]

Whilst Goodin emphasises the unique in green thought, the next contributor, Ariel Salleh, attends to a set of relationships between radical greenery and two close relatives amongst schools of left social critique: feminism and anarchism. Pointing to the strong feminist content within the eco-anarchist vision of Murray Bookchin's social ecology and noting especially the liberatory potential of women's mutualism within the theory, Salleh examines the manner in which neither Bookchin nor his personal and political companion Janet Biehl prove able to truly recognise or develop this potential. Arguing that these failings derive from an ambivalence over the historic significance of patriarchal power in Bookchin's case and a tendency towards a liberal rationalist version of progress in Biehl's, Salleh puts ecofeminist stress on the material, distributive aspects of human freedom in order to conclude that attaining a fair, green society embodying gender equity may require us to properly develop the mutualism of ecofeminist praxis and 'to re-think the unbridled Eurocentric fetish for the transcendent'.

A similar emphasis on the dangers of excessive abstraction may be found in Piers Stephens' chapter, which addresses the relationship between liberalism and green thought, especially liberalism of the neutralist modern type manifested in Marcel Wissenburg's groundbreaking book *Green Liberalism*. Stephens deploys historical analysis to argue that the fashionable neutralism and formalism of contemporary liberal thought must invariably revert to overt or covert background accounts of human nature, agency and the good life when placed under justificatory pressure, and that given this, we must face the fact that some forms of account are far more conducive to green outcomes than others. Championing J.S. Mill's variant of liberalism as against the economistic and atomistic assumptions of Lockean liberalism that he sees as tacitly reproduced in much contemporary liberal thought, including Wissenburg's, Stephens argues that motivating real green change within a liberal framework requires the sort of embodied, naturalistic virtue-inclusive liberalism that Mill's relational account of the self and many-sided conception of human flourishing exemplifies, as well as the direct physical presence of nature and re-constructive practices to go along with this.

These chapters, testifying to the growing significance of green thought in relation to more established traditions, are complemented by Robert Brulle's chapter to conclude the part, in which a further significant collision is dissected, as Brulle examines the sort of ecocentric green political theory popularised by

Robyn Eckersley in relation to the Critical Theory of Jurgen Habermas. Pointing to the tendency towards the naturalistic fallacy found in Eckersley's critique of Habermas' Critical Theory, Brulle maintains that Eckersley overlooks vital foundational work in Habermas' account, and that her attempt to reconstitute it as an ecocentric project of democratic politics based on the intrinsic value of nature is intellectually mistaken as well as politically inappropriate. Brulle's chapter points instead to the prior re-construction of the public discursive arena as a pre requisite to the proper recognition of ecological values; it thus contributes to the burgeoning wider debate over discursive democracy as well as connecting to the tensions between social and ecological values already touched upon by Salleh and Stephens and later looked at in policy terms by Hugh Ward's chapter on citizen's juries.

Part II: Green movements

This attention to the discursive realm leads to the next part, which is devoted to environmental movements and organisations and opens with Stephen Rainbow's paper on the genesis of the world's first green parties, both originating in the Antipodes: the United Tasmania Group in Australia and the Values Party in New Zealand. Rainbow maintains that these parties, which remain relatively little studied by comparison with (for instance) the reams of research devoted to the German Greens, were brought into being as a result of a confluence of local factors, with similar initial rallying points – the desire to protect sites of natural beauty from industrial depredation, in this case particular lakes – being politically drawn out into wider critiques of the development path and ideals of industrial society. In an absorbing study, Rainbow suggests that in both cases, the deep commitment of the dominant party of government to the industrial status quo and the relative ease of media access for minority groups necessitated and enabled a rapid growth of green oppositional ideas to spread from a small base, whilst the presence of inspiration from wilderness preservation in Tasmania and New Zealand pushed both groups towards characteristically ecocentric perspectives. He also strikingly suggests that a future green politics will need to be far more sensitive to urban issues, a development that is now identifiably occurring but which was long-sighted on the chapter's original publication in 1992.

An indication of just how far the influence of environmental politics has come since the early days charted by Rainbow comes with the next chapter, in which Eric Laferrière examines the different types and the influence of environmental groups on the globalising international stage. In a significant linkage of environmental politics to the study of international relations, Laferrière's carefully constructed analysis not only identifies environmental degradation as a key source of likely transformation in the dynamics of the North–South divide but also illustrates the way in which environmental NGOs have increasingly found ways to co-operate across this divide and to pioneer novel and successful policy initiatives. Presciently observing the implicit tensions in both the NAFTA treaty then being negotiated and between the environmentalisms of North and South, Laferrière provides an engaging overview of a set of conflicting international actors and values that have, in many cases, since become significantly more polarised.

A shift of key away from the electoral and international domains of politics and towards the organic and personal concerns of protest is represented by the last chapter in the part, Ben Seel's discussion of the Pollok Free State road protest community in Glasgow, Scotland. Seel examines the creative imagination displayed in the mid-1990s British roads protest movement and the manner in which active practices of local resistance informed and helped spread wider radical theoretical ideas in opposition to the socio-economic status quo, prob-lematising private ownership of land, consumerist accounts of well-being and economic growth, car culture and the democratic status of the British polity. Observing both the radical participatory challenge made by the direct action movement and the reformist residue that it habitually helps create in policy, Seel argues that such environmental groups and actions, contrary to customary cate-gorisations, represent far more than single-issue campaigning and can even be seen as a type of counter-hegemonic resistance to the dynamics of consumerism and state corporate power.

Part III: Green political economy

This radical challenge to socio-economic orthodoxy and examination of the relationship between radical and reformist strategies sets up a vexed set of ques-tions about the role of market institutions and the extent to which contemporary reformist solutions may be able to deal with environmental crisis, and thus it prepares the way for the next part, geared to political economy. In an admirably clear and concise chapter that has helped support much subsequent critique, Robyn Eckersley examines the broad brush claims made for free market solutions to a series of environmental problems, teasing out some of the oft-hidden under-lying normative assumptions involved and arguing that because the free market environmentalist (FME) focuses only on a rather narrow vision of efficiency, their preferred ideas cannot act as a full solution to environmental problems. Although FME policies may sometimes be appropriate for some limited goals, Eckersley argues, they are partly inspired by historical conditions that no longer hold and cannot of themselves act as a clear solution to most of the problems which greens diagnose, due to being insufficiently receptive to the demands of social justice and strong sustainability, and this problem, she maintains, holds across the diversity of FME approaches, be they of the libertarian, Austrian or public choice schools of thought.

These reflections are followed by John O'Neill's more fine-grained chapter which, in the context of considering the management and understanding of envi-ronmental goods, engages with the fashionable literature of public choice theory. Maintaining that public choice theory constitutes a new form of institutional economics in its attempt to draw motivational assumptions from economics and transplant them to the political realm, O'Neill contrasts the diffuse egoism of the public choice school with the greater contextual sensitivity of the old style of institutional economics, arguing that the latter's superior understanding of the roles and character played by institutional settings in human action should mandate its return to centre stage in attempting to deal with the new challenges represented by environmental goods. Such an associational-centred focus, he maintains, should be invoked to replace both state-centred and market-centred approaches, perhaps ultimately even transcending both.

This concern with reformist diversity helps introduce the themes of the part's final chapter, Peter Christoff's pathfinding and influential essay on ecological modernisation and modernities. Rather as Eckersley and O'Neill examined the typology and applications of FME and institutional economics, so Christoff provides a stimulating analysis of that range of thought and reformist state responses to environmental crisis that evolved from the late 1980s and has come to be known as ecological modernisation. In a rigorous and wide-ranging examination, Christoff examines not only some of the empirical and institutional settings and goals denoted by the term but also, mindful of the confusion and conceptual pollution that has befallen the term 'sustainable development', he attempts to clarify the range of the ecological modernisation concept. To this end, he elaborates some important distinguishing marks that may separate weak, technocentric and basically instrumentalist variants of the creed that stress market competitiveness from more genuinely ecologically motivated, democratic and engaged versions of the concept. Finally, Christoff critically locates the idea's dynamics within the overall economic dynamics and cultural themes of the modern era, connecting the notion of ecological modernisation to such contemporary social developments as the loss of faith in science-based grand narratives and the rise in consciousness of technological risk, thus concerning the chapter not only with economic change but also with the wider cultural concerns of green politics and the policy focus of our final part.

Part IV: Policy

Risk and distributive inequalities are also key foci of the first chapter in the policy part, namely Andrew Blowers and Pieter LeRoy's analysis of the dynamics of environmental inequality and the siting of environmentally hazardous facilities or 'locally unwanted land uses' (LULUs). In an important chapter that combines case studies from the UK and Belgium with an attempt at a theoretical structuring of the dynamics whereby certain regions are rendered peripheral and targeted for LULUs, Blowers and LeRoy set out their central thesis. They argue that LULUs tend towards being located in already backward or deprived areas and thus reinforce environmental inequalities and advance eleven explanatory propositions dealing not only with the general characteristic dynamics of peripheral communities but also with the ways in which resistance to LULUs can cut across typical modern socio-economic divisions. This influential chapter thus has wide significance, and North American readers familiar with the burgeoning environmental justice movements in their own countries are also likely to find their understanding enriched by this important European work.

Still wider concerns of environmental and social justice, meanwhile, are implicated in Joyeeta Gupta's evaluation of the World Bank's controversial Global Environmental Facility (GEF), which focuses on the power asymmetries identified and criticised by NGOs and representatives of the South. Noting the reluctance of Southern governments to accept the GEF as the financial agency for Agenda 21 implementation, Gupta identifies three different institutional levels at which their suspicions of the GEF apply – the interpretation of issues in GEF documents, the GEF's wider institutional context and the deeper problems of North–South power differentials – and analyses the criticisms, arguing that whilst these may be being addressed at the first of these levels, the two wider issues remain recalcitrant, and accordingly that the (then ongoing) restructuring of the GEF will need to seriously promote transparency and greater democracy. Donor countries too, Gupta argues, may help in this process by re-considering the current mechanisms of expenditure for the money given, and while she stops short of arguing that shifts in the North–South international power balance are or should be preconditions for addressing global environmental problems, she nonetheless regards the longer-term resolution of such global problems to be fundamentally entwined with tackling their economic causes at the systemic level.

A similar focus on institutions and international comparison, but one more tightly attuned to a particular environmental problem, is found in Markus M.L. Crepaz's essay on national variations in air pollution levels. Crepaz sets up a dichotomy between states with corporatist, goal-orientated co-operationist political cultures on the one side, such as Sweden, Austria and Norway, and nations with pluralist, process-orientated political cultures that feature interest groups engaged in adversarial struggles over access to the legislative process, as exemplified by countries like the United States, Canada and Britain. Having clarified the distinction, he advances a systematic comparative analysis of the differences in effectiveness between the two types of institutional set-up in minimising air pollution, covering 18 countries over 2 time periods; the examination is thus unusually comprehensive in bridging significant customary gaps between some of the typical foci deployed in environmental management, international relations, policy analysis and political theory. Concluding that corporatist states appear significantly better equipped to deal with pollution problems because the 'institutional logic of corporatism has a built-in incentive to represent "public interest" in a more effective way than pluralism does', Crepaz's concluding reflections, noting the deflating effects of corporatist political institutions upon democratic vitality, point to a worrying source of tension between the likely vigour of democratic institutions and success in resolving concrete environmental problems, a tension that the book's concluding chapter by Hugh Ward partly seeks to relieve.

Ward advances a proposal that has since proved highly influential in the debates over cost-benefit analysis and the political valuation of nature, namely the use of citizen's juries as either adjunct or replacement for standard economic cost–benefit analysis in environmental decision-making. Adducing a range of advantages to the approach, of which better informed evaluation, greater democratic inclusivity and legitimacy, greater sensitivity to distributional effects and superior opportunities to representatively include nature's interests are just a few, Ward's chapter also suggests an optimal geographical-cum-political range for the use of citizens' jury valuations and connects green valuation importantly to the wider and increasingly significant debate over both deliberative democracy and the current health of the liberal democratic state.

In doing this, Ward's chapter brings the compilation full circle, for these are not only significant themes for political theory in general but testify to the way in which environmental politics – and indeed *Environmental Politics*! – has provided a new political voice whilst contributing to transformations and resurrections of far older schools of thought: anarchism, utopianism, feminism, aesthetic socialism, Millian liberalism and even the revival of a republicanism that might not have been wholly unfamiliar to the Roman satirist with whom we began. The book you have in your hand thus represents the best of more than a decade of development in green political thought, as represented in the pages of one of its most influential academic journals. To trace the record of that development, and to gain an appreciation of the multi-faceted character of environmental politics as thus represented, read on....

Notes

1 Juvenal (1974), *The Sixteen Satires* (trans. Peter Green), Harmondsworth: Penguin.
2 Robert E. Goodin (1992), *Green Political Theory*, Cambridge: Polity Press.

Part I

Theory

2   The high ground is green

Robert E. Goodin

Chimneys belching black smoke have never been popular. Scenic vistas and cuddly creatures have long been the stuff of picture postcards. Politically, there have always been people prepared to act on those sorts of preferences. The Sierra Club has been with us for virtually as long as the US National Park system itself. The Council for the Preservation of Rural England may date only from the inter-war years, but its precursors – the National Trust and the Commons, Open Spaces and Footpaths Preservation Society – are of respectably Victorian vintage. Various national societies for the prevention of cruelty to animals have been around for even longer. In all those ways, green politics are old hat. In recent years, though, they have taken on an importantly different hue.

I

Changing symbols serve as clues to the changing substance of environmental concern. In the America of my youth, Smokey the Bear could be seen on billboards across the country warning of the dangers of forest fires ignited by cigarettes carelessly tossed out of open car windows. Today such placards are tokens of a bygone era: an era when most people still smoked; when people still opened their cars' windows for a breeze, rather than turning on air-conditioners; when billboards were not yet regarded as unacceptable eyesores on public highways.

All that has now changed. So too has the sort of issue figuring centrally in environmental politics. Smokey – the brown bear cub burned in a forest fire – was representative of that earlier generation. More characteristic of present environ-mentalist campaigns is the smiling sun of the 'Nuclear Power: No Thanks' campaign mounted by the Friends of the Earth. Cute is out: cosmic is in.

Rather than worrying about localised forest fires burning individual bears, environmentalists now tend to worry about the destruction of whole forests and entire ecosystems. Instead of fixating upon individual animals, we now worry about whole species. While still worrying about smoking chimneys blighting the landscape, dirtying people's laundry and lungs, we now worry rather more about the acid rain that they cause destroying downwind lakes and the carbon dioxide that they emit altering the global climate. Rather than disapproving of aerosol cans merely as a source of litter along roadsides, we now worry about the hole that their contents have punched in the ozone layer.

Green causes seem to me somehow more compelling in those newer manifestations. The arguments of animal liberationists notwithstanding, I, for one, have remained at least a half-hearted carnivore; I wear leather shoes; I did not dissuade my aged mother from buying a fur coat. I commit all those sins against the sterner forms of the ecological creed only vaguely apologetically. At the end of the day, I simply do not think that caring about animals one-by-one is what the environmentalist movement is – or ought to be – most centrally all about. The whole point of a self-styled ecology movement, surely, is that we must learn to see things in their largest possible contexts. In those terms, it is global forms of the issues that really matter.

I suspect that I am not alone in such sentiments. Similar concerns are arguably what fuelled the emergence of the green movement in its present form and especially the formation of explicitly green political parties that in many places now overshadow the older and more specialised environmentalist crusades out of which they have grown.

Any movement has many beginnings. That is particularly true of one such as the green movement, which emerged independently in many different places at once. Still, those parallel movements share many of the same inspirations (McCormick, 1989). Intellectually, formative tracts for green movements on both sides of the Atlantic would standardly be said to include Rachel Carson's *Silent Spring* (1962), *The Ecologist* magazine's *Blueprint for Survival* (Goldsmith *et al.*, 1972) and the Club of Rome's report on *The Limits to Growth* (Meadows *et al.*, 1972).

Politically, the green movement in its contemporary form might be said to date from Earth Day 1970. At least in the United States, that was in effect the constructive face of the anti-Vietnam war movement then at its peak. Just as the message of earlier anti-war campaigns was that we in the United States could no longer expect to bend the nations of the world to our will, so too the analogous message of that first Earth Day was that we of the industrialised world could no longer expect to bend the physical fabric of the earth to our will.

The announcements of eco-doom heard on that occasion and so often since were of course overstated. Still, it was clearly concern with issues of a global sort that motivated participants in those events: pictures of tortured dogs were vastly outnumbered by pictures of dead lakes. And for at least an important subset of environmental activists, those global issues seem to have predominated ever since.

Over the intervening years, the ecology movement has travelled hand-in-hand with the peace movement, especially in its nuclear disarmament phase. Thus, when Jonathan Schell was casting about for a title for his powerful tract against nuclear weapons, he chose *The Fate of the Earth* (Schell, 1982). Similarly, the conjunction contained in the name of the organisation 'Greenpeace' is no accident. Neither is the fact that, in Europe and America alike, pro-ecology movements have piggybacked powerfully on movements opposing nuclear weapons and their civil equivalents, nuclear electricity generating plants. In Germany, this strategy helped to take the Greens into parliament.

Like all contrasts, this one is drawn too sharply, and like all potted social histories this one suppresses many nuances and counter-tendencies. Cuddly creatures – seal pups, whales and such like – still do figure largely in the campaigns even of Greenpeace. But they function, it seems, more as targets of opportunity, good ways to garner mass support. That is no criticism. After all, Greenpeace activists genuinely do care about seal pups and whales, among many other things; and politically we must all take our opportunities where we find them. My point is just that our present concerns are not *limited* to cuddly animals, in the way that previously they seem to have been much more tightly focused on 'our furry friends'.

II

Neither are our present concerns limited, in a way they were even on that first Earth Day, to remedial actions which might be taken by countries one-at-a-time. Of course, environmentalists of that earlier era were acutely aware of the global threat, as is evident from many of the more popular tracts of the time. The unofficial manifesto of the UN Conference on the Human Environment reminded us that there was *Only One Earth* (Ward and Dubos, 1972). *The Limits to Growth* no longer referred to scarcities that were merely domestic in nature (Meadows *et al.*, 1972). The environmental feedback loops that constituted *The Closing Circle* would eventually threaten the entire biosphere, not merely a single lake (Commoner, 1971). Overpopulation, localised though it may seem, actually puts pressure on entire ecosystems (Ehrlich and Ehrlich, 1972).

What is distinctive about those earlier understandings of the global nature of the threat, and what is different with more recent understandings of it, is not the scope of the threats but rather the scope of the required solutions. Roughly speaking, all those earlier arguments suggested that the world was at risk, sure enough, but that there was something useful that could be done at the local level to stem the threat. In the spirit of 'every litter bit hurts', households were admonished to use biodegradable detergents, to confine themselves to (at most) 2.1 children, to moderate their own consumption. National governments, likewise, were admonished to pass tough environmental protection laws domestically, whether or not their neighbours did.

Of course it would be better – the biosphere would be more secure – if all households and all nations did likewise. Responsible environmental practices were universal recommendations, in that sense. But in that earlier era, there was little appreciation of threats that could only be tackled by concerted worldwide action. There was always something useful that could be done by individual households and individual nations, whatever their neighbours might be doing.

We are no longer so sanguine. We rather suspect that concerted action on the part of all – or virtually all – nations of the world will be required if catastrophic changes in the ozone layer or in the global climate are reliably to be averted. That is not to say that individual nations and individual households will not still have a role to play. It is merely to say that, to play their role efficaciously, they will have to play it in league with others, according to some properly elaborated plan of joint action.

The sphere within which such co-ordination of joint plans of action takes place is, of course, the sphere of politics. So all of that is merely to say that the contemporary understanding of the environmental crisis carves out a much larger role for politics – both nationally and internationally – than previous understandings, which saw much more scope for individual initiatives making all the difference (Goodin, 1990).

III

There exists a role in all this for theorists as well as for theoreticians, for political analysts as well as for political activists. What green parties and self-styled green activists do, and what they say or think they are doing when they do it, is important too. And assessing that is not a purely factual matter. At the very least, it requires a fair bit of careful listening, if not outright hermeneutics or philosophical anthropology. Andrew Dobson's *Green Political Thought* (1990) is a model of this crucial kind of work.

There is, however, a crucial contribution that can only be made from a greater critical distance. Besides studies of what greens do say, there is an important place for an analysis of what they *should* say. What positions should greens take, given their core concerns, whether or not that is what they actually do so? Here we are involved in something more like a 'critical reconstruction' of green theory – an exercise which is, in that sense, intentionally revisionary, at least at the margins. It is designed as a guide *for* greens, much more than as a guide *to* them.

My own work on *Green Political Theory* (Goodin, 1992) falls squarely into this latter camp. In it, I try to show greens how to cast their position in the strongest possible form, even if that means shifting some of their ordinary emphases and perhaps even abandoning certain of their views altogether.

The reason for this repackaging of the green programme has at least as much to do with political strategy as philosophical purity. The greens have a package of policy proposals that is – or can be shown to be – unusually tightly integrated, logically. That in turn puts them in what is at least potentially an unusually strong position, politically.

Mainstream parties confronting challenges from minority parties and single-issue movements typically try to mollify their supporters by giving them a little of what they want. They try to satisfy some, but by no means most and certainly not all, of the demands made by such single-issue groups. Ordinarily it is perfectly right and proper for them to do so. The policy demands made by most parties or pressure groups are largely separable from one another, both logically and pragmatically. Accepting their position on one score rarely commits you to accepting it on any, much less all, others as well.

My aim in tidying up the green position is to show that in this respect the demands of the greens can be seen to be quite out of the ordinary. Theirs, unlike those of most parties, genuinely constitute a logically tightly integrated package. This being so, it would be logically illegitimate for mainstream parties to try to pick and choose items off it in the ordinary way. And, insofar as the electorate can be made to see that logic clearly, it would prove politically pointless for them to try.

The upshot would be that the green position would have to be taken on an all-or-nothing basis. Saying that would ordinarily be tantamount to courting disaster, politically. Those with no intention of giving the greens all that they want would be thereby excused from giving them any of it. But here again, I take it that the greens enjoy an unusually strong position.

At least some of the issues that the greens have made their own are truly compelling ones. Virtually no one, presumably, would care to court any serious risk of the sorts of global catastrophe that might be associated with the greenhouse effect or depletion of the ozone layer. Insofar as the greens have given the most credible account of what has gone wrong, socially, to produce those dangers and what must be done to avert them, it is difficult to dismiss the green position altogether. They, then, are in the uniquely privileged position of being able to expect that, demanding all-or-nothing, they just might get it all.

IV

In another sense, there might be a fair bit of work to be done in uncoupling bits of the familiar green package. I think, for example, that people can legitimately insist upon the substance of the green public policy agenda – and insist upon *all* of it – without necessarily committing themselves to all other forms of greenery.

The 'complete green' is, in fact, a composite, combining (in caricature) an environmental ethic with a new-left political style and a countercultural 'hippie' lifestyle. Those, I would argue, are separable components of a larger green package. One can – indeed, I do – embrace the public policy positions that follow from their environmentalist ethic without necessarily embracing any of the rest of the package. If I am right in this, you would not have to practice holistic medicine or have some wild-eyed faith in the powers of grassroots democracy in order to be green to the core, in the public policy terms that matter most to the fate of the earth.

Politically, this sort of argument amounts to an attempt to rescue greens from themselves. It tries to carve out and bolster what is strong in their position, while insulating that portion of the theory from other aspects that I – and, more to the point politically, many among the electorate at large – find less persuasive. That strategy is designed to win support for green positions, but inevitably it will win me few friends among greens themselves. They will warm to my all-or-nothing thesis, but they will want it applied more broadly. The last thing they want to hear is that you can consistently demand all green public policies be implemented, without being prepared to adopt any other peculiarly green personal or political practices along with them.

There is, perhaps, a certain measure of pragmatism in my attempt to separate out the bits of green theory that are politically saleable from those that are not. But it is not purely a matter of pragmatism: there is an element of logic to this position, as well. Accidentally or otherwise, the bits of green theory that are politically less saleable arguably rest on altogether different foundations from the bits that are politically more popular. So there is a reason, as well as a motive, for separating out those aspects of the green doctrine – remembering all the while that that does not necessarily mean that those bits of green theory are wrong, merely that they require that separate arguments be given in their defence.

V

That is, I hasten to add, a very personal perspective on some highly contentious issues. Some of those controversies define greens, others divide them. Greens differ in their views of the history and defining features of their movement. There is no agreement on just how shallow or deep one's ecology ought to be. Some self-styled greens would content themselves with pollution taxes, resource conservation and wildlife protection; others would insist upon the need for radical reorderings of socioeconomic and political relations. In short, there are many different shades of green.

What the green movement most needs, in light of that fact, is a place where all these intra-mural disputes can be conducted in a constructive fashion. There should be one central place where information can be pooled and experiences shared, where arguments can be tried out on a sympathetic but critical audience, where diverse factions of the movement can square off at a respectful distance to thrash out the issues that divide them and where those who do not regard themselves as greens can nonetheless learn more about green issues.

Therein lies the promise of the new journal now before you. *Environmental Politics* aspires to provide a forum for the discussion of green issues, to blend theory and practice from all continents, to serve as a broad church open to all of the movement's several sects. It is a noble aspiration. It is one that can be realized only with the active co-operation of all greens everywhere – whatever their hue, nationality or academic specialism.

We join, at its launch, in wishing it well. Given the seriousness of the problems to which it is a response, 'long may it prosper' may not be quite the right salutation: perhaps 'soon may it render itself irrelevant' would be more appropriate. Either way, let us all hope that it soon fixes its indelible mark upon environmental debates worldwide.

References

Carson, Rachel (1962), *Silent Spring*, Boston, MA: Houghton Mifflin.

Commoner, Barry (1971), *The Closing Circle*, New York: Knopf.

Dobson, Andrew (1990), *Green Political Thought*, London: Unwin Hyman.

Ehrlich, Paul R. and H. Anne (1972), *Population, Resources, Environment*, 2nd edn, San Francisco, CA: W. H. Freeman.

Goldsmith, Edward (1972), 'A Blueprint for Survival', *The Ecologist*, Vol. 2, No. 1, pp. 1–44.

Goodin, Robert E. (1990), 'International Ethics and the Environmental Crisis', *Ethics and International Affairs*, Vol. 4, pp. 81–105.

Goodin, Robert E. (1992), *Green Political Theory*, Oxford: Polity Press.

McCormick, John (1989), *Reclaiming Paradise: The Global Environmental Movement*, Bloomington, IN: Indiana University Press.

Meadows, Dennis and Donella H., Randers, Jorgen and William W. Behrens III (1972), *Limits to Growth*, London: Earth Island.

Schell, Jonathan (1982), *The Fate of the Earth*, London: Jonathan Cape.

Ward, Barbara and René Dubos (1972), *Only One Earth*, Harmondsworth: Penguin.

3 Social ecology and 'the man question'

Ariel Salleh

Persistently exorcising her powers

After the Marxist doldrums of the 1970s, anarchist Murray Bookchin's essays in *Toward an Ecological Society* offered an exhilarating release for some women activists stymied by unrelenting economism and male Left hierarchies.[1] For Bookchin, Marxism had become 'an ideology of naked power, pragmatic efficiency and social centralisation almost indistinguishable from the ideologies of modern state capitalism' (1971: 92). But more importantly, Bookchin's social ecology, born but yet unnamed as politics, focused on ecological crisis and its social origins just as ecofeminists were beginning to do. Among would-be fathers of ecopolitical thought, Bookchin alone intuited the ecofeminist connection: an understanding that men's oppression of nature and of woman are fundamentally interlinked. As he wrote in *The Ecology of Freedom*: 'The subjugation of her nature and its absorption into the nexus of patriarchal morality forms the *archetypal* act of domination that ultimately gives rise to man's imagery of a subjugated nature' (1991: 121 (italics added)). Bookchin's impressive history of hierarchy coincides with this key ecofeminist idea in a number of places, despite an assertion that gerontocracy was the earliest social stratification.

The following passage demonstrates the tension between gerontocracy and patriarchy as causal principles in his work, yet it ultimately favours patriarchal authority as prior. Why, after all, this concern with the specific relation of father and son? 'Until well into the sixth century BC, the son "had duties but no rights; while his father lived, he was a perpetual minor". In its classical form, patriarchy *implied* male gerontocracy, not only the rule of the males over females' (Bookchin, 1991:120 (italics added)). Of course, the question which form of hierarchy came first historically – gerontocracy or patriarchy – is fairly scholastic and can never be determined with any methodological certainty. We could settle for recognising a relative autonomy of the two faces of domination perhaps. On the other hand, it might be argued that the motive behind formation of a geron-tocracy was itself a patriarchal need to secure resources for sexual gratification by less vibrant older males – for example, rule by ageing females is never the issue. Besides, while older men may use cunning over males and females of all ages, younger men in most societies threaten physical violence over both men and women. Then again, even without brute force, Bookchin notes, women are physically disadvantaged by their reproductive capacities.

If classical patriarchy was based on the subjection of sons, we scarcely seem to have moved beyond it. Older men sending younger men off to war has the double benefit of reducing sexual competition and protecting their accumulated property. The inequities of capitalism can be seen as a precise transmutation of a dynamic where young people, women and outsiders are kept impoverished and powerless by the corporate greed of a few big men, usually but not necessarily in the over-fifty age bracket. Looking at which system of domination has a tighter hold on our lives today, it has to be said that patriarchal power, embodied in capitalist economics and state bureaucracies, is certainly more glamorous and pervasive than gerontocracy. In addition, a handful of liberated women reaching positions of authority in these institutions does nothing to change that structural domination.

If the Oedipal logic of totem and taboo still seems to apply, Bookchin's formulation, unlike that of Freud or fellow anarchist Kropotkin, is far removed from any social-instinct theory. Social ecologists, like ecofeminists, understand that power relations develop by historical convention. Bookchin sounds especially ecofeminist when he writes that woman was the first victim, her oppression being reinforced by appearance of the civil sphere:

> Woman became the *archetypal* Other of morality, ultimately the human embodiment of its warped image of evil ... the male still opposes his society to woman's nature, his capacity to produce commodities to her ability to reproduce life, his rationalism to her 'instinctual' drives.
>
> (1991: 120)

Again, he acknowledges that it is the material productivity of women everywhere that makes life possible. Here, he supports a model of gender exploitation that precedes both slavery and the class-divided society of Marx. Bookchin suggests that denigration of women's 'nature' has been an all but universal phenomenon and notes how unremitting hatred of women's 'inquisitiveness' reaches from pygmy Africa to ancient Greece. Her posture must always reflect renunciation and modesty.

Even so, the masculine will to power is not quenched:

> A gnawing sense of inferiority and incompleteness stamps every aspect of the newly emergent male morality ... It is utterly impossible to understand why meaningless wars, male boastfulness, exaggerated political rituals, and a preposterous elaboration of civil institutions engulf so many different, even tribal, societies without recognising how ... the male is over-active and 'over-burdened' by his responsibilities – often because there is so little for him to do in primordial communities and even in many historical societies.
>
> (Bookchin, 1991: 122)

While, in an enlightened world, Hobbes' social contract appears to abnegate the patriarchal self, in fact it simply sublimates the roles of fathers, priests and warriors. The modern state comes to colonise and absorb every facet of daily life, replacing custom and loyalty by depersonalised law and bureaucratic supports. As Bookchin reminds us, 'the entire ensemble is managed like a business' (1990: 182). Thanks to Locke and his brothers, the possibility of vigorous participatory democracy gives way under bourgeois capitalism to representative government by a mostly male propertied elite. Social production becomes mineralisation of the earth and civil society a fragmented mass that now celebrates its identity in the electronic glitz of the shopping mall.

Against this postmodern condition, Bookchin pits a fundamentally ecofeminist vision by outlining what he sees as the feminine contribution to civilisation. This contribution, created in the communication between mother and child, lays out the very foundations of consociation and thought. While Bookchin's discussion tends to use unexamined, some would say essentialist notions of gender, ecofeminists break with patriarchal dualisms by inviting men to join this radical nurturant activity. Social ecology points to such labour as a very specific form of reason – one 'concealed by the maudlin term mother love'. It is a rationality of otherness, grounded in symbiosis. Consistent with his modernist framework, Bookchin calls this nurture an 'earlier' model of rationality, but clearly it is a skill current among women care workers across many cultures. Further, as I have argued in an ecofeminist critique of deep ecology, the apparent invisibility of techniques and values that make up this paradigm of sociability is holding back ecopolitical change: 'if women's lived experience were...given legitimation in our culture, it could provide an immediate 'living' social basis for the alternative consciousness which (radical men are) trying to formulate as an abstract ethical construct' (Salleh, 1984: 340). Such a move would also further the gender revolution by de-stabilising fixed masculine and feminine work roles.

Compared with the bourgeois ethic of egoism, Bookchin contends that the sensibility women learn in caring labour expresses

> a rationality of de-objectification that is almost universal in character, indeed, a resubjectivization of experience that sees the 'other' within a logical nexus of mutuality. The 'other' becomes the active component that it always has been in natural and social history, not simply the 'alien' and alienated that it is in Marxian theory and the 'dead matter' that it is in classical physics.
>
> (1991: 306)

Without any sense of appropriation, Bookchin claims the mutualism of feminine labour and its techniques as the practice of libertarian reason *par excellence*. In the light of this pervasive force, it is curious, then, that he should wonder how to define the historical subject (Bookchin, 1991: 139). Nevertheless, he goes on to reflect that what passes for civilisation now is precisely the undoing of this empathic capacity in order for individual adults – that is, men and a handful of so-called emancipated women – can take part in patriarchal institutions:

> growing up comes to mean growing *away* from a maternal, domestic world of mutual support, concern, and love (*a venerable and highly workable society in its own right*) into one made shapeless, unfeeling and harsh. To accommodate humanity to war, exploitation, political obedience, and rule involves the undoing not only of human 'first nature' as an animal but also of human 'second nature'.
>
> (Bookchin, 1991: 305)

Based on such destructive de-socialisation, Western pretensions to personal autonomy become psychologically hollow and unsustainable, for their very substrate is vitiated. Women, meanwhile, are obliged to forge a cunning accommodation with patriarchal requirements, and feminists must exercise a double duplicity. Bookchin contrasts Hopi Indian peoples (and we can recall the tale of Margaret Mead's Samoans) whose luck it was to carry their socialisation for reciprocity into adult life. According to social ecology, the organic evolution of humans (Eurocentered ones, he means) towards awareness of their 'free nature' demands recovery of this repressed sociability – a recollection as Frankfurt Marxists would say; a renewal of the semiotic, according to poststructuralist Julia Kristeva. Social ecology, etofeminism, critical Marxism and semanalysis converge at this turn, despite Bookchin's desire to differentiate his work from other radicalisms.

Nevertheless, both social ecology and critical theory posit men's control of woman as pivotal to the establishment of hierarchy. The implication is that being less sullied by the commodity society, women are potential agents of liberation. But, as noted, Bookchin does not explore this line further, preferring a pluralist analysis. Accordingly, *The Ecology of Freedom* reads:

> The dialectical unfolding of hierarchy has left in its wake an ages-long detritus of systems of domination involving ethnic, gendered, age, vocational, urban–rural, and many other forms of dominating people, indeed, an elaborate system of rule that economistic 'class analyses' and strictly antistatist approaches do not clearly reveal.
>
> (Bookchin, 1991: xxv)

Bookchin urges us to understand the complex interaction between these various stratifications, but in doing so, he does not seem to have assimilated the implications of his generous proto-ecofeminist insight. For once the complementarity of otherness, so well-understood by women care-givers and reciprocity-based indigenous communities is overtaken by self-interested calculation, the sexually fetishised dualisms of the Eurocentric patriarchy become a complementarity of domination.

Bookchin ultimately bypasses his proposition that men's historical power over women is archetype of this polarising style, and so he loses the hidden political opportunity for actualising the free nature expressed in women's labours. Instead, and in seeming self-contradiction, his writing turns derisive of contemporary women's struggle: 'It will do us little good to contend that all the evils in the world stem from a monolithic "patriarchy," for example, or that hierarchy will wither away once women or putative female values replace "male supremacy" ' (1991: xxv).[2] After long passages spelling out the liberatory significance of women's nurturant activities in his philosophy of dialectical naturalism, Bookchin mocks 'putative feminine values'. Then, in the face of his own ambivalence, he projects ecofeminism as irrational.

What is he saying here? It seems that woman as glorified object of man's contemplative gaze is one thing, but the feminine voice itself becomes a different matter. When can the subaltern speak?[3] As we have been, in dealing with women who dare to speak as women, a number of ecopolitical writers adopt defensively rejecting postures. So much so that discursive strategies such as denial and omission, refusing to connect, projection and personalisation, caricature and trivialisation, discredit and invalidation, ambivalence and appropriation are now familiar responses to women who presume to enter the masculine domain of theory. Given Bookchin's path-breaking recognition of men's domination of women as archetypical, could the politics of social ecology itself be compromised by the man question?

Domestic agendas

In 1991, Janet Biehl, intimate companion of Murray Bookchin, published a small book called *Rethinking Ecofeminist Politics*. This set out the terms of a long overdue political debate between social ecology and the spiritually oriented culturalist ecofeminism prevalent in the USA.[4] The tension between these two ideological tendencies became clear at the first National Green Gathering in Amherst, Massachusetts in June 1987. Eco-anarchist Bookchin was a key speaker at this event, and spiritual ecofeminist Charlene Spretnak, a mother of green politics, was another. As the nascent US green movement struggled for self definition, a sense of competing hegemonies hung over it like a cloud. Some described it as a collision between New England rationalists versus California mystics. Spretnak was also identified with deep ecology – another West Coast approach to green thought and total anathema to Bookchinites.

The subsequent rise of a Left Green Network and Youth Greens organised by Howie Hawkins near Bookchin's home base in Vermont was another practical outcome of the Amherst encounter – a concerted effort by social ecologists and others on the Left to ensure that an adequate social analysis would inform the development of green politics in the USA.[5] A further issue introduced by the East versus West Coast divide at the first US National Green Gathering was a tacit struggle over the body of ecofeminism. Where should it belong? Was it to affirm the life-giving potency of woman and nature through ritual celebration of the earth goddess? Or was ecofeminism to walk hand-in-hand with social ecology, helped along by Chiah Heller and Ynestra King, teachers at Bookchin's Institute for Social Ecology? An Ecofeminist Seminar hosted by the Institute of Social

Ecology in July 1994 drawing together women from all regions of North America played out the residue of that agenda.

From the perspective of women in an international ecofeminist community now some twenty years old these ideological schisms are very much a product of social conditions domestic to the USA. Ecofeminists in Scandinavia or Australia, for example, enter a political scene where broadly socialist ideas have currency even in establishment circles, where the famous L word so precious to American progressives is even seen as conservative and where politics itself is felt to be a spiritual commitment. The mainstream community temper in the wider Western world tends to be secular humanist, too, rather than shaped by religiosity as it is in the USA. In India or Venezuela, ecofeminism encounters different conditions again. For the fact is, that the problems facing green activists around the world, including ecofeminist activists, vary with the unique historical trajectory of their region.

This fact indicates a serious limitation in Biehl's *Rethinking Ecofeminist Politics*, for that re-think depends on omission and a falsely universalised notion of what ecofeminism is. Her ecofeminist textual sources were Susan Griffin's *Woman and Nature* (1978), Carolyn Merchant's *The Death of Nature* (1980), Charlene Spretnak's *The Politics of Women's Spirituality* (1982) and *The Spiritual Dimension of Green Politics* (1987), Riane Eisler's *The Chalice and the Blade* (1987), Starhawk's *Truth or Dare* (1988), Andree Collard's *Rape of the Wild* (1989) and essays from anthologies such as Plant's *Healing the Wounds* (1989) and Diamond and Orenstein's *Reweaving the World* (1990). While Biehl claims to engage with a movement, her bibliography deals only with North American material. The upshot of this inadequate research base is that ecofeminists in the wider international community have their political contribution marginalised. Yet, equally unfair, they have to wear criticism that does not necessarily apply to their articulations of ecofeminism. Biehl comments somewhere in her book that the US education system is notably remiss in conveying a sense of history and geographic relativity to its people. Clearly, this serves the impoverished imperialist consciousness in many ways, but it is sad to see this same limitation reflected in radical American writing as well.

Of course, the mis-match between Biehl's rather home-grown project and the global reach of its title may have issued from publication editors with a keen eye for commodity export. The political impact of that decision will nevertheless continue to ripple outward into the international scene. To take an example: on the Island Continent where green parties first began, *Rethinking Ecofeminist Politics* has been embraced by Trotskyists who operate under a Green Alliance banner and used as a means of invalidating the work of independent ecofeminist activists.[6] These Left cadres, never much troubled by ideological consistency when scoring a political point, are too unread to be inhibited by the message of Bookchin's *Listen Marxist!*. (Perhaps the time is right for Murray to look at a revised, updated version of his earlier essay? A number of ecofeminist activists and scholars on our fatal shore would value his efforts.) It is not Biehl's fault that others have used her writing in this opportunistic way, although there is a salutary lesson in taking stock of the political landscape on all fronts before setting out to attack potential allies. The other lesson in all this is a reminder that history is made up of internal contradictions – ecofeminism having no prerogative on them.

Now, because ecofeminist politics grows out of a plurality of social contexts, it will have many complexions. Biehl asserts that it is marred by 'massive internal contradictions'. But one cannot expect the spontaneous organic voice of a worldwide democratic groundswell such as ecofeminism to show the same degree of philosophic grooming as a statement such as social ecology, born of the pen of a singular charismatic figure. Despite differences among ecofeminists, there is always a common strand to women's experiences – things shared by dint of the patriarchal ascription of womanhood and things beyond that. The knowledge of this unity is empowering to women and a delight. Women are discovering themselves as re/sisters outside the divisive legacies of patriarchal capitalism, colonialism, even Marxism and some green ideologies. In a global context women, 53 per cent of the world's population are the largest minority group. Never to forget that it is women who put in 65 per cent of the world's work for 10 per cent of the world's pay. This is what marks women out as a significant political category – not an essentialist fabrication as antifeminists want to claim. But *Rethinking Ecofeminist Politics* forgets this material fact, preoccupied as it is with the status of political ideas. In this respect, New England rationalists display a bourgeois idealism equal to that of the West Coast spiritual feminists who bother it so.

Bearing in mind that US ecofeminism is Biehl's focus, she expresses disappointment in a literature that '[fails to] draw upon the best of social theory and meld it with radical concepts in ecology to produce a genuine anti-hierarchical, enlightened, and broadly oppositional movement' (1991: 1). She is disturbed by ecofeminists who seem to situate themselves 'outside' the emancipatory legacy of Western – read Eurocentric – political culture. Not surprisingly, she offers Bookchin's social ecology as the most promising model in this legacy for ecofeminists and other greens to espouse. Now Biehl is rightly concerned, in that there is no well-developed Left ecofeminist account among the US texts she addresses. But she is wrong to go on to conclude that ecofeminism as such lacks this analysis or, more seriously, that it lacks the intellectual resources for arriving at the same. German ecofeminist Maria Mies' study *Patriarchy and Accumulation* (1987) provides a coherent analysis of an internationally predatory capitalist system and of how it uses patriarchal violence on women and nature to secure economic ends. Mies steps outside the Eurocentric legacy to look for an empirically grounded feminine voice, then brings this voice into dialogue with the basic presuppositions of Marxism itself. Vandana Shiva's postcolonial *exposé* of development in *Staying Alive: Women, Ecology, and Development* (1989) is a further example. Other ecofeminist positions again have developed from the interplay of gendered living, environmental struggle and intensive study of dialectical philosophies. This scarcely represents a turning away from social theory, as Biehl charges.

More to the point, Biehl does not seem to recognise that it is patriarchal attitudes that put women's knowledges and feminine values outside of reason – a long established procedure and one that she herself now partakes of. But what is important for ecofeminists is that loss of women's wisdoms and skills through this marginalisation has devastating social and ecological impacts. Perhaps more than a double irony is involved when Bookchin reminds us that 'In a civilisation that devalues nature, she is the "image of nature"... Yet woman haunts this male "civilisation" with a power that is more than archaic or atavistic. Every male-oriented society *must persistently exorcise her ancient powers*' (1991: 121). Thus, Merchant has demonstrated how the rise of the European scientific hegemony went hand-in-hand with a systematic elimination of knowledgeable women healers as witches. Mies documents how their property was appropriated by executioners finding its way into the bureaucratic coffers of what has grown into the nation-state. Considerable booty was to be had from an estimated 12 million women tortured to death. Before long, the trajectories of state and science became interwoven with capitalism. Today, we witness successful capture of the knowledge industry by corporate interests – masculinist enterprise in yet another guise – and Shiva points out how women's centuries-old agricultural expertise is displaced in India by the import of so-called development: the advanced dust-bowl-technologies perfected by Western scientific men.

Dichotomies: nature/culture; body/mind; private/public

Biehl is not well-read in feminist epistemology and so misses the deeper impli-cations of ecofeminist critiques of patriarchal politics and science. Women's approaches to making knowledge are not simply weak and irrational but posi-tively committed to principles of participation, embodiment, connectedness and wholism.[7] Conversely, the Eurocentric patriarchal legacy from religion to science exorcises nature, body and self as contamination. The nature/culture split is replicated in the rationalist dichotomy between body and mind and echoed in turn by the political device of separating private from public sphere. For many ecofem-inists, these binary representations are symptomatic of masculine struggles for independence – to be understood as transcendence from the originary body of the mother. The bodies of lovers and wives bring back the sense of need and dependency, the terror of reabsorption, dissolution. Rousseau's Emile is telling in this respect. If women were not kept restrained by modesty 'the result would soon be the ruin of both [sexes], and mankind would perish by the means established for preserving it... Men would finally be [women's] victims... All people perish from the disorder of women' (Pateman, 1988: 97–9). Women's passion is nature, which must be controlled and (note) transcended, if social order is to be maintained.

In contrast to the simple pleasures of immanence contained in women's various labours, Eurocentric history shows hegemonic masculinity as a defensive ego-oriented system, engorged with transcendent projects such as monotheism, global empire, scientific mastery and the cult of Reason. Carol Pateman was early to conclude that such institutions originate in sublimation of men's fear of women's otherness: 'Men have denied significance to women's unique bodily capacity, have appropriated it, and transmuted it into masculine political genesis' (1988: 216). At any rate, it is no surprise to find masculinist thinkers railing against an immanence which tells of our human embeddedness in nature or more recently, railing against ecofeminists who are said to collapse mind into body. What ecofeminists are actually insisting on is restoring acceptance of the organic flow between body and mind – the link that Eurocentric men so compulsively check. This is an existential prerequisite to unmaking the destructive nature/culture split. Biehl, on the other hand, by reading ecofeminism literally back into the body, unwittingly sides with unreconstructed misogynist attitudes which, since Aristotle if not before, have tried to contain women by association with nature. But we are no longer living in such unreasoned times. Ecofeminist arguments address a postmodern conjuncture, where subaltern voices have new currency.

By looking at the relation of men and women to the natural body and its metaphors, ecofeminism is paving the way for an ecological ethic based on a profound re-thinking of the human condition. Susan Griffin puts it aptly:

> We know ourselves to be made from this earth. We know this earth is made from our bodies...For we see ourselves and we are nature. We are nature seeing nature. We are nature with a concept of nature. Nature weeping. Nature speaking of nature to nature.
>
> (1978: 226)

There is little about this statement that Bookchin should have difficulty with – unless it is the speaker's gender. Compare *The Ecology of Freedom* where he describes nature as 'writing its own philosophy and ethics'. For, 'from the biochemical responses of a plant to its environment to the most willful actions of a scientist in the laboratory, a common bond of primal subjectivity inheres in the very organisation of matter itself' (Bookchin, 1991: 276).

Speaking from a position of masculine privilege, Bookchin can afford to be less inhibited on the question of our human relation to nature than is Biehl. So, comfortably reviving Kropotkin in tandem with Bloch's neo-Marxist concept of co-productivity, he theorises that: 'Labour's "metabolism" with nature cuts both ways, so that nature interacts *with* humanity to yield the actualisation of their common potentialities in the natural and social worlds' (Bookchin, 1991: 33).[8] In contrast, Biehl's old style patriarchally identified feminist contempt for the body and nature becomes confusion in discussion of the nature/culture nexus. She agrees with ecofeminism that men and women are not ontological opposites but rather differentiations in human potential. But her antagonism to social constructionists means that she cannot concede this potential as discursively mediated. In other words, lacking a dialectical understanding of links between nature and nurture she is forced back into the very reductionism that she would like to fault ecofeminism with.

Losing sight of Bookchin's acknowledgement of women's mutualism as libertarian reason *par excellence*, Biehl asserts that if feminine otherness is put forward as a political identity, then ecofeminists 'root themselves outside of

Western culture altogether' (1991: 15). Yet how else is the Eurocentric patriarchal tendency to essentialise masculinity as humanity to be negated without such an antithesis? Leaving the dialectical naturalism of *The Ecology of Freedom* aside, Biehl shapes her argument with ecofeminism squarely within the classic binarisms of liberal politics. In consequence, she characterises the ecofeminist argument that women and men are in and of nature as anti-Enlightenment and regressive. In fact, ecofeminists are like deep ecologists in endorsing a continuum between human and natural spheres, but they are even more like those social ecologists who argue dialectically that human and non-human nature is simultaneously continuum and disjunction.

Biehl's support for Bookchin's rejection of autonomous ecofeminist voices also adopts the classical distinction between private and public as a political given. Hence, the text of *Rethinking Ecofeminist Politics* echoes the terror that Hegel and Rousseau had of women's subversive potential: here, feminine piety versus public law represents the supreme opposition in ethics. That opposition is played out today in debates over the adequacy of caring as a feminist ethical principle. Again, forgetting Bookchin's writing on women's practice of libertarian reason, Biehl dismisses ecofeminists such as Plant, Diamond and Orenstein for seeking 'to extend the very concept of "women's sphere" as home to embrace and *absorb* the community as a whole' (1991: 132). While she agrees that ecofeminism coincides with the communitarian emphasis of social ecology, and with the ecological struggle of rural women in the Two-Thirds World, Biehl is not happy to reinforce this convergence in green thought. Rather, she remarks that 'decentralised community, seen abstractly without due regard to democracy and confederalism, has the potential to become regressive...Homophobia, anti-Semitism, and racism as well as sexism, may be part of a parochial "communitarian ethos" ' (1991: 134).

In light of recent feminist political theory, *Rethinking Ecofeminist Politics* comes down inappropriately on King's critique of a masculinist political legacy that is 'founded on repudiation of the organic, the female, the tribal, and particular ties between people'.[9] Biehl calls this 'convoluted thinking and atavism with a vengeance, especially if one considers that the Western democratic tradition produced a consciousness of *universal* freedom that ultimately opened the public sphere to women' (1991: 136).[10] Ecofeminists do not deny some ideological inspiration in the North's universalism so-called, though re/sisters in the South may have another view of the origins of their emancipatory struggle. The real issue though is the question of why our Eurocentric democratic tradition has so consistently failed to deliver. Twenty years after Second Wave feminism began, the leading nation of the Free World still has not accorded women legal possession of their own bodies. Hence the work of Mary O'Brien, Hilkka Pietila, Shiva and others to diagnose the source of this fraternal incapacity. To repeat: it is not ecofeminists, but the Western legacy itself, that puts women outside. Biehl worries about possible loss of political objectivity in ecofeminist communal dealings based on any feminine principle, but perhaps she should examine her own stance. For as she herself notes: 'In any democratic polity worthy of the name, one is accountable to one's fellow citizens [including sisters], not only to one's friends and lovers' (Biehl, 1991: 153).

Eco-anarchist Bookchin rightly regrets the arrival of factory production which killed off the principle of usufruct and self-reliance in community life. In related vein, he opposes the disempowering effect of representative government by an elected elite. Councils and political parties simply mirror the bureaucratic state in his view. As Biehl relates it:

> Social ecology distinguishes between statecraft, as a system of dealing with the public realm by means of professionalised administrators and their legal monopoly on violence, on the one hand, and politics, as the management of the community on a grass roots democratic and face-to-face level by citizen bodies.
>
> (1991: 150)

Bookchin recognises, but does not dwell on the role of a restless, transcendent masculinity in undermining its own political institutions. His lack of systematic gender analysis equally affects his treatment of usufruct – a favourite economic theme, referring to communal availability of resources by those who need them, as opposed to ownership or exchange based on the monetary principle of equivalence. Now usufruct is precisely what continues to mark the daily rounds of a global majority of women, excluded as they are from the commodity society. Pietila's account of the pink economy among Finland's domestic workers or Shiva's North Indian forest dwellers are clear illustrations. Here is 'an immediate living social basis for the alternative consciousness which [radical men are] trying to formulate as an abstract ethical construct' (Salleh, 1984: 340). But social ecology remains too compromised by traditional binarisms to make connections of this sort.

The same problem contaminates its political vision based on a rejuvenated Athenian model. *Polis* was, and is, premised on a separation of culture from nature and, as such, is ill equipped to steer an ecological future. The divide between *polis* and *oikos* was also a gendered and ethnic stratification, as women and slaves were excluded from citizenship. The gender stratification in turn reinforced the separation of humanity and nature by compounding men with culture and women with nature. With the advent of the market, *polis* effectively split *oikos* apart into economy on the one hand and ecology on the other. And so *oikos* as economics was detached from its grounding in daily needs, breaking the rational tie between household and sustainability. Further, *polis* implies severance of its own ethical universalist orientation from *oikos*, supposedly limited to particularistic ends. However, feminism now teaches us that political and personal ends are intrinsically tied, while environmental crisis teaches that we split economy from ecology at our peril. Biehl's *Rethinking Ecofeminist Politics* states that 'the essence of democracy is precisely its latent capacity to cut across particular, gender and other cultural lines' (1991: 149). Not only is democracy even in the twentieth century still latent, but the cultural line that Biehl does not mention here is that which cuts humanity off from the rest of nature. As we move towards a green understanding, it is essential to address the full gamut of Eurocentric domination.[11] Ecofeminism, like deep ecology, is concerned about the oppression of all life forms.

It goes without saying that against the dreary, alienating, exploitative society of transnational corporate capital, Bookchin's Rousseau-style neighbourhood assemblies and confederation of city states offers an inspiring alternative. Emerging first as land trusts and shadow councils, they could mobilise communities around reforms, gradually gaining legitimation and at the same time fostering autonomous co-ops, organic gardens and market places.[12] But as deep ecological greens and most ecofeminists believe, a real political shift means letting go of the culture versus nature polarity. A regressive humanity/nature split is certainly a domain-assumption of the Eurocentric political legacy that Biehl's conventional liberal feminism wishes to preserve. And although Bookchin's neo-Hegelian image of nature contemplates a continuum of life potentials rather than dualism, he also speaks of consciousness as delineating a specifically human realm separate from the rest of nature. In this rationalist vein, *Rethinking Ecofeminist Politics* would have women place themselves with men over and above nature. By contrast, ecofeminist politics enlists men to give up their originary fears of embeddedness, to join women in reaffirming their place as part of nature and to formulate new social practices and institutions in line with that perception.

Conclusion

The gulf between Bookchin's radical, if occasional, celebration of women's mutualistic rationality and Biehl's liberal disdain of feminine values is a profound theoretic fracture within social ecology. It is plain from women's ecological actions across the globe – the 300-year-old tradition of Chipko tree huggers, the peasant mothers of Seveso, Australian Koori women anti-base activists – that it is empathic nurture rather than any sophisticated social theory that guides these sound and genuinely universalised political stands. Most women in general, and ecofeminists in particular, do not have great difficulty applying concern to strangers and others outside their immediate kin community. Mutuality as an ethical basis is no more fragile than the objective basis of democratic rights legitimated by the polity of men. In fact, as ecofeminist Marti Kheel has observed in an environmental ethics context, the emotional substrate of caring is prerequisite for a rights-based ethic to function at all – an invisible feminine underbelly, whose social labour makes possible the public world of fraternal relations (1985).

Biehl's primary misgiving over ecofeminist 'immanence' is that its ontology is cyclic rather than progressive and she feels that this goes against a transcendent liberatory politics. But the logic of ecology is also cyclic, which is why human intentionality cutting a linear path to its unreasoned ends leaves so much destruction behind. Moreover, looking at green priorities, a trajectory of pure subjective choice is rationalist illusion – an embourgeoisement of freedom, to borrow Bookchin's insightful phrase. The absolute freedom of some is always enjoyed at the expense of others. Freedom was an important piece of ideology at a time when the classical liberal notion of human agency occurred to the North. But democratic citizenship, really fraternal emancipation, was only ever gained at the cost of women tacitly absorbed in social provisioning through the hidden sexual contract.

On a global scale, the freedom that men and a few women in a postmodern commodity culture believe they enjoy still rests on the labours of an underclass of women domestics, food growers and silicon slaves (Salleh, 1994). As Commoner put it: there is no such thing as a free lunch. We live in a material world and freedom has material parameters. Beyond women's labours stands the resource substrate of nature, next in the chain of appropriation. In order to arrive at a green society, where gender equity is global and a sustainable reciprocity is established with nature, we may have to rethink the unbridled Eurocentric fetish for the transcendent. True freedom involves limits and an acceptance of our embodied condition. Without awareness of this, the most enlightened citizenry is as free as infant children are.

Notes

1 On p. 15 of the 1979 Introduction to *Toward an Ecological Society*, feminism is commended for recognising the originary domination, though no woman author is cited. See also Bookchin (1980: 40). On p. 265, Bookchin acknowledges damage done to the women's liberation movement by the Left and specifically by Marxism as bourgeois sociology.

2 Bookchin's ambivalence towards feminism is deep. In *Remaking Society*, p. 64, he argues that feminists are wrong to see women as prototypal victims of hierarchy. On p. 156, he notes that feminism brought an opportunity to 'existentialise' the concept of hierarchy. His further claim that feminists have drawn 'heavily from the language and literature of social ecology' in order to do this is undocumented and patently false.

3 In connection with silencing the subaltern voices of ecofeminism, see the examination of typical defensive strategies in Salleh (1993) and for a depth analysis, Lederer (1968).

4 Bookchin's own caricature of ecofeminism can be found in *Remaking Society*, p. 163. Despite his theoretical departure from Marxism and importance as a counter-cultural thinker, this text demonstrates an Old Left difficulty in understanding the link between personal and political.

5 This work has since been formalised as Principles of the Left Green Network, First Conference of the Left Greens, Ames, Iowa, 21–23 April 1989.

6 The world's first Green Party is now recognised as the United Tasmania Group, formed in March 1972, during the heady days of struggle for Lake Pedder. The New Zealand Values Party appeared one month later.

7 Compare Salleh (1982), Keller (1985), Harding (1986), Haraway (1990). There is a useful thematic summary of feminist epistemologies in Lichtenstein (1987). See also the foundational critiques of rationalism by Gilligan (1984), Lloyd (1984) and Irigaray (1985).

8 The reference is to Kropotkin's *Mutual Aid* and Ernst Bloch's *Das Prinzip Hoffnung*.

9 This recent feminist political literature includes Okin (1979), O'Brien (1981), Hartsock (1983), Ferguson (1984), Pateman (1988) and Naffine (1990).

10 The reference is to Ynestra King's essay 'Healing the Wounds' in Diamond and Orenstein (1990).

11 Compare Salleh (1993) and *Ecofeminism as Politics: Nature, Marx and the Postmodern* (London: Zed Books, 1997).

12 Bookchin's vision of transitional practices in Chase (1991: 83–4) is especially heartening.

References

Biehl, Janet (1991), *Rethinking Ecofeminist Politics*, Boston, MA: South End Press.

Bookchin, Murray (1971), *Post Scarcity Anarchism*, Montreal: Black Rose Books.

Bookchin, Murray (1980), *Toward an Ecological Society*, Montreal: Black Rose Books.

Bookchin, Murray (1990), *Remaking Society: Pathways to a Green Future*, Boston, MA: South End Press.

Bookchin, Murray (1991), *The Ecology of Freedom* (Rev. edn, 1991), Montreal: Black Rose Books.

Chase, Steve (ed.) (1991), *Defending the Earth*, Boston, MA: South End Press.

Collard, Andree (1989), *Rape of the Wild*, London: Women's Press.

Diamond, Irene and Orenstein, Gloria (ed.) (1990), *Reweaving the World*, San Francisco, CA: Sierra Club.

Eisler, Riane (1987), *The Chalice and the Blade*, San Francisco, CA: Harper.

Ferguson, Kathy (1984), *The Feminist Case Against Bureaucracy*, Philadelphia, PA: Temple.

Gilligan, Carol (1984), *In a Different Voice*, Cambridge, MA: Harvard University Press.

Griffin, Susan (1978), *Woman and Nature*, New York: Harper.

Haraway, Donna (1990), *Primate Visions*, New York: Routledge.

Harding, Sandra (1986), *The Science Question in Feminism*, Ithaca, NY: Cornell University Press.

Hartsock, Nancy (1983), *Money, Sex, ana Power*, New cork: Longman.

Irigaray, Luce (1985), *Speculum of the Other Woman*, Ithaca, NY: Cornel University Press.

Keller, Evelyn Fox (1985), *Reflections on Gender and Science*, New Haven, CT: Yale University Press.

Kheel, Marti (1985), 'The Liberation of Nature: A Circular Affair?' *Environmental Ethics*, Vol. 7.

Lederer, Wolfgang (1968), *The Fear of Women*, New York: Harcourt.

Lichtenstein, Benyamin (1987), 'Feminist Epistemology: A Thematic Review', *Thesis Eleven*, No. 21.

Lloyd, Genevieve (1984), *The Man of Reason*, London: Routledge.

Merchant, Carolyn (1980), *The Death of Nature*, San Francisco, CA: Harper, Brace.

Mies, Maria (1987), *Patriarchy and Accumulation*, London: Zed Books.

Naffine, Ngaire (1990), *The Law and the Sexes*, Sydney: Allen & Unwin.

O'Brien, Mary (1981), *The Politics of Reproduction*, London: Routledge.

Okin, Susan Moller (1979), *Women in Western Political Thought*, Princeton, NJ: Princeton University Press.

Pateman, Carol (1988), *The Sexual Contract*, Cambridge: Polity Press.

Plant, Judith (ed.) (1989), *Healing the Wounds*, Philadelphia, PA: New Society Publishers.

Salleh, Ariel K. (1982), 'On the Dialectics of Signifying Practice', *Thesis Eleven*, No. 5–6.

Salleh, Ariel (1984), 'Deeper than Deep Ecology: The ecofeminist connection', *Environmental Ethics*, Vol. 6.

Salleh, Ariel (1993), 'Class, Race, and Gender Discourse in the Ecofeminism/Deep Ecology Debate', *Environmental Ethics*, Vol. 15.

Salleh, Ariel (1994), 'Nature, Woman, Labour, Capital: Living the Deepest Contradiction', in M. O'Connor (ed.), *Is Capitalism Sustainable?* New York: Guilford Press.

Shiva, Vandana (1989), *Staying Alive: Women, Ecology, and Development*, London: Zed Books.

Spretnak, Charlene (1982), *The Politics of Women's Spirituality*, New York: Anchor.

Spretnak, Charlene (1987), *The Spiritual Dimension of Green Politics*, Santa Fe, NM: Bear & Co.

Starhawk (1988), *Truth or Dare*, San Francisco, CA: Harper.

4   Green liberalisms

Nature, agency and the good

Piers H.G. Stephens

The tension between green political prescriptions and the standard political priorities of liberal political theory, as instantiated in the contemporary liberal democratic state, has now been a staple of debate in the field for some time. It has manifested itself at several levels: in the arguments between moral monists and moral pluralists in environmental ethics, in the apparent linkages of liberal thought with atomism and instrumentalism in green accounts of the history of ideas and in the vexed question of the compatibility of green political ideals with liberal democratic institutions.[1] Yet with the publication of Marcel Wissenburg's *Green Liberalism*, the first full-length argument for the capacity of the liberal democratic state to deliver much of the green agenda, the debate has entered a new phase. Wissenburg's work, with its 'restraint principle' (a revamping of the Rawlsian 'just savings' principle) to account for sustainability issues and do away with arguments for intrinsic value, its thought-provoking reflections on procreative rights and its stimulating attempt to map out a weakly anthropocentric rough path between 'the short-term ecological modernisation and the often politically unfeasible long-term ecological Utopianism approaches' (Wissenburg, 1998: 3) is now required reading; green thinkers, whether they are of anti-liberal persuasion or, like this writer, supporters of a broadly green critique of the status quo but fearful of throwing out the liberal baby with the extraneous Enlightenment bathwater, will have to engage with Wissenburg's arguments and respond to them if they can. In this chapter I want to sketch out the areas of Wissenburg's argument which I regard as most problematic and then set out the initial elements of my response.

We should note first of all that Wissenburg's project is liberal first and green second; his focus is avowedly on 'the rules used by the political system at the moment of decision-making' and his guiding question that of whether 'the rules of a liberal democratic system *themselves* [can] in any way accommodate g's type of preferences for a greener world, regardless of the current type of preferences of the individuals who accidentally happen to be around?' a question which he broadly answers in the affirmative (Wissenburg, 1998: 17–18). In this respect, to contextualise the debate, Wissenburg and I are coming to the same rough point on the political territory, namely that of a middle path between the excesses of green utopianism and the technofix of ecological modernisation,[2] but we are coming from different directions and carrying different epistemological baggage.

Part of this baggage, as should become clear later, is my attachment to classical American pragmatism, a theory which shares the liberal emphases on fallibilism, pluralism and toleration, but also insists upon the situated and environmentally embodied status of any judging agent, and in this analysis I intend to focus on Wissenburg's conceptions of human nature and agency, along with the related concerns with liberal neutrality and the good, only obliquely using my criticisms here to argue against Wissenburg's instrumentalised view of subjectivist value, and thus for a more fully greened type of liberal society. In doing so, I shall argue that the implicit human nature and agency models present in liberalism, when taken in conjunction with the way in which elements of human nature may be either encouraged or suppressed through the choices of particular liberties advocated by particular liberal thinkers, in practice tend to reverse into a broad regulative ideal of the moral and political agent, and moreover that some such regulative ideals are healthier for green outcomes than others. In other words, an appropriate theory of the self, however abstract this topic may be, is a *conditio sine qua non* for the justification/legitimisation of ecological policies in the concrete context of modern liberal democratic societies. With these points flagged in advance, let us now move on to the essential outlines of Wissenburg's scheme that will be examined.

Wissenburg conceives of contemporary liberal democracy as resting on three pillars of principle: those of liberty, equality and democracy. Within this framework, liberal democratic politics is represented as 'the existence, on a collective level, of mediating and reconciliatory mechanisms (state, market, education, etc.), transforming the *claims* of individuals to benefits and the reduction of burdens into formal rights via the recognition of valid claims by means of *principles* of social justice'; the system is thus 'a particular form of input–output machine, transforming the preferences of individuals into rights for individuals' (Wissenburg, 1998: 9, 11). Within Wissenburg's treatment, preferences are treated as given, a move which he acknowledges to be practically unrealistic but maintains is predominantly methodological in intent, and similarly he repudiates any 'interference by higher authorities [i.e. the state] in the process of preference formation' (Wissenburg, 1998: 220). Human agency is thus represented at a high level of formal abstraction, and though Wissenburg does devote some space to the history of liberal political thought and its increasing abandonment of formal metaphysical grounding in conceptions of human nature, as well as taking care to distinguish political from full-blown economic liberalism, his own version of agency is typically modern in its formalism. Just as Rawls's agents in the original position are abstract genderless beings who are unaware of their conceptions of the good or the talents and social stations which await them once the veil of ignorance is lifted, so Wissenburg's model of agency is effectively that of a black box which projects preferences into the political mechanism.

This formalism is continued in a further area of focus, and the one which I shall begin with in earnest. This is Wissenburg's effective acceptance, though he does not explicitly use the terminology, of the definition of a liberal state as being one which is neutral between competing conceptions of the good; in his own characterisation of the matter, he argues for 'the "liberty of life" to design and pursue any reasonable plan of life' where 'no moral standard, hence no individual plan of life... should be privileged over any other' and allocates it as a defining duty for a liberal democratic polity that it must 'show equal respect, i.e. not to favour any plan or conception of life over any other' (Wissenburg, 1998: 43). This type of definition of the liberal state is, of course, very much a standard of contemporary political theory, though as I shall try to indicate later, it is perhaps less contentious as a characterisation in general theoretical discourse than it properly ought to be when viewed in the wider liberal historical context.

The final main element of Wissenburg's characterisation that I plan to give critical attention to is that which is by his own admission the least developed area of the book, namely his invocation of civic virtue. Wissenburg, in a defence of economic liberalism that places the onus on the consumer but none the less stops short of libertarian extremes, appears to place a great deal of weight on this concept, as arguably he must do given his refusal to countenance state intervention in preference formation.[3] Indeed, he explicitly argues that 'green liberalism requires individual responsibility to be viable: citizen virtue but even more civic virtue, and particularly virtue in the market place' (Wissenburg, 1998: 90). Yet remarkably, beyond a few remarks on virtue in the medieval market, the idea remains largely undeveloped. I shall argue that Wissenburg is right to acknowledge the need for this component, but that the combination of his highly abstract human agency theory with his conflation of subjective with instrumental values and refusal to engage in speculation on preference formation leaves him bereft of sufficient theoretical tools to make the presence of this notion convincing in the face of the corrosive effects of market instrumentalisation of the world.

With these main targets for analysis now outlined, let us begin with an examination of the standard characterisation of the liberal state as one defined by its neutrality between competing conceptions of the good.

Neutrality and agency: Wissenburg, Locke and Mill

Wissenburg's implicit characterisation of the liberal state as one which is neutral between competing conceptions of the good is one that is characteristic of twentieth-century liberalism, and it is important to recognise the provenance of the notion. First, as Jeremy Waldron observes, this neutrality 'is not and cannot be the doctrine that legislation should be neutral in relation to all moral values', nor the equally incoherent claim that legislation should somehow be 'value-free' (Waldron, 1989: 72). Rather, neutrality is itself a value, a value which is instrumental in securing some good, in the same way that the impartiality of a judge is instrumental in achieving justice. The point is thus that neutrality is the *right position to adopt*, rather than that neutrality is legitimated by virtue of there being no good to be promoted or ill to be combated in legislation. There must, of course, be reasons, either directly or indirectly to do with some formulation of citizens' welfare, as to why neutrality is the correct procedure, and in what follows I shall argue that such a formulation will itself be value-laden and necessarily involve either overt or covert recourse to regulative ideals of human nature, to what a human being is and what they may or ideally ought to become.

We must now turn to why neutrality is a good, and thus we come to the indirect character of the liberal values of individual liberty and diversity. As the impossibility of a liberal legislator being neutral about the value of neutrality implies, liberalism may be agnostic as to the nature of the good life, but it must contain some conception of the necessary requirements for a good life; as Rawls would put it, it must have a notion of primary goods. Since much of the justification of the state's official agnosticism on the nature of the good is precisely to enable the flourishing of a plurality of differing conceptions of the good, chosen by different free agents, then the most obvious and central values here are those of individual liberty and social diversity; the core intuition is perhaps best summed up by Mill, in his assertion that 'if a person possesses any tolerable amount of common sense and experience, his own mode of laying out his existence is the best, not because it is the best in itself, but because it is his own mode' (Mill, 1984: 135). The two values interconnect in that the practical worth of liberty, the exercise in self-reliance and self-creation which acting freely involves, will necessarily require a diverse range of options to choose from, and inevitably, the choice of primary goods will frame the broad character of the polity.

Though the notion of neutrality does indeed appear to articulate long-standing liberal concerns, it is well worth recognising that the use of this rather abstract term as a defining characteristic of liberalism is, as Goodin and Reeve note, a recent development; indeed, Waldron sees no explicit formulation in these terms before 1974 (Goodin and Reeve, 1989: 1; Waldron, 1989: 62). This habitually high level of theoretical abstraction is a striking characteristic of modern liberalism more generally, as already noted in relation to Wissenburg and Rawls, though one that has not gone uncriticised in recent times.[4] Yet I believe that as a characterisation of the essence of a liberal state, it should be seen as what it is: effectively a scholastic device, an explanatory hook on which to hang a variety of theories, rather than a characterisation of liberalism *tout court* as Wissenburg appears to assume. Notoriously, of course, what it means to treat individuals equally under a neutral state is itself an immensely morally contested field, with contests becoming especially notable when liberal values are deployed against the prevailing interpretation of neutrality within the state at the time. I want now to bring up some historical examples, those of Locke and Mill, which may shed light and also cast doubts upon the adequacy of the contemporary characterisation of the liberal state and in particular on Wissenburg's ahistorical, formalistic variant of this.

The first example is that of Locke – a, and perhaps the, major source of inspiration for liberals over the past centuries. I have provided an extensive reading of Locke's political philosophy in relation to nature and property elsewhere (Stephens, 1999) and shall not go into the full details of that reading here. Rather, what concerns us are those areas of Locke's thought which pertain to agency, neutrality and the good.

We should note first that while Locke's philosophy explicitly abandons any search for a classically definitive summum bonum of human life and happiness, this was not due to any agnosticism on his part as to the nature of the good. On the contrary, Locke was adamant to the last that the injunctions of the natural law could be known and proved, that reason was the faculty that would reveal 'right reason', the dictates of the natural law itself, and that the field of morality was an area in which demonstrable truths could be found, given patient application, with mathematical certainty (Locke, 1958: 149, 1975: 549–50). We find his own working out of these issues in the writings on Christianity, education, toleration and, of course, politics, but also in his reflections on human nature in the *Essay Concerning Human Understanding*. Key in these areas is the classic Protestant concern with the individual and the related work ethic associated with Weber's analysis; it is this which is focal in Locke's statement that God gave the earth 'to the use of the Industrious and Rational', especially when set against his sarcasm about the 'irrational untaught Inhabitants' of 'Woods and Forests' who 'keep right by following Nature' in the First Treatise (Locke, 1988: 294, 291, 183).

Locke, for all his status as an icon of liberal toleration, had no time for the conceptions of freedom held by the folk traditions of sylvan liberty and was a fervent apologist for enclosure and Baconian agricultural improvements that would maximise production, even being prepared to extend royal prerogative for 'God-like Princes' who promote the 'increase of lands and the right imploying of them' (Locke, 1988: 378, 298). What matters from our perspective here is not only that those who appropriate for productive and transformative purposes are acting under the divine injunction to 'subdue the Earth' and 'lay out something upon it' that was their own (Locke, 1988: 291), but that in doing so they are simultaneously *expressing moral rationality*, generating value by their labour and expanding the sphere of concrete human freedom against determinate nature.

Locke, then, had little doubt about the existence of an objective good and was strongly convinced of the character of this good. In relation to the goal of state neutrality noted earlier, we can see merely from these extracts that the state may be granted additional powers to promote a core goal, that of a particular conception of liberty, a conception which closely ties liberty and moral rationality to a dynamic of transformative labour. Locke's praise of the industrious farmer who maximises production could not be more explicit on this transformative dynamic; it is, he informs us, '*Labour* indeed that *puts the difference of value* on every thing', use-value being 99 per cent 'on the account of labour', whereas 'Land that is wholly left to Nature' is 'called, as indeed it is, wast' (Locke, 1988: 296–7).[5] The imparting of value is given by a manifestation of free will, and this manifestation is initiative; since only man has this dimension, then only man can appropriate and transform nature. Hence a particular conception of liberty, a conception which ties it to productive expansionist labour, is intimately tied to the conception of neutrality involved; the state should not violate particular rights of property, not merely for theological-cum-deontological reasons, but because productive labour manifests the distinctly human trait of initiative. Economic enrichment, provided that it is carried out without violation of others' rights and done for the right reasons rather than through mere greed and the quest for power, is regarded as an unquestioned morally laden objective good – hence Locke's comparison of the English day labourer with a native American king, in which he ignores consideration of status or relative utility to pronounce the lot of the former, who has transformed nature for economic advantage, to be unequivocally better.[6]

In this instance, then, neutrality is not only constructed in a particular way – that is, based on a particular notion of liberty – but is intimately tied to and justi- fied by particular ideas of objective goods to be promoted through it. Neutrality is thus adopted not merely to rule out certain activities whilst leaving a free space elsewhere, but also to promote a particular conception of liberty as the good life; the system, though not attempting to enforce a set uniform morality by directly coercive state methods, can thus be none the less seen to possess a dynamic which will implicitly promote some goods while downgrading others. And this impres- sion is reinforced by a consideration of Locke's views on human nature and agency, as manifested in the *Essay*.

To begin with, we should note that in the treatment which follows, I am not assuming any form of naturalistic fallacy, of a simple 'reading off' of the good from human nature. Rather, what is significant is that conceptions of the good must require as background some notion of the type of being that a human is, and in this sense the differing accounts of human flourishing, of what it is to be a free, autonomous human individual self of integrated and fulfilled type, found in Locke and Mill are significant. To start with the issue of liberty, it is notable that the anti-naturalistic transformative dynamic manifested in relation to outer nature is equally present in his treatment of human inner nature. Here it seems proper to invoke two significant *Essay* passages in which Locke discusses desire and the will. He notes that man has 'a power to suspend the execution and satisfaction of any of its desires, and so... is at liberty to consider the objects of them; examine them on all sides, and weigh them... In this lies the liberty Man has... in this seems to consist that, which is (as I think improperly) call'd *Free will*' and more- over ''tis as much *a perfection, that desire or the power of Preferring should be determined by Good*, as that the power of Acting should be determined by the Will'.[7] This seems important. Humans have the power to evaluate their desires and suspend the will, interposing rational judgement before activating it to the best course of action, whereas animals merely operate instinctively; in the same manner, humans can interpose appropriation between their desire for subsistence and the satisfaction of it. Freedom is thus partly defined in terms of external action and the repression of internal nature. In both cases the result is an increase in value and a manifestation of distinctively human autonomy.

Moving on to the related topic of the self, the main touchstone for Locke may be found in his analysis in Book II of the *Essay*. Locke's treatment of the self here clearly runs the passive cognitive self into the active conative self, constantly link- ing together the ego with egoism. We hear, for example, that the self is 'that con- scious thinking thing... which is sensible, or conscious of Pleasure and Pain' and is therefore concerned for itself 'as far as that consciousness extends'; that 'all the Right and Justice of Reward and Punishment' is founded in personal identity, both happiness and misery being that 'for which every one is concerned for himself, not mattering what becomes of any Substance, not joined to, or affected with that consciousness', and further that the personality 'extends it *self* beyond present Existence to what is past, only by consciousness, whereby it becomes concerned and accountable', at root because we find 'a concern for Happiness the unavoidable concomitant of consciousness, that which is conscious of Pleasure and Pain, desiring, that that self, that is conscious, should be happy' (Locke, 1975: 341–2, 346).

Not only is the account here clearly egoistic, but it is an identifiably utilitarian egoism. Indeed, one contemporary utilitarian thinker prominently includes Locke amongst Bentham's intellectual ancestors in the tradition (Hayry, 1994: 4, 10–11, 20–1, 24–5). Moreover, Locke sees desire as an uneasiness, brought about by the absence of something enjoyable, but an uneasiness to be positively used, 'the chief if not only spur to Humane Industry and Action' (Locke, 1975: 230). Importantly, this demonstrates that for Locke, not only were men basically self-interested, but their actions were fundamentally driven by the uneasiness of desire, especially *acquisitive* desire. And here Locke's utilitarian and possessive concerns are curiously linked, for he tells us that the 'greatest Happiness consists in having those things which produce the greatest Pleasure', rather than in enjoying them, whilst at the same time insisting that the acquisitive quest is dynamic, propelled by 'a constant succession of uneasinesses', desires which 'take the will in their turns' (Locke, 1975: 269, 262).[8]

By implication, nature primarily exists to possess and remould, not to respect as it is, and such desires are in principle infinite, giving a powerful expansionist dynamic to his Baconian vision of increased agricultural production through enclosure, private ownership and experiment. We should also note the radical atomism of the approach: subject and object are not linked, but primordially separate, whereby 'every one is concerned for himself, not mattering what becomes of any Substance, not joined to, or affected with that consciousness'.

The moral key for Locke is to acquire the right desires, training acquisitiveness to economically productive impact whilst restraining desires that would violate Christian natural law; as such, the model of the human agent involved and the values attributed to particular liberties in the Lockean account of neutrality are deeply intertwined with a particular ideal type. Locke did not believe that one could or should impose this ideal directly by physical coercion, but it nonetheless informs his entire project: it is, so to speak, a regulative ideal of the human agent, a vision of what the human being is and should (if possible) ideally become, an implicit benchmark linking nature and ethics, is and ought. In appropriation, the atomised agent projects themselves on to the world, annexes a spiritual domain of initiative on to Newtonian matter, making it an owned productive object, and natural acquisitiveness, tempered by self-control, should promote this 'only spur to Humane action'.

To draw on a phrase from Bob Brecher's sharp little recent critique of liberal morality, the Lockean human being is, at root, 'a wanting thing', with the added presupposition that wants should, in principle, be satisfied.[9] The self is thus a disconnected subject, and this disconnection, I believe, naturally lends itself to instrumental modes of perception. We may note in passing the striking resemblance between this atomised self, projecting desires onto the world and Wissenburg's model of agency, in which the human agent is represented as a black box which projects preferences into the polity, and should recognise how alarming the implications of this type of formalism are from a green perspective. For the more fully the subject is conceived as an impermeable, disconnected 'wanting thing', then the less any mutual and fluidic interchange between subject and object or full-blown experiential encounter are possible; as with the separative self of neoclassical economics, relationship will necessarily be increasingly modelled on egoism, ownership, annexation and instrumental extraction of worth, since altruism, for example, would imply that one subject's happiness depended on what made another happy and thus violate the assumption of independent preferences.[10] In addition, precious little room is left for appreciation of nature in any sense other than as resource.

Moving on to Mill, we have a similar insistence on the priority of liberty, but differently conceived so far as the weighting attached to particular liberties is concerned, and as a consequence, different attitudes to inner and outer nature are both implicit and made feasible. Mill's defences of freedom of speech, and the worries over the harm principle, are already exhaustively analysed, but here I wish to focus more on the themes developed around human agency and nature in his writings, as a counterpoint to the previous example, drawing especially on the themes of *On Liberty* developed in his chapter on individuality. Mill's work, as I have argued elsewhere (Stephens, 1996), is surely the classical liberal theory with which greens can find common ground, and a key factor in this is precisely the difference between the views of human agency and the self, and the different emphases on the particular liberties that may be held most important, that we find in his work.

Mill's scheme differs from Locke's, superficially, through its defence of individuality for its own sake. Social toleration of diversity is to be justified not merely because intolerance is irrational, as in Locke's account of religious toleration, but through the need for a diversity of options from which the individual may form themselves as an individual, through the possibilities of social experiments in living and through a fallibilism which insists on resisting any closure which might result in the rejection of possible truths. Just as Locke's defence of his scheme was bound up with a particular conception of significant liberties that were ultimately tightly linked to results, so Mill's more explicit consequentialism is anchored in a notion of social progress. Yet, and critically for green acceptability, this notion differs from the Lockean scheme of progress in the form of maximised productivity, and I broadly agree with John Barry in his recent pronouncement that it is a particular conflation of the idea of progress with its dominant present instantiation, the dream of ever-increasing economic growth and technological transformation, that really lies at the heart of green scepticism about 'progress' (Barry, 1999: 249–55).

Mill's emphasis is quite different from this Lockean-inspired dream. He explicitly repudiates the idea that human progress is logically necessary and automatic as being fallacious (Mill, 1974: 790–1), while his famous advocacy of an eventual 'stationary state' of economic growth rejects the equation of moral progress with such growth, instead affirming that such a state would allow 'as much scope as ever for all kinds of mental culture, and moral and social progress...and much more likelihood of its being improved, when minds ceased to be engrossed by the art of getting on' (Mill, 1987: 750–1). Yet his idea of human development is also broader than a merely intellectualist one. In fact, it is derived from a classical ideal, and economic and productive liberties are far from being the focus for Mill that they are for Locke.[11] *On Liberty*, all too often thought of as a handbook of arguments for free marketeers, is certainly not a defence of possessive individu-alism, and Mill is quite explicit in what limited treatment he does give to the ques-tion of state action on economic affairs in the last chapter of the work: 'these are questions which, though closely connected with the subject of this *Essay, do not, in strictness, belong to it*...cases in which the reasons against interference do not turn upon the principle of liberty' (Mill, 1984: 178). Rather, what animates it, and similarly impacts upon the notions of neutrality and agency involved, is the apho-rism from Von Humboldt which opens the work: 'the absolute and essential importance of human development in its richest diversity' (Mill, 1984: 69).

This emphasis, it should be made clear, does not merely appeal to diversity across society, but also to the development of the individual within it. Whereas Locke's model of motivation and agency is ultimately a training of the wants of a 'wanting thing', time and again Mill invokes the notion of balancing a variety of diverse factors both in the society outside the individual personality and within the agent's own personality, factors which include material desires but are not exhausted or primarily defined by them. Indeed, it is precisely the narrowness of the Lockean formulation that Mill objects to: 'There is now scarcely any outlet for energy in this country', he protests, 'except business'. Against this, he argues for both the widest range of development of faculties and the greatest integration of them. 'He who chooses his plan for himself', he argues, 'employs all his fac-ulties', an integration and development that is vital because it is 'of importance, not only what men do, but also what manner of men they are that do it'; in the perfecting of human works, 'the first in importance surely is man himself' (Mill, 1984: 138, 126–7).

What is significant about this vision is that it provides a set of naturalistic background assumptions of what the human agent may become, allied to an emphasis on individual liberty as the best manner of encouraging this develop-ment. Just as with Locke, the neutrality of the state, and the liberties it should allow, are set in the context of an account of human agency that employs a regu-lative ideal of human potentiality and development of inner nature. Against the Lockean egoist model, Mill has deployed a classical ideal of well-rounded devel-opment according to the inner nature of the individual and even emphasises this with his insistence that ' "Pagan self-assertion" is one of the elements of human worth, as well as "Christian self-denial"...It may be better to be a John Knox than an Alcibiades, but it is better to be a Pericles than either.' We may also detect the presence of this vision in Mill's otherwise bizarre invocation of Socrates as a utilitarian at the beginning of his essay Utilitarianism; both this and Mill's division of higher and lower pleasures may be seen as a recasting of utilitarian morality into a variant of Aristotelian eudaemonia, not so much happiness as fulfilment and flourishing through development of faculties. Most significantly, in his other significant citation from Von Humboldt in *On Liberty*, Mill makes this regulative ideal quite plain: 'the end of man, or that which is prescribed by the external or immutable dictates of reason, and not suggested by vague and transient desires, is the highest and most harmonious development of his powers to a complete and consistent whole', and as such, this goal is that 'towards which every human being must consistently direct his efforts...the individuality of power and development' (Mill, 1984: 125).

We should also note that Mill, unlike Locke, implicitly takes on board the idea of the agent as a social and *relational* being. His complaints, about the homogenising effects of media, the compression of personality through the power of public opinion and the dangers of uniformity through mass market pressures were voiced as early as 1836 in the essay *Civilisation* and not only have a strikingly contemporary ring,[12] but necessarily involve a conception of the agent as *primarily* interactive; subjects do not merely confront a determinate natural world, are not mere impermeable black boxes projecting given preferences into the void, but are in constant development and flux through the pressures of the information flowing from this process of encounter. In his writings on education and nature, Mill is eager to stress the need for respectful cultivation of innate natural energies rather than the imposition of information on to a Lockean *tabularasa*, maintaining that it is 'through such fostering, commenced early...that...the most elevated sentiments of which humanity is capable become a second nature, stronger than the first, and not so much subduing the original nature as merging it into itself' (Mill, 1969: 396).

The latter part of this statement is especially significant, for genuine progress is to be conceived on a model of cultivation, of development informed by nature and its potentialities, a theme which I shall return to. What is significant here, however, is that Mill's liberalism differs from Locke's in being a form of evolutionary liberalism (to use Gus diZerega's happy phrase) in which the individual is essentially a relational being, 'more verb than thing, a gestalt of relationships' rather than a disconnected atom, and the model of agency thus allows space for the forms of encounter and experience which greens habitually invoke against modernity's ethos of estrangement.[13]

What I have tried to demonstrate in these examinations is that the neutrality of the liberal state is, in a fully developed theory, intimately linked to goods of, or resulting from, liberty, and indeed to particular liberties, which may be ranked differently. The definitions of liberty and the ascriptions of priority to particular liberties (as, for example, in the limiting or expansion of the bundle of liberties involved in a property right) necessarily involves the assumption that *these* goods and liberties are more important and morally fitting than others. Moreover, these goods are themselves necessarily conditioned and informed by ideas of human agency in the world and goods of human development, conceived either in a narrowly economistic way or more broadly across an ideal of wide potentiality. This necessarily involves recourse to some background model of human nature and potential against which the evaluative judgments must be mapped; unless it is taken as a Moorean non-natural property or suchlike metaphysical oddity, good cannot mean anything except by reference to some account of what sort of organism the good is good for, and classical liberals did not shirk such accounts.

Thus a Benthamite liberal will ultimately be driven back to the justificatory ground of pleasure/pain moral psychology when pressed, while Kant, whose ethics appear far removed from naturalism, none the less insisted on a 'pure' rational and universalist ethics precisely because he regarded reason as the home in which humans could find and act upon the transcendent demands of the moral law; emotional inclination was unsuitable for moral purposes because moral action must be free action and inclination, as the part of the human which shared in the determinate order of nature, opposed freedom. Hence an implicit human nature theory is still very much present. Nor did Kant's scheme wholly abandon teleology in its understanding of human nature and its optimal course of development.[14]

The lesson to be drawn is that regulative ideals of the human agent and his or her nature and goods are practically unavoidable, for to state that some liberties are more important than others is effectively to make a moral choice, to state that some goods are more worth promoting than others; for this to have *general* justificatory backing it must appeal in turn to some broader vision of human nature and potential. Thus to say in a general political theory that consumer choice liberties are to trump liberties of political choice is effectively to say that human agents are more paradigmatically consumers than political animals and that it is at least implicitly better for them to be so.

Two points seem to follow from these considerations. The first is that regulative ideals of the nature of the human agent, of the linkage between is and ought in terms of human potentialities and goods, are like the air bubble under the carpet: try to press them out and they will pop up unexpectedly somewhere else. Even the most abstract of models will tend to sit far more easily with certain naturalistic assumptions than others, as my earlier comments about Wissenburg's preference-projecting black boxes may indicate. Second, if regulative ideals of the type I have outlined are unavoidable, then surely a liberal who truly upholds the values of liberty and diversity should opt for whichever model offers the *widest range* of developmental options.

Mill's account, habitually thought of as a 'thick' theory in its many-sidedness, surely fits the bill here. It is probably true that not everyone can be Pericles, but Mill's claim is not that only such a paragon may be considered possessed of 'true' human nature, and thus that a higher good must be invoked against those who fail to match it. Rather, it is that the ideal of the person who possesses the fullest breadth of talents and capacities is the best (because broadest) regulative ideal that we can employ as a guide at both the individual and social level, and this is precisely because of the central importance of liberty and diversity. The reality of specialisation in skills and knowledge today militates against this ideal, whilst the pervasive pressures to conceive of almost every human activity in terms of production and consumption does likewise by persistently squeezing out 'soft' non-material values like concern for nature; accordingly, it would appear all the more necessary to affirm the breadth of the Millite ideal precisely in the interests of diversity.

By comparison to these full-blown examples of classical liberalism, we can see that Wissenburg's characterisation of the liberal state and human agency is rather descriptively anaemic. Moreover, in its refusal to question preferences and its disconnected 'black box' model of the agent, it bears a far stronger resemblance to the Lockean scheme than the Millite one: the preference-projecting 'black box' is identifiably a successor of the Lockean 'wanting thing'. Indeed, the extent to which wants and Lockean mechanism dominate Wissenburg's scheme becomes obvious when we recall again his explicit characterisation of the liberal polity: 'a particular form of input–output machine, transforming the preferences of individuals into rights for individuals' (Wissenburg, 1998: 11).

Wissenburg might reply that this resemblance is irrelevant, for his characterisation is intended methodologically rather than normatively. Yet given that the significance of his work is that his theory could (hopefully) at some stage be manifested in practice, the characterisation will need to be cashed out, and any consistent translation must retain the idea of the agent as essentially a disconnected being with given preferences. Indeed, Wissenburg himself insists on this aspect of disconnected agency, maintaining in an endnote that 'pragmatism, unlike liberal political philosophy, links the observation that mind and its products develop in dialogue with their environment(s) to a sceptical attitude with regard to given preferences' and thus 'has a far less disinterested perspective on the value of nature than liberalism' (Wissenburg, 1998: 230, fn.10).

Pragmatism is indeed emphatic on the linkage between the mind and environment; yet in my view, that is precisely the cause of pragmatism's supremacy for these purposes. Nor, on the reading given, can Lockean political philosophy really be characterised as having a disinterested perspective on preferences in relation to the value of nature. One need not suppose any causally idealist view of history to assert that in its atomism and its expansionist motivational dynamic, as well as the well documented formative impact of these on the economic thought of Adam Smith and the neo-classical marginalists (Cropsey, 1977; Wolin, 1960), Lockean political philosophy can be seen to stand at the historical root of the productionist imperative which greens set their faces against.

The revolution in values represented by Locke and by Baconian science was one which abandoned the original meaning of culture, *cultus*, the idea of cultivation (as later represented in Millite education) in which nature was one's guide rather than one's enemy, the idea of nature as a principle of development from which one learned through receptivity. With the ideal of culture as cultus dethroned, then from that point in history, as Strauss observes, it is not 'resigned gratitude and consciously obeying or imitating nature but hopeful self-reliance and creativity' that 'become henceforth the marks of human nobility' (Strauss, 1953: 248); it is also this latter dynamic which informs the economistically inspired accounts of human motivation and agency that have dominated liberal political thought in the twentieth century and which Wissenburg's formalistic model is most closely related to.

A pragmatist perspective, by contrast, can be seen as closely related to the core values of liberalism – fallibilist toleration, moral pluralism, a democratic approach to truth and the encouragement of social experimentation – while lacking the commitment to economic instrumentalisation found in Lockean inspired liberal thought. In ethical approaches, pragmatism stands for an attempt to interweave and coherently balance values (Weston, 1992), just as Mill sought to balance the human agent's impulses, rather than to formalise the individual into a purely choosing agent and resolve clashes by a head-count of given preferences. Indeed, the closeness of the connection between classical pragmatism and Mill's brand of liberalism is illustrated by William James' decision to dedicate his book *Pragmatism* to the memory of Mill, 'whom my fancy likes to picture as our leader were he alive today' (James, 1907).

This issue of agency and interaction with environment leads us on to our concluding considerations, focused on Wissenburg's treatment of intrinsic value and the issue of virtue.

Value, virtue and practices

The fact that Wissenburg's commitment to the disengaged agent must run deeper than a methodological device would is indicated by his treatment of intrinsic value. Here his typology, which reduces to four possible interpretations, is careful and probably represents the most definitive categorisation of types currently available. Yet his treatment of them is, to put it mildly, odd. Whilst arguing, I think correctly, that 'there can be no value without a valuer', he gives the examples of staring at the night sky or meditating about infinity to claim that if we gain something from such cases, then 'the stars above have a use, they are instruments in our attempts to fight boredom or depression or to relax'; because 'anything we choose to do we do by definition for a reason...and the reason makes the act (looking up) and its prerequisites (the stars) means to whatever end our reasons are'. Later, following on from this argument for the necessary instrumentality and subjectivity of value, he even goes so far as to 'use "external" and "instrumental" value as synonyms unless explicitly noted otherwise' (Wissenburg, 1998: 96, 98), thus linking together subjectivism with instrumentalism as a necessary cognitive posture of valuing. This, I think goes too far.

My reason for holding this invokes Jamesian considerations of psychology and radical empiricism (James, 1912, 1918). These are that in the data of real experience, consciousness selects and does so on the grounds of worth and interest to us. We can of course give reasons as to why consciousness does this and why we attend to what we do: we attend to what interests us. But whilst these are reasons, it does not follow that the reasons *precede* the act and thus make the value in question instrumental. If I am walking in the country and have my eye drawn by a pheasant flying from the undergrowth, I may watch the pheasant, and *after-wards* say that I found this pleasurable, interesting or whatever. But at the moment of contact, of being aware of something happening, I do not know, and may not have, a *conscious reason* for my eye being drawn; the instrumentality, the use-value if you prefer, is ascribed after the fact, not before. Yet clearly, from the mass of sensory data, I focused, I valued one portion of experience more highly than another and did this before I could ascribe any instrumental value to it – quite simply, because I did not yet know what it was.

Hence from the fact that the experience was mine, and that I subsequently gave instrumental reasons for it. it does not follow that the value of the experience occurred for instrumental reasons, that I 'used' the pheasant as a means. On the contrary, it is precisely in moments of simple receptivity that the jaws of instrumental rationality are temporarily closed, and this may account for much of what is accounted special about nature experience, its role as a counterbalance to the instrumentality of technology and mass production that surrounds us at other times.[15] At the wider political level, the point may also stand against Wissenburg's wider classification of nature as instrumental resource (albeit one which should be sparingly used).

What I think this conflation of instrumentality with subjectivism illustrates is that Wissenburg has, however unwittingly, bought into the Lockean account of motivation that goes along with the baggage of the disengaged reasoning agent engaged in projecting preferences onto the world, thus squeezing out the possibility of appreciating nature other than in predefined use-value terms. If it is the case that we are self-interested detached social atoms, then it will also naturally follow that our reasons for action and perception will be predominantly instrumental, for the world will essentially look to us like a container of items for use, rather than (say) a set of possibilities for engaged relationship. Though it is logically possible to detach methodological assumptions of the Wissenburg type from the forms of rationality and assumptions that habitually go with them, this example may illustrate just how difficult that is, in practice, to do. Theories of agency and the self tend automatically to suggest fitting accounts of motivation and nurture abhors a vacuum.

The example also illustrates a pragmatic point: though consciousness is informed by previous experience and will select accordingly, there is none the less a priority of experience to conceptualisations about experience. This in turn is significant from the perspective of Wissenburg's invocation of virtuous practices, for the central issue raised by an agent who values instrumentally is that their activity will be geared to external goals: they turn up for work so that they will get paid, not because they are engaging in a practice of work that contains internal goals that they appreciate. This issue of cognitive posture towards experience is significant in several ways.

First, there is the issue of what we experience. Numerous green positions stress the role of direct experience of nature, and this stress does not only apply to wilderness experience in the American context. Rather, it can be seen to connect to green critiques of the modern self as disconnected, instrumentalised and narrow. In this respect, the critique links also to green communitarianism, attacks on the alienation of the modern subject and to the sometimes unfortunate demand from deep ecologists and their ilk for the 're-enchantment of the world'. What all these themes have in common is, I believe, a single core intuition, the intuition that what is missing about contemporary views of experience and the self is the sense of relational connection, and that as Anthony Weston has it, 'this disconnection, on the deepest level, *is* "the environmental crisis"' (Weston, 1994: 8).

The extent to which we should disconnect from immediacy of experience in order to control the world according to our free will is, as we saw in our examination of Locke, a demand that was originally motivated by expansionist intent. Yet it was motivated also by fear, for Locke is concerned that the 'wanting thing' that is the human agent must be *restrained* by reason, and the suppression of elements of inner and outer nature go hand-in-hand, replacing an earlier model of human culture and development in which the key demand was on employing nature as a principle of development. *Cultus*, in the original Latin, carried no implications of denying nature or opposing the human and natural as such. Rather, it implied being informed by nature, working *with* its own dynamics rather than imposing preset patterns upon it. And in order to do this, to recapture a model of harmonious interaction, it is necessary to have some nature to experience, and by this I do not necessarily mean wilderness; rather, I mean nature as counterpointed to human instrumental artifice of the Lockean era.

This links to my second point, that of how we experience, of our cognitive posture towards what we experience. Wissenburg's assumption that the fact that our looking at the stars may render some utility to us means that we must necessarily regard the experience as instrumental posits the conscious reason for the action as being *prior* to the experience and geared to a further end of satisfaction. By doing so, he is then able to argue that we *have an instrumental interest beforehand*, and that this is projected outwards to the objects. But it does not follow that we must have an interest in a predefined sense; on the contrary, it may be that we look because we *are interested*, that, like every human child before they learn to instrumentalise the world, we remain open to experience and wonder. To *have an interest* is already to have to some extent limited and defined the subject matter of that interest, to regard it as something which one has a particular orientation towards, and in our present era, over which the shadow of Lockean possessive individualism hovers so powerfully, such interests are habitually thought of in possessive and consumptive terms; to *be interested*, by contrast, is to be engaged, to be open to the possibility of surprise in encounter and to the possibility of being guided by the object in the manner of the earlier notion of culture advanced, *cultus*. The initial cognitive posture is as significant as the presence of nature itself, since what we experience will be partly conditioned by how we approach it.

This point is easy to recognise if we take an example from intra-human relationships, that of friendship. Friendship involves numerous internal goods but can also sometimes produce external goods, as when a friend informs us of a bargain or an opportunity. Yet to regard friendship as a social institution geared to the production of external goods is to fail to understand the nature of friendship, and this failure is obvious if we consider the likely fortunes of someone who attempted to acquire friends solely with a view to attaining external goods from the relationship; we all recognise the insincerity of the sycophant or the fair-weather friend. Such a person would fail to attain friends because their starting point was of having an interest rather than of being interested, and our recognition of the insincerity would come about precisely through their social failure to acknowledge the other person as a subject with a point of view, their refusal to allow their conduct to take this adequately into account, their failure to engage in genuine mutuality. The result of an individual's attempts to form friendships depends very greatly on the initial cognitive posture involved, and hence *what* their resultant experience is will be to a large extent conditioned by how they initially oriented themselves to the other.[16]

These two points, that experience precedes conceptualisations and reasons about it, and that the manner of our initial cognitive comportment will impact upon what we experience, links to the difficulties with Wissenburg's account of civic virtue. For the key point about the characteristic excellences is that they are learned through initial experience, immersion in practices; as such, the internal goals are learned through experience, through willingness to absorb without at first knowing the goals inherent to the practice (MacIntyre, 1981: 187–9). Aristotle's moral theory, in fact, was written explicitly for Greeks who already lived well; it was intended as an intellectual guide to enrich lives that were already good, not to answer the question of what worth there was in being good, as was the case for Plato.

This is no accident, for the point about practices is precisely that you cannot know what internal goals you will get out of them until you engage in them and learn about the worth of these goals. But by instrumentalising agency and motivation, by emphasising disconnection, Wissenburg robs us of the chance to have any motivation to engage in the practices to begin with. The necessary openness to experience is missing, for the characterisation of agency is one which assumes the existence of predefined instrumental motives for further external goals. It may (perhaps) be the case that economic liberalism 'contains many elements that impede sustainability, but none of these threats seem invincible' if we assume 'the right kind of preferences', but in the practical situation in which we find ourselves, we shall need some means of generating the right kind of preferences, and Wissenburg's refusal to countenance any 'interference by higher authorities in the process of preference formation' (Wissenburg, 1998: 219–20) is less than encouraging. Moreover, given Wissenburg's treatment of value and instrumentalism, it will not do simply to invoke eloquent appeals to virtue from the medieval era, a period in which religious bonds, strong local economic ties and an effective guild system of craft workers, all of which have now largely vanished from public consciousness in the Western world, helped keep restraining virtues alive (Wissenburg, 1998: 218–19). Civic virtue cannot do the job which Wissenburg wants it to, for on his own conception of value and motivation, there is no obvious reason or cognitive space for wishing to learn to care about it to begin with.

It follows that, if we do indeed need to inculcate virtues of care in relation to the natural, we shall require both a cognitive reorientation and the existence of some nature in our lives to begin with to give an experiential base. I do not mean by this that we should or practically can radically repopulate the countryside from city regions for as Barry notes, this would be more than a little problematic

(Barry, 1999: 256–61). But Barry overlooks the alternative: if we cannot take the city people to nature, we can still reintroduce greater natural components to the city. This can be done, in the spirit of what was once called culture, by paying attention precisely to *points of contact* between the human and nonhuman, by emphasising connection and relationship as the point at which we must epistemologically, ethically and politically start, if only to know what our disconnected urban, consumerist selves might actually be missing. The use of 'city–country fingers' into the hearts of towns, the presence of more parks and green spaces, the encouragement of practices in city garden agriculture, the redesign of houses – all of these are options for Millite social experiment in reinvigorating our relationship to nature, and many of them would even be cheaper than yet more thousands of suburbs (Weston, 1994, 1996). But we will not be able to do these things in contemporary society, we will not even know any clear *experientially grounded* reason to care, if we regard the preferences promoted by contemporary consumer society as given, and assume, as Wissenburg does, that a virtue which we have no reason to learn can protect us from the corporate promotion of preferences that the democratic state is not allowed to restrict.

Notes

1 See respectively Callicott (1990), Weston (1991), Mathews (1991), Doherty and De Geus (1996).
2 We are, of course, not alone in this. Similar efforts to find a middle ground are manifested in Marius de Geus's concept of 'ecological restructuring' and John Barry's democratised model of virtuous ecological stewardship. See De Geus (1996) and Barry (1999).
3 I confess to being slightly puzzled as to precisely what it Wissenburg means by this, since much would seem to hang on what would be classified as interference; at one extreme, this injunction might rule out any regulation of advertising, state promotion of (for instance) traditional craft opportunities or perhaps even state education, but I suspect and hope that Wissenburg simply means that the state should not intervene in the formation of preferences that do not adversely impact on other assignable individuals or the common good.
4 I am not only thinking of familiar communitarian critiques of liberalism, but also attempts to recast liberal thought in a less physiphobic and disembodied form; see Zvesper (1993) and Stephens (1996).
5 That one per cent of value is not made by human labour is best explained by Locke's not wishing to imply that God's creation was wholly worthless, rather than by the argument that the one per cent stake restrains the extent of ownership powers, as claimed by Shrader-Frechette (1993: 78–80).
6 Locke states despite their occupation of fertile land, Native Americans 'for want of improving it by labour, have not one hundredth part of the Conveniencies we enjoy: And a King of a large and fruitful Territory there feeds, lodges, and is clad worse than a day Labourer in England' Locke (1988: 297), emphases mine.
7 Locke (1975: 263–4). We should not worry here over Locke's 'I think improperly' clause, for the reference is to will as being determined by uneasinesses (desires) and thus not 'free' in that sense.
8 Though the emphases are mine here, we should note that chapter 21, from which both quotes are taken, is the longest in the *Essay* and is significantly titled 'Of Power'.
9 Brecher (1998: 32–83). Brecher argues that the liberal emphasis on wants is one that leads liberal thinkers to continually slide between wants as motivation and wants as

justification for moral positions. Whilst I think his position rather overblown – Brecher, in neo-Kantian fashion, does not regard wants as having moral relevance at all – and unfair, most notably in his treatment of J.S. Mill, I believe his critique none the less deserves rather more attention than it has so far attained.

10 For an excellent critical summary of the problems of the separative self model in neoclassical economic theory, see England (1997).

11 For an extended scholarly treatment on the theme of Mill's grounding in classical virtue, see Semmel (1984).

12 Mill reviled the moral complacency and passive consumerism of the wealthy and strikingly attacked the manner in which the honest self-reliant craftsman was being driven out of business, due to the turbulence of industrial expansionism, by the capitalist con-man. 'Success', he complained,

> in so crowded a field, depends not upon what a person is but upon what he seems: mere marketable qualities become the object instead of substantial ones, and a man's labour and capital are expended less in doing anything, than in persuading other people that he has done it.
>
> (Mill, 1977: 133)

13 See diZerega (1997: 7–8, 70).

14 This understanding comes out in connection with the 'Formula of the Law of Nature' in the *Groundwork of the Metaphysic of Morals*. While Kant saw physical nature as being primarily a realm of cause and effect, in which moral freedom must constantly struggle against the determinist push of the physical world and of inner impulse, he also seems to have believed that human nature, through its possession of reason, had other factors: human nature was capable of moral progression, of moving towards the goal of a better and morally more perfected world through discovery of the moral laws laid down by reason and obedience to them, and the 'Formula of the Law of Nature' was designed to bridge the gap between pure reason and the empirical (natural) realm of the senses. Accordingly, Kant too supposes that human nature has developmental potentialities which ought ideally to be actualised. In this sense, human nature at least is not a mere mechanism but can be seen as teleological, as what Kant later calls a 'kingdom of nature' (Paton, 1989: 30, 84–101).

15 This resonates with Leopold's complaint about mass-market objections to wilderness recreation, that the 'basic error in such argument is that it applies the philosophy of mass-production to what is intended to counteract mass-production' (Leopold, 1987: 193–4).

16 For an extended treatment of this theme in relation to the natural world, see Weston (1994).

References

Barry, J. (1999), *Rethinking Green Politics: Nature, Virtue and Progress*, London: Sage.

Brecher, B. (1998), *Getting What You Want?: A Critique of Liberal Morality*, London: Routledge.

Caldwell, L.K. and K. Shrader-Frechette (1993), *Policy for Land: Law and Ethics*, Lanham, MD: Rowman & Littlefield.

Callicott, J. Baird, (1990), 'The Case Against Moral Pluralism', *Environmental Ethics*, Vol. 12, No. 2. Summer, pp. 99–124.

Cropsey, J. (1977), *Polity and Economy: An Interpretation of the Principles of Adam Smith*, Westport, CT: Greenwood Publishing.

De Geus, M. (1996), 'The Ecological Restructuring of the State', in Doherty and De Geus (eds), *Democracy and Green Political Thought: Sustainability, Rights and Citizenship*, London: Routledge, pp. 188–211.

diZerega, G. (1997), 'Empathy, Society, Nature and the Relational Self. Deep Ecology and Liberal Modernity', in Gottlieb (ed.), *The Ecological Community*, London: Routledge pp. 56–81.

Doherty, B. and M. De Geus (eds) (1996), *Democracy and Green Political Thought: Sustainability, Rights and Citizenship*, London: Routledge.

England, P. (1997), 'The Separative Self: Androcentric Bias in Neoclassical Assumptions', in Goodwin, Ackerman and Kiron (eds), *The Consumer Society*, Washington, DC: Island Press, pp. 204–7.

Fairweather, N.B., S. Elworthy, M. Stroh and P.H.G. Stephens (eds) (1999), *Environmental Futures*, London: Macmillan.

Goodin, R.E. and A. Reeve (1989), 'Liberalism and Neutrality', in R.E. Goodin and A. Reeve (eds), *Liberal Neutrality*, London: Routledge, pp. 1–8.

Goodwin, N.R., F. Ackerman and D. Kiron (eds) (1997), *The Consumer Society*, Washington, DC: Island Press.

Gottlieb, R.S. (ed.) (1997), *The Ecological Community*, London: Routledge.

Hampsher-Monk, I. and J. Stanyer (eds) (1996), *Contemporary Political Studies 1996*, Vol. 1, Oxford: Political Studies Association of the UK.

Hayry, M. (1994), *Liberal Utilitarianism and Applied Ethics*, London: Routledge.

James, W. (1907), *Pragmatism*, London: Longmans, Green.

James, W. (1912), *Essays in Radical Empiricism*, New York: Longmans, Green.

James, W. (1918), *The Principles of Psychology* (2 vols), London: Macmillan.

Leopold, A. (1987), *A Sand County Almanac and Sketches Here and There*, Oxford: Oxford University Press.

Locke, J. (1958), *Essays on the Law of Nature* (ed. and trans. W. von Leyden), Oxford: Clarendon Press.

Locke, J. (1975), *An Essay Concerning Human Understanding* (ed. P.H. Nidditch), Oxford: Clarendon Press.

Locke, J. (1988), *Two Treatises of Government* (ed. P. Laslett), Cambridge: Cambridge University Press.

MacIntyre, A. (1981), *After Virtue*, London: Duckworth.

Mathews, F. (1991), *The Ecological Self*, London: Routledge.

Mill, J.S. (1969), 'Nature', in J.M. Robson (ed.), *Collected Works of John Stuart Mill*, Vol. X, Toronto: Routledge & Kegan Paul, pp. 373–402.

Mill, J.S. (1974), 'A System of Logic', in J.M. Robson (ed.), *Collected Works of John Stuart Mill*, Vol. VIII, Toronto: Routledge & Kegan Paul.

Mill, J.S. (1977), 'Civilisation', in J.M. Robson (ed.) (1977), *Collected Works of John Stuart Mill*, Vol. XVIII, Toronto: Routledge & Kegan Paul, pp. 117–47.

Mill, J.S. (1984), *Utilitarianism, On Liberty and Considerations on Representative Government* (ed. H.B. Acton), London: Everyman.

Mill, J.S. (1987), *Principles of Political Economy*, London: Augustus M. Kelley.

Paton, H.J. (1989), *The Moral Law: Kant's Groundwork of the Metaphysic of Morals*, London: Unwin Hyman.

Semmel, B. (1984), *John Stuart Mill and the Pursuit of Virtue*, London: Yale University Press.

Shrader-Frechette, K. (1993), 'Locke and Limits on Land Ownership', in Caldwell and Shrader-Frechette (eds), *Policy for Land: Law and Ethics*, Lanham, MD: Rowman & Littlefield, pp. 65–83.

Stephens, P.H.G. (1996) 'Plural Pluralisms: Towards a More Liberal Green Political Theory', in Hampsher-Monk and Stanyer (eds), *Contemporary Political Studies 1996*, Vol. 1, Oxford: Political Studies Association of the UK, pp. 369–80.

Stephens, P.H.G. (1999), 'Picking at the Locke of Economic Reductionism', in Fairweather, Elworthy, Stroh and Stephens (eds), *Environmental Futures*, London: Macmillan, pp. 3–23.

Strauss, L. (1953), *Natural Right and History*, Chicago, IL: University of Chicago Press.

Waldron, J. (1989), 'Legislation and Moral Neutrality', in R.E. Goodin and A. Reeve (eds), Liberal Neutrality, London: Routledge, pp. 61–83.

Weston, A. (1991), 'On Callicott's Case Against Pluralism', *Environmental Ethics*, Vol. 13, No. 3, Fall, pp. 283–6.

Weston, A. (1992), *Toward Better Problems: New Perspectives on Abortion, Animal Rights and the Environment*, Philadelphia, PA: Temple University Press.

Weston, A. (1994), *Back to Earth: Tomorrow's Environmentalism*, Philadelphia, PA: Temple University Press.

Weston, A. (1996), 'Self-Validating Reduction: Towards a Theory of Environmental Devaluation', *Environmental Ethics*, Vol. 18, No. 2, Summer, pp. 115–32.

Wissenburg, M. (1998), *Green Liberalism: The Free and the Green Society*, London: UCL Press.

Wolin, S. (1960), *Politics and Vision: Continuity and Innovation in Western Political Thought*, Boston, MA: Little, Brown.

Zvesper, J. (1993), *Nature and Liberty*, London: Routledge.

5 Habermas and green political thought

Two roads converging

Robert J. Brulle

Scientific-technical civilization has confronted all nations, races, and cultures, regardless of their group-specific, culturally relative moral traditions, with a common ethical problem. For the first time in the history of the human species, human beings are faced with the task of accepting collective responsibility for the consequences of their actions on a world-wide scale.

(Apel, 1980: 23)

The events of the first year of the new millennium do not bode well for the future of the global environment. Biodiversity loss continues to accelerate. Global climate change, with its manifold adverse ecological impacts, continues to advance. Portending future climate disruptions, the El Niñõ effect is re-emerging in the Pacific Ocean (*New York Times*, 8 Sept. 2001, p. A14). International efforts to reverse global warming continue, with few tangible results. Quietly, bureaucrats and financial managers have assessed these trends, made their conclusions, and begun to take actions that anticipate the impacts of global climate change. Planners at LaGuardia and Kennedy International Airports are drafting construction plans to keep the runways above the expected rise in sea level. The US Army Corp of Engineers is studying where to build dikes to preserve shorefront property. Insurance companies are divesting themselves of coverage of such property in anticipation of increased storms and associated damage. Exxon-Mobil is studying ways to keep the Trans-Alaska pipeline stable after the permafrost on which it rests melts. Finally, on Wall Street, scientists are tutoring financiers on how best to manage their investments to maximise profits in view of climate change (*New York Times*, 19 Nov. 2000, p. B1).

It seems as if our social institutions have surrendered any attempt to deal effectively with environmental degradation. Rather, these institutions make marginal, reactive adjustments instead of the significant proactive changes that are required. Absent these significant changes, the future we can anticipate is one in which we must resign ourselves to the inevitability of mass extinctions of numerous species due to human activities and loss of entire ecosystems due to climate change. Thus, the development of an ecologically sustainable society is one of the most sweeping and crucial challenges our social institutions will ever face. So far, however, the efforts undertaken make this imperative seem only a Utopian fantasy, fast receding from our grasp.

The social learning capacity of our society must be expanded to generate new ways to respond to the process of ecological degradation. One key component in fostering social learning to address ecological degradation is through the development and instantiation of binding ecological norms (Brulle, 2000: 49–73). To enable large-scale, multicultural action among numerous human communities, an ecological ethics must work within the pluralist, postmodern world. This requires an ethics that can accommodate a wide range of cultural viewpoints, including conflicting notions of what is sacred and profane, what constitutes truth and heresy, and even basic notions regarding what it means to be human (Cooper, 1996: 257).

One important approach to this problem has been developed by the intellectual project that is defined by Critical Theory. This perspective holds the possibility of defining a means through which such an ecological ethics can be developed. As noted by Dobson: 'Critical Theory might provide a historical and material analysis of the relationship between human beings and the natural world, together, perhaps with a non-utopian resolution of the contemporary difficulties with this relationship' (Dobson, 1996: 298). However, Critical Theory has been criticised extensively as unable to meet this task. In this Chapter, I defend the use of Critical Theory in the creation of environmental ethics. I start with a short description of the key concepts in Critical Theory and how this perspective has been applied in the area of environmental ethics. In the second section, I summarise the objections to the use of Critical Theory in environmental ethics by focusing on the robust and articulate work of Robyn Eckersley. My response to this critique is provided in the third section. I conclude the Chapter with an overview of efforts to integrate Critical Theory into environmental decision-making and how these efforts could be extended to foster the development of an ecologically sustainable society.

Critical Theory and environmental ethics

A cogent argument has been developed for the use of Critical Theory for the development of a social science that unites theory with practice, thus enabling us to develop the cognitive, moral and aesthetic cultural resources to expand the social learning capacity of our society.[1] The area of Critical Theory that I focus on centres on the work of Jürgen Habermas, as defined by his 'Theory of Communicative Action' (Habermas, 1984, 1987a). This theory starts with the development of a post-metaphysical world. Habermas maintains that in previous historical eras, the justifications for classical ethics were based in encompassing metaphysical or spiritual belief systems that provided a philosophical definition of the 'good life'. However, we now encounter in modern societies 'a pluralism of individual life styles and collective forms of life, and a corresponding multiplicity of ideas of the good life' (Habermas, 1993:122). As a result of this pluralisation of world-views, the critique of metaphysics by postmodernism, and the growth of science, classical ethics has been challenged and, in the opinion of Habermas, has broken down (Baynes *et al.*, 1987: 4; Habermas, 1984: 2). Thus 'if we take modern pluralism seriously, we must renounce the classical philosophical claim to defend one uniquely privileged mode of life' (Habermas, 1993: 123).

In this post-metaphysical situation, Habermas seeks to avoid a cultural relativist position. His project is to develop a philosophy that can fully acknowledge the insights of postmodernism and cultural pluralism, while at the same time, serve to preserve some form of reason as a guide in everyday life practice (Habermas, 1987b). To accomplish this task, Habermas turns to an analysis of language use. By using philosophy and empirical social science, he seeks to demonstrate how the use of language and social interaction necessarily rely on norms of speech use. These norms form the pragmatic presuppositions of speech and define rational universal moral principles (Habermas, 1993: 163).

Habermas's analysis of language focuses on how communication creates and maintains social order. To examine the presuppositions of language use, Habermas bases his analysis on a thought experiment of social interaction based only on 'pure communicative sociation' (Habermas, 1996: 323) which he defines as the Ideal Speech Situation. In this situation, it is assumed that the actors can express their goals truthfully and without reservation, that all pertinent evidence can be brought into play in the discussion and that the agreement is based on reasoned argument (Habermas, 1984: 294, 1996: 4).

This analysis allows Habermas to identify the functionally necessary resources for communication to exist which exist as 'formal-pragmatic presuppositions and conditions of an explicitly rational behavior' (Habermas, 1984: 2). These presuppositions, in the form of three types of validity claims of truth, normative adequacy and sincerity, enable the communication process and are embedded in the use of any natural language. By fulfilling these validity claims, a mutually agreed upon definition of the situation is constructed which describes the relevant states in a situation, places the interaction within the ethical criteria of a specific historical and social context and ties the individual's personal identity to the interaction (Habermas, 1984: 136). Thus language and social interaction necessarily rely on norms of truth, rightness and sincerity.

The process of developing mutual agreement defines a universal and rational moral framework. In coming to mutual agreement, the claims of the speaker must be validated for the discourse to be rational. Validation requires an open speech community in which the unforced force of the better argument prevails. This allows Habermas to define a universal morality from which the rationality of a social order can be evaluated in a Discourse Principle (Habermas, 1987a: 141), which states that 'The only regulations and ways of acting that can claim legitimacy are those to which all who are possibly affected could assent as participants in rational discourses' (Habermas, 1996: 458).

Habermas (1996) builds on this perspective to develop the links between rationality, law and constitutional democracy. He argues that the legitimate reciprocal behavioural expectations in a pluralist modern society now take the form of rational law. In such a society, law can no longer be legitimated by metaphysical arguments. Rather, 'Under post-metaphysical conditions, the only legitimate law is one that emerges from the discursive opinion and will formation of equally enfranchised citizens' (Habermas, 1996: 408). This requires that citizens understand themselves as authors of the laws to which they are subject and to see public decision-making as a process of self-determination through an open and rational discourse. This ties the rationality of an open discourse to the formation of legitimate laws in a democracy. To institutionalise this process, the constitutional state has developed with a formal separation of powers (Habermas, 1996: 132–93). Thus the normative content and structure of a representative constitutional democracy arise 'from the structure of linguistic communication' (Habermas, 1996: 297).

The development of representative constitutional democracy is an attempt to implement the Discourse Principle in a political system. To realise this principle, all citizens must have basic individual rights, including freedom of speech, individual legal protection and rights of political association. In addition, there is a need for political rights, to ensure broad and inclusive public participation in political decision-making. Habermas defines these requirements in the Democratic Principle: 'The establishment of the legal code…must be compelled through communicative and participatory rights that guarantee equal opportunities for the public use of communicative liberties' (Habermas, 1996: 458). This principle then defines a number of specific criteria for a democratic and socially rational political process (Habermas, 1996: 305–6).

In addition, Habermas also identifies a need for Social and Ecological Rights, which are defined as the 'basic rights to the provision of living conditions' (Habermas 1996: 123). These rights define the empirical conditions that are necessary 'insofar as the effective exercise of civil and political rights depends on certain social and material conditions such that citizens can meet their basic material needs' (Habermas, 1996: 78). It is important to note that these rights are not conceptually derived, but empirical requirements to enable citizens the necessary means to realise their political rights (Habermas, 2001: 77).

Habermas' analysis thus points away from ethics based in metaphysical inquiry and towards sociological inquiry into a critical assessment of existing social institutions compared to the standards of rationality defined by Critical Theory. The presuppositions of language use provide a basis from which the rationality and legitimacy of the political decision-making institutions can be judged and also form a guide for reconstructing these institutions (Habermas, 1996: 5). Thus Habermas seeks to preserve reason as a guide in everyday life practice and to enhance the social learning capacity of society. As a result, there is a division between morals and ethics within Critical Theory. Questions of morals involve who are to be considered as morally competent agents entitled to be considered as ends-in-themselves – that is, how do we make decisions and who participates in this process? In this area, the Democratic Principle specifies that to take joint action, the process must involve the active and democratic participation of all of the affected human parties. On the other hand are ethical questions regarding what should we do?, that is, what is the 'good life'? Here, Critical Theory can provide no guidance regarding what ethics should be used. It can 'only show the participants the procedure they must follow if they want to solve moral problems and must leave all concrete decisions up to them' (Habermas, 1993: 128). It does not define any particular ethics or specify any requirement that joint action be based on only one set of cultural beliefs.

What this means is that Critical Theory cannot specify an ethical standard for the treatment of nature. Ecological Rights are concerned solely with protecting aspects of nature strictly for human utilitarian purposes. Critical Theory does not provide guidance beyond this utilitarian perspective regarding treatment of the natural world. Instead, an ecological ethics is seen as a concern about what constitutes the 'good life' and thus outside of the purview of Critical Theory. Instead, Critical Theory recognises that there are many different forms of reasoning about the value of the natural environment (Oelschlaeger, 1991). These different perspectives inform multiple ethical arguments for the preservation of nature, and their acceptance is dependent on the cultural context in which the argument is made. Hence no one universal argument for the preservation of nature will fit all cultures. Which one of these ethics would apply to a particular circumstance is a matter to be decided by the participants themselves. Critical Theory can contribute to this debate over environmental ethics by defining the social conditions in which a morally binding ethics can be constructed and enacted (Habermas, 1983: 1–20).

There is no theoretical barrier to the development of an ethics for the treatment of nature in Critical Theory. Critical theorists have argued that there are good reasons to believe that a democratic decision-making process would consider treatment of nature a significant ethical concern. First, it is clear from the ecological sciences that humanity and nature are interdependent. In an undistorted communication situation, this relationship would have to be recognised and taken into account in human deliberations (Torgerson, 1999: 120). Additionally, the dependence of nature on our actions would also be made clear. Thus our responsibility for and treatment of nature would become an ethical concern of the human community in an undistorted communication situation (Caterino, 1994: 32; Habermas, 1993: 111; Vogel, 1996: 165–71). However, in none of these formulations does nature attain the status of a moral subject. Rather, nature is seen as an object of moral concern for the human community, and it is through our deliberations that we would decide how it should be treated. In short, apart from anthropocentric utilitarian concerns, Critical Theory provides no guarantee that we will decide to preserve the natural world.

The green critique of Critical Theory

The critique over the application of Critical Theory to ecological ethics has been engaged in by a number of authors, starting more than 20 years ago (Whitebook, 1979). The core of this critique is that Critical Theory cannot adequately integrate concern for non-human nature, since it only considers the development of norms between mutual participants in a discourse. This omits consideration of the fate of other species that are not capable of participating in this dialogue. Thus Critical Theory is an anthropocentric belief system that separates and privileges human emancipation over the emancipation of non-human beings and cannot serve as a basis for informing a cultural practice that would fully protect biodiversity.

One of the most influential critiques has been the work of Robyn Eckersley. Since the publication of *Habermas and Green Political Theory: Two Roads Diverging* (Eckersley, 1990), she has developed a persuasive critique of the use of Critical Theory in defining environmental ethics. For Eckersley, there is much to commend about Critical Theory. She sees it as adequate for human affairs and also notes that public participation enhances deliberations for the preservation of the natural environment. She also agrees that community decisions should be reached through democratic deliberations among representatives of the various groups of the society (Eckersley, 1999: 33).

However, Eckersley believes there are limits to its utilisation. Specifically, she argues that Critical Theory 'does not attempt to restructure the ground rules of decision-making to provide any explicit protection or recognition of non-human interests' (Eckersley, 1995a: 179). Critical theory is not adequate for the full preservation of nature because it is based only on human concerns and as such, fails to justify the preservation of species that do not have a utilitarian value for humans. In addition, aesthetic arguments are also inadequate in themselves to guarantee protection of nature. Aesthetic values are selective, based on the particulars of taste, and see the protection of nature as secondary to ensuring the protection of a particular human experience. Hence, aesthetic arguments are particular, weak and anthropocentric. Thus utilitarian or aesthetic arguments alone cannot provide a general basis for environmental protection (Eckersley, 1998a: 178–9).

To reliably protect nature, Eckersley argues that we need to develop a concept of nature as a an end-it-itself, not as just one more criterion in the 'good life'. Hence we need 'reliable grounds for the protection on nonhuman nature' (Eckersley, 1998a: 165). This calls for the development of an expanded ethics that can include the non-human community in our decision-making process. To provide for this ethics, she argues that there is a need to develop a scientifically informed moral line of argument (Eckersley, 1998a: 178). Eckersley maintains that science 'may be enlisted to inform and support arguments concerning the desirability of either existing or potential human orientations toward the rest of nature' (Eckersley, 1998b: 83).

At the core of her argument is the autopoietic intrinsic value theory (Eckersley, 1992: 60–1). Developed by Fox (1995: 165–76), this ethics is based on the characteristic of autopoietic entities as 'primarily and continuously concerned with the regeneration of their own organizational activity and structure' (Eckersley, 1995a: 188). All living entities that make up nature have the capacity to define themselves through evolutionary processes and thus are autopoietic entities (Eckersley, 1999: 39). It is this capacity for 'self-directedness' which provides the ultimate ground upon which we recognise humans as moral subjects. Since nature also has a capacity for self-directedness, it should be 'recognized as a morally considerable being, deserving of recognition and consideration in human deliberation' (Eckersley, 1999: 42).

Based on this formulation, Eckersley seeks 'to inscribe ecocentric norms into the procedures of discursive dialogue in an impartial way – as a matter of morality and justice rather than ethics in Habermas' sense of those terms' (Eckersley, 1999: 25). She notes that moral concern is not limited to individuals who have the ability to participate in community dialogue. The ability to engage in the conversation is thus not a requirement to be treated as a subject of moral concern. Arguing that Habermas' Critical Theory is 'ultimately based on respect for the relative autonomy of the human subject', she maintains that the treatment of the other as moral subjects should be extended to nature, regardless of its level of communicative competence (Eckersley, 1999: 44–5). To realise this moral requirement requires an addition to Habermas Discourse Principle as follows: 'A just common structure of political action must be common to all those affected, irrespective of whether they happen to be able to speak or gesture' (Eckersley, 1999: 46). The question that this ethics formulates regarding nature is 'If they could talk and reason, would they agree to the proposed norm' (Eckersley, 1999: 44)?

However, there is a problem in designating a particular human group or individual to serve as a representative of nature. Since all of our knowledge of nature is socially constructed and particular, there can be no authentic human representative of nature (Eckersley, 1999: 40). Her solution to meet the moral requirement of including the concerns of non-human beings in human decision-making processes is to mandate institutional procedures that would 'guide human decision makers away from putting "the silent environmental constituency" at grave risk' (Eckersley, 1999: 45–6). She then cites the Precautionary Principle as one such procedure which would institutionalize the moral mandate to consider the impacts of human actions on non-human beings (Eckersley, 1999: 46).

Analysis of Eckersley's critique

Eckersley develops an interesting argument for the inclusion of the concern of nature within Critical Theory. One can sympathise with and favour her aim of developing ecocentric morals. However, I believe that her argument has a number of serious theoretical and political limitations.

Theoretical concerns

My first concern is the scientific basis for autopoietic intrinsic value theory. Autopoietics is not a concept that is used by evolutionary ecologists to describe the behaviour of different species or ecosystems. Seeing nature as an autopoietic system is based rather on the application of systems ecology to construct a philosophy of nature. In systems ecology, nature is seen as a bio-cybernetic entity that regulates itself (Hazelrigg, 1995: 295; Keulartz, 1998: 149). This view was commonly held by many ecologists throughout most of the 1960s and 1970s. However, the notion of community, and the supposed self-ordering properties of these communities, was robustly critiqued in the 1980s (Schrader-Frechette and McCoy, 1994b: 111–12). As a result of this debate, systems ecology was supplanted in the 1980s and 1990s by evolutionary ecology. Evolutionary ecology centers on the idea that nature evolves through the generation, diffusion and selective retention of random mutations. Nature is involved in a process of continual adaptation, which is not an active structuring process. Accordingly, evolutionary ecology rejects the idea that nature can be seen as a self-regulating mechanism. Rather, nature is seen as a chaotic system, in which chance and random events, as well as linear and non-linear interactions govern (Hazelrigg, 1995: 295–6; Zimmerman, 1994: 12).

The result of this progression of thinking is that one cannot use ecological science to define what the essence of nature really is. As Schrader-Frechette and McCoy note:

> If one cannot tell what a community or stability is, then it is likely not possible to determine – in any precise way – what a natural community or ecosystem is and when it is in some equilibrium or homeostatic state...then ecological science has little that is precise and firm to contribute to disputes over environmental ethics and values.
>
> (1994b: 112)

While a review of the debate between systems and evolutionary ecologists is beyond the scope or concern of this chapter, it is fair to conclude that 'If the controversy between systems ecology and evolutionary ecology makes one thing clear, it is that the constant appeal to the ecology is misleading, to say the least' (Keulartz, 1998: 155).

The notion of autopoietics is thus based on the selective use of ecological science to forward a particular view of nature. Eckersley's argument 'orients itself one-sidedly toward system ecology's account of nature, thereby doing scant justice to the multiplicity of views of nature circulating both in science and society' (Keulartz, 1998: 21). In her argument, she conflates living processes into the agency of nature. This is a social construction that highlights the self-determining components of nature and downplays the more mechanistic and random models of nature.

The autopoietics of nature, and thus the endowment of agency to nature is not a universal and objective idea, firmly grounded in ecological science. Rather, it is a social construction of nature that suits a particular political aim. As Hazelrigg (1995: 292) notes: 'Preserving nature means preserving a particular construction of what nature is supposed to be.' Eckersley's nature needs to be an agent to have worth, and therefore, she constructs this particular definition through the selective use of ecological theory.

It is obvious that ecological science can, provide information about practical impacts on the natural environment. However, this science holds no special competence in providing moral or aesthetic reasoning. Thus there are limits to the use of scientific and biological reasoning, especially in regard to human ethics (Schrader-Frechette and McCoy, 1994a). Greenwood (1984: 202) has persuasively argued that such moral tales have very little to do with evolution, because

> without fixed natural categories, without a fixed boundary between nature and culture, without a fixed 'human nature', and without any overall direction

in the life process, it is impossible to make nature into a source of ethical and political prescriptions.[2]

In addition, the uncritical use of a systems ecology perspective sets up an artificial dichotomy between human and non-human nature. From a systems ecology viewpoint, human activities are artifices that upset the balance of the self-regulating system of nature. This informs a particular treatment of nature as apart from man. Hence 'systems ecology views functional disentanglement as an essential precondition for a healthy nature' (Keulartz, 1998: 173, 1999). This dichotomy is not present if an evolutionary ecology perspective is adopted. Humans are seen as part of the complex interactions between living entities, and the apparent dichotomy between human and non-human nature disappears into a consideration of specific interactions (Keulartz, 1998: 173; Yrjö, 2000).

The society/nature split is also scientifically and historically inaccurate (Yrjö, 2000). Many of the supposed natural systems have been found to be the result of human artifice (Beck, 1985: 80–1; Keulartz, 1998: 152–5; Richerson *et al.*, 1996). Humans have played a role in the evolution of life on earth for millions of years. In that time, they have exercised an important influence on virtually all of the natural world. In his examination of the evolutionary history of North America, Flannery (2001: 173–254) shows the extraordinary impact of humans on the shape of the ecology of the entire North American continent. His analysis shows that the impact of humans began more than 13,000 years ago and significantly altered the type and distribution of both flora and fauna. For example, in examining the evidence related to the co-evolution of the plains Indians and the giant bison herds, Flannery concluded that

> All this leads me to believe that while a symbol of the 'wild west', beloved of the wildest of 'wild' Indians and a victim of the likes of Buffalo Bill, the bison is a human artifact for it was shaped by Indians and its distribution determined by them.
>
> (2001: 227)

So not only are our ideas about nature socially constructed, but also nature itself is partially the product of human social interaction (Vogel, 1996: 165–71). The dichotomy between nature and society has been empirically, historically and intellectually falsified (Yrjö, 2000). The imprint of humans on the globe has become so ubiquitous, that at the beginning of the twenty-first century, there are virtually no places beyond human influence.

My second concern regards the structure of the argument for an ethics based on autopoietics. From a rhetorical perspective, Eckersley constructs a bio-rhetoric, in which biology is used to infer moral necessities. As such, a bio-rhetoric 'is thus talk on its way from an is to an ought, making that connection only in the play of language' (Lyne, 1990: 38). While this may be an interesting rhetorical strategy, it does not make up for its theoretical deficiencies. I agree with Lyne, who noted in his analysis of other bio-rhetorics that 'Like the motion of an arrow, it will seem to dissolve under an analytic stare' (Lyne, 1990: 38). To link ecology and ethics is a highly problematic enterprise (Kitcher, 1994: 440), and in a previous writing, Eckersley (1998b: 90) states that 'we cannot "divine" a telos from nature's unfolding for the purposes of developing an ecological ethics'. However, in her attempt to extend communicative ethics to include nature, it appears that she does exactly this. This problem originates in the development of the autopoietic intrinsic value theory. Eckersley's work builds on the development of this perspective by Fox (1995), and an examination of his work reveals the origins of this problem.

Fox's argument for the intrinsic value of nature starts with the characteristics of living systems. Citing biologists, Fox argues that

> more recent thinking regarding the nature of living systems...emphasizes the fact that living systems can be distinguished from nonliving systems by particular kinds of ends for which they strive. Specifically living systems are seen as being characterized by the property of autopoiesis...[which] refers to the fact that living systems continuously strive to produce and sustain their own organizational activity and structure.
>
> (1995: 169)

Based on the authority of science, Fox then argues that

> The fact that autopoietic processes are primarily and continuously engaged in the recursive process of regenerating themselves means that they are not merely means to ends that are external to themselves, but rather that they are ends in themselves...[and] therefore deserving of moral consideration.
>
> (1995: 172)

Ignoring other scientific perspectives, Fox creates an unproblematic and reified nature with a specific 'essence', that of an autopoietic entity. This essence then legitimates a specific form of moral treatment of nature, as an end-in-itself. Here Fox engages in a bio-rhetoric by deriving norms for the treatment of nature from ecological facts, and thus his argument can be thus seen as a variety of ethical naturalism (Glacken, 1967: 36–49). In effect, the autopoietic intrinsic value of nature is based on a claim to be able to 'discern the essence of nature, and to require us to act in accordance with it' (Cheney, 1989: 294). As a result, Fox and Eckersley by inclusion commit the naturalistic fallacy (Kerr, 2000).

Could not this same criticism be applied to the development of the Discourse Principle by Habermas? This criticism is based on a misunderstanding of the links between validity claims and speech acts. Universal Pragmatics identifies the unavoidable presuppositions of language use, which define, metaphorically speaking, a necessary 'moral' grammar of justice and solidarity that are the presuppositions of communicative action. We cannot engage in communicative action without invoking these principles, just as we cannot form comprehensible sentences without the use of grammar. To argue against these presuppositions places one in the state of a performative contradiction – that is, 'systematically disputing the necessary presuppositions of communicative action while engaging in it' (Habermas, 1993: 162). Based on this logic, Habermas argues that one can link the use of language to the values of justice and solidarity 'without committing a naturalistic fallacy' (Habermas, 1993: 50).

My third theoretical concern relates to Eckersley's extension of autopoietics into Critical Theory. By attributing agency to nature, Eckersley seeks to extend the realm of moral concern to all of nature. She maintains that communication abilities are not a relevant consideration for whether a living entity should be treated as an end-in-itself. In contrast, Kant's criteria for the treatment of humans as ends-in-themselves is based on the capacity to act as a rational, self-defining being, with consciousness, will and freedom to act based upon ethical choices (Kant, 1785: 75–8). The ability to speak is not just an arbitrary endowment. Consciousness and self-awareness are bound up with the acquisition of language. The ability to act in the world based on reasoned choices is based on conscious choices and creates the ethical requirement to treat every rational being as an end-in-itself. Communicative competence is thus not arbitrary from a moral point of view. Rather, it is a fundamental precondition of rational existence. Furthermore, self-directedness and agency cannot be reduced to merely the unfolding of biological processes (Vogel, 1996: 160–1). Moral subjects are others with whom we can enter into a normative and reciprocal relationship. Nature cannot make choices about what it will do or not do, nor can we enter into a binding reciprocal relationship with nature. To extrapolate agency into a property of all living entities, whether or not they are endowed with any sentience, or ability to choose, is a fundamental distortion of this idea.

In addition, Eckersley misrepresents the rigorous foundations of Critical Theory. She argues that the basis for the acceptance of Critical Theory is that this ethics provides the best means for ensuring a free dialogue that protects the autonomy and integrity of human actors (Eckersley, 1999: 44). Habermas is certainly concerned with individual autonomy. However, this argument ignores the robust foundations of Critical Theory in Habermas Universal Pragmatics. Habermas does not derive his ethics as a means to uphold individual dignity and autonomy. If he did the latter, he could be correctly critiqued as developing a Eurocentric metaphysics. The values of solidarity, respect, truthfulness, authenticity and autonomy are not metaphysical assumptions or values in their own right. Rather, these norms are the implicit assumptions of the use of everyday speech. By ignoring this foundational work of Habermas, Eckersley misrepresents the cognitive argument for the acceptance of Critical Theory and produces a weak and arbitrary argument for its extension to include nature.

Political concerns

The next set of concerns regards the implications of attempting to translate this form of ethics into political practice. First, this position is likely to have little appeal to environmental groups not directly concerned with wilderness preservation. The split between human and non-human nature systematically devalues the urban environment as something outside of nature (Light, 2001: 17). This creates a geographic dualism between human-impacted areas and wilderness. Since human-impacted areas are no longer seen as part of nature, the end result is a systematic blindness of this ethical argument to urban environmental problems (Light, 2001: 17–18). This limits its political acceptability and creates a division between environmental groups concerned with environmental justice and those dealing with ecological sustainability (Dobson, 1998; Light, 2001: 27). Additionally, this argument, by asserting its basis in science, serves to delegitimate other sources for the ethical treatment of nature. For example, American Evangelical Christians argue that it is the Biblical story of Noah that defines an ethical duty to act for the preservation of nature. By establishing one justification for the protection of nature, this argument limits the political acceptability of this ecological ethics and thus limits the possibility to form a broad based political movement to protect the natural environment.

Second, even if accepted, it is not at all clear that an 'ecocentric' perspective would result in an ecologically sustainable society. While the need for such a belief system has now become virtually taken-for-granted within environmental philosophy, I am in agreement with Light (2001: 9) who sees this uncritical acceptance of an ecocentric norm as 'an accepted prejudice, [rather] than as a proven position'. Even a casual review of the historical record shows that virtually all human civilizations have been unsustainable. There are several examples that can be drawn from the anthropological literature of nomadic peoples, endowed with an ecocentric view of nature, creating serious permanent ecological disruptions (Flannery, 2001: 173–254; Ponting, 1992: 18–36; Richerson *et al.*, 1996: 286–9). Philosophical arguments alone do not provide a compelling case for the efficacy of an ecocentric ethics (Yrjö, 2000: 160). Rather, what is needed is the provision of anthropological, or sociological evidence of the real impact of an ecocentric perspective on a society's practices toward the natural environment. Absent this evidence, Eckersley's assertion remains just that.

Finally, there is an unresolved tension between Eckersley's advocacy of a neo-Aristotelian form of ethics and democratic political practice. The autopoietic intrinsic value theory defines a given value for nature, apart from any discussion by a human community. This brings a conflict between the democratic requirement for the participants themselves to determine the 'good life' through their own deliberations and this form of neo-Aristotelian morals (Habermas, 1993: 123–5). In examining similar arguments, Vogel (1996: 9) argues that 'instead of allowing the human community to decide these matters democratically, those who make such arguments attempt to short-circuit democratic discourse by labeling as "natural" – and hence unquestionable – what are inevitably really their own socially situated normative claims' (Vogel, 1996: 9). Such neo-Aristotelian ethics, derived apart from the active participation of the participants themselves, are 'beset with insuperable difficulties' (Habermas, 1993: 125). Eckersley does not explain how this dynamic would be resolved in a democratic and pluralistic society with multiple definitions of the good life.

Taken together, the theoretical and practical limitations of Eckersley's attempt to graft an ecocentric ethics onto Critical Theory is highly problematic. Since one can certainly argue for the Precautionary Principle from a number of different perspectives, including Critical Theory, the enactment of this approach to providing some legal protection for the natural world does not require acceptance of the autopoietic intrinsic value of nature. Accordingly, there is little compelling intellectual force or practical need for this viewpoint.

Critical Theory in practice

If Eckersley's attempted graft between Critical Theory and ecocentric ethics is unviable, then the question arises: what environmental norm can adequately protect the natural environment? I believe no one ethics or argument will fit all situations or cultural beliefs. Decisions regarding protection of the natural environment will always be partial, temporary and contingent. So a universal morality guiding our treatment of nature is most probably an impossibility. The question remains as to whether or not Critical Theory can inform a practice that is capable of protecting the natural world? If it is to realise this task, it must be capable of informing a political practice that could increase protection of the natural world. Thus the locus of efforts by Critical Theorists to protect the natural world is to enable a change in the conditions under which decisions about the natural environment are made. As Dobson (1993: 198) states, summarising Habermas' position, 'Healing the rift between human beings and the natural world ... is not a matter of joining what was once put asunder, but of getting the relations between human beings right first.'

There are many useful examples of this type of analysis. Here I can only quickly point to three such projects. The first project focuses on changing the decision-making processes of government agencies that deal with environmental issues.[3] Individuals working in this area have developed and tested a decision-making process which integrates scientific analysis and community deliberation into a comprehensive strategy for environmental decision-making. Known as Analytic Deliberation, this process defines a democratic method for development of government policies that recognises the link between social rationality and public involvement. It also provides techniques for integrating practical, normative and aesthetic concerns into a democratic decision-making process (NRC, 1996). This process has been verified and expanded in a number of reports on watershed planning (1999c: 240–53), environmental justice (1999b: 64–8), and valuing biodiversity (NRC, 1999a). This project, while very useful, is limited. Its focus is on administrative decision-making and small group processes. While this process can help a society make better decisions regarding the application of existing laws and scientific evidence with community concerns, it fails to deal with the vast power differentials that exist outside of this process. It also fails to consider the larger decision-making structures in society.

The second project focuses on the relationship between different planning approaches and their potential to realise a deliberative and democratic practice.

Over the past decade, a number of scholars and planners have worked to develop and test planning practices that can better realise the democratic morality of Critical Theory. This approach has expanded beyond Analytic Deliberation to include an analyses of the power and institutional relationships within which government planning activities are conducted. These efforts have initiated the development of a planning practice that is both sensitive to issues of power and ethics and able to assess issues in situated political processes (Forster, 1989, 1993, 1999).

The final project attempts to deal with society level decision-making processes (Habermas, 1996: 299). As Dryzek (2000: 142) has argued, values alone are not sufficient to reform our social order. Rather, what is required is also structural change in our political and economic structures. This leads to considerations of institutional structures and the role they play in either promoting or hindering an ethical consideration of nature. Some of the major works in this area focus on the role of the state and environmental degradation (Eckersley, 1995b; Janicke, 1990), economic structure (Schnaiberg, 1980; Jaeger, 1994), risk decision-making (Beck, 1985) and the public sphere and social movements (Brulle, 2000; Dowie, 1995; Torgerson, 1999).

Conclusion

There is no necessary conflict between ecocentric norms and Critical Theory. Rather, the relationship is one of mutual reliance. One key task for the realisation of the aims of both Critical Theory and ecocentric norms is the development of a strong public sphere. In this discursive arena, the industrialist presuppositions of profitability would not be the deciding force. Rather, the public space defines an arena in which ecological politics would take place and meaningful disagreements and debates about our society and the actions necessary to foster ecological sustainability would be carried out (Brulle, 2000: 64–8; Torgerson, 1999: 162). To create the public space defines a political task that would be accomplished 'through legally institutionalised procedures of democratic deliberation and decision-making, and gain sufficient strength to hold its own against the other two social forces – money and administrative power' (Habermas, 1998: 249). This would open up the possibility of a fair hearing for the protection of the natural world. So while the creation of a public sphere would not necessarily result in decisions always to protect nature, it is a necessary prerequisite for us to even consider these questions in a meaningful way.

We need to develop and institutionalise more adequate procedures to integrate the consideration of ecological values into the decision-making process. To accomplish this task, we do not need to look to metaphysical arguments, but to ourselves and our beliefs, political actions and social institutions. Constructing an ecologically sustainable society has never been accomplished before, and so we do not know in advance what will or will not work, including ethics, institutions or individual personality characteristics. Thus any efforts to create this society should proceed through a practice of trial and error in a 'logic of justified hope and controlled experiment' (Habermas, 1971: 283–4). Critical Theory can provide valuable intellectual resources toward the realisation of this project. It is in the democratic conversation about our fate and the fate of nature that Habermas and green political theory converge

Notes

1 There has been an extensive debate between Critical Theory and the other major schools of thought. For summaries of the epistemological arguments on which the Theory of Communicative Action is based, see Radnitsky (1973), Bleicher (1982) and Holub (1991). The Communicative Ethics developed by Habermas has been the subject of intense debate. For a discussion of the viability of this ethical position, see Benhabib and Dallmayr (1990).
2 Also Gould (1988) and Keulartz (1998: 156).
3 There is an extensive literature that examines the legal and administrative efforts to protect the natural environment (Cranor, 2001; Lindstrom and Smith, 2001; NRC, 1995; Taylor, 1984). In addition, there is also a large amount of research on public involvement in environmental decision-making. For an excellent review of these perspectives, see Webler (1995, 1999), Webler and Tuler (2000).

References

Apel, K.O. (1980), *Toward a Transformation of Philosophy*, Boston, MA: Routledge.

Baynes, K., J. Bohman and T. McCarthy (eds) (1987), *After Philosophy: End or Transformation?* Cambridge, MA: MIT.

Beck, Ulrich (1985), *Risk Society: Towards a New Modernity*, New York: Sage.

Benhabib, Seyla and Fred Dallmayr (1990), *The Communicative Ethics Controversy*, Cambridge, MA: MIT.

Bleicher, Josef (1982), *The Hermeneutic Imagination*, Boston, MA: Routledge.

Brulle, Robert, J. (2000), *Agency, Democracy and Nature: The U.S. Environmental Movement from a Critical Theory Perspective*, Cambridge, MA: MIT.

Caterino, Brian (1994), 'Communicative Ethics and the claims of Environmental Justice', paper presented at Annual Conference of the American Political Science Association, Washington, DC.

Cheney, J. (1989), 'The Neo-Stoicism of Radical Environmentalism', *Environmental Ethics*, Vol. 11, No. 4, pp. 293–326.

Cooper, Marilyn, M. (1996), 'Environmental Rhetoric in the Age of Hegemonic Politics: Earth First! and the Nature Conservancy', in Carl Herndl and Stuart Brown (eds), *Green Culture*, Madison, WI: University of Wisconsin Press, pp. 87–106.

Cranor, Carl (2001), 'Learning from the Law to Address Uncertainty in the Precautionary Principle', *Science and Engineering Ethics*, Vol. 7, No. 3, pp. 313–26.

Dobson, Andrew (1993), 'Critical Theory and Green Politics', in A. Dobson and Paul Lucardie (eds), *The Politics of Nature: Explorations in Green Political Theory*, New York: Routledge, pp. 190–206.

Dobson, Andrew (1996), 'Democratizing Green Theory: Preconditions and Principles', in B. Doherty and M. de Geus (eds), *Democracy and Green Political Thought*, New York: Routledge, pp. 132–50.

Dobson, Andrew (1998), *Justice and the Environment: Conceptions of Environmental Sustainability and Theories of Distributive Justice*, Oxford: Oxford University Press.

Dowie, Mark (1995), *Losing Ground*, Cambridge, MA: MIT Press.

Dryzek, John S. (2000), *Deliberative Democracy and Beyond: Liberals, Critics, Contestations*, Oxford: Oxford University Press.

Eckersley, Robyn (1990), 'Habermas and Green Political Theory: Two Roads Diverging', *Theory and Society*, Vol. 19, No. 6, pp. 739–76.

Eckersley, Robyn (1992), *Environmentalism and Political Theory: Toward an Ecocentric Approach*, London: UCL Press.

Eckersley, Robyn (1995a), 'Liberal Democracy and the Rights of Nature: The Struggle for Inclusion', *Environmental Politics*, Vol. 6, No. 1, pp. 169–98.

Eckersley, Robyn (ed.) (1995b), *Markets, the State, and the Environment: Towards Integration*, South Melbourne: Macmillan.

Eckersley, Robyn (1998a), 'Beyond Human Racism', *Environmental Values*, Vol. 7, No. 2, pp. 165–82.

Eckersley, Robyn (1998b), 'Divining Evolution and Respecting Evolution', in Andrew Light (ed.), *Social Ecology after Bookchin*, New York: Guilford Press, pp. 59–91.

Eckersley, Robyn (1999), 'The Discourse Ethic and the Problem of Representing Nature', *Environmental Politics*, Vol. 8, No. 2, pp. 24–49.

Flannery, T. (2001), *The Eternal Frontier: An Ecological History of North America and its People*, New York: Atlantic Monthly Press.

Forster, John (1989), *Planning in the Face of Power*, Berkeley, CA: University of California Press.

Forster, John (1993), *Critical Theory, Public Policy and Planning Practice*, Albany, NY: SUNY Press.

Forster, John (1999), *The Deliberative Practitioner: Encouraging Participatory Planning Processes*, Cambridge, MA: MIT Press.

Fox, Warwick (1995), *Toward a Transpersonal Ecology: Developing New Foundations for Environmentalism*, Albany, NY: SUNY Press.

Glacken, Clarence, J. (1967), *Traces on the Rhodian Shore: Nature and Culture in Western Thought from Ancient Times to the End of the Eighteenth Century*, Berkeley, CA: University of California Press.

Gould, S.J. (1988), 'Kropotkin was No Crackpot', *Natural History*, Vol. 97, No. 7, pp. 12–21.

Greenwood, D. (1984), *The Taming of Evolution: The Persistence of Non-evolutionary Views in the Study of Humans*, Ithaca, NY: Cornell University Press.

Habermas, Jürgen (1971), *Knowledge and Human Interests*, Boston, MA: Beacon Press.

Habermas, Jürgen (1983), 'Hermeneutics and Critical Theory', paper presented at Bryn Mayr College, 19 Feb.

Habermas, Jürgen (1984), *The Theory of Communicative Action, Volume One, Reason and the Rationalization of Society*, Boston, MA: Beacon Press.

Habermas, Jürgen (1987a), *The Theory of Communicative Action, Volume Two Lifeworld and System: A Critique of Functionalist Reason*, Boston, MA: Beacon Press.

Habermas, Jürgen, (1987b), 'Philosophy as Stand-In and Interpreter', in K. Baynes, J. Bohman and T. McCarthy (eds), *After Philosophy: End or Transformation?* Cambridge, MA: MIT Press, pp. 296–315.

Habermas, Jürgen (1993), *Justification and Application: Remarks on Discourse Ethics*, Cambridge, MA: MIT Press.

Habermas, Jürgen (1996), *Between Facts and Norms: Contributions to a Discourse Theory of Law and Democracy*, Cambridge, MA: MIT Press.

Habermas, Jürgen (1998), *The Inclusion of the Other: Studies in Political Theory*, Cambridge, MA: MIT Press.

Habermas, Jürgen (2001), *The Postnational Constellation: Political Essays*, Cambridge, MA: MIT Press.

Hazelrigg, Lawrence (1995), *Culture of Nature: An Essay on the Production of Nature*, Gainesville, FL: University Press of Florida.

Holub, Robert, C. (1991), *Jürgen Habermas: Critic in the Public Sphere*, New York: Routledge.

Jaeger, Carlo, C. (1994), *Taming the Dragon: Transforming Economic Institutions in the Face of Global Change*, New York: Gordon & Breach.

Janicke, Martin (1990), *State Failure: The Impotence of Politics in Industrial Society*, State College, PA: Pennsylvania State University Press.

Kant, I. (1785), *Groundwork of the Metaphysics of Morals in Practical Philosophy*, Cambridge: Cambridge University Press.

Kerr, Andrew, J. (2000), 'The Possibility of Metaphysics: Environmental Ethics and the Naturalistic Fallacy', *Environmental Ethics*, Vol. 22, Spring, pp. 85–99.

Keulartz, Jozef (1998), *The Struggle for Nature: A Critique of Radical Ecology*, New York: Routledge.

Keulartz, Jozef (1999), 'Engineering the Environment: The Politics of "Nature Development"', in Frank Fischer and Maarten A. Hajer (eds), *Living with Nature: Environmental Politics as Cultural Discourse*, Oxford: Oxford University Press, pp. 83–102.

Kitcher, Philip (1994), 'Four Ways of "Biologicizing" Ethics', in Elliott Sober, (ed.), *Conceptual Issues in Evolutionary Biology*, Cambridge, MA: MIT Press, pp. 439–50.

Light, Andrew (2001), 'The Urban Blind Spot in Environmental Ethics', *Sociology*, Vol. 35, No. 1, pp. 7–35.

Lindstrom, M.J. and Z.A. Smith (2001), *The National Environmental Policy Act: Judicial Misconstruction, Legislative Indifference, and Executive Neglect*, College Station, TX: Texas A&M University Press,

Lyne, J. (1990), 'Bio-Rhetorics: Moralizing the Life Sciences', in H.W. Simons (ed.), *The Rhetorical Turn*, Chicago, IL: University of Chicago Press, pp. 35–57.

National Research Council (NRC) (1995), *Science and the Endangered Species Act*, Washington, DC: National Academy Press.

National Research Council (NRC) (1996), *Understanding Risk: Informing Decisions in a Democratic Society*, Washington, DC: National Academy Press.

National Research Council (NRC) (1999a), *Perspectives on Biodiversity: Valuing Its Role in an Everchanging World*, Washington, DC: National Academy Press.

National Research Council (NRC) (1999b), *Toward Environmental Justice: Research, Education, and Health Policy Needs*, Washington, DC: National Academy Press.

National Research Council (NRC) (1999c), *New Strategies for America's Watersheds*, Washington, DC: National Academy Press.

Oelschlaeger, Max (1991), *The Idea of Wilderness: From Prehistory to the Age of Ecology*, New Haven, CT: Yale University Press.

Ponting, Clive (1992), *A Green History of the World: The Environment and the Collapse of Great Civilizations*, New York: St Martin's Press.

Radnitzky, G. (1973), *Contemporary Schools of Metaphysics*, New York: Regnery.

Richerson, P., M. Mulder and B. Vila (1996), *Principles of Human Ecology*, Needham Heights, MA: Simon & Schuster.

Schnaiberg, Alan (1980), *The Environment: From Surplus to Scarcity*, Oxford: Oxford University Press.

Schrader-Frechette, K.S. and Earl, D. McCoy (1994a), 'What Ecology can do for Environmental Management', *Journal of Environmental Management*, Vol. 41, pp. 293–307.

Schrader-Frechette, K.S. and Earl, D. McCoy (1994b), 'How the Tail Wags the Dog: How Value Judgments Determine Ecological Science', *Environmental Values*, Vol. 3, pp. 107–20.

Taylor, S. (1984), *Making Bureaucracies Think: The Environmental Impact Statement Strategy of Administrative Reform*, Stanford, CA: Stanford University Press.

Torgerson, Douglas (1999), *The Promise of Green Politics: Environmentalism and the Public Sphere*, Durham, NC: Duke University Press.

Vogel, Steven (1996), *Against Nature: The Concept of Nature in Critical Theory*, Albany, NY: SUNY Press.

Webler, Thomas (1995), ' "Right" Discourse in Public Participation: An Evaluative Yardstick', in O. Renn, T. Webler and P. Wiedemann (eds), *Fairness and Competence in Citizen Participation: Evaluating Models for Environmental Discourse*, Boston, MA: Kluwer, pp. 35–86.

Webler, Thomas (1999), 'The Craft and Theory of Public Participation: A Dialectical Process', *Journal of Risk Research*, Vol. 2, No. 1, pp. 55–71.

Webler, Thomas and Seth Tulcr (2000), 'Fairness and Competence in Citizen Participation: Theoretical Reflections from a Case Study', *Administration and Society*, Vol. 32, No. 5, pp. 566–95.

Whitebook, Joel (1979), 'The Problem of Nature in Habermas', *Telos*, Vol. 40, pp. 41–69.

Yrjö, Haila (2000), 'Beyond the Nature-Culture Dualism', *Biology and Philosophy*, Vol. 15, No. 2, pp. 155–75.

Zimmerman, Michael, E. (1994), *Contesting Earth's Future: Radical Ecology and Postmodernity*, Berkeley, CA: University of California Press.

Part II
Green movements

6 Why did New Zealand and Tasmania spawn the world's first green parties?

Stephen L. Rainbow

Writing in 1990 Marion Wescombe asked:

> How can a small island, remote from the great centres of intellectual discourse, and sustaining a population smaller than that of individual suburbs in the world's great cities, be of any account? Can it play a pivotal role in the reinvigoration of political theory? Can it provide signposts to a future that is a quantum leap forward from the present?

> (1990: 172)

Wescombe was referring to Tasmania, but her question had in part been answered by Hazel Henderson twelve years earlier when she had written optimistically that the 'politics of reconceptualisation is perhaps most advanced and articulated in New Zealand, where the new Values Party and its intelligent, globally oriented manifesto *Beyond Tomorrow* captured five per cent of the vote at their last election' (1978: 368). Small island nations, she clearly suggested, could be of account.

This Chapter will examine the similarities between the growth of the green movements in Tasmania and New Zealand from the early 1970s, suggesting reasons why green parties should have first arisen in these antipodean locations. The Chapter is also an attempt to put the New Zealand experience, in particular, into some perspective, by comparing its experiences with another country which shares a very similar pattern of historical development. The study of green politics is a growth field and the experiences of the formative green parties in an antipodean context sheds potentially valuable light on what has largely been a Eurocentric field of study to date. Reading the European literature on green politics one could be forgiven for thinking that green parties had not existed in New Zealand and Tasmania almost a decade before they became popular parts of the European electoral landscape.

Green parties have enjoyed mixed fortunes during the 1980s. Recent setbacks cannot detract from the overall impact of green parties, with greens represented in the parliaments of most advanced industrial nations. The German Greens lost their representation in the Bundestag after six years in 1990, while the Swedish Greens lost their parliamentary representation in 1991, after only three years in the Riksdag. They had, in 1988, been the first new party to enter the Swedish parliament in seventy years. However, in neighbouring Finland the Greens increased their parliamentary seats from four to ten in 1991. A better indication of the general level of support for green parties is the 7.7 per cent of the vote which greens won in the 1989 European elections (as compared to the 2.7 per cent they gained in 1984). Even in countries with hostile electoral systems, such as Britain, the Greens gained 15 per cent of the vote. The impact of green politics has been as significant, some suggest, as the rise of socialist parties around the turn of the century.

Theoretical background

The rise of green politics has been explained in a variety of ways, summarised by Andersen as class perspectives, values perspectives, Marxist perspectives and industrialist perspectives (1990: 102). The most common explanation links widespread socio-economic change to a change in political orientation and issues. This change engenders a new set of societal values which have been described as post-materialist. These new values are distinct from the preceding set of dominant values, which are predominantly materialistic and attach a high value to security, whether financial or strategic.

This values perspective draws heavily on the works of Inglehart (1981, 1987). The new values have led to the rise of a 'new politics' which stands in marked contrast to the 'old politics' of preceding generations and the established parties. The old politics is characterised by representative forms of decision-making and by conventional political behaviour (Kolinsky, 1989: 21). The new values are associated with increasing affluence and progression up a Maslowian hierarchy of needs. As basic life needs for physical security and material well-being are met, people are able to focus on non-material needs, such as the quality of life, a beautiful environment and political participation.

A main problem identified with this values-change model is that, taken to its logical conclusion, it can be argued that there is no causal relationship between environmental problems and the green movement itself (Andersen, 1990: 104). Increased environmental awareness can be interpreted simply as a reflection of changing values, unrelated to any actual environmental problems. This effectively excludes from proper consideration the concrete issues that catalyse and motivate green parties. As Rüdig and Lowe have argued, 'the development of green parties cannot be understood without consideration of the emergence of particular issues and protest movements, and the concrete circumstances of party formation' (1986: 265).

The class perspective draws on the theories of value change and especially on the class changes which occur as a result of the same socio-economic developments that are engendering the new values. In particular the class perspective notes the disproportionate incidence of 'new values' within the 'new middle class' (Anderson, 1990: 102). The 'new politics' is disproportionately associated with a 'new class' of professional workers most often employed in the public sector and distinct because of their distance from the interests of production

(Eckersley, 1989). The new class is comprised above all of younger age groups and people who have enjoyed access to higher education. Being financially secure, they are at the forefront of demands for greater participatory democracy, environmental protection and opportunities for self-actualisation. They have provided a sizeable constituency for the 'new politics' agenda advocated by the new social movements, green parties and parts of the established political left. This amounts to what has been described as a realignment of the electorate based on the new middle class and the young (Papadakis, 1989: 79)

The class perspective has also been used to suggest that the new politics simply expresses the self-interest of the new middle class. This argument is based on the assumption that any kind of social movement must be based on the maintenance or improvement of the material conditions of that particular group. The content of the movements is disregarded in this analysis, as is the heterogeneity of the occupational groups and interests involved in the new class (Eckersley, 1989: 211).

Much has been written about the validity or otherwise of explanations for the rise of green politics based on changing values and space precludes other than a cursory summary here. Suffice it to say that doubts have been raised about the universal validity of such a model. For example, value change theories do not adequately explain why the environmental cleavage has been the most enduring catalyst for the 'new politics', as if environmental issues themselves have no role to play. Nor do they explain contradictions such as the fact that environmentalists have had to fight so hard against economic or bureaucratic elites which include actors who should, according to the model, have post-materialist sympathies (Andersen, 1990: 105). Both class-based analyses and arguments based on the assertion of changing values downplay or ignore the fact that 'the actual, multi-faceted social and ecological crises facing the world today are the *sine qua non* of the green movement' (Eckersley, 1989: 223).

Structural perspectives are based on a sense of crisis involving such issues as the future of humankind, rather than on the view that environmental conflict has arisen out of affluence and changing values (Andersen, 1990: 105). The Marxist perspective is the first of two structural perspectives arid draws upon analogies between the capitalist exploitation of labour and the capitalist desecration of nature. The relentless pursuit of profit and growth destroys natural resources in the same way that it destroys labour. The environmental conflict is not between capital and labour but between 'the people' and capital (Andersen, 1990: 106).

The Marxist model has difficulties in explaining pollution by reference to sources other than capitalist industry, for example activities in the home. Furthermore it fails to offer convincing arguments why pollution has tended to be most serious in the socialist countries. Capitalist industry, observation of the socialist economies suggests, does not have a monopoly on externalising the environmental costs of production. By concentrating on the ownership and control of industry the Marxist view detracts from the core green concern with the very process of industrialisation, regardless of whether it is privately owned or 'socialised'. Importantly, too, the Marxist view cannot account for the association between environmentalism and the broader set of anti-industrial values embodied by the 'new politics' (Andersen, 1990: 107). For the 'new politics' embraces a range of issues extending well beyond environmentalism.

The second structural perspective, based on a model of industrialism, focuses on the fact that the 'new politics' embodies a generalised reaction against the negative side-effects of industrialism. The 'new politics', Andersen asserts, could be labelled 'anti-industrial' politics (1990: 107). Industrialism is more than simply a mode of production, it is a total culture representing a particular stage of social evolution. The hallmarks of the industrial era are bureaucracy and overbearing rationality. The new politics represents the possibility of a general transformation towards a qualitatively different kind of society. This next stage of social evolution can be called 'post-industrial' society, and green politics is one of its harbingers.

Much analysis of green politics to date has almost disregarded the *content* of green politics, but from the industrialist perspective, environmental problems *of themselves* are worthy of study because they motivate movements and frequently generate an alternative political agenda embracing a full range of policies. The structural perspective of industrialism enables the most plausible explanation why immediate environmental concerns have the potential to inspire a full political programme which extends beyond environmental issues.

Environmental issues often conspicuously symbolise a more general problem with the direction of development and the destruction wrought by the pursuit of progress. Particular issues take on a wider significance for greens, signifying a general unease with the way in which industrial societies are developing. From the conception of industrialism, Andersen asserts, it is possible to derive a relatively coherent green discourse (1990: 108).

This Chapter will focus on this second structural perspective of industrialism. The cases of Tasmania and New Zealand lend themselves to this analysis because of the concrete environmental issues that have arisen since the early 1970s and the simultaneous creation of green parties. It is argued here that concrete issues generated by industrial development have acted as the catalyst for green movements in the antipodes. The particular patterns of industrial development, and the opposition they aroused among a minority with a critical view of the costs of industrialisation, help to explain why the first green parties in the world arose in New Zealand and Tasmania.

Concrete issues may have been of greater significance in explaining the rise of green politics in the antipodes because of unique political–cultural factors. Frontier societies, for example, value practical skills and attach less importance to ideas and to intellectuals than their European equivalents. Caute captures these differences in his analysis of the New Left which, he asserts, 'was divided between its intensely intellectual platoons – preponderant in Europe – and the apostles of instinct and feeling, whose sacramental playground was America' (1988: 23).

The specific issues that catalysed the early green movements in Tasmania and New Zealand evolved around the defence of two lakes: Pedder in Tasmania and Manapouri in New Zealand. The defence of these lakes was rarely couched in intellectual terms, but arose from an emotional rejection of environmental destruction as the price of progress. Decision-makers involved in hydroelectric development had become over-concerned with economic and technical considerations and short-sightedly unimaginative about the aesthetic and cultural implications of the onrush towards industrial development (Cleveland, 1972: 34).

In both cases the defence of these lakes was related to a broader rejection of the consequences of industrial development by a growing minority of people. To these people, the continued destruction of the environment in the name of progress was no longer defensible. The Save Manapouri Campaign generated a good deal of 'collectivism symbolism' about natural assets and national heritage, and confronted government, for the first time, with 'the necessity of weaving a strand of aesthetic consideration into its public-policy making' (Cleveland, 1972: 96). The threat to the lake, which had become 'a symbol of nature despoiled in the name of progress', showed that 'the existing political parties seemed to be have been an inadequate channel for the articulation of the feelings and sentiments of large masses of people in an area of public affairs which is of great importance' (Cleveland, 1972: 135).

Also important politically was the fact that the Save Manapouri Campaign, more than conflicts over sporting contacts with South Africa or involvement in the Vietnam War, gave liberals and radicals 'common cause' at the beginning of the 1970s (James, 1986: 321). The involvement of prominent professionals and business people also gave the campaign credibility as the model of economic development based upon 'the single purpose planning of the NZED (New Zealand Electricity Department)' (Howell, 1975: 184) was fundamentally challenged for the first time. Ending the harnessing of lakes and rivers for hydro-electric development became central to the objectives of the conservation movement in both Tasmania and New Zealand.

The United Tasmania Group and the Values Party

The United Tasmania Group: a brief history

The United Tasmania Group (UTG) was formed at a public meeting on 23 March 1972, two months before the Values Party was formed in New Zealand. The UTG was the first political party based on an environmental platform to contest elections anywhere in the world (Walker, 1989: 161). The UTG was made up of concerned but politically inexperienced citizens, alarmed at the lack of public participation over major issues and at the dominance of industrial values in the decision-making processes of Tasmania (Walker, 1989: 161).

The UTG was formed to take the battle to save Lake Pedder into the political arena. When the Liberal–Centre Party coalition collapsed in March 1972, members of the Lake Pedder Action Committee (LPAC) saw a chance to deny an absolute majority to either major party by contesting the electoral arena. The Labor Party had originally approved the Lake Pedder Scheme and was as implicated in the technocratic and economic values of the Tasmanian programme of hydroelectric development programme as the governing Liberal–Centre Party coalition. Unable to use the Tasmanian ALP (Australian Labor Party) to achieve their ends, Tasmanian conservationists 'had to go outside the established political forms and construct a new movement from scratch' (Lynch, 1990: 152).

Primary among the targets of the LPAC was the Hydro-Electric Commission (HEC). The close relationship between the HEC and the mainstream parties was exposed for the first time by the UTG who claimed at a pre-election symposium that certain instruments of government had become subverted and that parliament had become a 'rubber stamp for public administrators' (Walker, 1989: 162). The UTG was formed as a direct result of the intransigence of the established decision-making processes in the face of pressure group activities by LPAC. Led by Dr Richard Jones, the UTG fielded 12 candidates in four electorates but concentrated its efforts in the southern urban electorates where it gained approximately 7 per cent of the vote, insufficient to win a seat in parliament, but a strong showing nevertheless for a party formed only four weeks before the election.

Rather than fade away after its failure to gain election, the UTG set about developing an extensive policy platform based on ecological and humanitarian principles. The consequences of unfettered economic growth and the increasing encroachments of official power were major UTG concerns (Walker, 1989: 164). As well as its environmental platform the UTG explicitly rejected exclusive ideologies; the misuse of power; individual wealth; the tyranny of rationality; social alienation and the loss of community. The UTG platform committed members to regulating their individual and communal needs in order to reduce resource-demand. UTG members were to do the minimum of damage to the web of life on an island 'uniquely favoured with natural resources, climate, form, and beauty' (UTG, 1990: 34). The institutions of politics and government, according to the UTG, were central to the problems of unbridled economic growth and the suppression of non-material values in industrial society. The UTG addressed the political problems of technological society and called for a shift in social values. The decision about Lake Pedder was but one example of how centralised parties and bureaucracies prevented involvement by the public and gained advice from only a limited perspective.

The UTG developed a detailed range of policies in a short period of time, dealing with the major issues facing Tasmania and including a commitment to zero economic growth among its platforms. By 1974 the main Tasmanian newspaper, *The Examiner*, conceded that the UTG had initiated more new policies for Tasmania in a short space of time than either of the mainstream parties had in years. The organisation of the party revolved around Dr Jones and a core of dedicated members in an organisational style described as 'open oligarchy' (Walker, 1989: 166). The party's strongest period electorally was between 1974 and 1976. But contesting nine elections during its four years of existence without gaining a single seat took its toll on the party's activists. Therefore when the opportunity came in 1976 to put energy into a new organisation – the Tasmanian Wilderness Society (TWS) – 19 of the 23 people who attended the inaugural meeting were UTG members.

The TWS was primarily concerned with the protection of the Franklin River in the south-west of Tasmania and the immediacy of its goals had an appeal among those disillusioned with the unsuccessful pursuit of political representation. After 1977 UTG faded away, unable to sustain itself 'because continuous demands of electioneering and policy formulation, and the decline in resources (financial and human) weakened the base of the party' (Walker, 1989: 167). The UTG had been unable to produce tangible benefits or outcomes for its members, its potential constituency was limited, and its lack of resources hampered attempts to fight elections credibly or to campaign against undesirable development.

Importantly, UTG had mobilised previously unpoliticised sections of the community. It was the first medium through which the environmental issues which have dominated Tasmanian politics ever since were presented to the public, and it made a substantial contribution to what Hay has described as 'one of the most highly skilled and politically advanced environment movements in the world' (Walker, 1989: 169). The UTG provided the first experiences in the political arena for many TWS activists, an experience and degree of political skill which would later be used to influence the federal Labor Party in its policy against the Franklin Dam at the 1983 federal elections. The UTG presented Tasmanians with an alternative view of the world for the first time, as well as challenging the hegemonic assumptions of the hydro-industrialisation process (Walker, 1989: 171).

The Values Party: a brief history

The Values Party was formed on 30 May 1972 at a meeting convened by Tony Brunt and Norm Smith, former journalist colleagues who had become disillusioned with the political process in New Zealand. A subsequent nationwide television programme about the fledgling party on October 17 drew an enthusiastic response and resulted in the party's putting up candidates in 43 of the 87 electorates in the November 1972 elections. The party was publicly endorsed by public figures as diverse as a national student leader, Tim Shadbolt, and the ageing Mayor of Auckland, Dove-Myer Robinson. Values went on to win 2.7 per cent of the national vote and 3.9 per cent of the vote in the seats it contested.

The Values Party, Brunt claimed, was 'the political expression of widespread environmental concern' (interview, 5 February 1987). While the Labour Party had by 1972 adopted a policy of *not* raising Lake Manapouri, Values reminded the electorate that it was the Labour government that had originally made the decision to raise the lake in 1959 'without public debate' (*Beyond Tomorrow*, 1972: 13). Labour also remained committed to hydro-development on the Clutha River. The Values Party's 1972 manifesto, *Blueprint for New Zealand*, took its title from *The Ecologist* magazine's 1972 *Blueprint for Survival*, and unashamedly included a reading list, featuring titles such as *The Limits to Growth*, and Commoner's *The Closing Circle*. The manifesto, while including specific environmental policies, claimed to be concerned with 'the environment in its broadest sense' (1972: 5) and made a strong case against increased industrialisation on the basis of the need for zero population growth (ZPG) and zero economic growth (ZEG): 'Ecologists throughout the world are warning that population and economic growth must be stabilised in order to stop pollution and ease the pressure on natural resources' (1972: 8).

The party's 1973 conference decided that Values should operate solely at a community level, and that a centralised party with a leader was too much in the mold or conventional political parties. The party subsequently disappeared in all but name, a situation which was remedied after a year with the adoption of a new constitution at the 1974 conference, which re-established a national leadership. An Auckland lawyer, Reg Clough, became the new leader and Cathy Wilson was elected deputy leader, the first woman to hold such a high ranking position in a New Zealand political party.

Values went into the 1975 election with a manifesto – *Beyond Tomorrow* – and television advertising which was notable for its creative and original approach to political promotions. The party was able to capitalise on disillusionment with the third Labour government which had been elected on a great wave of hope after 12 years of Conservative rule. Energy policies were a particular focus of Values' attentions. The Labour government had continued to promote 'hard' energy policies – with one minister even advocating a nuclear power programme – as part of what Values described as 'a prehistoric obsession with development' (Sunday Herald, 24 March 1974).

Labour's illiberal social policies, especially on the issues of abortion and homosexual law reform, also attracted Values' critical comment. The Labour Party at the beginning of the 1970s was still dominated by the concerns of the materialistic 'old politics' agenda and it failed to meet the expectations of those who thought that a Labour government would radically reshape New Zealand society after years of conservative government. The Values Party went on to win 5.2 per cent of the national vote, with candidates standing in all electorates. Polls show that Labour lost a lot of its idealistic supporters to the Values Party at the 1975 election (Evening Post, 6 Nov. 1975; James, 1986: 36).

Winning nine per cent of the vote in the Nelson by-election in January 1976 represented the high-point for the Values Party. From then on two processes in particular worked against its continued viability. The first of these was the modernisation of the Labour Party, a process begun by party leader Bill Rowling, and new party president Jim Anderton. The Labour Party modernised its structures and attracted a large number of new members, fundamentally changing the make-up and outlook of the party. New policies and new personnel made Labour less unattractive to those who had previously voted for Values (Rainbow, 1989). The prospect of Values voters turning (or returning) to Labour was further enhanced by the effect of the new national prime minister (now Sir) Robert Muldoon, who polarised the population with his aggressive and populist style. Opinion polls show that among all voters, Muldoon was liked least of all by Values' voters (Rainbow, 1989).

Second, the Values Party began a process of comprehensive policy development in response to negative feedback from candidates and the public at the 1975 election, particularly about the lack of economic policy. This process served to exacerbate existing tensions within the party between those described as 'middle class environmentalists' and the more politically experienced faction who saw Values' role in conventional party-political terms. This latter group believed that Values could be used to bring about much needed radical political and social change. The environmentalists tended to see Values as an umbrella group for a variety of causes, including alternative lifestyles, and less as a party in the conventional sense of a power-seeking political grouping. These intra-party divisions were exacerbated geographically, with the more politically oriented group tending to be concentrated in Christchurch, while those frequently described as 'armchair liberals' or 'the love and peace brigade' tended to be based in Auckland. The more politically oriented members consciously manipulated party processes so that by the 1978 elections Values had been publicly discussing the possibility of policies such as the nationalisation of land and the compulsory 'co-operatisation' of private businesses, leading to claims by some members of a Marxist take-over of the party.

For those disillusioned with mainstream parties but unimpressed with policy developments in the Values Party, a third factor worked against Values by the time of the 1978 election. For the Social Credit Party had been relaunched as a viable third party after the election of its appealing leader, Bruce Beetham, in a parliamentary by-election early in 1978. Unlike the Values Party, Social Credit had no qualms about the pursuit of political power, which it embraced with a vengeance and – for a short period – with some success.

The Values Party went into the 1978 campaign better organised and with a more detailed policy than at previous elections, but won only 2.8 per cent of the vote. This was a severe setback to members who had seen the party's success increasing at an exponential rate from election to election. The 1979 conference brought existing feuding and antagonisms to a head, with the result that the politically oriented faction, which included the defeated party leader, Tony Kunowski, withdrew from Values, depriving the party of many of its most active and visionary members. From that time on Values was dominated by those who had seen the party more as a 'social movement', as distinct from a political force. While Values continued to contest some seats at subsequent elections, its fortunes rapidly declined after 1979. The small remnant of remaining members joined with the new Green Party in 1990 prior to contesting the general election of that year. The new Green Party included several former Values Party activists, but former Values Party members have appeared in a variety of public positions, including that of a Labour Party Deputy-Mayor of Wellington and a National Party Member of Parliament.

Patterns of economic development in Tasmamia and New Zealand

A country's politics will be shaped by a variety of factors, including its history, political institutions and culture *and the nature of its economy* (author's emphasis) (Gold, 1989: 2). The importance of pressure stemming from economic development as a determinant of green fortunes is confirmed by Rüdig and Lowe's 1986 study of the British Greens. Rüdig and Lowe argue that low growth had constrained development in Britain, therefore preventing the expansion of environmentally controversial projects – *in particular in the energy sector* – (author's emphasis) which would act as a stimulus for the development of a viable green party (1986: 281). In both Tasmania and New Zealand relatively low but steady rates of growth had aroused little opposition until the campaigns to save Lake Pedder in Tasmania and Lake Manapouri in New Zealand. Both lakes were threatened as a result of energy policies which were inextricably linked to particular models of economic development.

There are remarkable similarities between the economic pressures and development patterns in Tasmania and in New Zealand, in part because of their geographical location and the sense of 'marginality' this has engendered. Both nations were settled predominantly by Europeans, in the case of Tasmania from the late eighteenth century onwards and in the case of New Zealand from the mid-nineteenth century onwards. The relationship between settlers and the indigenous peoples has been an ongoing issue for both states ever since. Both, countries developed economies based on the extraction and exploitation of natural resources, including sizeable agricultural sectors. In the absence of large quantities of private capital, the state always took a major role in the promotion of economic development. History was seen as a pattern of unending progress, and the inevitability of this unfolding of events led to any opponents being perceived as 'irrational' (Jesson, 1987: 175).

In order to overcome the disadvantages associated with distance from overseas markets, both states embarked on similar developmental paths, particularly after the Second World War. This developmental path concentrated much power in the hands of those responsible for the respective national policies of hydroelectric development. Hydro-electric development was seen to be a 'natural advantage' the potential of which both states could develop. It was a natural advantage that could be harnessed to produce cheap electricity which could, in turn, be used to encourage industry to develop in the antipodes.

The process of energy planning is an inherently political one, encapsulating certain assumptions about models of society and development. In New Zealand this process was driven by the New Zealand Electricity Department (NZED), who made the energy planning decisions, and the Works Department (later to become the Ministry of Works). The Works Department built the dams and also played a large role in planning through their access to important committees of officials and to Cabinet. It was the Works Department, for example, which through its minister initially brought the proposals to raise Lake Manapouri before Cabinet (Sutch, 1969: 340).

In Tasmania the process was driven by the Hydro-Electric Commission, which enjoyed the patronage of successive Labor Premiers and took an unashamedly political role at times (Herr and Davis, 1982). For example, the HEC went as far as to place full-page advertisements against the UTG in the run-up to the 1972 elections. The HEC received support from the dominant trade-union factions in the Tasmanian labour movement. They would have no part in Jack Mundey's proposal for a 'blue ban' to save Lake Pedder. Mundey was Secretary of the New South Wales Builders' Labourers' Federation whose 'green bans' had saved large parts of Sydney's heritage from 'redevelopment'. But the majority of unionists in both New Zealand and Tasmania remained committed to conventional patterns of development and had no truck with the way in which Mundey used union power. In New Zealand the dam-building programme received particular support from the Workers' Union, which was affiliated to the Labour Party. The Workers' Union Covered most of the workers on the dam sites, ensuring a healthy supply of revenue both to its own coffers as well as to those of the Labour Party, through affiliation fees.

McQueen writes that in the Tasmanian context,

> the HEC had gone on, year after year, decade after decade, for more than half a century, choosing its own projects, building its dams, completely free of ministerial control, and supported by a succession of Labor premiers.
>
> (1990: 45)

Central to this hydro-electric programme was the role of energy planners. The work of the energy planners and their apparent inability to make accurate forecasts of energy needs was a key focus of the environmentalist criticism in both countries:

> In spite of the fact that year after year, projections made by the planners were proved to be absurd, governments continued to plan for power stations that were not needed, and then to save face were forced to seek industries to use the power.
>
> (Wilson, 1982: 39)

Energy planners predicted an increase in New Zealand's electricity consumption from 1974 to 1975, for example, of 12.9 per cent. In fact electricity consumption decreased by 1.4 per cent (Howell, 1975: 187).

Energy planners investigated the prospect of nuclear power for New Zealand from the late 1960s and a cabinet minister in the third Labour government, Tom McGuigan, publicly advocated a nuclear power programme for New Zealand. His successor as Minister of Electricity, Ron Bailey, responded to criticism of the energy planners by asserting that 'it would be a good idea for uninformed people to leave the power production projections of New Zealand to the experts' (Wilson, 1982: 42). Both major parties promised a commission of enquiry into nuclear power if elected in 1975, a promise the new National Government kept. During 1976 the Campaign for Non-Nuclear Futures launched a petition which gained 333,087 signatures by the time it was presented to parliament that October. The Royal Commission began hearing evidence in 1976 and presented its report in May 1978, recommending that there was no need for an urgent decision, but that a significant nuclear programme should be economically possible for New Zealand in the early part of next century.

Significantly, this debate and several others in the energy field had dented the credibility of the New Zealand Electricity Department, which was primarily responsible for promoting the dam building programme because of its continued predictions of increased future energy demands. The NZED, and the government, had underestimated the ability of the environmental movement to provide credible and coherent technical counters to the NZED/Works juggernaut. The hydro-electric complex was also subject to scrutiny through a new medium: television. The widespread advent of television visually conveyed the controversial wilderness areas, such as Lake Manapouri, directly into the public's homes. Chapman asserts that the more critical and powerful news media was one of the chief factors bringing to a close the extraordinary degree of social consensus in post-war New Zealand (1989: 22). The role of the media, and particularly television, cannot be over estimated in examining the roots of the rise of environmental opposition movements in both the Tasmanian and New Zealand contexts. Both hydro-development proposals also aroused concern because they were more dramatic than any other projects attempted beforehand, and in the case of Lake Pedder, there was a unique quartz beach which would be destroyed.

The debate about Manapouri was succeeded by controversy over the damming of the Clutha River, a project described by an opponent as a 'hydrocrat's dream' (Wilson, 1982: 61). Both major parties were equally committed to a scheme which, the Commission for the Environment said, showed that the Ministry of Works had become blinded by the supposed need to produce electricity (Wilson, 1982: 62). The Treasury and the Planning Tribunal gave credence to environmentalists' views that the electricity was not needed, but the government procured the support of the Social Credit minority in Parliament to pass empowering legislation which allowed the Clyde Dam to proceed. As Wilson argues in his history of the New Zealand environmental movement, 'twenty years of controversy had not improved the level of debate – the principal factor in Clutha's decisions remained a rigid determination by the government to dam the river' (1982: 67).

Historian Keith Sinclair claims that 'for most of New Zealand's history, politics have been about economic development... The typical New Zealand leaders have seen their chief task as to initiate and administer development' (1980: 288). Mitchell reiterates this view, quoting early Liberal Premier, Richard Seddon, to the effect that 'party and the higher reaches of politics vanish into thin air before the public works statement' (1969: 14, 24). Mitchell goes on to assert that the predominant fact of New Zealand history has been development. Economic development largely meant industrialisation, a model designed to increase New Zealand's self-sufficiency, to generate employment and to insulate New Zealand from an over-dependence on a limited range of raw material exports. Essential to industrial expansion would be the continued provision of cheap hydro-electricity which the government would effectively subsidise in order to encourage industry (Wilson, 1982: 39). These policies were particularly pursued by the first and second Labour governments, who doubtless saw their electoral prospects enhanced by a growing industrial proletariat.

In both nations disadvantages of distance were to be overcome by the provision of cheap hydro-electricity, a technological advantage which would attract industrial development. In the case of Tasmania this has been described as public policy driven by a bipartisan vision of the island at the end of the world as a sea-bound equivalent of the Ruhr Valley. Such a vision reduced any ideological component of politics to a competition about which party would be best qualified to administer the technocratic state (Wescombe, 1990: 170). Green parties arose in both countries to challenge technocratic anti-politics (Wescombe, 1990: 171) and it may be no coincidence that given the similarity of the patterns of development between the Tasmania and New Zealand that there is also a remarkably consistent pattern of environmental disputes. For what Pybus writes of Tasmania could equally be applied to New Zealand:

> The focus of protest, invariably followed by direct action and civil disobedience, has been the protection of wild country against exploitation for hydro-electric power, for woodchips, for mining. The rallying cries in these environmental battles (for battles they were) have emphasised the right of the rivers or forest to remain in their natural state without human and technological intervention.
>
> (1990: 63)

The wilderness orientation of antipodean greens

It provides useful insights to draw on Eckersley's distinction between green orientations in the relatively human-dominated European environment and that in societies with large tracts of wilderness:

> the existence of large tracts of relatively 'undeveloped' wilderness areas in North America, Australasia and Scandinavia has meant that wilderness preservationist conflicts ... have tended to be a more significant feature of the green debates in these countries compared to 'domesticated' Europe. This is especially applicable to Tasmania, where wilderness preservation campaigns have been in the forefront of the state's environmental controversies since the Lake Pedder campaign of the early 1970s.
>
> (1990: 70–1)

Eckersley differentiates between anthropocentric greens and ecocentric greens, suggesting that different environmental issues can generate different ecological orientations (1990: 71). The prominence of wilderness issues has given the green movements in both countries an ecological, rather than an anthropocentric view, confirming cultural patterns in both states of isolation and the dominance of the landscape. This has led to an environmental movement which has concentrated on wilderness issues at the expense of social issues.

While the Green/ALP Accord[1] of 1989 in Tasmania included the promise of homosexual law reform, the problems of a green politics divorced from traditional socio-political considerations is demonstrated by recent opposition to homosexual law reform in the same state. A group called Concerned Citizens Against Moral Pollution has campaigned against homosexual law reform on the basis that homosexuality is a moral toxin in the social ecosystem which should be eliminated with much the same compunction with which we would deal with pollution in the environment (Croome, 1990: 116).

In both New Zealand and Tasmania the concentration on issues related to protecting the 'natural' world has given the green movement an anti-cosmopolitan bent which is often perceived as moralistic and puritanical. But perhaps most importantly this 'wilderness' focus has prevented the greens from developing a coherent approach towards a crucial factor in the environmental debate, as well as in the lives of the majority of people in both states: the city. An anti-urbanism pervades the greens, and rather than the 'urban commons' view – which suggests that cities are necessary but that they must be in sympathy with the environment – a 'rural commons' view associated with a suspicion of city life and a rural romanticism grips large parts of the green movement (Newman, 1991: 20–1).

Trainer, for example, has written that small-scale and highly self-sufficient local socio-economic systems will form the basis of the necessary, sustainable, conserver society. Most of us will live well without cash incomes, Trainer claims. He suggests that we will have less urge to seek entertainment in our solidaristic communities and that we must share more things as part of a more communal and co-operative lifestyle (1991: 32). Even ignoring the totalitarian overtones of such a utopian plan, such a lifestyle will hold little appeal for many. For those to whom it does appeal there are already opportunities to live in the intentional communities which proliferate in both Tasmania and New Zealand.

In contrast to the 'natural world' to which Trainer's Utopia defers, there is a sense that culture is artificial: removed from authentic relations between humans as well as between humans and nature. Wilderness is held up as a mirror against which the artificiality of culture can be measured. The wilderness, Tasmanian Green MP Bob Brown asserts, 'is an environment for finding a new kind of self, something better than the self that exists in the everyday world' (McQueen, 1990: 43). The natural world stands as a limit to the manipulative power of social control and 'once wilderness is gone, once there is no longer a reference point outside the manipulations of culture, the state, corporations, or other powerful interests, they will be able to shape and form citizens any way they want' (Manes, 1990: 221).

This ecocentric view fits easily with the traditional cultural patterns and myths in both Tasmania and New Zealand.[2] Sinclair asserts that the stereotypical character in New Zealand literature is a bachelor, a 'man alone', an outsider and misfit *'at odds with society'* (author's emphasis) (1980: 329). Regardless of how accurate this portrayal was in post-pioneering New Zealand, the stereotype has persisted. Raymond Sole, the narrator of Maurice Gee's *Sole Survivor* (the final part of Gee's highly perceptive trilogy tracing New Zealand's development through the lives of one family) ends up alone, passing time in a caravan on an alternative community in isolated Golden Bay (Gee, 1983).

This cultural stereotype is paralleled in a Tasmanian context by the notion of 'Tasmanian gothic', which emphasises the landscape as no mere backdrop to human settlement, but rather as an interventionist, and even dominant, force: 'In this gloomy and fatalistic scenario the notion of "society" is minimal and the emphasis is on the lone individual' (Lohrey, 1990: 91).

Competing visions of Utopia

The vision of nature tempered was particularly attractive for those who had lived through the great depression and one or two world wars. For them hydro-industrialisation signalled the march of progress and security through economic development. In New Zealand, industrialisation – a process that depended upon electricity – was connected quite explicitly with the survival of the Labour government's welfare state (Sutch, 1969: 240). Labour's 1935 Plan explicitly mentioned the role of hydro-electric development in establishing a qualitatively better society (1935: 9). The vision of hydro-industrialisation, symbolic of so much, 'was a grand and majestic vision that moved a great many people' (Flanagan, 1990: 125).

This vision saw power stations as the fulfilment of the Utopian goal of harnessing nature's energies to the benefit of the good life. Nature was there not to oppress people, as in the gothic vision, but to be improved upon in the interests of a better society. Hydro-electric development was symbolically significant for other than economic reasons, as Bolton's argument in an Australian context shows:

> Australians have been so much at the mercy of their environment in planning economic development that their morale and self-confidence are lifted by major co-operative engineering feats such as the Snowy Scheme. Soon the opening up of the Australian Alps led to a growing tourist traffic, [which] found much to admire in a great work of construction co-ordinating the work of men of many nationalities.
>
> (1990: 490)

This utopian vision – encapsulated by the mainstream parties and the dam-building juggernaut – was confronted by a qualitatively different type of utopian vision in the 1960s and 1970s. This new utopia was often the creation of a minority who had either consciously chosen to make Tasmania or New Zealand their home, or who had travelled abroad and did not want their countries to make the same mistakes as had the industrialised north. For another cultural stereotype which has relevance to Tasmania and to New Zealand is that of the utopian account of antipodean escape from the worst excesses of northern industrialism and artificiality, New Zealand has at times had the image of 'an Eden for the spiritually emaciated Europeans flocking to its coasts in a great escape bid from an original sin whose workings they suffered in their industrialising homelands' (Trussell, 1982: 32). The landscape in both Tasmania and New Zealand was seen as confirmation of the uniqueness of the place, of islands of great potential.

Many of those involved in the UTG were from outside of Tasmania, and one of the first environmentalist MPs, Norm Sanders, was a Canadian. Bob Brown is from New South Wales. In New Zealand the number of foreign born people in the Values Party was frequently commented upon. These were people 'who seemed intent on trying, after getting away from it all, to stop it coming here' (*Critic*, 6 May 1975).

This was a vision which also appealed to many young New Zealanders who had travelled abroad. For them, New Zealand was an unspoiled haven which should be kept so. Hence the Values Party's strong anti-immigration policies which saw them joining the National Party and the Federation of Labour in attacks on what were claimed to be the over-generous immigration quotas of the third Labour government.

This negative attitude to immigration was rather ironic given the number of foreign-born people in the Tasmanian and New Zealand green movements. A growing group of 'environmental refugees' have consciously chosen to live in New Zealand or Tasmania and they have provided an activist constituency for those committed to preservation and the prevention of hyper-industrialisation. Many of these immigrants have contributed to the proliferation of intentional communities and craft-based industries in both countries. Their utopian vision directly conflicts with the utopian vision still held by many locals, in spite of the fact that most of the long-term locals are themselves the descendants of people who fled the worst excesses of northern hemisphere industrialism in earlier times. But long-term locals fear that their limited employment prospects may depend upon just those developments that the environmentalists challenge. Considerable tension can exist as a result, and Tasmania has been described as a 'polarised society' because of these factors (Bingham and Ramsay, 1991). Similarly, in certain parts of New Zealand considerable tension exists between long-standing local communities and their late-comer environmentalist neighbours (for example on the West Coast of the South Island).

Summary

Several factors emerge to explain why green parties evolved at a similar stage in both Tasmania and New Zealand.

First, the creation of green parties signalled the emergence of opposition to similar processes of industrialisation based on an exploitative attitude towards the natural environment. It is maintained here that the simultaneous controversy generated by concrete environmental issues in both states was sufficient to explain why new political movements arose, movements whose concern was with particular issues which symbolised a more general uneasiness with industrialism. Because of the particular nature of the issues that catalysed the movements in both states, the green movement also came to be dominated by a concern for the wilderness and nature conservation, rather than for social and urban issues. The pattern of environmental issues is similar in both countries, and the continued concentration on issues of nature protection has been cemented by the relative lack of population pressures which have brought urban environmental issues to the fore elsewhere.

Second, new parties arose because of the inability of the Labour parties in either state to represent the attitudes of the new opposition to industrial expansion. This is an inevitable outcome of the situation where 'the labour movement is the product of industrial society, and it has always tended to build organisations and institutions based on the fundamental principles of industrialism' (Andersen, 1990: 115). Therefore even though Labour parties may adopt certain environmental or quality-of-life policies, to challenge economic development is to compromise their electorate as well as the funding base for social reforms, which are dependent upon the profits of capital (Przeworski in Denmark (1987: 272)).

In both Tasmania and New Zealand the Labour parties had been the main articulators of the industrial image of society in response to which the new green parties arose. In addition, the lack of other bureaucratic or established machinery to accommodate environmental demands made the seeking of political influence for the groups involved a logical strategy. This confirms Rüdig and Lowe's assertion that 'ecological parties will be more likely to develop the less the political system is able to integrate environmental demands by other means' (1986: 283).

Third, the similar patterns of development in both states made industrialisation increasingly conspicuous and inspired opposition from a conscious minority who rejected the alleged benefits of hydro-industrialisation. Conspicuous among these opponents were foreign-born people who had consciously chosen to live in either Tasmania or New Zealand precisely because of the peripheral status of these states in relation to the core industrial nations. This group provided a constituency and a potential activist elite with an investment in conserving the status quo. For some the peripheral status of a particular place is a positive asset, while the established decision-making processes see peripheral status as something to be overcome in their desire to gain closer links with industrial core nations (hence the case for cheap hydro-electricity as compensation for distance).

Fourth, energy issues were of crucial significance to the rise of green parties in both Tasmania and New Zealand, particularly as they were so closely connected to an industrial vision of society. The oil shock of 1973 also gave credibility to the greens' dire predictions about the depletion of resources. The importance of energy issues – and in particular the advent of nuclear power – to the rise of green parties in Europe has been noted by Rüdig and Lowe (1986).

Fifth, the electoral systems in both Tasmania and New Zealand initially thwarted attempts at green political influence. This meant that early forays in the electoral arena tended to leave activists disillusioned and willing to put their energies elsewhere (Tasmanian Wilderness Society or the Campaign for Non Nuclear Futures in New Zealand) because the prospects of political power seemed so remote. Not until 1984 were the Tasmanian Greens able to capitalise on their electoral system to gain parliamentary representation. The Tasmanian electoral system affords far more influence to the Greens in Tasmania now than is in prospect for the Greens under New Zealand's current electoral system.

Finally, the green parties that developed in both Tasmania and New Zealand initially revolved around key figures – Richard Jones in Tasmania (and later Bob Brown) and Tony Brunt in New Zealand – who were successful in making the intellectual connections between concern for environmental issues and a broader critique of industrialisation and the process of modernisation. Their subsequent visions captured the imagination of significant minorities in their respective environments. The task of these early activists may have been made easier because of the small size of the population in both Tasmania and New Zealand – easing access to the media as well as to the inter-locking networks which exist in smaller societies (Smith, 1987).

Conclusion

This Chapter has focused on the emergent stage of the first green parties in the world and has analysed some of the reasons why they were formed almost simultaneously in two similar states. More recent developments such as Resource Management Law Reform in New Zealand and the Green/ALP Accord in Tasmania have not been investigated in detail, but it is interesting to consider whether or not there is a connection between these contemporary developments of international significance and the fact that green movements emerged at a relatively early stage in both states.

Nor has the Chapter touched upon the implications of this historical analysis for the future of the greens. Suffice to say that if greens are serious about addressing issues of relevance to the majority of people they will need to devote far greater attention to the urban environment. In particular, greens need to promote practical ways in which sustainable economic development can be achieved at a local level, ensuring that 'local government be revitalised in the service of the whole community rather than the vested interest of a few' (Downton, 1991: 28). The relative lack of urban development pressures in both countries is no longer an excuse for greens in Tasmania and New Zealand to ignore urban issues. Population and pollution pressures will eventually impact upon even the remotest wilderness areas if steps are not taken now to address the way in which our cities function.

One issue which political processes in both New Zealand and Tasmania may have to take into account in future is the perception among a portion of the community that peripheral status is a positive attribute, to be protected and preserved.[3] This perception has considerable implications for approaches to economic development, but – given the will – it may be possible to turn the peripheral status of such countries into an economic advantage, through the promotion of tourism, secure information storage and so on.

The similar patterns of development in both states made industrialisation increasingly conspicuous and inspired anti-industrial movements in both countries. Given the choice of class perspectives, value perspectives, Marxist perspectives and industrialist perspectives addressed at the outset of this Chapter, the industrialist structural perspective is given credibility by the examples of the Tasmanian and New Zealand green experiences. The industrialist perspective has the added advantage of helping to explain the differences within green politics. These differences can be attributed to the fact that opposition to contemporary industrialism can give rise to both pre-industrial and post-industrial responses, represented by the dark-light green spectrum within the green movement.

The industrialist perspective also helps to explain why relationships between the greens and Labour parties are fraught with irreconcilable tensions, as the Tasmanian Green/ALP Accord showed. For on a spectrum with industrial growth and development at one end and ecology and conservation at the other (as Vedung (1989) suggests), greens and 'labourism' are clearly at polar opposites.

Opposition to previously unchallenged patterns of development may have been enhanced in the early 1970s by changing social values. But there is sufficient evidence in both countries of concrete issues, and the concerted green response they engendered, to explain the rise of green parties in both states. The experience in Tasmania and New Zealand suggests that in explaining the growth of green movements in the late twentieth century the escalation and visibility of concrete environmental problems can not be ignored. Similar patterns of development, similar economic pressures, shared cultural and political traditions and the inability of the respective Labour Parties to facilitate concerns about the negative effects of industrialisation, help to explain why these movements arose in two separate settings simultaneously.

Notes

1 The Tasmanian Green/ALP Accord of 1989 was an agreement between the Greens and the Australian Labor Party which assured the ALP of a majority in the Tasmanian Parliament in return for certain policy concessions. It collapsed after the Labor Party withdrew from the compact, but the five Green Independents who hold the balance of power in the Tasmanian parliament refused to support the motions of no-confidence moved by the Liberal opposition. This allowed the ALP to keep governing Tasmania as a minority government. For details of the Accord and a discussion of its implications see Pybus and Flanagan (eds) (1990).

2 For a discussion of myths and society in a New Zealand context see P. Harris, (1975), 'Mythology and Society: Three Examples from New Zealand Politics and Culture', *Political Science*, Vol. 27, Nos. 1 and 2; also L. Cleveland, (1979), *The Politics of Utopia* (especially ch.1 'The Symbolic Life of New Zealanders'), Wellington: Methuen; and W.H. Oliver, 'The Awakening Imagination', in Oliver (ed.) (1981).

3 Particularly after the fourth Labour government implemented anti-nuclear policies in New Zealand following its election in 1984, there were a number of prominent headlines about foreign perceptions of New Zealand which celebrated its isolation from the rest of the world. Headlines included 'Swedes opt for nuke-free NZ' (*Evening Post*, 10 Jan. 1986); 'NZ popularity increases with would-be migrants' (*Evening Post*, 19 June 1987); and 'Nuclear fear exiles pregnant Trixie to NZ' (*The Dominion*, 16 July 1986). Frank Alack summed up this view of New Zealand when he wrote to the *Nelson Evening Mail* on 28 May 1982:

> Our greatest poverty is our inferiority complex because we are a small nation at the bottom of the world. But being small and down here is to our advantage. Because of our geographical position, our reliable climate, fertile soil, raw materials, combined with our creative ability, and by tightening our belts a little, we could go it alone and be our own masters, bowing to no one, accepting no defeat.

Such sentiments may not be widespread but they do suggest an alternative point of view to that currently in vogue and may have to be taken into account by future decision-makers.

92   *Stephen L. Rainbow*

References

Andersen, J.G. (1990), ' "Environmentalism", "New Politics" and "Industrialism": Some Theoretical Perspectives', *Scandinavian Political Studies*, Vol. 13, No. 2.

Bingham, R. and J. Ramsay (1991), interview, Department of Environment and Planning, Hobart, 23 Aug.

Bolton, C.C. (1990), '1939–1951', in F. Crowley (ed.), *A New History of Australia*, Sydney: Heinemann.

Brunt, A.J. (1987), interview, former Values Party leader, Wellington, 2 Feb.

Caute, D. (1988), *Sixty-Eight. The Year of the Barricades*, London: Hamish Hamilton.

Chapman, R. (1989), 'Political Culture: The Purposes of Party and the Current Challenge', in H. Gold (ed.), *New Zealand Politics in Perspective*, Auckland: Longman Paul.

Cleveland, L. (1972), *The Anatomy of Influence*, Wellington: Hicks Smith.

Critic, 6 May 1975.

Croome, R. (1990), 'At the Crossroads: Gay and Green Politics', in Pybus and Flanagan (eds), *The Rest of the World Is Watching*, Sydney: Pan.

Denemark, D. (1987), 'Social Democracy and the Politics of Crisis in New Zealand, Britain, and Sweden', in J. Boston and M. Holland (eds), *The Fourth Labour Government*, Auckland: Oxford.

Downton, P.F. (1991), 'Ecopolis Now! Building Tomorrow Today', *Habitat*, Vol. 19, No. 4, Aug.

Eckersley, R. (1989), 'Green Politics and the New Class: Selfishness or Virtue?' *Political Studies*, Vol. XXXVII.

Eckersley, R. (1990), 'The Ecocentric Perspective', in Pybus and Flanagan (eds), *The Rest of the World Is Watching*, Sydney: Pan.

Evening Post, 6 Nov. 1975.

Flanagan, R. (1990), 'Masters of History', in Pybus and Flanagan (eds), *The Rest of the World Is Watching*, Sydney: Pan.

Gee, M. (1983), *Sole Survivor*, London: Faber & Faber.

Gold, H. (1989), 'The Social and Economic Setting', in H. Gold (ed.) *New Zealand Politics in Perspective*, Auckland: Longman Paul.

Henderson, H. (1978), *Creating Alternative Futures*, New York: Perigee.

Herr, R.A. and B.W. Davis (1982), 'The Tasmaman Parliament, Accountability and the Hydro-Electric Commission: The Franklin River Controversy', in J.R. Nethercote (ed.) *Parliament and Bureaucracy*, Sydney: Hale and Iremongr.

Howell, J. (1975), 'The Environment', in R. Goldstein with R. Alley (eds), *Labour in Power-Promise and Performance*, Wellington: Price Milburn.

Inglehart, R. (1981), 'Postmaterialism in an Age of Insecurity', *American Political Science Review*, Vol. 75.

Inglehart, R. (1987), 'Value Change in Industrial Societies', *American Political Science Review*, Vol. 81.

James, C. (1986), *The Quiet Revolution*, Sydney: Allen & Unwin.

Jesson, B. (1987), *Behind he Mirror Glass*, Auckland: Penguin.

Kolinsky, E. (1989), *The Greens in West Germany*, Oxford: Berg.

Labour Party (1935), *Labour Has a Plan*, election literature.

Lohrey, A. (1990), 'The Greens: A New Narrative', in Pybus and Flanagan (eds), *The Rest of the World Is Watching*, Sydney: Pan.

Lynch, M. (1990), 'Uncharted Territory', in Pybus and Flanagan (eds), *The Rest of the World Is Watching*, Sydney: Pan.

McQueen, J. (1990), 'More Than A River', in Pybus and Flanagan (eds), *The Rest of the World Is Watching*, Sydney: Pan.

Maier, J. (1990), 'Elections in Germany: Kohl's Landslide Victory, Greens Out', unpublished analysis.

Manes, C. (1990), *Green Rage: Radical Environmentalism and the Unmaking of Civilisation*, Boston, MA: Little, Brown & Co.

Mitchell, A. (1969), *Politics and People in New Zealand*, Christchurch: Whitcombe & Tombs.

Newman, P. (1991), 'Sustainable Settlements. Restoring the Commons', *Habitat*, Vol. 19, No. 4, Aug.

Oliver, W.H. (ed.) (1981), *The Oxford History of New Zealand*, Wellington: Oxford.

Papadakis, E. (1989), 'Green Issues and Other Parties: *Themenklau* or New Flexibility', in Eva Kolinsky (ed.), *The Greens in West Germany*, Oxford: Berg.

Pybus, C. (1990), 'Commentary', in Pybus and Flanagan (eds), *The Rest of the World Is Watching*, Sydney: Pan.

Pybus, C. and R. Flanagan (eds) (1990), *The Rest of the World Is Watching*, Sydney: Pan.

Rainbow, S.L. (1989), 'New Zealand's Values Party: The Rise and Fall of the First National Green Party', in P. Hay, R. Eckersley and G. Holloway (eds), *Environmental Politics in Australia and New Zealand*, Hobart: University of Tasmania.

Rainbow, S.L. (1991), 'The Unrealised Potential of Green Politics: A Study of Four Green Parties', PhD thesis, Victoria University of Wellington.

Rennie, N. (1989), *Power to the People, 100 Years of Electricity Supply in New Zealand*, Electricity Supply Association, Wellington.

Rüdig, W. and P.D. Lowe (1986), 'The Withered "Greening" of British Politics: A Study of the Ecology Party', *Political Studies*, Vol. XXXIV, No. 2.

Sinclair, K. (1980), *A History of New Zealand*, Auckland: Penguin.

Smith, N. (1987), interview, founding member of Values Party, Wellington, 5 March.

Sunday Herald, 24 March 1974.

Sutch, W.B. (1969), *Poverty and Progress in New Zealand*, Wellington: Reeds.

Trainer, F.E. (1991), 'The Conserver Society', *Habitat*, Vol. 19, No. 4, Aug.

Trussell, D. (1982), 'History in an Antipodean Garden', *The Ecologist*, Vol. 12, No. 1.

United Tasmania Group (UTG) (1990), 'The New Ethic', in Pybus and Flanagan (eds), *The Rest of the World Is Watching*, Sydney: Pan.

Values Party (1972), *Blueprint for New Zealand*, election manifesto.

Values Party (1975), *Beyond Tomorrow*, election manifesto.

Vedung, E. (1989), 'Green Light for the Swedish Greens', unpublished paper, Uppsala University.

Walker, P. (1989), 'The United Tasmania Group: An Analysis of the World's First Green Party', in P. Hay, R. Eckersley and G. Holloway (eds), *Environmental Politics in Australia and New Zealand*, Hobart: University of Tasmania.

Wescombe, M. (1990), 'From World's End the Greening Starts?', in Pybus and Flanagan (eds), *The Rest of the World Is Watching*, Sydney: Pan.

Wilson, R. (1982), *From Manapouri to Aramoana*, Auckland: Earthworks Press.

7 Environmentalism and the global divide

Eric Laferrière

Introduction

The purpose of this chapter is to explore the theoretical and empirical links between environmentalism, as a transnational new social movement, and globalisation, as a new phenomenon in politics. It poses an essential question: in what ways is the global environmentalist network shaping patterns of global relations, as they converge over the general issue of environmental sustainability? This is indeed a pertinent question in the current political context: states are ill-equipped to handle environmental issues; such issues have arisen through the impulse of environmental groups; the latter have proliferated globally in recent years; finally, environmental problems best illustrate the global (or 'total') character of politics.

The chapter will proceed as follows in answering the question. First the issue of globalisation in contemporary international relations theory will be discussed, with specific reference to social networks; second, the way in which environmental issues fit into an analysis of global politics will be explained; finally an analysis will be presented of how environmentalism operates as a global force and how it seeks to influence global elite relations.

As the logic of environmentalism drives towards the goal of sustainability, and as the logic of globality leads to the geographic whole, it will seem appropriate to focus the empirical discussion on North–South issue: the crucial test of environmentalism, as a global force, hinges precisely on resolving the 'environment-development dilemma' – common to both rich and poor countries. If there is meaning to the educative phrase 'global environmental polities', it must be ascertained from an examination of the link between environmentalism and global reform. Probing that link should help us understand if environmental groups, for better or for worse, play a role in either instigating or discouraging co-operative relationships across the global divide.

Defining the contours of globalisation

The discipline of international politics has long focused on the state as a unit of analysis and, in various instances, has insisted on the preeminent 'logic' of the state system as an explanation for interstate behaviour. However artificial the conceptualisation of an institution as 'behaving', the extensive attention paid to the most resourceful actors in the world is understandable: state decisions are ultimately responsible for peace and war among nations, for the international redistribution of wealth and for the success or failure in managing common problems. The state, long anthropomorphised by realists using the Hobbesian concept of survival in anarchy, is also central to liberals and Marxists alike who appreciate its role in buttressing world order.

If the importance of the state as a political actor is not denied, there has been, nonetheless, a long-standing criticism of its privileged position in theories of international relations. The state may be defending a national interest and mobilising its constructive and destructive powers in the process, but the definition of this national interest cannot be assumed merely from an analysis of 'anarchy'. The complexity of political life beyond the confines of structured polities reveals as much hierarchy as anarchy, while unveiling distinctive exchanges among less recognised actors which contribute significantly to patterns of co-operation and conflict among nations. Liberal theorists, from early functionalists to recent institutionalists, have described the various links connecting societies and thus explained international outcomes in a much more nuanced fashion. Neo-Marxists have outlined a very hierarchical model of the international system, centred on the domination of monopoly capital at the global level: here, the international links among the capitalist elite create a parallel system to the system of states, using the latter system to its advantage in what amounts to a single, integrated 'logic' (Chase-Dunn, 1981).

These qualifications to the realist paradigm, reducing the centrality of states as actors in international politics, have rendered a great service to our theorising efforts. They have demonstrated the necessity of looking at social groups and forces in order to understand state behaviour and international outcomes. They have also modified the conception of the 'internal' and the 'external': whereas traditional realist theories identify external and internal threats to the state (here, the country) and thus consider the two issues as intrinsically different, rival paradigms have shown that such threats converge to upset state positions.

The richness of a theory of international politics rooted in specific considerations of state–society relations is today widely accepted and increasingly promoted (e.g. Milner, 1992). This remark is especially important to those accepting the premise of a globalisation of politics. The concept is a logical extension of popular notions of 'inter-dependence' and 'world system', but is also eminently empirical in its depiction of common problems facing societies (Campanella, 1990). It conveys a description of reality whereby: (a) states depend essentially on other states for the resources necessary to satisfy societal demands; (b) social and economic 'externalities' have spilled over most or all countries on the planet; (c) organised non-state actors are increasingly drawing popular loyalties away from the state *and* are recognising their own sovereignties by regrouping across state boundaries (Rosenau, 1990). The argument is, thus, that global politics within global structures represents a distinctive reality to describe and analyse.[1]

While the postulate of 'globality' may initially suggest a reformulated 'systemic' (macro) approach, it can also insist on a micro-sociology of societal groups and new social movements.[2] Indeed, the globalisation of society is a key dimension of the investigated process and must be understood politically and culturally. In the latter instance, the concept of globalisation extends beyond the converging influence of the telecommunicative revolution to a particular cultural ethos disseminated by new social movements; as Albert Bergesen stated (1990) in his critique of international relations theory, the definition of a system must be culturally based, and new social movements have surely contributed to the definition of a global system in which new sets of values (peace, co-operation, respect of nature, respect of minorities, community-based empowerment) increasingly take hold and become meaningful for most people. Therefore, in a political sense, social globalisation designates effectively the purposive joining of non-governmental organisations working autonomously for the resolution of specific problems. From the perspective of international relations theory, the globalist approach can guide the analyst to a largely unexplored research agenda – one exploring the impact of transnational movement activity on patterns of global co-operation and conflict.[3]

The analysis of international relations from a social perspective is, then, decidedly far from the theoretical mainstream. Most 'globalists' concentrate on the role of international organisations in the adoption of 'global policy',[4] and are not concerned, even indirectly, with the impact of social organisations on global relations and/or global problem solving. Yet, so as to heed the calls of many critics of international relations theory and effectively integrate the perspectives from comparative politics, it is essential to appreciate the relevance of social analysis (and, thus, of 'local' social processes) to our discipline.

In sum, the globalist perspective to politics, upheld here, is a direct call for an analysis of the global polity – decentralised, acephalous, both anarchical and hierarchical, and fully shaped by the dialectical relationship between parallel systems of elites (state, corporate) and challengers (movements).

The environment as a case of global political analysis

The political ramifications of the environmental crisis illustrate well the dynamics of globalisation, which can be represented by a conceptual triangle, linking: (a) the state and economic system; (b) threats to human security and dignity and (c) new social movements. The dialectic is explicit:[5] 'established' elite institutions eventually display serious weaknesses (such as environmental crises) which stimulate the creation of politicised movements (organised, for instance as environmental groups); the latter, in turn, question the legitimacy of the system and encroach upon elite relations. In addition to environmental problems and environmentalism, this model applies especially well to the problems of nuclear proliferation and human and gender rights, from which new social movements all stemmed.

Admittedly, those problems, all crises of the *status quo* which invite political change, could be and have been analysed within 'domestic' systems – indeed, problems and movements always originate within a propitious locality or region. However, the point here is, precisely, that the characteristics of domestic state and economic systems are replicated globally, and that social organisations, emulating the multinational corporations, not merely extend beyond borders but thrive in their global reach.

Nonetheless, there remains a difference between environmental problems (and nuclear proliferation) and the other 'globalised' problems mentioned above, for the alleviation of environmental stresses often depends on global policies. In this sense, the globality of environmental problems stems not merely from the replicated institutions which create them and the spread of environmental activism, but also from both the very transboundary nature of pollution and depletion problems *and* the reliance on co-operative mechanisms for problem solving. From this angle, environmental problems resemble others such as terrorism, drug trafficking, migration or disease spread – all eminently global in a problem-solving sense, but easily handled by mainstream international relations theory. In sum, environmental problems straddle both fences: they can be, and have been, analysed (though only as regional issues) from conventional regime perspectives focused strictly on elite dynamics (states or epistemic communities (Haas, 1990; Young, 1982, 1989a,b)), or they can invite a 'globalised' reflection encompassing both state and social actors.

Environmental degradation is perhaps, then, the quintessential global problem. Some environmental issues exemplify the 'tragedy of the commons', where the unregulated exploitation of a common resource, driven by short-term rational calculation, leads to its extinction.[6] The image is applicable to such issues as stratospheric ozone depletion, global warming and ocean pollution;[7] in all cases, problem solving necessarily depends on global co-operation, where rules of behaviour are co-ordinated so as to ensure the respect of a 'maximum' threshold of production in relation to consumption. However, globality exists at an even deeper level, for environmental problems are conditioned by various principles of world order: militarisation, industrialisation and capital concentration are some of the most serious causes of environmental abuse, and they reflect micro-structures and micro-activities shared by the planet as a whole.

Environmental problems and the global divide

While the assumptions of the globalist perspective may direct the analyst towards certain kinds of processes and actors, they do not, *a priori*, specify the particular political arena in which the explanandum must reside; in other words, a globalist approach can be used to understand political events or relations equally well in local, national, regional, continental or global contexts. A focus on environmental politics, however, leads naturally to a discussion of the relationship between rich and poor: income inequalities are indeed part and parcel of the dynamic of environmental degradation. The rich–poor gap, as environmental *problématique*, would ideally be approached in its entirety – that is, both within countries and between countries. In other words, a thorough study of the impact of environmental problems and environmentalism on political relations would seek to identify commonalities or differences between national and non-national experiences. In this study, the less ambitious objective is to focus on the global rich–poor gap and on the North–South patterns of relations which are associated with it. The association of 'North–South' with 'the global', however, does not void the utility of the latter concept. In fact, it seeks to emphasise that, in this integrated global polity, the North–South divide represents probably the single most important political problem, a 'critical issue' around which elites and challengers gravitate in the pursuit of their respective utopias.[8]

The significance of the environmental crisis for North–South relations thus clearly unfolds. The mutual dependence inherent in globality is displayed most clearly, of course, in the 'commons' problems mentioned above. But it extends beyond them. Southern dependence on the North is quite real in local matters related to health care and sustainable production. These are typical Southern problems, intricately linked to pollution and ecologically destructive practices, whose alleviation 'requires' (at least according to elites) Northern capital and technology/knowledge.[9] On the other hand, Northern dependence, and the consequent 'power of denial' claimed by the South, is rooted in the political demands of the North's globalist environmentalism: Northern environmental groups are keenly interested in curtailing environmental problems in the South, and the latter is fully aware of the bargaining chip which it can extract from such 'emotional attachment'.[10]

Recognising environmental degradation as a global issue of concern, what is its existing and likely impact on North–South relations? A global problem such as environmental degradation can just as much create or increase conflict (if parties cannot agree on a solution) as it can prompt affected actors to initiate a dialogue on broader issues.[11] Indeed, existing evidence suggests that although Northern governments have used coercive mechanisms of environmental problem-solving (such as lending conditionality), they also have accepted the principle of compensatory funding for Third World expenses linked to environmental protection and sustainable development (of course, the sheer level of compensation can, and has, become a serious issue of contention).[12]

There are several reasons why the environmental question can worsen North–South relations. For instance, as hinted above, the types of environmental preoccupations differ from North to South. The North carries a globalist discourse, laced with scientific interests and aesthetic considerations: for instance, Northern countries want the South to protect its tropical forests so as to reduce global warming, preserve access to untapped reservoirs of organic materials necessary for biotechnological and medical research and maintain nature's grandeur. Northern actors want to minimise the South's existing and potential contribution to environmental problems affecting Northern interests. As for the South, it perceives environmental problems through the lenses of public health and sustainable local production and insists that these problems be addressed internationally before yielding on commons issues and conservationist policies.

Charges of 'neo-imperialism' under environmental garb are thus often levied, especially with existing and opportunity costs involved. Not only does the environmental agenda differ between the two hemispheres, a definite Northern reluctance to bear the full costs of global environmental policies is viewed with much suspicion in the South. The latter correctly claims that Western development policies are most responsible for global pollution and resource depletion while the world economic order has institutionalised Southern impoverishment, which itself fuels local environmental abuse. In other words, Southern elites perceive environmentalism as a Northern phenomenon designed either to legitimise protectionism or aid restraint or to forestall the growth of an autonomous industrial power base for the South.[13] Burdened by debt and the socio-economic problems that it fuels, the South is hardly willing to delay growth projects and 'waste' money on pollution control.[14]

In sum, assuming that environmental concerns are solidly implanted on the global agenda and actively pursued by at least some sectors of the Northern political elite, there are many reasons to believe that the urgency of environmental crises induces sustained pressure on the South for domestic sacrifices; at the same time, Southern states are well aware of their power of denial in environmental affairs and have used it in the hope of extracting Northern commitments.[15] The potential for increased North–South conflict is especially evident in current recessionary times.

On the other hand, some market-based factors could be invoked to link environmental issues to North–South co-operation. Many opponents of the proposed North American Free Trade Agreement have argued that disparities in the implementation of environmental legislation would act as a magnet for polluting industries wishing to avoid American and Canadian standards in favour of looser restrictions in Mexico.[16] If this assumption is valid, and if liberal forces do have the upper hand in coalition politics, then environmental problems, far from being the object of international dispute for their resolution, become an impetus for increased levels of trade depending precisely on the *status quo*. However, the argument can just as easily be turned around: protectionist and environmentalist forces may well exaggerate the extent to which environmental control costs are indeed uppermost on industry's priority list,[17] and effectively discourage instances of North–South co-operation (which, if pursued, may in fact generate the necessary wealth for environmental policies – though this benign view of the market can be debated). In other words, the environment, as it relates to trade, either raises barriers between North and South or, perversely, brings inter-hemispheric *rapprochement*.

Another market-based example will illustrate the point. The North–South trade in toxic wastes has been the object of virulent denunciations from African governments, prompting a sharply worded resolution at the OAU and setting the stage for the drafting of a global convention, in 1989.[18] However, this weak display of international law has yet to be ratified by the necessary minimum of parties for its implementation. Most probably, this reflects the tremendous economic benefits, for both North and South, of using the Third World as a dumping ground for hazardous wastes:[19] waste disposal in the South is ten times cheaper than in the North,[20] while the South gets access to a source of revenue which would vanish under a strong North–South environmental regime.

This said, the market does not necessarily violate the interests of nature, at least in principle. Americans have long advocated market mechanisms to control pollution. Having introduced the concept of tradeable pollution permits, which sets a 'tolerable' aggregate ceiling of emissions but allows efficient plants to sell their share of pollution rights to less efficient ones, and having implemented the idea domestically,[21] the US has urged the adoption of a similar mechanism at the global level. Applied to the problem of global warming, the scheme would use the country rather than the plant as an emitting unit and authorise 'excessive' individual greenhouse gas emissions, providing that a global maximum be respected.[22] This problem-solving mechanism might hence elicit the co-operation of key, reticent Third World countries (such as China and India) into a global regime. However, the numerous obstacles (political, definitional, practical) facing the adoption of such a revolutionary plan are overwhelming. Moreover, market-based environmental problem-solving may say relatively little about the impact of environmental problems on global relations. It may demonstrate that the *market* is an appealing approach, enticing co-operation for the resolution of *any* common problem; but it does not suggest that common environmental problems are, in their essence, conducive to co-operation.

To summarise, the global problem posed by environmental degradation may well modify North–South relations. An optimist would argue that the urgency of the situation has ensured the presence of environmental issues on the global agenda, that the North cannot extract environmental compliance from the South through traditional means of coercion and that the intensity of the South's economic crisis and own environmental crisis must stimulate its participation in co-operative schemes destined to reduce pollution and implement sustainable development patterns. The pessimist, on the other hand, would assume that the same urgency is pushing Northern countries to harden their economic policies towards the South so as to elicit rapid compliance to Northern environmental dictates, while the South cares relatively little about environmental questions and seeks to extract huge commitments from the North by the use of the environmental bargaining chip. Optimism and pessimism could also drive arguments assuming little or no efforts at North–South problem-solving: trade could benefit from the *status quo* in the regulatory gaps, but could suffer from attempts at using environmental arguments as disguised non-tariff barriers;[23] left untouched, pollution and resource depletion would also, in the long run, cause serious conflict (directly or indirectly) as rich and poor societies become embroiled in finger-pointing exercises.[24]

What role for environmental groups?

Having discussed the manifold impact of environmental problems on North–South relations, we must determine the extent to which environmental groups have been responsible for any new outcome. In other words, while environmentalists are responsible for raising environmental issues on the agenda of states, they do not necessarily control this new agenda.

Many important theoretical questions thus come to mind. For instance, what aspect of international relations are environmental groups more susceptible to influence? Also, can any pattern of co-operation or conflict be deduced from 'environmentalist ideology'? Finally, is the global structure of political environmentalism conducive to a particular tendency in global relations?

Environmentalism, as a social movement, is a relatively new phenomenon. Environmental groups have existed for decades in Britain, North America and Oceania, but the early groups were strictly conservationist and never articulated a broader social discourse.[25] Conservationist objectives are still important today, but the portrait of environmentalists has become much more differentiated, both in terms of ideology and membership.

In developed countries, environmental activism is a phenomenon of the extended middle class opposing the defects and abuses of capitalist society: this is often described as a symptom of a 'post-materialist' stage of development, where the financial security of the salaried individual leads to an emphasis on non-materialist values, while the openness of the political system allows for the politicisation of these new demands (Inglehart, 1989; Milbrath, 1984).

Northern environmental groups may all pursue reductions of environmental stresses, but they cannot be seen as homogeneous.[26] Most groups ire oriented towards local pollution problems and are scarcely concerned with global issues or the global implications of their local activism. Some groups are more research-oriented, globalist in their outlook and tactically subtle with governments; such groups are very much involved in North–South issues and are usually staunch (yet controversial) defenders of the South.[27] The most famous groups, such as Greenpeace, Friends of the Earth (FoE) or the World Wildlife Fund (WWF), are similar to the previous ones except for their wider scope, their often flamboyant tactics (except for FoE) and, in the case of Greenpeace, its financial independence.[28] Meanwhile, the WWF is a conservationist group, and is joined in this respect by several others. Conservationists tend to be less sympathetic to the demands of the impoverished South, although, as we will see below, they have sponsored very creative (and disputed) methods of environmental problem-solving through co-operation.

Environmentalism in the South has originated in a very different context and is much more homogeneous than in the North, though poorly integrated. The emergence of environmental groups in developing countries, in the 1980s, is a specific reaction to the economic failures of military regimes and/or command planning policies[29] (the experience of Eastern European countries is similar and should provide useful comparisons). The groups should be seen as part of a wider network of activists working for the democratisation of Southern countries (Durning, 1989). The context of activism is thus not the postmaterialism of Northern societies, but the struggle for survival in societies long repressed economically and politically. Southern environmental groups are largely focused inward and are most concerned with breaking the links of dependence on Northern capital and knowledge, eminently responsible for local environmental degradation (Shiva, 1989).

Examined globally, the environmental movement appears to be a very differentiated force. However, assumptions about environmentalist ideology do not always converge. At the most simple level, all environmentalists are united in a common cause – to fight against the destruction of nature. Moreover, a basic tenet of ecological thought (which is otherwise very diversified[30]) is the inter-related structure of the natural world, which suggests the idea that elements in a system must be synchronised so as to ensure either its stability or its steady evolution. Finally, the environmental movement is, quite correctly, recognised as one expression of a multifaceted social movement incorporating peace, human rights and feminist activism; these new social forces all believe in international co-operation for solving the particular problems which they are addressing and/or the larger problems facing the planet. For all these reasons, one may well assume, as a matter of fact, that environmental groups do form an integrated whole, successfully establishing 'global dialogue' (Friberg and Hettne, 1988: 358).

There is validity to this assumption, buttressed by selected evidence. Environmental groups have indeed established structural links between North and South while devising co-operative mechanisms of environmental policy between the Northern group and Southern state: there is no doubt that environmental problems, through the work of activists, have brought a North–South *rapprochement* on at least those two dimensions of relations.

At the inter-societal level, many well-known groups have expanded their operations, formally establishing offices in key Third World countries where policy coordination can take place on, usually, local issues with global implications. This is especially the case for Greenpeace, one of the least decentralised international groups. In the case of Friends of the Earth, a very decentralised network, learning exchanges between Northern and Southern groups have significantly increased since the publication of the Brundtland Report, in 1987.[31] Bilateral co-operation between independent groups is now common: two recent examples include the support of American groups for Peruvian and Ecuadoran colleagues' opposition to the 'development' of local tropical forests.[32] Multilateral interaction occurs within NGO secretariats and at NGO conferences.[33] In this latter case, an interesting by-product of the UNCED process was the drafting of 'parallel treaties', whereby NGOs dioplayed their critiques of official arrangements and offered their own version of a new global compact. Such activities are good examples of a vibrant political life within the non-state system; they may well institutionalise inter-societal co-operation and heighten the credibility of NGOs within diplomatic circles (Padbury, 1991).

Encouraging evidence also extends to the relationship between states and foreign NGOs, as suggested by the expanding use of an innovative mechanism of sustainable development, combining debt reduction and environmental protection: the debt-for-nature swap. The principle, conceived by the WWF and first applied in 1987 by Conservation International (an American environmental group), can be explained as follows. An environmental group purchases 'debt rights', at a discount rate, from a chartered bank (many creditor banks today prefer to secure an immediate lump sum rather than wait for uncertain complete payments). The environmental group then negotiates an agreement with the targeted Third World debtor state, by which the latter will pay directly to nature the debt now owed to the group. In other words, instead of merely reimbursing a Northern creditor (which does nothing for the country), the Third World state is asked to spend the same amount into a project of conservation (which is a productive and sustainable action). Furthermore, there is no obligation to use hard currency. Finally, the agreement usually requires the state to channel its funds through a local environmental group: this increases local empowerment while enhancing North–South NGO links, as the (Northern) debt purchaser works with the local environmental group in implementing the project of conservation.[34]

The debt-for-nature swap demonstrates most interestingly the role of new elites in establishing co-operative links across the global divide. Despite criticisms of the principle[35] and reservations as to its general relevance,[36] it has surely contributed to the improvement of global security.[37] Yet, more importantly for our purpose here, the swap mechanism has proved to be a model of North–South co-operation for state elites *per se*: indeed, several Northern governments have embraced the concept in dealing with the Third World,[38] while, conversely, debtor states of the South have manifested a strong willingness to participate in extensive swap programmes.[39]

In sum, there is evidence that Northern environmental groups have defended the interests of the South and worked purposively to foster co-operation; Southern groups, for their part, have sought guidance and obtained financial backing from Northern counterparts. Of course, the objectives pursued by Northern environmentalists are not merely altruistic. What matters to them, as the end result, is more environmental protection than local empowerment. They will defend Southern states in some global environmental negotiations, but not others.

One 'positive' experience can be discerned in the ozone process. The 1987 Montreal Protocol, following the 1985 Vienna Convention, had tackled rather inadequately the problem of stratospheric ozone depletion. One shortcoming pertained to the regulatory scope of ozone-depleting substances. Yet another failing, of special interest here, was the absence of a compensatory principle for Third World countries. The latter were not prepared to restructure the industrial sectors targeted by the ban on chlorofluorocarbons and other products unless they secured access to the necessary technology and funds. The 1990 London Amendments, perhaps a landmark in North–South relations, successfully filled the two aforementioned gaps.[40] Almost all harmful substances were banned (and the deadlines advanced, in most cases from 2000 to 1997), and a Multilateral Fund of, initially, $240 million was instituted so as to channel compensatory funds to the Third World (technology transfer was mostly left hanging). The major environmental groups, relatively silent through the early years of the Convention and Protocol, abruptly came to the fore in 1988 and vehemently endorsed Third World demands for compensation. There is little doubt that their active lobbying and their articulate argumentation helped convince the recalcitrant states of the North (especially the US) to accept the principle of the Fund.[41] Admittedly, there is no claim here that environmental groups or the broader NGO community were solely responsible for the acceptance of a distributive mechanism, for delegates from Southern states themselves made impassioned pleas and issued fair warnings in relation to the issue.[42] Nonetheless, these Southern concerns had existed for a long time and were seriously addressed only when other actors became involved.

If environmental groups can entice Northern governments into accepting Southern demands for resource transfers, they can also oppose unsustainable policies for which the Third World bears direct responsibility. The struggle against species extinction is one particular instance where group activity is enforcing the co-operation of Southern states into a global regime. The recent agreement on the protection of elephants is worth noting in this respect. The 112-country Convention on International Trade in Endangered Species (CITES) has worked, for several decades, to prevent the disappearance of threatened species of flora and fauna. Elephants, awe-inspiring in the North, yet both detested (as they can damage crops) and prized (for their products) by many in the South, have preoccupied CITES seriously. Economic crises in Africa, combined with attractive Northern markets, have put serious pressures on the elephant. Although no binding agreement exists on the trade of ivory, trade in hides and meat is forbidden. Five African countries recently sought a partial lift on the trade ban and were initially backed by Washington. However, the staunch opposition of the WWF and other conservationist groups effectively persuaded the five states (and the US) to retreat from their positions, which they formally did at a CITES conference, in March 1992.[43] Environmental groups hence succeeded in maintaining the support of Southern states for a global agreement. However, unsurprisingly, half-hearted participation by the South may well turn a seemingly co-operative endeavour into a long-term thorn in relations.

The groups thus clearly adhere to their own agenda; although they defend the South's demands for global economic reform, they will not accept income-generating policies which might harm the environment. Their position on international trade indeed suggests that they will readily oppose instances of (economic) co-operation which do not satisfactorily address environmental issues. This is an important observation in the context of North–South relations and the global assertion of new social movements. In spite of a value system which emphasises co-operation, new social movements will not hesitate to undermine interstate co-operation, rejecting the (admittedly liberal) argument that such elite co-operation might instill a common understanding, generate wealth and shape institutions which, in the long run, could further sustain development and other objectives.

As mentioned earlier in the text, the impending North American Free Trade Agreement (NAFTA) symbolises a new North–South elite *rapprochement* based on the virtues of neo-liberal policies (which nonetheless parallels Southern demands for redistribution and structural reform at global conferences).

These negotiations and the broader trade framework have both neglected (at least initially, with NAFTA[44]) the environmental implications of international trade. The trade-environment dynamic is, in fact, a relatively new issue in trade theory, and environmental groups became seriously active on the matter only in 1990, urging the GATT (though yet unsuccessfully) to form a working group which would study the possibility of tolerating legitimate cases of environmental protectionism. Such activities are resented by the South, whose poverty largely emanates from decades of Northern agricultural protectionism, ignored by GATT rules.

Environmental groups are not against the principle of liberalisation.[45] However, they are against the internationalisation of unsustainable patterns of development, which they see embodied in NAFTA. Their lobbying in Congress initially managed to delay the process of co-operation. Along the way, they received participation rights in advisory councils, thus allowing them more input in decision-making. Although they may have come short of constituting an essential force in this particular exercise in negotiations, they have nonetheless established the inevitability of an environmental agenda in non-environmental affairs, while indicating their readiness to abort interstate co-operative endeavours which might worsen environmental conditions.

A general assessment of environmentalist influence over North–South interstate relations must therefore acknowledge the growing presence of environmental groups in the negotiating process, which is a consequence of their long-standing, yet diffuse, impact on agenda setting. In other words, the 'greening' of elite institutions and its implications for inter-state relations are much more vivid today. Environmental groups have sponsored co-operative mechanisms[46] and delayed others. Nonetheless, it would be incorrect to exaggerate the extent of their influence, as it stands now. In diplomacy, state autonomy from 'non-established' movements remains quite strong.[47] This is especially the case with inter-governmental organisations. Although environmental groups have achieved observer status with many IGOs, they have yet to penetrate policy circles.[48] Interstate co-operation on environmental matters between North and South has recently attained new heights, but the inputs of non-governmental organisations have been essentially limited to implementation (which nonetheless remains an essential task);[49] and of those NGOs, most are problem-oriented groups rather than 'typical' environmental activists.

Finally, a note of caution pertaining to the high degree of pluralism inherent in global environmentalism. Although fundamentally united under the same banner, environmental groups do compete for resources and display varying ideologies and political tactics. This happens across and within hemispheres. In the South, such societal divisions can be especially detrimental to the environmentalist cause, for Southern NGOs are, *a priori*, much more vulnerable to the state than in the North (Yap, 1989–90). As a result, Southern states are often much less constrained by environmentalist pressure than their Northern counterparts. In the context of North–South interstate relations, different levels of domestic pressure might entail different understandings as to the importance of particular issues, such as the environment. For this reason, the potential for conflict seems more palpable, although the political weakness of Southern environmental groups might be compensated by the political reach of Northern groups. However, as stated earlier, Northern environmentalism is often perceived as intrusive in the South. Sustained conflict is, therefore, just as plausible.

Conclusion

This chapter attempts to relate themes of globalisation, environmental degradation, new social movements and North–South relations. The purpose is to explore the impact of a global problem on global relations, as mediated by trans-societal groups critical of world order. Inspired by alternative approaches to international relations, one underlying concern pertains to the centrality of states in international relations and their permeability, in that context, to social forces; evidence suggests that states remain vibrant and largely autonomous actors, though increasingly challenged.

Parallel investigations of the specific links between environmental group activity and North–South relations are also launched: one emphasised plurality and conflict, the other unity and co-operation. Mixed evidence indicates the need to clarify how relations are affected by the structures and ideologies of environmentalism. If the initial intention was to explore how changing values (symbolised by environmentalist activity) are modifying existing patterns of relations across the global divide, it will require further research on the various actors submitted to this new type of political pressure. More probing of the link between the various political strategies of environmental groups and the reaction of established elites is necessary.

Such considerations underlie the complexity of global analysis, whose eclecticism is heuristically powerful yet empirically perplexing. Whereas traditional research in social sciences seeks to solve 'puzzles' by isolating and comparing completed phenomena, this type of research concentrates on ongoing processes and is necessarily much more speculative. Therefore, global analysis is best appreciated as a long-term, multidimensional project. This chapter is only a small part of a much larger effort, and its various theoretical components will likely remain in a constant flux.

Nonetheless, it is crucial to remember the importance of explanation, as distinct from a more limited exercise in analytical description. For students of international relations, the goal is precisely to relate, theoretically and empirically, observed structures and processes to co-operative and conflictual tendencies. Very few authors have ventured into explanations linking new social movements, environmental problems or even structural interdependence to patterns of global relations. The field is new, evidence is elusive and, most importantly, the links usually depend on a myriad of related factors. Using North–South categories, for instance, is replete with problems; the US is not Norway, while the Middle Eastern region has displayed protracted conflicts rarely seen elsewhere (and these are just two examples among many).

This said, the chapter can point to several observations on which to build. At the most basic level, the 'North–South issue' is very much a preoccupation for the political elite, old and new, in environmental problem-solving: the issue may be far from settled, but, to quote again Vasquez and Mansbach (1983), it is undoubtedly 'critical'. Second, the presence of environmental groups, as actors in international relations, is solidly anchored and will likely wane only after bringing structural change. Third, environmentalist activity has not been ineffective in shaping patterns of interstate relations, although the conflictual/co-operative direction of relations is not uniform and remains open-ended. Perhaps the most interesting development in this regard is the debt-for-nature swap, conceived by enviromentalists and endorsed by Northern and Southern states.

As a final thought, it is worth remembering the essential lesson taught by any analysis of so-called environmental relations. Indeed, unless one's study is cast squarely in regime approaches and treats the environment as a mere case study, the concept of 'environmental relations' is at best unhelpful and, at worst, misleading. Environmental issues are not self-contained and, in the North–South dynamic, their impact on relations can only be understood in a broader socio-economic context; they can only be measured by what they do to other policy fields. As such issues can hardly be dissociated from a wider *problématique* of reform, an analytical perspective from the new social movements seems indeed appropriate.

Notes

An earlier version of this chapter was presented at the annual meeting of the Canadian Political Science Association, University of Prince Edward Island, Charlottetown, 31 May–2 June 1992. The author acknowledges the comments of EP's two anonymous reviewers; Robert Boardman, Mark Brawley, Ronnie Lipschutz and Patricia Romano were also helpful with early versions. The Social Sciences and Humanities Research Council of Canada provided financial assistance in the initial stages of the project.

1 The research agenda explored by Robert Cox and his colleagues at the United Nations University is perhaps the most ambitious in this regard (Cox, 1990). In many ways, Cox's thought, rooted in a Gramscian analysis of hegemony and emphasising the link between historic blocs and world order, is a most inspiring source for contemporary 'globalist' challenges to mainstream theories of international relations; cf, his path-breaking book (1987).

2 A key volume in the field is Mendlovitz and Walker (eds) (1987); see especially the chapter by Walker and Mendlovitz, Shiva, Alger and Mendlovitz and Falk (most other chapters are themselves excellent); and see also Cox (1990). For a recent collection of articles, see the special edition of Social Research, Vol. 52 (1985), pp. 684–890. For a detailed case study (though restricted to developed countries), see Inglehart (1990).

3 A rare article somewhat touching on the topic is Dorsey (1993). A good conceptual piece on social movements and global politics is Thiele (1993).

4 A valuable work is Soroos (1986). The approach receives strong criticisms in Donnelly (1990) and in J. Martin Rochester (1990) (though the latter is a little less stinging).

5 Similar conceptions are found in Hettne (1990), Friberg and Hettne (1988) and Cox (1990).

6 Garrett Hardin (1968) used the parable of the English pasture to illustrate his famous model.
7 The image is indeed similar, though not identical. Here, the atmosphere and the oceans are apparently bottomless sinks in which are dumped previously unimaginable quantities of hazardous materials.
8 The conceptualisation of a 'critical issue' was forcibly argued by Vasquez and Mansbach (1983) who foresaw the North–South conflict as the emerging such issue announcing a new era in world politics. The importance of the global rich–poor gap to ecological sustainability was expressed in landmark reports from the Brandt Commission (1980), the World Commission on the Environment and Development (Brundtland Commission) (1987) and the South Commission (1980). The famous report to the Club of Rome had set the tone for the others which followed (though not all shared its neo-malthusian assumptions); cf. Meadows *et al.* (1972).
9 Shiva (1989) makes the powerful argument that current unsustainability in the Third World is precisely rooted in the use of Northern methods of development and that the goal of Southern environmental groups (at the very least in India) is to re-introduce traditional approaches to, especially, agriculture. However, state elites are turning back to the North in their efforts to overcome the economic crisis.
10 The expression is derived from Nadelmann (1990), who explains how 'transnational moral entrepreneurs' (reform-oriented NGOs holding strong non-instrumental values) have succeeded in 'proselytising' world elites and prohibiting common, tolerated practices (such as piracy or opium trade). He mentions the environment as a new 'cause' and singles out Geenpeace's efforts to combat whaling as a telling example of the power of such 'moral entrepreneurs'.
11 Gourevitch (1986: 240) makes basically the same point, noting that international economic crises can either lead to aggressive, imperialist policies (such as in Nazi Germany) or stimulate very constructive responses based on domestic and international co-operation (such as in Sweden).
12 Examples (some to be detailed later) include the Multilateral Fund for the Montreal Protocol ($240 million for the first three years), the World Bank's Global Environment Facility ($1 billion for three years) and the US's $75 million global warming fund for the Third World.
13 The economistic argument is well articulated in Juda (1979): this is an early yet still authoritative piece on North–South environmental relations. The power argument is derived from Krasner (1985).
14 Of course, when the intensity of pollution reaches unbearable effects, any government will likely take action and, if necessary, sacrifice some economic assets. The recent shutdown of Mexico City's biggest oil refinery is a case in point; cf. *New York Times*, 19 March 1991, pp. A1, A6.
15 This strategy yielded success in the case of ozone depletion, with the creation of the $240 million Multilateral Fund responsible for channelling necessary funds to the South's efforts at implementing the provisions of the Montreal Protocol (technology transfer does remain a moot point, however). The best account of the tractations surrounding international negotiations over ozone is in Benedick (1991).
16 For a succinct analysis of the link between environment and trade, see Far Eastern Economic Review, 19 September 1991, p. 50.
17 See Gene Grossman's letter to the *New York Times*, 1 March 1992, section 3. p. 11.
18 This is the Basel Convention, signed by fifty five countries from both North and South.
19 Lawrence Summers, chief economist at the World Bank, exposed this cold logic in an internal memo – which was leaked to the press and drew severe criticism for its implicit support of dumping activities; cf. *The Economist*, 8 February 1992, p. 66.
20 Precise figures on this matter remain difficult to gather. Cf. Brady (1989) and *Le Monde diplomatique*, August 1988.

21 Sulphur dioxide (SO_2) emission permits are now being traded at the Chicago futures market (SO_2 is the essential contributor to the problem of acid rain). The 1990 amendments to the Clean Air Act sanctioned the use of this market mechanism for pollution control.

22 An ardent proponent of the approach is Grubb (1990), who nonetheless acknowledges the various practical problems inherent in the method.

23 It is always difficult to establish with certainty whether environmental barriers to trade are tools of economic policy or reflections of genuine environmental commitments. The GATT ruling of August 1991, striking down an American law forbidding the import of tuna (whole or canned) caught with sub-American 'dolphin standards', is a perfect example; the case also had a definite North–South component, for many Third World countries were targeted by the law (especially Mexico, which filed the complaint with GATT). The ruling, in fact, de-emphasised the success of environmentalist lobbying and assumed the preeminence of traditional protectionist lobbies in Congress.

24 There are few clear examples, at this point, for what remains a scenario (migration often results from environmental degradation and is a potential irritant between North and South; Haitian migration patterns to North America are partly explained by the extent of deforestation in Haiti, now at 90 per cent). Thomas Homer-Dixon [1990] has perhaps best articulated the hypothetical (and existing) links between environmental degradation and conflict, though mostly at the dyadic or regional levels.

25 The Audubon Society and the Sierra Club are two well-known examples of traditional environmental groups; however, the objectives of both (especially Sierra) did evolve through the decades.

26 A great debt is owed to André Beaulieu for helping with the following classification. On similar lines, see Porter and Brown (1991: 57–8).

27 Good examples are three American groups: the World Resources Institute (WRI), the Worldwatch Institute and the Natural Resources Defense Council (which is also very active on national issues). The WRI's positions on sustainable development issues and global co-operation are well reflected in an article written by its President, Gus Speth (1990). The sensitivity of Northern groups to Third World development needs did take time to evolve. John McCormick (1989: 197–8) credits Third World countries themselves for 'inject[ing] a note of realism into environmentalism in Western Europe and North America', and convincing Northern groups of the validity of sustainable development, as a concept.

28 For an insider's analysis of FoE, see Weston (1989). For interesting though unsystematic notes on Greenpeace and the WWF, see Pearce (1991).

29 Notable cases of popular environmental 'awakening' include the Philippines, Kenya, Chile and Brazil; the latter case is especially indicative and is well analysed by Viola (1988). The experience is somewhat different in India, where environmentalism has much deeper roots in history and is greatly influenced by Gandhian anti-industrialism; of all Third World countries, this brand of environmentalism is perhaps the closest to Northern non-materialist objectives, though it is very different from the 'wilderness thinking' of American groups; cf. Guha (1990).

30 Useful books on the matter are Eckersley (1992), Mellos (1988) and Paehlke (1989).

31 Personal interview with Guy Buron, coordinator and project director at Friends of the Earth, Montreal.

32 For the Peruvian case, cf. *New York Times*, 2 July 1991, p. C4; for Ecuador, cf. *New York Times*, 26 February 1991, p. C4.

33 NGOs have access to two secretariats: in Nairobi (within the structure of the United Nations Environment Programme) and in Geneva ('Our Common Future' centre). Global NGO conferences form a new trend, launched at the December 1991 meeting, in Paris. The Global Forum, a NGO parallel to the official 1992 Earth Summit, fully concretised this new process.

34 For a concise article on the issue (yet with ample case references), see Page (1989).
35 Usual criticisms pertain to an alleged violation of state sovereignty (this assumes a certain manipulation on the part of the environmental group) or to the 'sacrifice' entailed by the swap – in other ends, money thus spent could have been allocated for other ends (health, education, a more 'rational' use of resources or, of course, pollution reduction). As well, debt-for-nature swaps may run to exhaustion: not all banks have accepted to forgo the billions of dollars owed to them while environmental groups do not possess sufficient financial clout to organise large-scale swaps. Finally, if not most importantly, the creation of parks can take place at the expense of indigenous groups while, in practice, doing little to prevent illegal logging and mining. Cf., *inter alia*, Mahony (1992) and *Le Monde diplomatique*, September 1989.
36 Approximately twenty swaps were negotiated between 1987 and 1991, for a total of less than $100 million worth of debt rights. This amount is obviously tiny if compared to the $1.3 trillion owed by Third World countries. Cf. Mahony (1992).
37 Positive spin-offs can thus be summarised: the improvement of the local environment; a more productive use of the debt; the creation of or the support to a Southern NGO; a demand for local currency; the stimulation of environmental consciousness in Southern governmental circles; the partial satisfaction of banking interests. All these security-enhancing processes imply co-operative links between various actors, domestically and internationally.
38 Noteworthy cases include the Netherlands ($33 million) and Sweden ($24.5 million) with Costa Rica and the United States ($16 million) with Chile.
39 Brazil has offered to swap $100 million worth of debt, yearly. Poland has proposed 10 per cent of its debt, for a $3.1 billion total by 2011.
40 Specialists in international law are often optimistic as to the potential of new mechanisms of public allocation. Political analysts might rather stress the US's insistence on the 'exceptional' distributive character of the Amendments.
41 Benedick emphatically suggests (1991: 166) that environmental groups were 'a new element' in negotiations. In fact, the groups' influence came through in two special ways: from their access to UNEP top officials (especially its executive director, Mostafa Tolba, who played a key leadership role through the years) and to the American chief negotiator, Mr Benedick himself, whose former employment at the WWF and Conservation Foundation undoubtedly predisposed him to environmentalist discourse. The more general point about the persuasiveness of environmental groups in international conferences was stated in a personal interview by Pierre Marc Johnson, former Premier of Quebec and currently special advisor to UNCED General Secretary Maurice Strong.
42 See especially India's Manekha Gandhi's speech at a meeting of the parties, referred to in *The Economist*, 1 July 1990, pp. 43–44.
43 Cf. *New York Times*, 11 March 1992, p. A8. The five African countries are Zimbabwe, Botswana, Malawi, Namibia and South Africa.
44 Negotiators deliberately circumvented environmental debates at the outset. See the excellent paper (titleless) presented by Mike Feinstein, from the Green Party of California, at the North American Green Summit in San Francisco, 27–29 September 1991.
45 Jay Hair, President of the National Wildlife Federation, stressed the point in an op-ed contribution to the *New York Times*, 19 May 1991, s. 4, p. 17.
46 Another noteworthy – but very controversial – example is the Tropical Forestry Action Plan, a long-term assistance project for the preservation and (sustainable) development of tropical forests; it was conceived by the WRI and the FAO in 1985 and secured an initial budget of $8 billion for five years.
47 Perry (1986: 13) writes about the general tendency by which career diplomats displace NGO representatives at 'important' meetings. Referring to a mid-1980s World Meteorological Organization congress on nuclear war, he explains: 'new faces

suddenly appeared in virtually every delegation as meteorologists were pushed aside by political officers – probably the same officers who appeared at the World Health Organization when a similar issue was debated'. FoE International (1991), for its part, decries the UNCED process, claiming that 'environmental NGO views appear to have been marginalised in favour of those presented by official organisations'.

48 The former Greenpeace Director for Eastern Canada, Brigitte Gagné, had no qualms in admitting to the author her organisation's 'minimal' influence at the World Bank. However, the Bank is much more receptive to allegedly less 'radical' groups.

49 A good example of this tendency is noticeable in the World Bank's Global Environment Facility, instituted in 1990. The Facility is distributing $1 billion of new money to the Third World (at least until 1993) for selected (yet, from a Southern perspective, not necessarily crucial) environment protection programmes; the implementing capacities of NGOs are essential to the programme. Cf. United Nations Environment Programme (1991).

References

Benedick, Richard E. (1991), *Ozone Diplomacy: New Directions in Safeguarding the Planet*, Cambridge, MA and London: Harvard University Press.

Bergesen, Albert (1990), 'Turning World-Systems Theory on Its Head', *Theory, Culture and Society*, Vol. 7, Nos 2–3, pp. 67–81.

Brady, Diane (1989), 'New Curbs on the Commerce of Poison', *Our Planet*, Vol. 1, Nos 2–3, pp. 18–20.

Brandt Commission (1980), *North–South: A Programme for Survival*, Cambridge, MA: MIT Press.

Broad, Robin, John Cavanagh and Walden Bello (1990–91), 'Development: The Market Is Not Enough', *Foreign Policy*, No. 81, pp. 144–62.

Campanella, M.L. (1990), 'Globalization: Processes and Interpretations', *World Futures*, Vol. 30, pp. 1–16.

Chase-Dunn, Christopher (1981), 'Interstate System and Capitalist World Economy: One Logic or Two?' *International Studies Quarterly*, Vol. 25, No. 1, pp. 19–42.

Cox, Robert (1987), *Production, Power and World Order*, New York: Columbia University Press.

Cox, Robert (1990), 'Multilateralism and the United Nations System (MUNS)', United Nations University Programme, 1990–95, unpublished manuscript.

Donnelly, Jack (1990), 'Global Policy Studies: A Skeptical View', *Journal of Peace Research*, Vol. 27, No. 2, pp. 221–30.

Dorsey, Ellen (1993), 'Expanding the Foreign Policy Discourse: Transnational Social Movements and the Globalization of Citizenship', in David Skidmore and Valerie M. Hudson (eds), *The Limits of State Autonomy: Societal Groups and Foreign Policy Formulation* (Boulder, CO: Westview Press), pp. 237–66.

Durning, Alan (1989), 'People, Power and Development', *Foreign Policy*, No. 26, pp. 66–82.

Eckersley, Robyn (1992), *Environmentalism and Political Theory*, Albany, NY: SUNY Press.

Friberg, Mats and Björn Hettne (1988), 'Local Mobilization and World System Politics', *International Social Science Journal*, Vol. 40, No. 117, pp. 341–61.

Friends of the Earth International (1991), 'A Critical Review of Efforts to Establish Global Consensus on the Conservation and Wise Use of Forests', unpublished manuscript.

Gourevitch, Peter (1986), *Politics in Hard Times: Comparative Responses to International Economic Crises*, Ithaca, NY: Cornell University Press.

Grubb, Michael (1990), The Greenhouse Effect: Negotiating Targets', *International Affairs* (London), Vol. 66, No. 1, pp. 67–89.

Guha, Ramachandra (1990), 'Toward a Cross-Cultural Environmental Ethic', *Alternatives*, Vol. 15, pp. 431–47.

Haas, Peter M. (1990), *Saving the Mediterranean: The Politics of International Environmental Cooperation*, New York: Columbia University Press.

Hardin, Garrett (1968), 'The Tragedy of the Commons', *Science*, Vol. 162, pp. 1243–8.

Hettne, Björn (1990), *Development Theory and the Three Worlds*, Burnt Hill: Longman Group.

Homer-Dixon, Thomas (1990), 'Environmental Change and Violent Conflict', Cambridge: International Security Studies Program, American Academy of Arts and Sciences, Occasional Paper No. 4.

Inglehart, Ronald (1990), *Culture Shift in Industrial Societies*, Princeton, NJ: Princeton University Press.

Juda, Laurence (1979), 'International Environmental Concern: Perspectives of and Implications for Developing States', in David Or and Marvin Soroos (eds), *The Global Predicament*, Chapel Hill, NC: University of North Carolina Press.

Krasner, Steven (1985), *Structural Conflict: The Third World Against Global Liberalism*, Berkeley, CA: University of California Press.

McCormick, John (1989), *Reclaiming Paradise: The Global Environmental Movement*, Bloomington and Indianapolis: Indiana University Press.

Mahony, Rhona (1992), 'Debt-for-Nature Swaps: Who Really Benefits?' *The Ecologist*, Vol. 22, No. 3, pp. 97–103.

Meadows, Donnella H. and Dennis Randers, Jorgen and William W. Behrens III (1972), *The Limits to Growth*, New York: Universe Books.

Mellos, Koula (1988), *Perspectives on Ecology*, London: MacMillan Press.

Mendlovitz, Saul H. and R.B.J. Walker (eds) (1987), *Towards a Just World Peace*, London: Butterworths.

Milbrath, Lester W. (1984), *Environmentalists: Vanguard for a New Society*, Albany, NY: State University of New York Press.

Milner, Helen (1992), 'International Theories of Cooperation Among Nations: Strengths and Weaknesses', *World Politics*, Vol. 44, No. 3, pp. 466–96.

Nadelmann, Ethan (1990), 'Global Prohibition Regimes: The Evolution of Norms in International Relations', *International Organization*, Vol. 44, No. 4, pp. 479–526.

Padbury, Peter (1991), 'Getting UNCED Back on Track: The Role of NGOs', unpublished manuscript.

Paehlke, Robert C. (1989), *Environmentalism and The Future of Progressive Politics*, New Haven, CT: Yale University Press.

Page, Diana (1989), 'Debt-for-Nature Swaps: Experience Gained, Lessons Learned', *International Environmental Affairs*, Vol. 1, No. 4, pp. 275–88.

Pearce, Fred (1991), *Green Warrion*, London. Budley Head.

Perry, John S. (1986), 'Managing the World Environment', *Environment*, Vol. 28, No. 1, p. 13.

Porter, Gareth and Janet Welsh Brown (1991), *Global Environmental Politics*, Boulder, CO: Westview Press.

Rochester, J. Martin (1990), 'Global Policy and the Future of the United Nations System', *Journal of Peace Research*, Vol. 27, No. 2, pp. 141–54.

Rosenau, James (1990), *Turbulence in World Politics*, Princeton, NJ: Princeton University Press.

Scott, Alan (1990), *Ideology and the New Social Movements*, London: Unwin Hyman.

Shiva, Vandana (1989), *The Violence of the Green Revolution*, Debra Dun: Natraj Publishers.

Soroos, Marvin (1986), *Beyond Sovereignty: The Challenge of Global Policy*, Columbia, SC: University of South Carolina Press.

South Commission (1990), *The Challenge to the South*, Geneva: South Commission.

Speth, Gus (1990), 'Towards a North–South Compact on the Environment', *Environment*, Vol. 32, No. 5, pp. 16–20, 40–3.

Thiele, Leslie Paul (1993), 'Making Democracy Safe for the World: Social Movements and Global Politics', *Alternatives*, Vol. 18, pp. 273–305.

United Nations Environment Programme (1991), 'The Global Environment Facility', *Our Planet*, Vol. 3, No. 3, pp. 10–13.

Vasquez, John and Richard Mansbach (1983), 'The Issue Cycle: Conceptualizing Long-Term Political Change', *International Organization*, Vol. 37, No. 2, pp. 257–79.

Viola, Eduardo J. (1988), 'The Ecologist Movement in Brazil (1974–1986): From Environmentalism to Ecopolitics', *International Journal of Urban and Regional Research*, Vol. 12, No. 2, pp. 211–28.

Weston, Joe (1989), 'The FOE. Experience: The Development of an Environmental Pressure Group', Oxford: Oxford Working Paper in Planning Education and Research, No. 116.

World Commission on the Environment and Development (1987), *Our Common Future*, Oxford and New York: Oxford University Press.

Yap, Nonita (1989–90), 'NGOs and Sustainable Development', *International Journal*, Vol. XLV, Winter, pp. 75–105.

Young, Oran R. (1982), *Resource Regimes*, Berkeley, KA: University of California Press.

Young, Oran R. (1989a), *International Cooperation: Building Regimes for Natural Resources and the Environment*, Ithaca, NY: Cornell University Press.

Young, Oran R. (1989b), 'The Politics of International Regime Formation: Managing Natural Resources and the Environment', *International Organization*, Vol. 43, No. 3, pp. 349–75.

8   Strategies of resistance at the Pollok Free State road protest camp

Ben Seel

In 1939 Sir John Stirling Maxwell of Pollok, founder of the National Trust for Scotland, bequeathed Pollok estate to the citizens of Glasgow, stating: 'The said lands should remain forever as open spaces of woodland for the enhancement of the beauty of the neighbourhood and so far as possible for the benefit of the citizens of Glasgow.'[1]

In 1974 the National Trust for Scotland decided to waive the conditions of the 1939 agreement to enable the M77 Ayrshire link motorway to be built. Concerted protest by community groups began in 1978 (Kala, 1995). This first stage of the No M77 campaign involved submitting evidence to the Ayr Road Route public inquiry which lasted three months in 1988, as well as lobbying executive bodies such as the Strathclyde Regional Council and other influential local bodies such as political parties. Unfortunately for campaigners the Labour Party leaders who controlled the Strathclyde Regional Council supported the building of the road on the grounds that it would create more jobs for the region, and the 1988 public inquiry gave the go-ahead for the scheme.[2] Preliminary foundations were laid through Pollok Park in 1992 (Kala, 1995). The second stage of the campaign began in April 1994 when the Stop The Ayr Road Route Alliance (STARR) was launched, comprising 20 community and environmental organisations who opposed the motorway extension without success.[3] The Free State, founded in June 1994 by Colin McLeod in the Barrhead woods, was the rearguard, then, of a long anti-M77 campaign.

This chapter explores the strategy and effects of the 'core group' of resident protesters in their interaction with over 1,000 Free State passport-holding 'citizens', occasional visitors to the camp and the local No M77 campaign community and through the media the wider cultural and political environment and national state policy including its influence as part of the road protest movement. I define the 'core group' as those who were actually resident at the camp, living in benders, tents or occasionally tree-houses. Their numbers varied from ten to thirty. They were roughly two-thirds Glaswegians – often drawn from the immediate Pollokshaws locality – and one-third of English or other international origin. How long they stayed varied from individual to individual and the local – non-local balance of the group varied over time from the above rough mean. The ideological perspectives and strategies of the core group are best characterised as embryonic counter-hegemonic resistance, while at the same time their actions also contribute to a residue of reform.[4]

Counter hegemonic resistance via the temporary autonomous zone

On 20 August 1994, about two months after it was first established, the Pollok Free State declared independence:

> at this moment in time, we believe the ecological holocaust facing our lands and wider environment to be so great, that it is our right, our duty, to throw off such forms of government that allow such evils to continue, and provide for our future security. We take this step with great reluctance and it is our intention to maintain peaceful relations with Her Majesty's government of the United Kingdom and Strathclyde Regional Council. Nevertheless it is our view that the undemocratic activities of these two institutions, through the proposed [now law] Criminal Justice and Public Order [Act] and M77 motorway extension, are so unpopular, destructive and oppressive, and their behavior so unreasonable in the face of our appeals for mercy that we face no choice but to separate and determine our own future.
>
> (Pollok Free State, leaflet 1994)

It is interesting to note that this reads as a parody of John Locke's liberal idea of the right to withdraw power from and revolt against a government when it is no longer serving liberty, equality and survival, the purposes for which it was *supposedly* instituted.[5] Already we see how protesters sought to call into question hegemonic narratives about the function of the liberal state.

The Pollok Free State's declaration of independence is part of a recognisable tradition of 'temporary autonomous zones' (Bey, 1996: 101) traceable back to the Orange Free State of the Dutch Kabouter movement in 1970, which itself was a revival of some of the social and cultural strategies of the Dutch Provos from 1965 to 1967 (McKay, 1996: 157). 'The TAZ [temporary autonomous zone] is like...a guerrilla operation which liberates an area (of land, of time, of imagination) and then dissolves itself to reform elsewhere/else-when' (Bey, 1996: 101). McKay (1996: 156) has noted that the Free States of Britain are having a revival in the contemporary roads protest movement; the Pollok Free State follows Cuerdenia, Leytonstonia, Wanstonia and Avalonia in England, as the first Scottish road protest camp. That liberated area was instigated and upheld by the core group through their physical lived presence at the Free State camp in the Barrhead woods.

> That's the whole concept of the Pollok Free State – people make their own decisions about the way they want to live their lives; to a certain extent it's worked. It's been a bit of a gimmick, like declaring independence and giving out passports and stuff like that, but it's very much a definite space

here ... everybody has observed that, even the police. We've had the police out here telling us what to do and we've jokingly said, 'you can't tell us what to do, it's a Free State, it's a separate country'. But it's not a Free State so much as a geographical location, but a state of mind and it's very interesting to see how people observe that. Even people who have got the physical violent power know not to. That's weird, I mean it's good.

(Jake in interview)

The Pollok Free State TAZ played a dual function. First, it was primarily oriented towards oppositional *resistance*. This was made up of issue resistance to the building of the M77 through Pollok Park; resistance to the aspects of the CJA 1994 targeted against travellers, squatters and protesters, but especially sections 70–71 which increased police powers against 'trespassory assemblies'; and resistance to what the core group seemed to perceive as a more general hegemonic political, economic and cultural formation. Its secondary function was to offer positive cultural *alternatives* to that dominant hegemony. We will see throughout how protest and alternative fused in a strategy of symbolic challenges to the state and contracting company Wimpey to convey messages to the general populace about power, politics and culture. Resistance questioned the rationality of the M77 in particular and the government's 'Roads to Prosperity' transport policy more generally. It sought to reveal the interests that road construction served and the interests it did not serve. It highlighted vast power disparities and entrenched local disenfranchisement from control over local development. In this way the Free State strategy constituted what to traditional political categories is an awkward mix of single issue reformism and radical, though embryonic, counter hegemonic resistance.

In policy terms the M77 was passionately contested, but the focus upon the single issue was also designed to forward a wider political agenda and the development of a radical green social movement concerned with resisting elements of hegemonic ideology. After briefly demonstrating how hegemonic ideas are challenged in the core group's thought, publications and lifestyles I will show how the core group sought to practically empower local No M77 campaigners through the Free State venture. We will see how the core group sought to encourage protesters to learn from the process of protest in such a way as to contribute to the building of a radical green movement. There will be a brief look at the Free State's relationship with the media and the residue of reform that the road protest movement has contributed towards, before I elaborate upon the nature of the counter hegemony in evidence among the core group at the Pollok Free State.

Ideological challenge

It is first important to note that there was little evidence at the Free State of formal ideology in the sense of overarching unified explanations of society and economy or endpoint utopias and the stages required to attain them. Nevertheless, the core group undoubtedly saw their action as 'like a battle in a war' (Anna in interview) against dominant groups and especially dominant 'ideas that are destroying the planet which people have accepted and consented to' (Colin in interview).

Core group members stressed the importance of land rights, seeing the M77 construction as an appropriation of common land bequeathed to the people of Glasgow.[6] Their Declaration of Independence criticised the notion of owning the land. It documented the gradual enclosure of Scotland: from highlands in the past to the present Pollok Park commons:

> Our ancestors were cleared from their ancestral homelands by feudal greed... This process of *enclosure, the privatisation of a people's ultimate resource – land –* has ripped people away from the earth. The stable system that kept all alive without endangering the future, has been turned on its head in the interests of a selfish few. In... Scotland 500,000 people were cruelly evicted and deprived of what was rightfully theirs. Many were deported to 'the colonies' to drive the process of enclosure even further and inflict the same pains on other people of the earth. Those that remained had no choice but to flock to the cities and become part of the 'working class'. The age of industry is now dead and our labour no longer needed. We live poor lives on the pittance given to us from *the profits we have raised...* Today the process of enclosure continues as this land *our land*, is threatened with destruction in the name of 'infrastructure improvement'. Pollok Estate was returned to us in 1939 and now it is threatened by *privatisation* for a car owning elite, (emphasis).[7]

The first sense in which the core group's perspective is counter-hegemonic, then, is in that it challenges private ownership of land, a concept fundamental to the hegemonic capitalist economy and liberal democracy. There is also clear reference here to the linked exploitation of surplus value from sellers of labour by capitalist development. Welfare benefits paid by the state to these unemployed people are seen as a 'pittance' paid from accumulated profits dependent on surplus value. This implies a questioning of the legitimacy of private ownership of the means of production, and it also implies that the state works in close collaboration with business interests. But the declaration goes no further than this. Instead it moves on to focus on the CJA's (Criminal Justice Act) erosion of democratic rights of free assembly, which is seen as an extension of the same processes. The Declaration of Independence continues:

> At the same time in reaction to resistance by many good people, Her Majesty's government seeks to enclose us even further. Not content with 'owning' the land, private interests seek to stymie our protests and ban our access to our ancestral lands. It is proposed that those who wish to touch the earth will be criminalised for wishing to see *what is morally, but no longer legally, theirs* (emphasis).
>
> (Pollok Free State Declaration of
> Independence, 1994)

It is being suggested here that political rights were restricted in the CJA because the state is heavily implicated in enforcing and propelling development based on private ownership. Core group members, as well as Free State 'citizens' stressed again and again that they did not see the political system as democratic but as representing only moneyed interests. Lindsay, for example, explained how the political system just 'did not work' in a democratic sense:

> Once people become elected officials it seems they become a law unto themselves and just don't listen to reason. The thing is as well the financial factor here – fifty three and a half million pounds for this motorway, basically greases the wheels of industry. It's a lot of grease for a lot of wheels, like. At the end of the day it's corruption, there's a lot of corruption about and vested interest.

There was a clear opposition, then, to the purportedly 'representative' political system. We will see later how the core group sought to respond to this situation by encouraging extra-institutional participation among local people.[8]

A much less developed aspect of the core group's critique of the dominant hegemonic formation was their questioning of the nature or quality of 'development'. Earlier we saw a certain nostalgia in the description of the precapitalist 'stable system that kept all alive without endangering the future' but only in comparison to a form of development which they see as largely serving 'the interests of a selfish few'. Infrastructure improvement, industrialisation and economic growth were certainly not regarded as incontestable forms of 'development' or 'progress'.

> I kind of read a wee bit about the economic growth idea and the fact that it relies on motorways and all this kind of stuff and they argue for 'development' and that; and I didn't necessarily agree with those ideas. But at the same time it is not purely a theoretical, ideological stand I am making on these motorways.
>
> (Colin)

The rejection of a hegemonic mode of development actually emerged far more clearly at a cultural level in non-consumerist attitudes and lifestyles. Andrew Dobson has identified 'distance from consumption' as a crucial aspect of green social change. He suggests that it may be unemployed social groups marginalised from the process of consumption that are likely to become radical agents fighting for fundamental green social change.[9] Dobson refers to this as a 'materialist' approach to identifying a radical green movement agent (Dobson, 1995: 157–8). The evidence from Pollok certainly supports Dobson insofar as all of the core group were unemployed. However, it is clear that for the approach to remain distinctively 'materialist' it should have been participants' unemployed status which led them into their political ideas and action. This was applicable to many of the Glaswegian members of the core group, but it was also the case that many of the core group (especially the English members) had chosen unemployment as an ethical 'dropping out' from what they perceived to be an immoral economic system. In these cases political ideas led to material status and this discounts somewhat the materialist approach. Nevertheless, distance from consumption and radical green agency do seem to be complementary and expedient for the full-time instigation of a protest camp.[10]

Consumerism as a way of life was challenged more by deed than by word. Not surprisingly, it was car culture which was most directly reproached. The Pollok Free State 'carhenge' provided an example of the strategy of symbolic challenge to which Melucci (1996) draws attention as a common feature of new social movements. Old cars were driven up from Oxford via a route that stopped off at many other road protest camps and campaigns. This was the 1995 'To Pollok With Love' campaign organised by Earth First!. The cars upon arriving at the Free State were turned end up and cemented into holes in the M77 raised foundations to form a circular 'carhenge'. They were ceremoniously burned one night in a highly symbolic challenge to car culture.[11]

Acculturation of pre-modern forms seemed to be a response among protesters at the camp to what they saw as the paucity of the modern consumerist way of life. Gaelic themes waxed in significance at the Free State as time went on, noticeable for example in Celtic artwork around the camp. By 1996 the name 'Gal Gael' had been chosen for an organisation emerging out of the Pollok Free State hoping to initiate projects for ecological and cultural renewal in Scotland mainly focused on rural resettlement, reforestation and cultural regeneration. The Gal Gael peoples of Norse and Celtic origin originally emerged in the Hebrides and South West of Scotland. 'Gal Gael' means 'strange or foreign Gaels'.

> This name has been chosen for our society for two reasons. On the one hand, it symbolises our willingness to accept into our society anyone with similar ideals, irrespective of their race, colour or creed. On the other it symbolises the growing estrangement many Scots feel towards the culture in which they are increasingly living.
>
> (Gal Gael leaflet, 1996a)

The Free State also established contacts with Nuxalk Canadian Indians struggling against logging in their traditional territory. There was a visit to the Pollok Free State by a Nuxalk Indian and several hundred pounds were raised to send a stone eagle carving by Colin McLeod to the Nuxalk as a gesture of indigenous solidarity. The symbolic message to the wider public was to suggest the global free market was antagonising local traditions, ways of life and being.

The Free State's search for alternatives to the consumerist way of life made up counter-culture at the camp. The core group experimented with benders, wooden shelters, a tree lodge and tree houses as appropriate pointers to a perceived need to reconnect with the land and nature.[12] This was a beautiful, impressive and pioneering demonstration of the possibility of alternative abodes and 'in nature' architecture. There was also what Kala (1995) describes as 'eco-art'.

Colin McLeod, the initiator of the camp, is a skilled sculptor. The camp was scattered with carvings made from trees cleared for the M77. There were several totems and wooden and stone carvings of extinct Scottish birds and animals. Another carving depicted a chain saw cutting into a tree inside which was a human, highlighting the dependence of humans upon nature. Dumped plastic barrels were recycled to make drums which fuelled many late night 'jams'. Cans, glass and paper were recycled, and there was also a donated windmill at the camp which powered two caravans. Food was paid for and cooked communally on an open fire; when I first arrived an older core group member, Jimmy, gave me my dinner and proudly explained that 'no money changes hands here'. The fire served as the focus point for the camp, where plans and strategy would be discussed and from which communally organised 'pitch-in' style work parties would be organised.

These communal living arrangements and counter-culture at the Free State are part of 'the positive abolition of private property' (Heller, 1976: 55), part of a positive offering to society as an alternative to the destructiveness that protesters were negatively protesting against. Visitors are challenged to at least consider the merits of a more communal, outdoor lifestyle which is closer to nature. The opportunity is presented for visitors and supporters to try out such cultural alternatives and this may help them to develop further their own ideas about 'the good life'. Anna said in interview: 'It's more visible, people see more. It's fun, it's happening. You can't all just walk around with banners and leaflets; it's a way of living really.' In interview Colin said:

> So this is a message, everything that comes out of here is a message to the community that surrounds it because we are being watched... I came down here two years ago with leaflets and a lot of talk, and most people won't read a leaflet. The majority of people will glance through it just because you have given it, but it won't penetrate... so what we've done is make it interesting... we have tried to make it a bit different... Crazy carvings and that attracts people and they can make their own judgment about the situation; but if we can get their attention for a small moment as they are passing through then it becomes apparent to them in view of their own instincts and intelligence that the forest is a beautiful place.

A Tolkien image of Lothlorien harmony with nature and Mordor-like desolation was certainly difficult to resist in seeing the camp alongside the M77 construction site. There is a clear affirmation among these quotations from core group interviews of the force of example in facilitating cultural change. In Meluccian terms, 'movements operate as a "message" or "sign"' (Melucci, 1989: 206), in this case that alternatives to consumerist lifestyles and routes to happiness exist, and that people, their culture and nature are all being damaged together by much of the purported 'development' of infrastructure expansion and economic growth. The goals of greater communality in ownership of resources (food, benders, funds, etc.) and control over projects and work, more equitable relations between humans and a less exploitative relationship to the environment, were brought into the path to get there in the sense that the core group at least attempted to live out these values.[13] So as Melucci's analysis of new social movements suggests, Free State strategy cannot be reduced to achieving reform goals.[14] In so far as this wider pre-figurative strategy was applicable at the Free State, the core group could be regarded as 'nomads of the present' (Melucci, 1989). Contrary to Melucci's characterisation though, this did not mean that the core group had, 'no programme, and no future' (Melucci, 1989: 55), nor were their goals, 'temporary and to a certain extent replaceable' (Melucci, 1989: 56). The core group also had a longer term strategy and goal, that of *building a movement*. Concurrence of means and ends certainly did not serve to eclipse ends.

I have shown that the core group challenged hegemonic ideology and culture in four main ways. They challenged the legitimacy of ownership of land, the democratic status of Britain's liberal democratic polity, the notion of economic growth and 'infrastructure improvement' as being equal to development or progress, and commodity consumption as the route to personal satisfaction and happiness. It is important to stress that while these ideological challenges certainly were present, ideology was not the Free State's central articulating principle, nor was it developed in great detail in Free State literature. Deeds were preferred over words.

Empowering the No M77 campaign

The main practical focus of the core group's action was to encourage locals opposed to the M77 construction to escalate their protest to an extra-institutional level by getting involved in the Free State and non-violent direct action. The core group fought the M77 construction passionately as an end in itself but also, as we shall see, to pursue other longer-term aims.

Colin, who grew up in the Pollokshaws area, said in interview:

> The local people have always been against the motorway, so therefore, when we arrived in this woodland it was simply to assert an opinion that was already held in the communities. We weren't trying to convert anybody. The army's already there. It's just that they have been ignored; so what we are trying to do is we are trying to change that and push it forward.

The Pollok Free State provided an important practical focus for the M77 resistance movement; this aided campaign mobilisation and brought different interested people and groups together. The groups varied from local environmental organisations, 'Glasgow for People' and Glasgow Friends of the Earth, through to Militant Labour and Earth First! The roles of members of Militant Labour defending trees was unthinkable until recently but at the Pollok Free State it happened. The much-vaunted red–green alliance began to coalesce at a grassroots level. Many of those contacts will remain into future campaigns such as that against the proposed M74. The Free State was the place to go for people if they felt like getting involved in the campaign, and the camp was the source of numerous door knocking and leafleting parties as well as the destination of No M77 and anti-CJA marches (organised by the Scottish Defiance Alliance) which both started several miles away in the city centre. With there being a permanent base the opportunity existed for campaign supporters to contribute towards the campaign whenever they felt they wanted to and in whatever way they could. For some this meant going down to lend a hand with work, for others donating supplies (local Kwik Save employees, for example, always set aside a bag of vegetables for the camp), for others just going down to talk and offer moral support. Johan said in interview: 'It's sort of an attractive stall, the camp, and it's where people who are against [the motorway] can get together and discuss ways to move on...people are inspired to do all sorts of things.'

Some dug holes in the motorway foundations, some printed or handed out leaflets, some built benders or tree houses, some played music to others who chopped wood, some cooked and some discussed the issues at stake. A race was staged from the outskirts of Glasgow to the city centre between a bike, a car and a bus and they arrived in that order, highlighting congestion. Protesters used the stunt to put forward their argument that another road would just fill up with more cars, exacerbating pollution. A more unusual campaigning method still was used one afternoon when the 'Desert Storm' sound system filled its lorry up with pro-testers from the camp. The lorry then descended on various parts of the local Pollokshaws and Corkerhill estates and defiantly blasted music which could surely be characterised as something like the 'series of repetitive beats' proscribed under certain conditions according to the Criminal Justice Act (CJA, section 63). Protesters danced around the lorry and handed out leaflets to bemused locals. A spectacle was created and protesters used the opportunity to talk to people about the M77 and encourage them to visit the Free State.

By meeting and talking to others, visitors learnt about the connections between what may have previously appeared to be disparate issues. Bringing together dif-ferent types of people – different types of activists as well as non-activists – can push strategic thought and political awareness forward as different emancipatory and mundane concerns meet and how they are related can be drawn out. Johan described how the Free State had been:

> raising issues, especially in the local area which is predominantly working class and is pretty deprived...[people do not tend to] see environmental issues as particularly a concern in these places because obviously there are a lot of social issues to deal with. It's been good for unifying social and environmental concerns.

The Free State was a practical move towards what Seabrook has described as 'the most urgent task' of showing, 'how and why the poor would be the chief beneficiaries of Green politics' (Seabrook, 1988: 166). In this case, the M77 serves commuters to the city centre from the better-off areas of Eastwood and Newton Mearns. Meanwhile, according to the public inquiry, the poorer inner city areas of Corkerhill and Darnley will be 'losers' from the scheme and suffer from air and noise pollution, visual intrusion and obstruction to and from the green areas of the Pollok Estate (Morrison, 1995). Charles Gordon, the Labour Party councillor holding the Chair of the Roads and Transportation committee of the Strathclyde Regional Council, claimed that the M77 link to Ayr would mean, 'three things: jobs, jobs and more jobs'. This is a familiar rebuke to green ideas. The Free State challenged the evidence for his claim saying that the employment that would come from the construction and security for the road would be relatively short-lived and, especially in the case of the security, very poorly paid. Nevertheless, it was clear that the jobs argument did hold sway for some local people. The Free State's own ventures in this area were to encourage the passing on of, 'traditional craft skills...weaving, stained glass work, metal work and wood carving', at the camp. This was done, 'in a rough and ready way, but it would be good to formalise it' (Colin). It did not become formalised, but a small library was built up in the lodge and discussion groups were set up and publicised to attempt to get local people to discuss practical solutions and projects to deal with the problem of unemployment. One idea that came out of this was to twin the (pre-Free State) crofters of Assynt in Sutherland with the Pollok Free State. Land was bought at Assynt from the proceeds of an international campaign. The idea was to re-create a viable Highland economy but from talking to the crofters Colin had learnt that they were struggling with lack of people as well as skills. There was an attempt then to link the issue of de-populated highlands and absentee landlords with mass unemployment in cities. Colin said in interview:

> We have got to face the problem at hand and that is unemployment, bad land management, dying skills and all the rest of it...We would like this to be the venue for a modest attempt at doing that and even if we just build the ideas and throw them out, win or lose, the cat's out of the bag. I hope somebody else takes it up and moves the whole idea forward a step or two from the publicity we gain here.

The Free State also helped disseminate non-violent direct action techniques.[15] The Free State joined with Glasgow Earth First! in organising and providing people for a roadblock in central Glasgow. On other occasions heavy machinery was occupied and protesters chained themselves to chainsaws, trees and workers in order to disrupt work. Trees which were spiked were marked with an 'S'. Although that did not stop them being cut it did prevent Wimpey profiting from the sale of valuable old timber. Three chainsaws were confiscated by protesters on the grounds of 'criminal damage' one day in an opportunistic role reversal at the far end of the route near Newton Mearns! When English supporters visited with the 'To Pollok With Love' campaign they taught locals tree climbing skills using harnesses. But overall, the ingenious tactical innovation used in English campaigns to prolong occupations and escalate costs did not appear so much at Pollok.

Work started three weeks later than scheduled on 1 February 1995. Throughout February an elaborate game of cat and mouse was played out with protesters pursuing Wimpey vans around in order to raise the alarm once they saw where cutting was to begin. 'Do or Die', the Earth First! journal noted that

> Often the police would act as decoys getting between protesters' vehicles and allowing cutters to get away. Good communication links were desperately needed, although often our CB messages would be suspiciously jammed, and important phone contact [to the Free State emergency tree phone] would break down at crucial moments.

(Do or Die, 1995: 8)

The Barrhead Woods clearance began on 14 February and became known as the 'Valentine's Day Massacre'. At 6 am 500 police and 300 security guards closed roads and cordoned off the area isolating the Free State camp. The woods next to the Free State were destroyed, while emotional protesters held back behind police lines chanted, 'Shame on you!'. The clearance of just under half of the Free State occurred later in March. The flat land meant that 'cherry-pickers' (raised platforms) were easily utilised to bring protesters down from the trees. Nevertheless, the road was very slightly re-routed so that only half of the camp had to be cleared.[16] But the most famous disruption of the M77 works occurred at lunchtime of Valentine's Day. The police had used the Bellamine School playground, which was only four hundred metres from the clearance site, as a command centre. At lunch-time between 100 and 250 children (reports vary) swarmed the operation, going around and under the police line and security guards, waving No M77 banners they had made in class. The logging had to be halted for obvious safety reasons at 2 pm After this incident school lock-ins were implemented and opposed by a newly formed pupil union covering three local schools. Pupil strikes occurred when the demands of their new union for two hours off per day to protest were not met and direct action against machinery ensued. Twenty-six security guards quit that Valentine's Day and Earth First! attribute this to the effectiveness of Militant campaigners who knew which local communities security guards were from and used emotive solidarity demands to persuade them to switch sides (Do or Die, 1995: 9). It is interesting to note that most of the security guards I had contact with regarded the road as a bad thing but had been unemployed for years and had families to provide for. Some protesters regarded them with sympathy, while to others they were no more than 'spineless yellowbacks'. There were two other smaller camps temporarily established at different sites along the route. Most notably ex-Ministry of Defence buildings were squatted and converted to a vegan cafe at Patterton Woods where an 18-year-old girl spent a week up a tree and Wimpey employees set fire to tyres underneath her in an attempt to smoke her out. The Patterton camp fell after four clearance attempts. The other smaller camp at Corkerhill fell swiftly to a dawn raid.

There was considerable co-operation between Glasgow Earth First! and the core group at the Free State. Earth First! tends to emphasise cost escalation tactics. In an article about the Pollok Free State in 'Do or Die!' in early 1995, Kala satirically predicted, 'Giving free play to the imagination, all manner of direct actions will be effected to act as a "market force".' The basis of this tactic is that costing planners and business people money is the only way to make them take your opinions into consideration. Unlike the M11 case in London, in the construction of the M77 the construction company Wimpey did have to provide their own security so any extra security costs that protest forced them to incur cut into their profit margin. Free State initiatives certainly did cost Wimpey and the police considerable sums of money but it is worth noting that this was not the primary motivation of the core group:

> Escalating the costs of Wimpey is more, to me, it's more of a side issue … We want to escalate Wimpey's costs to make it difficult for them and hurt them in a financial way but in a more lasting kind of way we want to affect the consciousness of the local people really.
>
> (Johan in interview)

What was more important then was encouraging participation. This theme emerged again and again throughout interviews with the core group. When asked, 'What message do you want people to take from your action?' it was exactly this that the core group was aiming for: 'Do it yourself' said Anna.[17]

There was no faith whatsoever among the core group in 'representative' channels. The participative empowerment they sought to encourage was of extra-institutional collective influence via engaging in radical ventures such as the Free State and the non-violent direct action of obstruction. Doherty has observed that: 'Road protests began outside the existing environmental pressure groups and … the impetus of ecological protest has come from those who were dissatisfied with the passive character of membership of the existing environmental groups' (Doherty, 1996: 5). In line with this Jake stressed that the Free State was

> a direct, actual form of democracy … I often think groups like Greenpeace and Friends of the Earth are so much like companies. They're actually doing a service for people; they give them their money and they pretend to represent their views. This is more potent because its people directly representing their own views themselves.

Not all of the core group were as hostile as Jake (who had first hand experience of working for Greenpeace), but there was a clear affirmation of the green emphasis on participatory rather than representative democracy, as well as dissatisfaction with the institutionalisation of environmental pressure groups. An interesting discussion took place around the fire one night concerning how the Free State should react to an approach that had been made by a Greenpeace representative offering to assess the camp for financial aid and publicity. Jake was strongly of the view that what the camp needed was supporters prepared to give action, not money. Johan pointed out that pressure groups like Greenpeace can disempower because they encourage people to just give money and leave protest to the experts, rather than taking responsibility and acting themselves. The point was also made that Greenpeace was overly media-oriented in its methods. Jake said in interview:

> There are a lot of environmental groups which consider it [media coverage] an end in itself – just by achieving media coverage you are actually changing something, but I don't think that's the case. Everybody knows about the rain-forests getting chopped down which was one of the big news stories of the nineteen eighties, but it is still getting chopped down faster than ever.

There was a fear among many of the core group that if they accepted financial aid and publicity from Greenpeace that they might try to take credit for the venture and so endanger the sense of ownership of the initiative by Free State 'citizens'. Colin countered that the camp needed all the publicity it could get to try to stop the M77 and many of the core group agreed that environmental pressure groups could complement direct action rather than necessarily detracting from it. But the final outcome was that the Greenpeace offer was not followed up. The camp actually already had funds of £4,000 which had been raised at a Galliano benefit gig held at the Free State in December 1994.

In the internal organisation of the Free State there were no official leaders. Specific roles such as cook, builder, fire-wood collector, media spokesperson and organiser were considered as equal roles which were also interchangeable from one day to the next to a certain extent, though specialisation also emerged. Colin, who was a key figure at the Free State, often refused to tell people what to do because one of the purposes of the camp was to encourage local people to take responsibility for their own actions and create initiatives to deal with the situation they found themselves in. A person's power at the camp came from the extent to which people would listen to and take seriously their ideas and suggestions. Those that worked hard and saw through what they talked about gained credence while those that talked without backing it up with action did not. It is interesting to note that although the camp aspired to be a 'Free' State some exclusion was necessitated in practice. Local gangs were asked to stay away and fight elsewhere, and a sign was erected saying that the consumption of alcohol was banned on-site in order to prevent the campfire becoming a late-night drinking venue for local alcoholics.

Through the participation that did ensue the core group hoped that the wider Free State 'citizenry' and supporters would learn about power, structural links between the state and capital, and how these impact upon their everyday lives and environment. 'So here we are testing our power on our local environment', said Colin. The feeling of disenfranchisement, the belief that 'democratic' institutions are not so, seems to have been reinforced by the process. The local elected repre-sentatives on the Glasgow District Council were overruled by the Strathclyde Regional Council. Moreover, direct action forces the state to show its allegiances, and at Pollok Park this meant mobilising its coercive forces in favour of Wimpey. Morrison, writing for the Corkerhill Community Council, noted for example, that the 'invasion force' of 3 March 1995 at 4 am was made up of, '500 police and

300 over-zealous mercenary security guards, backed up by helicopters, video units, chainsaw gangs and snatch-squad vehicles' (Morrison, 1995). Jake said in interview: 'The fact that they need six hundred security guards and police to chop down fifty trees is very significant. The state has to go to war on behalf of the car culture and a multi-national company.'

Whether 500 or 600 police the message is clear: that local people are not allowed to control the process of development in their own area if it threatens vested interests – the car manufacturers, petroleum companies and construction company – or more generally if it threatens economic growth or the infrastructure expansion it requires. Therefore, testing their power amounted to exposing the links between the state and capital. Of course, being a government contracted scheme it is not surprising that the state's forces of law and order were used to protect the Wimpey contractors. It might be argued that a situation where police are used to protect a purely privately instigated business activity would demonstrate more about state–capital links. However, it is also important to remember that road building is a key infrastructure support to the capitalist economy, which requires the state to come into close contact with big business contractors both in the planning of the scheme and in outwitting protesters. It also heavily implicates the state in promoting hegemonic conceptions of progress as economic growth without proper regard to quality of life indicators, a perspective consistent with the 'externalising' of non-financial costs by business. At the same time the criminal justice system came to be seen increasingly as a mere appendage to a biased system. As the campaign went on more and more experienced activists were either jailed or given bail conditions disallowing any approach of the M77 site.

All of the core group and all of the Free State citizens that I came into contact with saw the forcing through of the M77 in these terms. There is a clear possibility that what participants learnt from the process of the campaign might have further radicalised them – akin to Marx's idea of a change in consciousness being produced by the process of struggle (McLellan, 1971: 198). The feeling of institutional disenfranchisement may well be complemented by a feeling of radical empowerment. This was clearly the reaction of the core group: 'Far from being defeated we're becoming more determined than ever to put our shoulder to the task of creating a positive future, realising that we alone can help ourselves' (Pollok Free State leaflet, 1995).

Of course, others might interpret this as just a 'brave face'; to judge this empowerment beyond doubt would require a longer-term process of studying participants.[18] Many participants (Free State 'citizens' as well as core group) seemed to become enmeshed in resistance culture and a wider resistance network. The harsh conditions at the camp, combined with the feeling of community, helped forge friendships and contacts which are likely to last through submerged cultural networks and which will probably re-emerge in other campaigns.[19]

Indeed the wider No M77 campaign itself was part of a long history of community resistance in Glasgow. It is worth noting that many of the core group will not go straight on to other overtly political campaigning. Some were planning time out after Pollok to live in a normal abode, travel or retreat to the country.

But most if not all are likely to re-emerge in other forms of green movement activity, though not necessarily protest. One such project was the setting up of a fund to try to buy a derelict church on Calder Street, Glasgow and convert it into a community centre. A 'Land Redemption Fund' was also set up, 'to begin to replace the common land that has been lost to development' and to pioneer environmentally sustainable community lifestyles (Land Redemption Fund leaflet, 1995).

It seems appropriate at this stage to point out that I am not claiming that the Free State venture was an unproblematic exercise in empowerment for all: core group, Free State 'citizen' participants, occasional visitors and those following the campaign in the media alike. Rather, it is far more likely that it had both empowering and disempowering effects on different people because the message the individual takes is dependent upon their own perceptual lens affecting their reading of events. Those that saw the campaign as simply a single-issue with a win/lose polarity depending upon whether the M77 construction was abandoned or completed are more likely to have experienced a sense of disempowerment or apathy because despite all the efforts made the outcome has been unaffected and the single-issue campaign lost.

Road protest actions, along with demonstrations such as those over the veal trade and CJA, have been widely characterised in the media precisely as 'single-issue' politics. To characterise campaigns in this way can be to actively encourage disempowerment, as single-issue campaigns are often lost. Of course, such campaigns do focus upon single-issues, but it should not be mistakenly inferred (and this is often implied) that road protests are concerned only with the single-issue and are intended as just a radical form of pressure group activity in the wake of Fukuyama's 'end of ideology' (1990). Although the core group's primary focus was the M77 being built through Pollok Park, they were well aware of issue linkages, seeing this as just one instance within a wider resistance movement against unfettered market forces, centralised (un-) 'representative' government and the erosion of rights.[20] The specific issue campaign was run as an end in itself, but *also* as a means of educating people about the wider processes driving social change and environmental degradation. It was through these processes of learning from the campaign and the tactical diffusion of direct action ideas and techniques through the Free State, that the core group hoped to contribute to the building of a radical green movement: 'We have trained up a lot of people which will last beyond this camp, creating a much more dynamic environmental movement in Scotland' (Jake in interview).

Symbolic challenges via the media

It is clear, then, that the primary strategic purposes of the Free State venture for the core group were to empower the No M77 campaign, facilitate learning about economic and political structures and to help build a radical green movement. We must view their relationship to the media as a secondary concern stemming from those primary ones. As such, media coverage was not valued as an end in itself (something we have already seen the core group criticise environmental pressure groups for) but primarily as a method of inspiring, empowering and motivating the wider public to take action. For example, Jake said in interview:

> I don't think you can use television to change the world because television is part of the world in which people are consuming something rather than participating. But if you use television as a media to get people out of their armchairs, to get them out by outraging them then it can be a first step. It's a means to an end rather than an end in itself.

Nevertheless, to inspire and motivate people to question and begin to think about changing the economic, social, political and cultural system they are living in requires a strategy of symbolic challenge to the values and assumptions of that system, and those symbolic challenges reach the larger audience through the media.

As well as seeking to empower activism then, the Free State venture can be seen as an example of 'theatrical politics' (Truett-Anderson, 1990: 171–6), whereby the 'purposeful and expressive disclosure of one's subjectivity (feelings, desires, experiences, identity)', through media exposure, 'to others who constitute a public for the participants' (Cohen, 1985: 706–7) can take on a dramaturgical strategic function. The medium is the message; that is, the identity, lifestyles and methods of protesters challenge hegemonic ideas and norms. Television viewers and newspaper readers may be faced with the heroic image of 'eco-warriors' resisting the onslaught of environmental degradation: a powerful and attractive altruistic antidote to the pollution, environmental plunder and naked self-interest about which we hear so much in the media. Counterpoised to the bulldozer was the fragile human body obstructing it; counterpoised to the uniformity of police and security were the colourful and diverse hairstyles and clothing of the protesters; counterpoised to the wasteland of the construction site was the 'in harmony with nature' architecture and art of the Free State. The core group hoped to stimulate viewers' identification with resistance to environmental degradation and their opinions of the modern projects such as road building which they are offered as 'development' or 'progress'. The Free State also successfully counter-posed local people to the developers, thereby drawing attention to the lack of control of people over their own local environment. The protesters were suggesting to the wider society their narrative and an alternative set of values and lifestyle.

In addition to providing a focus point for the local M77 and CJA resistance campaigns and inspiring others to participate in direct action, by building a protest camp directly in the way of the proposed M77, participants at the Free State deliberately escalated the conflict in order to make it clear to the widest number of people possible that the issue was passionately contested. They hoped that this would raise the profile of the issue and stimulate both neutral onlookers and proponents of the motorway to give further consideration to its opponents' viewpoint. Noisy clashes with tree-fellers, involving large numbers of protesters, security and police, create exciting news stories; especially since protesters engaged in direct actions such as chaining themselves to chainsaw operators and machinery and occupying bulldozers. By actually changing their abodes and lifestyles, enduring some extremely cold weather living in benders, risking arrest and perhaps even violent assault by police and private security guards, enduring the likelihood of MI5 surveillance and security files being kept on them and devoting large sections of their lives to their cause, the core group communicated something of their dedication and the depth of their beliefs, to onlookers.

This is not dissimilar to Gandhi's strategy of 'satyagraha' or 'truth-force' whereby it is hoped that self-sacrifice will open peoples' hearts to consider more deeply the protesters' point (e.g. Naess, 1965). There is a paradox here. Earlier I quoted Anna saying the way of life at the Free State was 'fun', and now I claim that what gave the protesters moral weight was the self-sacrificing nature of their action. The crux is that Free State lifestyle sacrificed modern luxuries such as the television, hot water and central heating which are considered by most people in our society today to be 'necessities'. The sacrifice was perceived by onlookers, and indeed felt by participants, especially, I can report from experience as a participant observer, during the harsh Scottish winter! What made those hardships worthwhile and satisfying for the core group was the belief that they have found a better, or at least an alternative, way of life. The well-being, enjoyment and sheer fun that can result from working together with a collective end and belief system should not be underestimated. The core group made sacrifices and reaped benefits; they perhaps believed this made them more 'alive to the aliveness of life' (Pollok Free State leaflet, 1994).

When considering how the Free State interacted with the media it is important to remember that powerful groups in society can manage the news far more effectively than protesters who are more dependent upon and vulnerable towards reporters' and journalists' characterisations of their struggle (Gamson and Wolfsfeld, 1993: 116–17). Some of the media coverage of the Pollok Free State was hostile towards it. The Scottish edition of the *Daily Mail*, for example, ran a story on 21 January 1995, headlined 'Why the English are Camping Out in Pollok' which claimed that half of the Free State participants were English. This was a blatant untruth designed to stir up nationalist sentiments and deliberately misportray local participation in the campaign and support for the Free State. The support and passionate involvement of local school children concerned about their future and the estimated 53,000 vehicles per hour which will be passing within a few hundred metres of school playgrounds, was skewed to become a story about subversive protesters and militants 'indoctrinating' poor innocent children to become law-breakers. On many occasions I witnessed core group and Free State 'citizens' dutifully answering questions about their cause, being requested to take up photogenic: poses for the camera and give personal details which could easily be placed on MI5 files, only to be faced the next day with journalism characterising them as nothing more than limelight-seeking, 'dole-scrounging' troublemakers wasting taxpayers' money. Free Staters used the media, but they were also used by it.[21]

The dramaturgical function of the Free State was its public role. The Free State camp was not 'staged' merely to allow the core group to claim themselves a heroic identity as fighters of evil while having, 'a great time on that big [media] stage' (Truett-Anderson, 1990: 173). Truett-Anderson's identity-based account of protests, by focusing upon the 'gratification' protesters get out of being in on the media act (Truett-Anderson, 1990), implies that appearances of publicly motivated protest behaviour simply hide another form of (albeit unusual) self-aggrandisement. This seems to reify self-interest as the only type of motivation there is. Of course the core group were not all altruistic angels and it is surely pertinent to be aware that if 'you have a rousing revolutionary-hero role and the whole world is watching, you don't really have to have a tangible political victory', or more importantly an effective, understanding enhancing role, 'to feel "empowered" ' (Truett-Anderson, 1990). But we should not neglect the fact that the core group believed in their cause and had a *strategy* of symbolic challenge designed to focus attention upon the ideas, politicians and economics which they saw as threatening people and the environment. A solely identity-based account of the Free State core group could overlook this publicly motivated and instrumental role of their action.[22] At the Pollok Free State the strategy of symbolic challenges via the media was only of secondary importance to the primary strategies of empowering local participation in the struggle, encouraging learning about political and economic structures from that struggle and thereby building a radical green movement.

The residue of reform

Despite the invigoration of the No M77 campaign, extensive media coverage and the heightened debate that the Free State venture contributed to, the M77 was still constructed through the Pollok Estate. It was opened on 6 December 1996 by the then Scottish Secretary Michael Forsyth, to the accompaniment of a direct action 'lock-on' to the motorway's central reservation by protesters. However, we need to look at the Pollok Free State as part of the wider road protest movement and the changes in road building policy as a whole to understand how the Free State contributed to achieving what Tarrow calls a 'residue of reform' (Tarrow, 1994: 186). The term is useful here because it implies that reforms come later as a by-product of movement activity rather than as their primary goal.

I have shown how the Pollok Free State was an expression of dissent to: unequal ownership and control of land and development; what they saw as the biased policy and politically oppressive role of the state's forces of law and order; seeing progress as equivalent to economic growth, and commodity consumption as the route to personal and social happiness; and failing to place sufficient value upon both natural and human environments. Those concerns could also be said to broadly characterise the wider road protest movement. Movement ideas slowly permeate political culture in a complex and often 'vulgarised and domesticated' (Tarrow, 1985: 185) or 'watered-down' form. They may become considerations in many types of debate and even decision-making procedures. In practice this may just mean paying lip-service to them, as demonstrated by political leaders' 'greenspeak' on sustainability while following largely the same policies which were originally criticised for their non-sustainability. Nevertheless, it should not be forgotten that roads protest, and the ideological perspectives it supports, will be one factor in a plurality influencing the perspectives of the general populace. At the very least their dissent renders power disparities and important questions of value and progress more visible (Melucci, 1996: 181). After the local people, it was precisely the general populace whom the core group were aiming their protest at. They saw no or very little chance of being considered by government through debate because of their marginal position in what they regard as an undemocratic system.

Nevertheless, some direct influence is exerted because, through protest, the contractor's security costs are escalated and road building becomes a more costly activity and so less attractive to government. The costescalation from protests and delays was relatively insignificant compared to the overall cost of road-building schemes (Doherty, 1996: 12).[23] But during a period when the Conservative government was trying to keep public spending down it is clear that protests made the 'Roads to Prosperity' programme an easier target for spending cuts. 'Initial cuts in 1994 led to the cancellation or indefinite postponement of around a third of the programme but the November 1995 budget saw the remaining roads programme cut back to around one third of its original size' (Doherty, 1996). When in opposition the Labour Party pledged a general review of all road-building schemes where construction had not started. This is now in progress and is due to report in March 1998 just before John Prescott produces his White Paper on transport. Twelve controversial schemes (some of which are packages of several road projects) are at the time of writing being subject to an 'accelerated review' which will give its decisions either way at the end of July 1997. At a more local level the M74 Glasgow extension is still formally planned though it is to be subject to a Scottish Office review which will report Spring of 1998. There also now seems to be greater political will among local authorities to confront traffic congestion (*The Independent*, 20 June 1997: 8). The road protest movement seems then to have influenced politicians' calculations of anticipated reactions to policies they might be considering.[24] This has made further road building a less attractive proposition in the light of past protests against similar policies. This new climate is in stark contrast to the cries of 'lunacy!' that pilloried Green Party suggestions in the 1980s that there should be limits on car use and road construction. By contributing to the general political climate protesters have influenced what policies can feasibly be carried through by policy-makers and politicians.

In contrast, the CJA remains firmly on the statute books. Through its outlawing of 'aggravated trespass' and unlicensed protest gatherings of over twenty people in a public place, it continues to pose a serious threat to both reformist and counter-hegemonic elements in the green movement. The Labour leadership, in its desire to be seen as 'tough on law and order' has failed to challenge it and at present there seems to be no prospect of it being revoked. Even though as yet only being implemented sporadically, it could be lawfully used in the future to repress larger-scale levels of collective action threatening to the government or big business. This would obviously be seriously deleterious to the ability of progressive social movements to communicate their message to a wider public and as such it threatens open debate.

Despite this, it seems that in terms of achieving reforms radical protest complements pressure group tactics. While the Pollok Free State and Glasgow Earth First! ensured the construction operation became a 'war on the ground' with a high media profile, Friends of the Earth were examining the possibility of using European Community legislation to challenge the legality of building the road and of getting compensation for those locals whose lives will be detrimentally affected (Friends of the Earth, 1994a). There is little doubt that environmentalist pressure groups such as Greenpeace and Friends of the Earth have used road protests as grist for their mill. So even for environmentalists who think of themselves as reformists and are happy that their concerns can be integrated into existing structures, there is good reason to appreciate the strategic publicity functions that a direct action protest camp like the Pollok Free State can play. This is a similar point to one of the strategic objectives outlined in relation to American Earth First!:

> The actions of monkeywrenchers [and similarly direct action protest such as 'squatting' the proposed route] invariably enhance the status of more 'reasonable' opponents. Industry considers mainline environmentalists to be radical until they get a taste of real radical activism. Suddenly the soft-sell of the Sierra Club and other whiteshirt-and-tie eco-bureaucrats becomes much more attractive and worthy of serious negotiation.
>
> (Foreman and Haywood, 1987: 22)

This phenomenon and the general residue of reform were regarded more as by-products than ends in themselves by the core group at the Pollok Free State.

Embryonic counter-hegemonic resistance

I have shown how the core group challenged four key tenets of the hegemonic political economy and culture while contesting the construction of the M77 through Pollok Park, seeking to empower local people and help build a radical green movement. The core group saw themselves as opposed to more than just the single issue of the M77, more than the 'Roads to Prosperity' policy and CJA and more than just the Conservative government or the dominant ideas in the liberal democratic arena at the time. The single issue and policy reforms were regarded as important but not sufficient goals in themselves. As such, the core group's Free State strategy was concerned with far more than a single-issue campaign, and neither should it be regarded as just one facet of a reform movement. They were opposed not just to the particular consequences of this particular system of political economy and polity, but to its general assumptions and ideals. As such, this was a kind of counter-hegemony. An exploration of the concept of counter-hegemony will now help us to pin down exactly what kind.

Gramsci's own original conception of 'counter-hegemony' involved two stages, the 'war of position' and 'war of movement'. The war of position was characterised as the war of ideas and culture, the battle for the hearts and minds of the general populace (Showstack Sassoon, 1980: 195), whereas the war of movement was an attempt at the revolutionary seizure of the state apparatus. It may be asked whether it is really legitimate to utilise the language of counter-hegemony considering the lack of even the briefest mention by the core group of a Marxist revolutionary perspective in the sense of war of movement. But Gramsci did stress that hegemony extended way beyond the economic sphere to the political, ideological, moral and cultural spheres. These spheres are not characterised as superstructural or secondary as in forms of 'vulgar' Marxism predicated on economic reductionism, but as having causal power of their own (Hall, 1987: 20–1). It was for these reasons that Gramsci advocated that the counter-hegemonic project should, 'be constructed [and] contested... on many different sites' (Hall, 1987: 20). Nevertheless, it is clear that Gramsci was working within the revolutionary Marxist tradition, and according to his notion of counter-hegemony the war of position would lead to the war of movement.

To what extent the concept of counter-hegemony can be meaningfully reconstructed without including the war of movement has been a controversial question. It is Laclau and Mouffe's desire to draw out Gramsci's non-reductionism that leads them to leave out the war of movement, seeing it as a remnant and a correlate of a reductionistic perspective where resolution of the issue of who owns and controls the means of production and polity can solve all other political problems (Laclau and Mouffe, 1985). Norman Geras has argued to the contrary that the belief in the need for a war of movement need not entail economic reductionism because one can regard certain (economic) aspects of a hegemonic formation as primary and crucial without stripping other aspects such as culture of all causal power. He has argued that Laclau and Mouffe's eschewal of (what he argues is an over-simplistic reading of the Marxist tradition's) economic determination 'in the last instance' and the need for a revolution (in the sense of war of movement) which goes with it, means that they have left behind all that is substantive of both analytical Marxism and its prescriptive counter-hegemony (Geras, 1987: 74–8). He describes this as a 'double void' in Laclau and Mouffe's work (1985: 69).

On the first (analytical) count, it is clear that to remain meaningful the concept of counter hegemony must entail challenging primary and fundamental systemic constants and assumptions concerning the organisation and goals of the capitalist political economy, since without the rich tradition of analytical Marxism, exactly what a counter-hegemony is working against would be unspecified and as such the concept would be redundant. I have shown that the core group at the Pollok Free State did have precisely such a concern through explaining four crucial ideological challenges to ownership tenets of the capitalist political economy, its assumptions about what constitutes 'development', the consumerist culture specifically related to it and to the democratic credentials of the 'liberal democratic' polity. It is clear that challenges to economic growth and infrastructure improvement go some way beyond the Marxist critique which was in many ways itself implicated in the industrialist expansionist project. Dobson, for example, writes of the need to press, 'for a change in the means of production themselves, towards a system that is sustainable' (Dobson, 1995: 158). This could feasibly be complementary to pressing for changes in ownership and control of the means of production. The counterhegemonic project shifts with the 'specificity of the historical conjuncture' (Hall, 1987: 16) and ecological issues today make such sustainability concerns a vital part of a contemporary counter hegemony.

On the second (prescriptive) count we should first note that it was the 'war of position', the war of ideas and culture, that Gramsci saw as the *decisive* counter hegemonic struggle in the West (Gramsci, 1971: 229–38). Furthermore, Gramsci saw the attempt at seizure of the state apparatus – the war of movement as merely a tactical instance within the war of position (Showstack Sassoon, 1980: 199). The core group at Pollok was involved in fighting a war of position, and the war of position is, in Gramsci's own version of counter-hegemony, the 'decisive' element of counter-hegemony. To utilise important insights of Marxist analysis of the capitalist political economy in specifying what systemic practices and ideas are being challenged does not mean that if a movement has no aspirations toward a war of movement it cannot be regarded as counter hegemonic. A revolutionary orientation towards a war of movement might or might not come from that ideological questioning. It certainly *did not exist in any way* among the core group during the period the research was conducted. What they did intend was a process of extra-institutional empowerment and learning about both political economic structures and tactical techniques from the process of protest. It is also the case that the Free State core group and many Free State 'citizens' did seem to be radicalised by the process of protest.

But what distinguishes the core group's perspective from a simple reformist perspective is that they saw their ideals as requiring the fundamental transformation of the existing hegemonic formation and as such reforms, concessions and individual 'battles' in the war of position were not seen as sufficient in themselves but as part of a much larger process of moving toward a totally different kind of society, culture and economic system.[25] Any counter-hegemonic project which is to emerge from the radical green movement of which road protesters are a part is faced with two different kinds of response to the issue of war of movement. Either one can argue that a war of movement could well result from a war of position but that orientation will only emerge when the time is ripe which it certainly isn't now. Alternatively one can suggest that in a green counter-hegemony the need for a war of movement is subsumed within a comprehensively waged war of position whereby opposition is largely *converted* by the power of ideas, by prefigurative example, by reasoned argument and changes in consciousness. This might be distinguished from the former by the label 'organic revolution'. Nevertheless, there is a continuum rather than a strict divide between a counter-hegemony of organic revolution and a counter-hegemony aiming at a war of movement, because an advanced counter-hegemony of organic revolution would have to confront the same difficult questions of how to organise a qualitatively different form of political economy and polity, and there would still be moments of important change even though the revolutionary upheaval would be more gradual and less conflictual.

The former war of movement strategy retains the causal primacy of economic factors while the latter moves further towards the causal power of ideas and culture. The former retains to some degree the notion of inevitable class conflict, whereas in the latter easy distinctions between friend and enemy break down. It is difficult to spy which, if either, of these strategies the radical green movement will, or should, move towards. At Pollok there was a very clear attempt to escalate the conflict in order to expose exactly which groups would gain from the M77 construction and which would lose, which had power and which did not. But at the same time the core group was hostile to class based analyses, stressing the variety of social groups visiting and supporting the Free State.[26] We have already seen how members of the core group themselves had no paid employment and so were not part of the wage labouring working class agent of Gramsci's counter-hegemony. Furthermore, we saw how their unemployment could not necessarily be claimed as support for a distinctively materialist analysis since many had chosen unemployment as a result of their ideas. Their refusal to specify a privileged historical agent to lead radical green struggles and the openness of the core group to anyone of the 'concerned class' (Colin) is in sharp contrast to Gramsci's more traditionally Marxist model of change where the working class were to seek an 'expansive counter hegemony' – to sites other than the workplace, issues other than the ownership and control of the means of production and classes other than the working class such as the Italian peasant class in Gramsci's own time. This is because Gramsci's 'expansive counter hegemony' was to be *led* and articulated around the principle of working class hegemony (Mouffe, 1988: 103), since in the Marxist schema the working classes' subjective interests are seen as melding with what is objectively needed to free other oppressed groups.

In making these long-term speculations about the possible nature of an evolving green counter-hegemony it is important to make clear that long term strategic theory certainly was not a central articulating principle amongst the core group. As such their orientation is best regarded as an *embryonic* form of counter-hegemony. This was primarily a propaganda of the deed over the word. There was sometimes a jocular attitude towards my theorisation of their actions. Colin got a laugh with, 'I'm not sure about this hedgehog money [hegemony] idea.' Nevertheless, core group members did assent to my characterisation of them as counter-hegemonic through a dialogical research process, and that characterisation was stimulated by the ideas *they* were raising in literature and interviews, combined with their phraseology of the No M77 campaign being a 'battle in a war' and so on. Behind Colin's comment lay some interesting pointers about the character of the counter hegemony they were engaged in. He emphasised in interview:

> I don't feel that we can be truly successful if we see 'an opponent'. I think that we must see the ideas that are destroying the planet which people have

accepted and consented to ... To me education is everything. We must teach people that they must respect the things that make our survival possible and then they can make their own decisions after that, and [we can] encourage them to make responsible decisions ... Ignorance is our opponent and that is ignorance in me, it's ignorance in you and it's ignorance in security guards. And let's help each other become more enlightened.

This seems, tentatively, to point in the direction of an 'organic revolution' – based counter-hegemony rather than working class led and war of movement-oriented strategy. That is as far as these speculations about the likely direction of a radical green counter-hegemony can go. Although the core group had cultural alternatives to offer, their primary motivation as a protest community was to raise political issues and dissent. As such, the counter-hegemonic orientation of their Free State venture is best characterised as counter-hegemonic *resistance* serving to invigorate debate and raise systemic level issues. The Pollok Free State core group's counter-hegemonic resistance was *embryonic* because the core group was not greatly concerned with questions of how different parts of a wider green movement would co-ordinate, nor with the more difficult questions of coalitions with other social movements or the potential role of a political party.

I have shown that the core group contributed to the No M77 campaign as both an end in itself and as part of a strategy to utilise the single-issue to raise wider policy questions about 'Roads to Prosperity' and the CJA and to raise systemic level issues about the ownership, control and nature of development. They aimed to empower locals to take extra-institutional political action and to contribute to the building of a radical green movement. The core group used the media to facilitate symbolic challenges to both the single issue and the hegemonic formation in the hope of motivating people to action, but they were also used by the media in some instances in a fashion detrimental to their cause. As part of the wider road protest movement they contributed to the residue of reform that is the decimation of 'Roads to Prosperity' and a new willingness to confront the problems of car culture. But this residue of reform is best seen as a byproduct of their more fundamental goals of facilitating learning about and challenge to the legitimacy of the hegemonic formation of capitalist political economy, liberal polity, development as economic growth and infrastructure expansion and consumerist culture. As such the perspectives, orientations and strategic actions of the core group at Pollok can be characterised as embryonic counter-hegemonic resistance, even though it is clear that this is quite different in some respects from Gramsci's original version of counter-hegemony.

Notes

1 A second less ambiguous version of the Maxwell Family Agreement was sent to the Lord Provost of Glasgow, John Johnstone, by Messrs Maclay, Murray and Spens, solicitors, on 21 November 1966 including this same sentence minus the words 'so far as possible' (Morrison, 1995).

2 Kala notes that

> The Region's Roads Department advanced a variety of justifications for the construction of the motorway extension. They argued that the motorway would:
>
> (i)   assist economic development;
> (ii)   save travelling time for road users;
> (iii) reduce road accidents;
> (iv)   reduce road congestion;
> (v)   improve the reliability of the public bus transport system; and
> (vi)   enhance environmental conditions by removing traffic from residential and shopping streets.

3 The STARR alliance comprised of: Corkerhill Community Council, Park Community Council, North Pollok Community Council, Templar Community Council, World-Wide Fund for Nature (Scotland), Scottish Wildlife Trust, Friends of the Earth (Scotland) (and Glasgow), Architects and Engineers for Social Responsibility, Earth First!, Transport 2000, Glasgow Cycling Campaign, Glasgow for People, Glasgow Building Guardians Committee, Glasgow Tree Lovers, Socialist and Environment Resources Association, Railway Development Society (Scotland), Ramblers Association (Strathclyde), Friends of the People's Palace, Friends of Kelvingrove Park; and Greenpeace supported the campaign (Glasgow for People, 1994). It had four goals:

> (i)   to have the M77 Ayr Road Route cancelled;
> (ii)   to re-direct financial resources saved from the cancellation into an alternative, environmentally sensitive transport strategy;
> (iii) to reinstate the land within Pollok estate to its previous condition as open space and woodland, as enshrined in the 1939 Conservation Agreement; and
> (iv)   to restore all open spaces and buildings blighted by the M77 Ayr Road Route, and give priority to provision of pedestrian and cyclist safety, public transport and park-and-ride facilities.
>
>   (Kala, 1995)

On 28 September 1994, the deadline for tenders from contractors bidding to construct the road, the STARR alliance submitted an alternative tender offering to modernise transport in the Glasgow-Ayr corridor by other means (Friends of the Earth, 1994b).

4 The focus here upon residents of the Free State is in no way intended to belittle the other roles in the No M77 campaign. It is simply a reflection of my interests and the temporal and financial limits to my research. This research was conducted from the winter of 1994–95 through to summer 1996. This was a mixture of participant observation, semi-structured interviews and examination of campaign literature, carried out with reference to Lather's dialogic research and theory building. Lather suggests three interrelated measures in research methodology: (1) a reciprocal learning relationship between researcher and researched, (2) dialogic theoretical construction including debriefing sessions with the researched in order that they may point out disagreements with and exceptions to emerging generaliasations, (3) multiple research sources and multiple theoretical schemes with systematised reflexivity allowing counter-patterns as well as convergence (Lather, 1986).

5 Whensoever...the legislative shall...by ambition, fear, folly, or corruption, endeavour to grasp themselves, or put into the hands of any other, an absolute power over the lives, liberties, and estates of the people, by this breach of trust they forfeit the power the people had put into their hands for quite contrary ends, and it devolves to the people, who have a right to resume their original liberty, and by the establishment of a new legislative (such as they shall think fit), provide for their own safety and security...

                                                                      (Locke, 1990: 229)

6 This is a similar emphasis to that of a radical environmental group based in Oxford and coordinated by George Monbiot, called 'The Land is Ours'.

7 Of course, car culture is actually mass culture. This 'privatisation for a car-owning elite' is largely a reference to the fact that the M77 serves commuters to the city centre from better-off areas while the local estates of the Pollokshaws and Corkerhill will suffer from air and noise pollution as well as restricted access to the Pollok Estate. Corkerhill also has the lowest per capita number of cars in Europe and one in five children there already suffers from asthma.

8 Catalysing and encouraging participation has been a tenet of many different strands of green political thought. Dobson, Achterberg and Barry all argue that green political projects require increased political participation (Doherty and de Geus, 1996). In contrast many liberals such as J.S. Mill and M.Weber argued that liberal democracies should minimise political participation, while Macpherson (1977) and Pateman (1979) have argued that liberal democracies do in fact minimise it, since representative procedures function to maintain no more than a facade of democratic participation.

9 Dobson has suggested, 'it is *the distance from the process of consumption and the degree of permanence of this isolation that currently determine the capacity of any given group in society for Green social change*' (Dobson, 1995: 158, his emphasis).

10 Note that I am not claiming that Free State 'citizens' and visitors were predominantly unemployed. This was beyond the remit of my research.

11 Stop-offs at different road protest campaigns on the 'To Pollok With Love' journey, and the burning of the carhenge itself, was filmed by an alternative news collective called 'Undercurrents' which has produced a series of videos utilising protesters' own recordings of direct action protests.

12 Benders are made by bending cut branches over and covering them with tarpaulin; their floors were often laid with pallets and lined with old carpet. The tree lodge was an impressive circular structure of 30–40 feet diameter, with a stone fire place and chimney in its centre. Its floor level was about fifteen feet above ground level. The central fireplace was built on the top of a freshly cut tree-stump and the rest of the structure was propped up by thick support branches.

13 Routledge (1996) provides an interesting description of how conflict ensued when the core group's ideal of 'consensus politics' was disregarded by an Earth First! organiser; clearly ideals were not always practically lived up to!

14 This discounts somewhat the value of the 'political process' school of social movement analysis to this sort of non-institutional social movement because it tends to concentrate upon how movement resources are mobilised to instrumentally achieve reform goals (see, for example, Tarrow (1994)), rather than drawing out symbolic challenges to dominant values, codes and modes of organisation as Melucci's approach does.

15   New forms of collective action...become modular...as their uses become known and they are learned throughout society, they become conventional forms of activity for others to use – even for some who do not share their originator's goals or preferences.

(Tarrow, 1994: 184–5)

16 Exactly why planners did this remains unclear; it could be regarded as a sop to protesters.

17 Routledge (1996) provides more detail about the role and organisation of Glasgow Earth First! in the No M77 campaign and their close relations with the Pollok Free State.

18 Such as McAdam's study of US civil rights activists in *Freedom Summer* (1988).

19 Mclucci has described how contemporary social movements depend upon submerged cultural networks, warning against a 'myopia of the visible' whereby analysis focuses only upon measurable aspects of collective action (Melucci, 1989: 43–4). The forging of a common identity through movement which strengthens future commitment has

been described by numerous social movement writers, for example, Blocker (1989); Mershon (1990); Percheron (1991); Mckay (1996).

20 Although the claims I can legitimately make about Free State 'citizens' and visitors to the camp are necessarily limited because they were not the main focus of my research and because I met only a small percentage of the total, it is worth noting that the vast majority of those that I had sufficient contact with to be able to tell also viewed the Free State as just a part of, or stage in, a wider social and ecological struggle.

21 Routledge (1996) offers further examples of newspaper hostility towards the Pollok Free State.

22 Nevertheless, it is clear that collective action at the Free State also had an important expressive element and that identity based analyses are an interesting *part* of social movement theory.

23 I am grateful to Brian Doherty for drawing my attention to a notable exception to this – the Newbury bypass protests of 1996 which probably increased the overall cost of the scheme by between 20 and 25 per cent.

24 The idea of environmental pressure groups influencing policy through policymakers' considerations of the likely reactions of pressure groups appeared in Newell (1995).

25 Of course, Marx himself argued that reforms and revolution are not mutually exclusive but that what is important in distinguishing a more radical perspective is the attitude to the sought after reforms – whether they are as sufficient in themselves as amelioratory measures or as part of a longer process of fundamental change in social structure (Marx, 1970: 77–8).

26 For example, in interview Colin said: 'I don't believe in looking at things in a class way. I do say I am of the concerned class, the class which is interested in nature rather than the financial or money class.' In interview, Johan, among others, emphasised the 'cross-over between classes on environmental issues', as a positive phenomenon.

References

Bellos, A. (1996), 'Protest Branches Out', *The Guardian*, Education section, 2 Jan. 1996, pp. 2–3.

Bey, H. (1996), *TAZ: The Temporary Autonomous Zone, Ontological Anarchy, Poetic Terrorism*, Camberley: Green Anarchist Books.

Blocker, J.S., Jr (1989), *American Temperance Movements: Cycles of Reform*, Boston, MA: Twayne Publishers.

Boggs, C. (1976), *Gramsci's Marxism*, London: Pluto Press.

Bray, J.S. and E. Must (1995), *Roadblock*, London: Alarm UK.

Clark, H., S. Crown, A. Mckee and H. Macpherson (ND), *Preparing For Non-Violent Direct Action*, London: A Peace News/CND Publication.

Cohen, J.L. (1985), 'Strategy or Identity: New Theoretical Paradigms and Contemporary Social Movements', *Social Research*, Vol. 52, No. 4.

Cunningham, F. (1993), 'Radical Philosophy and the New Social Movements', in R.S. Gottlieb (ed.), *Radical Philosophy: Tradition, Counter-Tradition, Polities*, Philadelphia, PA: Temple University Press, pp. 199–220.

Daily Mail (1995), 'Why the English are Camping Out in Pollok', 21 Jan. 1995.

Do or Die! (1995), 'Pollok Free State Lives On!', *Do or Die*, No. 5, pp. 7–10.

Dobson, A. (1995), *Green Political Thought* (2nd edn), London: Routledge.

Doherty, A. (1995), *Green Political Thought* (2nd edn), London: Routledge.

Doherty, B. (1996), 'Paving the Way: The Rise of Direct Action Against Road-building and the Changing Character of British Environmentalism', in C. Barker and M. Tyldesley (eds), *Alternative Futures and Popular Protest II*, Vol. 1, Manchester: Manchester Metropolitan University.

Doherty, B. and M. de Geus (eds) (1996), *Democracy and Green Political Thought: Sustainability, Rights and Citizenship*, London: Routledge.

Faol-Chu (1995), 'Pollok Free State Lives Wild and Free'.

Fendrich, J.M. and E.S. Krauss (1994), 'Student Activism and Adult Left-wing Politics: A Causal Model of Political Socialization for Black, White and Japanese Students of the 1960's Generation', in L. Kriesberg, M.N. Dobowski and I. Walliman (eds), *Research in Social Movements, Conflicts and Change*, Greenwich, CT: Jai Press, pp. 231–55.

Foreman, D. and B. Haywood (eds) (1987), *Ecodefense: A Field Guide to Monkeywrenching*, Tuscon, AZ: A Ned Ludd Book.

Friends of the Earth (1994a), 'Environmental Group Claims Ayr Road Route Illegal!', Press Release, 21 Sept. 1994.

Friends of the Earth (1994b), 'Environmental Alliance Bids for M77 Money', Press Release, 28 Sept. 1994.

Fromm, E. (1976), *To Have or To Be*, London: Jonathon Cape.

Fukuyama, F. (1990), 'Are We at the End of History?', *Fortune*, Vol. 121, No. 2.

Gal Gael (1996a), 'Ecological and Cultural Renewal in Scotland' (leaflet).

Gal Gael (1996b), 'Nuxalk Nation Consulate' (leaflet).

Gamson, W.A. and G. Wolsfeld (1993), 'Movements and Media as Interacting Systems', *The Annals of the American Academy of Political and Social Science*, Vol. 528, July.

Geras, N. (1987), 'Post-Marxism?', *New Left Review*, No. 163, pp. 40–82.

Geras, N. (1988), 'Ex-Marxism Without Substance: Being a Real Reply to Laclau and Mouffe', *New Left Review*, No. 169, pp. 34–62.

Glasgow for People (1994), 'Motorway versus Democracy', Newsletter.

Gramsci, A. (1971), *Selections From Prison Notebooks*, London: Lawrence & Wishart.

Hall, S. (1987), 'Gramsci and Us', *Marxism Today*, June, pp. 16–21.

Hall, S. and M. Jacques (1989), *New Times: The Changing Face of Politics in the 1990s*, London: Lawrence & Wishart.

Heller, A. (1976), 'Marx's Theory of Revolution and the Revolution in Everyday Life', in Heller, Hegedus and Vajda Markus (eds), *The Humanisation of Socialism*, London: Allison & Busby.

Howarth, D. (1996), 'Theorising Hegemony', in I. Hampsher-Monk and J. Stanyer (eds), *Contemporary Political Studies 1996*, Vol. 2, Exeter: Political Studies Association.

Kala, P. (1995), 'Pollok Free State: Roads Resistance Grows in Scotland's Dear Green Place', *Do or Die!*, 21 March 1995.

Laclau, E. and C. Mouffe (1985), *Hegemony and Socialist Strategy: Towards a Radical Democratic Politics*, London: Verso.

Laclau, E. and C. Mouffe (1987), 'Post-Marxism Without Apologies', *New Left Review*, No. 166, pp. 79–106.

Lather, P. (1986), 'Research as Praxis', *Harvard Educational Review*, Vol. 56, No. 3, pp. 257–77.

Locke, J. (1990), *Two Treatises of Government*, London: Guernsey Press.

McAdam, D. (1988), *Freedom Summer*, Oxford: Oxford University Press.

McKay, G. (1996), *Senseless Acts of Beauty: Cultures of Resistance since the Sixties*, London: Verso.

McLellan, D. (1971), *The Thought of Karl Marx*, London: Macmillan Press.

Macpherson, C.B. (1977), *The Life and Times of Liberal Democracy*, Oxford: Oxford University Press.

Marx, K. (1970), *Wages Price and Profit*, Peking: Foreign Languages Press.

Melucci, A. (1989), *Nomads of the Present: Social Movements and Individual Needs in Contemporary Society* (eds J. Keane and P. Mier), London: Hutchinson Radius.

Melucci, A. (1996), *Challenging Codes: Collective Action in the Information Age*, Cambridge: Cambridge University Press.

Merrick (1996), *Battle For the Trees*, Leeds: Godhaven Ink.

Mershon, C.A. (1990), 'Generazioni di leader sindicali in fabbrica. L'eredità dell' autunno caldo', *Polis*, Vol. 2, pp. 277–323.

Morrison, W. (1995), 'Pollok Estate: Glasgow's Last Legacy?' Glasgow: Corkerhill Community Council.

Mouffe, C. (ed.) (1979), *Gramsci and Marxist Theory*, London: Routledge & Kegan Paul.

Mouffe, C. (1988), 'Hegemony and New Political Subjects: Toward a New Concept of Democracy', in C. Nelson and L. Grossberg (eds), *Marxism and the Interpretation of Culture*, Chicago, IL: University of Illinois Press.

Naess, A. (1965), *Gandhi and the Nuclear Age*? New York City: Bedminister Press.

Newell, P. (1995), 'Environmental NGO's and the Politics of Global Warming', Paper given to British International Studies Association Conference.

Pateman, C. (1979), *The Problem of Political Obligation: A Critique of Liberal Theory*, Oxford: John Wiley.

Pepper, D. (1993), *Eco-Socialism: From Deep Ecology to Social Justice*, London: Routledge.

Percheron, A. (1991), 'La mémoire des générations: La guerre d'Algérie – Mai 68', in A. Duhamel and J. Jaffré (eds), *SOFRES: L'Etat de l'opinion*, Paris: Scuil, pp. 39–57.

Pollok Free State (1994), 'Declaration of Independence From the People of Pollok Free State' (leaflet).

Pollok Free State (1995), 'Land Redemption Fund' (leaflet).

Ramesh, R. (1997), 'Drivers May Have to Pay to Enter West End', 'Review Casts Doubt on Future of £1.5bn Road Schemes', *The Independent*, p. 8.

Road Alert! (1995), 'Polloks People', Road Alert! Newsletter, May.

Road Alert! (1997), *Road Raging: Top Tips for Wrecking Roadbuilding*, Newbury: Road Alert!

Routledge, P. (1996), 'The Imagineering of Resistance: Pollok Free State and the Practice of Postmodern Politics', Draft for *Transactions of the Institute of British Geographers*.

Seabrook, J. (1988), *The Race for Riches*, Basingstoke: Green Print.

Showstack Sassoon, A. (1980), *Gramsci's Politics*, London: Croom Helm.

Showstack Sassoon, A. (1982), *Approaches to Gramsci*, London: Writers and Readers Publishing Cooperative Society.

Tarrow, S. (1994), *Power in Movement: Social Movements, Collective Action and Politics*, Cambridge: Cambridge University Press.

Thompson, D. (ed.) (1983), *Over Our Dead Bodies*, London: Virago.

Truett-Anderson, W. (1990), *Reality Isn't What It Used To Be: Theatrical Politics, Ready-to-Wear Religion, Global Myths, Primitive Chic, and Other Wonders of the Post-Modern World*, San Fransisco, CA: Harper & Row.

Tyme, J. (1978), *Motorways Versus Democracy*, London: Macmillan Press.

Wall, D. (1990), *Getting There: Steps To A Green Society*, London: Merlin Press.

Welsh, I. and P. McLeish (1996), 'The European Road to Nowhere: Anarchism and Direct Action against the U.K. Roads Programme', *Anarchist Studies*, Vol. 4, No. 1, pp. 27–44.

Part III
Green political economy

9 Free market environmentalism

Friend or foe?

Robyn Eckersley

Scenario one

Elephant poaching in Eastern Africa has forced many elephant populations to the brink of extinction, prompting the issuing of a trade ban in ivory under the Convention on International Trade in Endangered Species (CITES). One East African country – X – has legislated an outright ban on elephant poaching and has set up a system of well policed national parks. However, over time, this protection has led to a swelling of the elephant population to the point where the elephants have become a threat to the habitat which sustains them. Debt-ridden and starved of foreign exchange, the government of X seeks the advice of a free market environmental economist, who advises the government to vest property rights in the elephants to the local villagers who could then earn revenue from these rights through such activities as tourism, the issuing of hunting licences to wealthy Western trophy hunters, and local 'harvesting' of elephants, for meat, hides and lucrative tusks. The free market environmental economist advises that the success of the scheme would require a relaxation of the ivory trade ban. The economist further advises that not only would the country reap more revenue than would be the case under a tourism regime only; the taking of elephants could also be controlled in a way that will ensure a sustainable population of elephants in relation to the habitat on which they depend.

Scenario two

Cornucopia Island lies off the coast of New Zealand and is under the jurisdiction of the New Zealand government. Its once abundant abalone fishery is threatened by over-fishing by local islanders and mainland interests. Although the government has introduced a licensing system, size limit, season limit, gear restrictions, and eventually individual quotas, the fishery still remains under threat. Enter a free market environmentalist, who suggests that the government set an overall catch limit and then issue Individual Transferable Quotas (ITQ) to fishers. This will enable fishers to enter and exit the market by buying and selling ITQs. The overall catch limit could be adjusted periodically by the government to accommodate changes in the size of the fish stock.

Scenario three

Greylands is an industrial region containing a range of heavy industries. The current regime of pollution control lays down individual emission targets for each polluter and stipulates the kinds of technology (say, the latest available technology) that must be used by each polluter. Many firms complain that this regime is discriminatory because the costs of installing the latest available technologies is higher for some firms than others and that a more flexible system is needed to enable firms to meet output standards in a more cost-effective way. Enter again the free market environmental economist. The advice is that pollution, or more accurately the right to pollute, should be turned into a commodity that can be bought and sold. The government is advised to set an overall emission target or pollution 'bubble' for the region and then allocate this total quota through the issue of tradeable emission licenses to each polluter in the region. The government could also enable companies to store emission credits for later use or sale ('banking'), trade-off between different plants in the one business ('netting') and allow emissions from new pollution sources if reductions can be made from other sources in the same plant ('offsetting').

Scenario four

A very large tract of old-growth, native forest on Crown lands administered by an Australian state government is recognised by scientists as being an outstanding example of natural heritage. The forestry industry is lobbying the government for licences to take saw logs from the area and to clearfell the remainder for woodchips. The Wilderness Society is opposing the application and arguing that the entire area of public land should be protected as a national park. The state government enlists the advice of a free market environmental economist, who suggests that the government sell perpetual (or long term) tradeable utilisation rights to the forest to both the forest industry and the Wilderness Society. Each party can then decide how it wishes to exercise or profit from these rights. This might include 'selling' the amenity value of the forest by charging an entry fee to walkers or a tour guide fee; selling various 'rights to take' from the forest such as charging a game fee to hunters or selling rights to cut saw logs or clearfell for woodchips. The parties can also swap or sell different bundles of rights to each other.

The consultant advises that the forestry commission's practice of focusing on maintaining a maximum sustainable wood volume has meant that it has failed to reap the economic benefits of non-timber forest values, which have been provided at a zero-price. This has contributed to the forestry commission's incurring substantial operating losses for the past 50 years. The consultant advises that the privatisation of the forests will not only put an end to the heated political controversy over the forests but also lead to a much more efficient use of the forest resources.

Scenario five

Acme Minerals Consortium is pressing the government to permit mining in an area of land contained within a national park. The Australian Conservation

Foundation (ACF) is strongly resisting the proposal. Again, the free market environmental economist advises that the political tug-of-war could be avoided if the environmental assets in question were taken out of the government's hands and vested in the 'interested parties'. Given that it is too time-consuming and complex for Acme Minerals to negotiate with every single person who has an interest in preventing mining in the park, the economist suggests that new private property rights could be held in common by those with an environmental interest in the area. For example, private environmental rights to the area could be formally vested in a group, say the ACF, that is officially recognised as democratically representative of those who benefit most from its preservation. Acme Minerals would then be in a position to make bids for these environmental rights from the ACF. The price offered by Acme Minerals would reflect what the company believed would be sufficient to compensate for the loss of environmental values that would result from the mining operation. This price would be a function of, *inter alia*, the degree of environmental damage that would be likely to occur from the mining venture and the estimated profitability of the venture. Whether the ACF accepted the price would be a function of, *inter alia*, the opportunities it has to use the money to purchase more significant threatened areas elsewhere (this scenario is adapted from a proposal put forward by Bennett (1991b: 284–5).

What is free market environmentalism?

The above mentioned scenarios – some of which are adapted from real life situations – provide examples of what has become known as 'free market environmentalism' or FME. In essence, FME refers to an approach defended by a certain school of environmental or resource economists who argue that most (ideally all) of our environmental problems can be solved by the creation and enforcement of tradeable property rights in environmental 'goods' and 'bads' (see Anderson and Leal (1991), Bennett and Block (1991) and Moran *et al.* (1991)).

Proponents of FME argue that their approach is far superior to what they variously refer to as 'command and control' solutions or 'state environmentalism' (i.e. government regulation), which they see as leading to the 'political' (and hence inefficient) allocation of environmental resources.

The market: not culprit but saviour?

Most greens usually attribute the growth of so-called enviromental externalities such as resource depletion and pollution to market forces. That is, the 'tragedy of the commons' is traced to the selfish (albeit economically rational) exploitation of the commons (air, waterways and so on) by private capital for short-term private gain. However, FME economists seek to turn this argument on its head by maintaining that the alleged culprit is in fact the saviour if we divide up the commons into private property rights. That is, environmental externalinities are seen to arise not form 'market forces' or self-interested behaviour but rather from *an absence of well-defined, universal, exclusive, transferable and enforceable private property rights* in respect of common environmental assets. 'The problem', as Moran explains, 'is the lack of the very institution that lies at the heart of the free enterprise system', namely, private property (Moran, 1991: 189). Indeed, FME economists maintain that it is not private capital but state regulation of, and 'political intervention' in, the economy (such as distorting subsidies, taxes or simply bad management) that is largely responsible for environmental degradation. As one FME economist from the Melbourne-based Tasman Institute has put it, 'Capitalism is naturally a conserver of resources, and an enemy of waste' (Porter, 1991: 4).

The loaded language enlisted by FME economists – *free* market environmentalism versus *command and control* mechanisms or government *intervention* – is illustrative of a quite zealous libertarianism on the part of some of the advocates of this school. The particular freedom guaranteed by such economists – 'freedom to' enter into voluntary contracts and trade, which requires a 'freedom from' government regulation of resource allocation decisions through such measures as bans, charges, taxes and penalties – may be seen as a concerted attempt to stretch the framework of classical liberalism and neo-classical economics to the point where they 'solve' the ecological crisis. Of course, FME economists acknowledge that the creation and enforcement of new property rights in respect of public or open-access environmental goods is something that can only be done by government legislation and administration. In the absence of this, profit-maximising behaviour by economic actors will lead to the over-use or degradation of open-access, zero-priced goods such as waterways and the atmosphere. However, as we have seen, such over-use or degradation arises not from market forces *per se* but rather from the *absence* of clearly defined property rights in the commons.

The return of the nightwatchman state

The state therefore has an important role to play under a FME regime in facilitating the division of the commons into private property rights. However, once this is achieved, the state's role is a minimal one of nightwatchman, whose principal job is to protect private property and uphold the rule of law. But there is one notable difference between this standard Lockean defence of government and that of the modern free market environmental economist. According to Locke, the Earth had been given to humans for 'the support and comfort of their being'; moreover, the simple act of mixing human labour with 'nature' was an act of appropriation that created something valuable (i.e. property) out of something otherwise *valueless* (the Earth in its state of 'natural grace') (Leeson, 1979: 305–6). In the Lockean world, the commons, or open-access environmental resources, were free and unlimited. There may have been environmental externalities in those times, but they were not considered significant. In today's world, the FME economist recognises the significance of environmental externalities and seeks to control the appropriation of the commons by *restricting* access to it (i.e. by dividing it up into tradeable property rights).

FME economists argue that voluntary exchanges between the holders of these new rights will enable the internalisation of environmental externalities and a more efficient allocation of resources. Wherever possible, state ownership, control and management of environmental goods and services (e.g. energy, timber, water, national parks and wastes) should be avoided on the grounds that bureaucracies are inefficient. The main proffered reasons are that bureaucrats do not have to pay for the costs of their actions, they are insulated from the consequences of their advice and decisions, and they are usually more interested in their career advancement or own self-interest than in the public good.

In contrast, the private property rights approach is defended as preferable to government regulation because it decentralises and depoliticises environmental resource allocation decisions; it enables the creation of a personal stake in the environmental asset that is the subject of the property right; and individual property holders will be better informed about the immediate consequences of different courses of action. Indeed, proponents of FME even maintain that their approach is *more democratic* than state environmentalism because governments are imperfectly informed of people's preferences and, in any event, they are likely only to pursue 'political' outcomes that will secure their re-election. In contrast, a free market environmental approach is defended as providing a more accurate and more efficient reflection of individual preferences.

Although, as we shall see, FME economists do concede that there are some situations where privatisation is impracticable, they argue that allocating private property rights should always be the first line of defence in. combating environmental problems (e.g. Bennett (1991b: 287)). As Moran explains, '*unfortunately*, there will inevitably remain a role for government over and above that of passively policing those [i.e. property] rights' (Moran, 1991: 268; emphasis added).

Free market environmentalism versus market-based instruments

Free market environmentalism should not be confused with market-based instruments, which are regulatory instruments such as taxes, penalties, charges, deposit-refund systems, financial assistance and sub-sidies that are designed to use economic incentives to encourage certain kinds of behaviour (although there is some overlap between the two). Whereas the advocates of FME seek the full privatisation option wherever possible by creating a market in previously free services or activities, the advocates of market-based instruments merely seek to modify existing markets by determining the costs of various environmental services and ensuring that these are incorporated into prices (Pearce *et al.*, 1989: 155). For example, market-based incentives such as taxes and charges can be used to give effect to the polluter pays principle (PPP), to ensure that total costs of production (i.e. marginal cost plus marginal external cost) are reflected in market prices. However, even here, the 'optimal' level of pollution resulting from such a system may not be an 'acceptable' level (Pearce *et al.*, 1989: 158) and a total ceiling on emissions may also need to be determined and imposed. Tradeable emission permits in fact involve a combination of privatisation, market-based incentives and government 'command and control' measures.

The libertarian versus public choice school

Even within the FME school, not all economists pursue the privatisation option with the same degree of zeal. While there are some 'heroic' or 'libertarian' environmental economists in this school (e.g. Terry Anderson and Michael Porter) there is also a more moderate 'public choice' school that recognises that market-based incentives have a role to play in those instances where the so-called transaction costs (i.e. the costs of establishing, assigning, trading or enforcing the new property rights) are too high to warrant the privatisation option (Bennett, 1991a: 3–4; Moran, 1991). For example, water pollution comes from a diverse range of sources and the number of people affected is very large. In such cases, it may be too intricate, time-consuming and costly to organise a system whereby the affected parties can negotiate successful contracts regarding the costs and benefits of using clean water.

Indeed, there are many instances where the privatisation option is effectively impossible. This arises in the case of pure public goods, which are characterised by not being excludable (i.e. it is impossible to target particular consumers and exclude others) and by being able to withstand non-rival consumption (i.e. as many people as want to can consume the good without jeopardising its availability) (Moran, 1991). Non-excludability is a characteristic not only of environmental 'goods' such as clean air but also environmental 'bads' such as air pollution. Here some form of government restriction, such as emission ceilings, is accepted by the public choice school as a necessary measure to reduce externalities such as air pollution (although this can then be combined with a tradeable emission permit system). This is especially so where the environmental damage is likely to be irreversible (as, for example, with species extinction, ozone depletion and global warming). Whereas the libertarian school argues that the initiative for addressing ecological problems should lie with private individuals (or, more accurately, private contracting parties) the public choice school recognises that there are some instances where the initiative must be taken by the government. Thus Moran proposes a hierarchy of actions to deal with externalities: first, allocate property rights; then regulate by granting tradeable rights; then adjust or establish taxation levels to reduce output of the externality; next, specify standards or particular technologies to reduce the externality; and, lastly, impose an outright ban (Moran, 1991; 256–8). The last two measures are anathema to most free market environmental economists on the grounds that they are inefficient and a threat to liberty.

As Bennett explains, the general thrust of FME is 'to integrate more environmental goods with the market economy, rely on government intervention only when transaction costs are extreme and then make most use of market forces when designing intervention mechanisms' (Bennett, 1991a: 9).

Despite the differences between the libertarian and public choice schools of FME economics, members of both schools share the view that environmental degradation and resource depletion are largely the result of the perversities of government regulation. Not surprisingly, both schools are highly critical of what they see as the green movement's reliance on greater government intervention in the economy. They maintain that greens have been unable to distinguish between market failures and wider institutional failures. Indeed, they go further and accuse greens of totalitarianism for seeking to use the coercive power of the state to realise their ideals. From a FME-perspective, the green call for more environmental regulations is seen as impairing or denying individual freedom of choice (Chant *et al.*, 1991).

What are the ideological stakes?

Before critically exploring the FME case and the green response, it is worth asking what has prompted the emergence and timing of FME economics (in particular, 1991 was a good year for FME; see, for example, Anderson and Leal (1991); Bennett and Block (1991); Moran, *et al.* (1991)). To what extent is free market environmentalism a new economic *initiative* (stemming, say, from a concern over the seriousness of the ecological crisis) and to what extent is it a *response* or rearguard action (say, to the growing influence of the green movement)? Has the green movement grown to the point where it poses a threat (whether real or perceived) to free enterprise? Has green economics come of age? What is at stake here?

What is at stake is a clash not only of economic ideologies but also of social, political and environmental ideologies. While the economic, social and political disposition of FME economists is quite apparent and familiar, their implicit environmental orientation deserves closer scrutiny. What is noteworthy about this orientation is that it closely approximates what Timothy O'Riordan has called a 'technocentric' environmental orientation (O'Riordan, 1981). It has four principal characteristics. First, it is sceptical towards the idea that there are limits to growth (e.g. the existence of scientific uncertainty is usually taken as a reason for not taking steps to respond to a particular ecological problem). Second, it involves an unrestrained development philosophy that is concerned to maximise economic output. Third, it is characterised by a scientific and technological optimism and a general belief that human ingenuity will solve any ecological problems that we may encounter (this includes a strong emphasis on the substitutability of resources). Finally, it emphasises material values and tends to downplay the significance of non-material values.

Underlying this orientation is a thoroughly anthropocentric or human-centred worldview – that is, a belief that the world was made for humans, that humans are the centre of value and meaning in the world, and that the rest of nature is merely raw material to be bent to human purpose.

This technocentric orientation stands in stark contrast to the ecocentric orientation towards which most greens lean. Such an orientation has the following characteristics. It recognises, first, that there are both ecological and social limits to growth. Second, it favours a development philosophy that is concerned to minimise the material and energy throughput in the economy and to operate comfortably within the carrying capacity of ecosystems. It appreciates, third, the complexities of ecosystems and the limits to human understanding and technological expertise, which gives rise to a cautious approach to technology and risk assessment and an emphasis on developing 'soft' energy paths and 'appropriate' technology. Finally, it recognises the importance of non-material or 'quality of life' values such as education, creativity, fellowship, civic responsibility and democratic participation, belonging and community, and aesthetic pleasure.

Underlying this development philosophy is a respect for all life-forms (not just humans) and a recognition that all life-forms should be given the opportunity to pursue their own destinies.

These technocentric and ecocentric orientations represent the opposing poles of an ecopolitical dimension which may be used to shed light on some of the *economic* differences between FME economists and green economists. This can best be done diagrammatically (see Figure 9.1) by superimposing the technocentric/ecocentric dimension on the conventional left/right political dimension; the latter we shall crudely define for present purposes in terms of

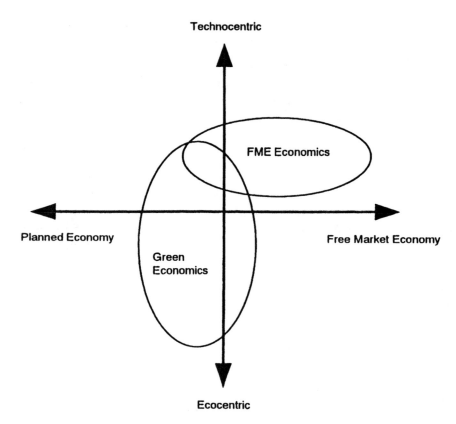

Figure 9.1 Orientational axes of green economics vs free market environmentalism.

the degree to which the state is prepared to constrain the operation of market forces.

Figure 9.1 illustrates the moderately left-of-centre leaning of greens on the conventional spectrum, which flows from the green ecological critique of both communism and capitalism. The green movement has been concerned to point out that while *social* relations between humans are theoretically different under communism and capitalism, the relationship between humans and the rest of nature appears to be the same. Greens are particularly critical of the technological optimism and indiscriminate growth ethos of these two forms of industrialism. Although many greens have drawn on, and in many ways bolstered, Marx's critique of capitalism, this has not led to an outright rejection of entrepreneurial activity or of the market as a method of resource allocation. Rather, greens are concerned to find an alternative economic framework that ensures that the market is *subservient* to ecological and social justice considerations. However, for many greens this search has largely remained within the fold of the social-democratic model, while others have pursued more local, communitarian models. Although some greens have defended state ownership of some capital assets and some degree of economic planning (for a discussion, see Eckersley (1992)) all greens reject a rigid and highly centralised command economy on the grounds that it provides little opportunity for participatory democracy and community initiative. In this respect, accusations by FME economists that greens are *totalitarian* because they seek 'command and control' environmental policies must be seen as considerably wide of the mark.

The green alternative: not one but three criteria

The green search for an alternative economic framework has been a challenging one and, for the most part, greens have had to be content with finding ways of modifying existing economic frameworks and institutions in order to channel, or in some cases force, the economy in new ecological directions (Eckersley, 1991). Part of the challenge has been to find ways of imposing ceilings on the level of material and energy throughput in the economy while simultaneously working toward a fairer distribution of environmental resources (and hence income) nationally and internationally. From a green perspective, conventional macroeconomics is blind to the relationship between the scale of the economy and the ecosystem in which it operates. As Herman Daly succinctly put it, it is like biologists looking only at the circulatory system, and ignoring the digestive tract. What is needed, argues Daly, is a picture of the macroeconomy as an open subsystem of the larger ecosystem upon which it is dependent as both a source of inputs and a sink for wastes (Daly, 1991: 34).

While the market can function very effectively within the economic subsystem in terms of the efficient *allocation* of resources, it cannot perform by itself the task of setting an optimal (in the sense of just) *distribution* of income nor an optimal (in the sense of sustainable) *scale* of the economy relative to the ecosystem (Daly, 1991: 36). The major concern of green economics is to find ways of synchronising these three objectives – efficient allocation, just distribution and sustainable scale (Daly and Cobb, 1989; Ekins, 1992; Jacobs, 1991).

Of course realising these three objectives is no easy task and there is a lively internal debate among greens as to how these goals might best be achieved. In general, it may be said that greens display a rather eclectic approach and a willingness to experiment with different policy instruments to achieve green goals. This means that privatisation options and market-based incentives are included in the range of policy measures considered by green economists. However, the measures espoused by FME economists are not given any special a priori ranking; rather they are selected if they can be shown to be effective in terms of bringing together the three objectives of resource allocation efficiency, distributional justice and ecological sustainability. The area of overlap between FME economists and green economists in Figure 9.1 may be seen as representing those instances where green economists and FME economists concur; it is noteworthy that the area is not particularly large.

Tunnel vision

From a green perspective, then, the FME economist is seen as suffering from tunnel vision in focussing only on efficiency. Indeed, many greens are wary of the idea that property rights and market forces can be put to work to solve so many diverse and complex ecological problems – problems that are inextricably linked with so many equally diverse and complex social problems. To tease this point out further, it is worth exploring in a little more detail the economic performance principle which is so central to the FME case, namely, the Pareto criterion of efficiency. According to this criterion, efficiency (i.e. Pareto-optimality) is achieved in a competitive market when economic exchanges take place to the point where it is impossible to make anyone better off without making somebody worse off. However, this approach provides a limited performance principle for environmental and social policy-making because it takes the original distribution of property rights as given – as we have seen, it only examines resource *allocation*, not property and income *distribution*. If we change the original distribution of property and income by, say, the imposition of new environmental taxes and charges, we will arrive at a different Pareto optimum solution in terms of resource allocation (Schmid, 1987: 218). The decision as to whether the original or the altered outcome is preferable is clearly a political decision, involving a consideration of not only efficiency questions but also questions concerning social justice and ecological sustainability. To argue, as FME economists do, against government environmental taxes that affect property and income, is effectively to endorse the existing distribution of property and income (something about which economists are *supposed* to remain neutral).

The above arguments can be illustrated by the simple example of an upstream polluter and a downstream fisher. The FME economist would suggest that it is preferable to create a market for water quality rights than for the government to regulate the pollution through, say, a tax designed to overcome the discrepancy between marginal private cost to the manufacturer and marginal social cost (i.e. to internalise externalities).

However, how this market operates, and the ecological outcome, will be a function of the distribution of rights and obligations with regard to the stream, and the individual preferences of the holders of those rights. For example, if the fisher owns the stream, then he or she can deny the polluter the use of the stream or charge the polluter for the use of the stream. If the fisher has a right to clean water, then he or she can demand damages from the polluter. However, if the polluter owns the stream, then the fisher would need to offer a price to the polluter that is worth more than the cost savings of continued pollution for the pollution to be discontinued. If the fisher cannot afford this price or is otherwise not bothered about the pollution, then the pollution will continue. In each case, the parties are free to choose when and how to exercise whatever property rights they may possess and to spend whatever income they may have at their disposal. However, the exercise of these rights will not necessarily result in the protection of river quality. Moreover, if one of the parties is poor and therefore in a weak bargaining position, then he or she will not be in a position to give effect to his or her preferences.

Free market environmentalism as an apologist for the status quo

Although FME economists place great store by the need for the creation of new property rights in respect of common environmental assets, they generally gloss over the contentious question as to how these rights might be defined and allocated in the first instance. In other words, the process of initial vesting and bidding is not an issue for FME economists; they simply assume that there is an economic and political process that allocates ownership. Greens, on the other hand, are vitally interested in questions concerning the ownership, control and distribution of environmental 'goods' and 'bads' and they insist that these issues remain firmly on the agenda.

The abalone fishery scenario sketched at the beginning of this chapter is a good case in point. The outline of this scenario, which is adapted from the ITQ experiment concerning the taking of paua (i.e. abalone) on the Chatham Islands, failed to mention the considerable conflict that has arisen concerning who should receive ITQs and at what price. It also failed to mention the contentious question as to how the total allowable catch should be regulated – for example, whether the government (i.e. taxpayers) should buy back a portion of each operator's quota or should simply enforce a proportionate drop in quotas from each operator in the industry without compensation. On the Chatham Islands, TTQs were allocated under the New Zealand Fisheries Act on the basis of catch histories, but this allocation has been contested by other interests who lay claim to the fishery. Local islanders who do not hold quotas are demanding some kind of return on the catch on the ground that the fishery belongs to everyone on the island, not just the fishers who hold ITQs. Maori representatives have also contested the quota system on the grounds that government ownership of the resource has not been established. Three sets of indigenous claims are now pending under the

Treaty of Waitangi. Yet FME economists are dismissive of these crucial questions. According to Peter Ackroyd and Rodney Hide, who have undertaken a case study of the ITQ system on the Chatham Islands from a FME perspective, the various claims for a stake in the fishery is lamentable because they involve 'replacing private investment with political [read unprofitable] investment' (Ackroyd and Hide, 1991: 202).

To recapitulate, the argument that a FME approach is preferable to government regulation because it 'depoliticises' resource use conflict by leaving the allocation of resources to the market must be seen as a thinly disguised endorsement of the existing distribution of property rights and income. In contrast, greens are concerned to ensure that questions concerning the nature and distribution of property rights are re-examined as part of the move towards a sustainable society. This is essential if we are to challenge and rethink the traditional liberal nexus between economic output and distributive justice. After all, basic liberal ideals such as possessive individualism, private property, limited government, and market freedom were born in, and have depended upon, a frontier setting which no longer holds. Traditionally, claims for distributive justice in a liberal setting have been appeased by the 'trickle down' effect, which requires that the stock of wealth continue to expand (even here relative inequalities in wealth and power are usually maintained). However, when we approach physical limits to growth, the prospects for social justice in such a setting are likely to become increasingly poor. Indeed, the long-term consequence of zealously pursuing the privatisation of environmental resources in an increasingly crowded world is likely to be the intensification of the already wide gap between the propertied and the propertyless, and the rich and the poor, both within and between nations.

A green stocktaking of FME

It is necessary to repeat that the above criticisms of FME should not be taken as a dismissal of the FME case. Rather, they merely counsel in favour of a very careful stocktaking of FME proposals. There may indeed be situations when facilitating commerce in certain ecological assets may be the only sensible means of achieving the desired ecological outcome.

For example, a FME solution readily lends itself to energy conservation. Amory Lovins has long advocated the advantages of creating a market in energy efficiency through the storage and sale of 'negawatts' (Lovins, 1977). Similarly, a tradeable emission permit scheme of the kind sketched in scenario three can prove to be both flexible and cost effective in those cases where the major sources of pollution can be identified, measured and monitored. However, as we have seen, where the number of polluters is large and where the sources of pollution are varied and difficult to identify, as is the case with greenhouse gases such as carbon dioxide and methane, the transaction costs involved in setting up a tradeable emissions scheme are likely to be prohibitive. In terms of domestic policy, a carbon tax is more likely to be a more effective policy option to reduce carbon dioxide emissions.

FME economists are also right to point to some of the inefficiencies of public sector management of environmental assets. For example, FME economists have identified government subsidies as having played a significant role in promoting poor land management, two major examples in Australia being the superphosphate bounty and native vegetation clearing subsidies (both of which have now been removed). Moreover, as we saw in scenario four, state forestry commissions in Australia have made substantial operating losses for lengthy periods. This can be attributed not just to a failure to reap the economic benefits of non-timber forest values (such as leisure amenities) as the FME economist advises, but also to the low royalties charged for timber resources. However, the operating losses of forestry commissions do not necessarily provide sufficient grounds for pursuing the privatisation option along the lines outlined in scenario four, as the situation can just as easily be remedied through better pricing policies with respect to timber. Moreover, as with the abalone scenario, the forest scenario glosses over the contentious question of what proportion of the forest should be vested in the respective private parties, and how much they should pay for the vesting. Here the forestry industry will have considerably more bargaining power than the Wilderness Society in terms of its ability to acquire rights to the forest, both at the initial vesting stage and in respect of its subsequent market transactions. Even if an equitable vesting could be negotiated, a more general case can be made that the state has a legitimate role to play as custodian of natural heritage on behalf of not only all members of society but also future generations and the non-human world, who cannot vote or otherwise register their preferences in the environmental policy-making process.

Indeed, when it comes to the preservation of biodiversity, FME solutions can be very problematic, particularly with regard to endangered species. For example, a FME argument of the kind illustrated in scenario one is currently gaining momentum in Zimbabwe with respect to saving the African elephant. The conflicting evidence and claims in this complex example (such as those concerning the accuracy of the estimates of the size of elephant populations, which will determine whether culling is indeed necessary to protect their habitat (Concar and Cole, 1992)) is such that it is too early to tell whether elephants must be forced to 'pay' for their protection with their own tusks, hides and meat rather than simply serve as admirable sights for tourists. These are knotty and painful questions for greens, who are decidedly ill at ease with FME solutions with regard to the protection of wilderness and biodiversity. To those who share an ecocentric persuasion, turning wildlife into a commodity is generally something that is to be fiercely resisted; after all, the flourishing of a rich and diverse nonhuman world is incompatible with the enslavement of that world. Few, if any, FME economists are likely to support a human slave trade, even if such trade may prove to be profitable. In other words, even FME economists would be prepared to concede that there are cases when moral arguments (such as respect for the autonomy and dignity of human beings) should override economic ones. Greens of a strong ecocentric persuasion are employing the same form of argument to oppose the ivory trade, only this time the argument rests on a respect for the autonomy and dignity of elephants. When it comes to showing consideration on moral grounds, greens see no reason why we should stop at the human border.

In any event, the commercial route is not even an option in respect of those species that are of no commercial value to humans. As we have seen, market rationality is incapable of valuing certain things, qualities, or beings *for their own sake*. Even the tourist trade is based on wildlife serving as scenery to those who are willing to pay for the view. It should be noted here that some environmental economists are now prepared to include in their cost/benefit analyses a non-use value known as 'existence value' which is a human valuation that certain species or ecosystems be allowed simply to exist. However, while these values might be usefully incorporated into more comprehensive cost/benefit analyses in project assessments, it is difficult to envisage *trade* in values of the kind contemplated by FME economists. To enable individuals to trade off the existence value of one species against another is in effect to grant extinction licences; from an ecocentric perspective, species preservation should be non-negotiable.

Conclusion

The foregoing examples are not meant to provide an exhaustive stocktaking of FME solutions. Indeed, there are many more areas of environmental policy that have not been covered (e.g. intractable wastes, transport and population). Moreover, this chapter has focused only on domestic environmental economic policy and has not addressed crucial economic issues in the international arena, such as 'dirty trade', Third World debt and overseas aid. Nonetheless, the domestic examples discussed are sufficient to make the major point of this chapter: that although there may be a range of specific environmental problems where a FME approach may prove to be the most appropriate solution, FME must be rejected by greens as a blanket solution to the ecological crisis. In short, the green message to the FME economist is that environmental and economic policy should be concerned with three broad goals – economic efficiency, social justice and ecological sustainability. To employ (and extend) another Herman Dalay analogy (Daly, 1991), if the economy were a boat, then FME economists might be able to assist in finding the optimal seating allocation of passengers to ensure that the boat remains on an even keel. However, they would not be able to assist those who were too poor to purchase seats; nor would they be able to provide seats to nonhuman species that have no commercial value. Finally, and this is the ultimate irony, they could do little to prevent the boat from sinking. The best they could do would be to ensure that the boat sank on an even keel.

References

Ackroyd, Peter and Rodney Hide (1991), 'A Case Study – Establishing Property Rights to Chatham Islands' Abalone (Paua)', in Alan Moran, Andrew Chisholm and Michael Porter (eds), *Markets, Resources and the Environment*, North Sydney: Allen & Unwin.

Anderson, Terry L. and Donald, R. Leal (1991), *Free Market Environmentalism*, San Francisco, CA: Pacific Research Institute for Public Policy.

Bennett, Jeff (1991a), 'Introduction', in Jeff Bennett and Walter Block (eds), *Reconciling Economics and the Environment*, Perth: Australian Institute for Public Policy, pp. 1–9.

Bennett, Jeff (1991b), 'Conclusion', in Jeff Bennett and Walter Block (eds), *Reconciling Economics and the Environment*, Perth: Australian Institute for Public Policy, pp. 269–87.

Bennett, Jeff and Walter Block (eds) (1991), *Reconciling Economics and the Environment*, Perth: Australian Institute for Public Policy.

Chant, John, McFetridge, Donald, Smith, Douglas and John Nurick (1991), 'The Economics of a Green Society', in Jeff Bennett and Walter Block (eds), *Reconciling Economics and the Environment*, Perth: Australian Institute for Public Policy, pp. 11–96.

Concar, David and Mary Cole (1992), 'Conservation and the Ivory Tower', *New Scientist*, No. 29, Feb. pp. 23–7.

Daly, Herman (1991), 'Elements of Environmental Macroeconomics', in Robert Costanza (ed.), *Ecological Economics: The Science and Management of Sustainability*, New York: Columbia University Press.

Daly, Herman and John, Cobb Jr (1989), *For the Common Good*, Boston, MA: Beacon Press.

Eckersley, Robyn (1991), 'Green Economics: Overcoming the Credibility Gap', Paper presented at the International Conference on Human Ecology, Gothenberg, 9–14 June 1991.

Eckersley, Robyn (1992), 'Green Versus Ecosocialist Economic Programmes: The Market Rules OK'? *Political Studies*, Vol. XL, No. 2, pp. 315–33. (Jon Mulberg's rejoinder to this article (ibid.) was not to hand when the present article went to press.)

Ekins, Paul (with the assistance of Mayer Hillman and Robert Hutchinson) (1992), *Wealth Beyond Measure: An Atlas of New Economics*, London: Gaia Books.

Jacobs, Michael (1991), *The Green Economy: Environment, Sustainable Development and the Politics of the Future*, London: Pluto Press.

Leeson, Susan, M. (1979), 'Philosophic Implications of the Ecological Crisis: The Authoritarian Challenge to Liberalism', *Polity*, No. 11, pp. 303–18.

Lovins, A. (1977), *Soft Energy Paths*, Harmondsworth: Penguin.

Moran, Alan (1991), 'Addressing the Limits of Market Solutions', in Jeff Bennett and Walter Block (eds), *Reconciling Economics and the Environment*, Perth: Australian Institute for Public Policy, pp. 249–68.

Moran, Alan, Chisholm, Andrew and Michael Porter (eds) (1991), *Markets, Resources and the Environment*, North Sydney: Allen & Unwin.

O'Riordan, Timothy (1981), *Environmentalism*, 2nd edn, London: Pion.

Pearce, David (1992), 'Green Economics', *Environmental Values*, Vol. 1, No. 1, pp. 3–13.

Pearce, David, Markandya, Anil and Edward, B. Barbier (1989), *Blueprint for a Green Economy*, London: Earthscan.

Porter, Michael (1991), 'Economics and the Environment – the Australian Debate', in Alan Moran, Andrew Chisholm and Michael Porter (eds), *Markets, Resources and the Environment*, North Sydney: Allen & Unwin, pp. 1–15.

Schmid, Alan A. (1987), *Property, Power and Public Choice: An Inquiry into Law and Economics*, New York: Praeger.

10 Public choice, institutional economics, environmental goods

John O'Neill

Most of the recent work on mainstream environmental economics has centred on the use of cost–benefit analysis in environmental policy formulation, either as an object of defence (Pearce *et al.*, 1989) or of criticism (Jacobs, 1991; O'Neill, 1993a; Sagoff, 1988). Cost–benefit analysis is taken to represent the standard attempt to bring the environment into orthodox market-based approaches to policy-making. It is defended on the grounds that it resolves the problems of 'market failures' that arise when real markets depart from 'ideal markets' which, according to the fundamental theorem of neo-classical economics, yield Pareto-optimal outcomes.

'Market failures' due to externalities or the existence of public goods are typically invoked as the rationale for the use of cost–benefit analysis to realise optimal outcomes by other, normally bureaucratic, means. Of special significance to environmental problems, its supporters note that it allows one to place a shadow price on environmental goods, preferences for which are not revealed in real markets (Pearce and Turner 1990: 41; Pearce *et al.*, 1989: 5ff.). Criticism of cost–benefit analysis often focuses just on this attempt to treat preferences for environmental goods as consumer preferences, and, hence, in particular, on the attempt to place a shadow price on environmental goods by ascertaining individuals' willingness to pay for them or accept compensation for their loss. Thus Sagoff, for example, distinguishes the preference an individual has as a consumer from those she has a citizen. The former express a person's private wants, the latter her public values, her judgements about 'what is right or good or appropriate in the circumstances' (Sagoff, 1988: 9). Thus go the main lines of the existing debate.

The challenge of public choice theory

A central problem with this debate, in particular for those who are critical of orthodox market-based approaches to environmental concerns, and I include myself in that category, is that cost–benefit analysis has its opponents within mainstream economics who are still committed to market-based solutions to environmental problems. These include not only the Austrian adversaries of the neo-classical paradigm, but also – from within the neo-classical paradigm – the proponents of public choice theory.[1] Whatever the influence of cost–benefit analysis as a justificatory ritual within policy-making processes, much of the most rigorous theoretical work within neo-classical economics represented by public choice theory is sceptical of its theoretical justifications and dismissive of it in its practice.[2] Moreover, many of the criticisms it makes of cost–benefit analysis are equally applicable to those of its opponents who, like Sagoff, appeal to a political realm inhabited by morally motivated citizens.

From the public choice perspective, the central weakness of cost–benefit analysis is its assumption of benign state actors. Cost–benefit analysis is a tool employed by bureaucrats, who never, in practice, leave the office and who standardly impute preferences to those affected by a policy rather than discover what they are. The results of cost–benefit analysis are then employed by politicians to justify their policies. The defender of cost–benefit analysis assumes that both bureaucrats and politicians are benevolent actors concerned to realise the common good or welfare of all (Olson, 1965: 98). However, making that assumption entails that the axioms that define the rational actor in neo-classical theory cease to apply behind the office doors of the bureaucrat or politician. The actors are no longer taken to make rational choices that maximise their own utility: they rather become altruistic channels through which the maximisation of the general utility is achieved. The axioms of neo-classical theory are assumed not to apply in the non-market setting of politics: 'The conventional wisdom holds that the market is made up of private citizens to trying benefit themselves, but that government is concerned with something called the public interest' (Tullock, 1970: v).

The starting point of public choice theory is the denial of that assumption. There is no reason to assume that what is true of actors in the market ceases to be true when they enter a non-market situation. Thus Buchanan writes: ' "Public choice" . . . is really the application and extension of economic theory to the realm of political and governmental choices' (Buchanan, 1978: 3).[3] The axioms that characterise the rational agent in economic life should be taken to apply also to the explanation of the behaviour of bureaucrat and politician in their political activities. There is no reason to assume that state actors suddenly become different and more benign when they enter the arena of government. If it is true that individuals act as rational self-interested agents in the marketplace, 'the inference should be that they will also act similarly in other and nonmarket behavioral settings' (Buchanan, 1972: 22). The assumption made in neo-classical defences of cost–benefit analysis of benign state actors represents a failure of theoretical rigour and nerve to apply consistently their axioms defining the rational actor.

For public choice theories cost–benefit analysis does not and could not produce the optimal outcomes of 'ideal markets' by other means. The state actors act to maximise their own interests not the 'public interest'. Bureaucrats are taken to aim at maximising the size of their bureau budget, since that is correlated with their utility:

Among the several variables that may enter the bureaucrat's motives are: salary, perquisites of the office, public reputation, power, patronage, output of the bureau, ease of making changes, and ease of managing the bureau. All except the last two are a positive function of the total budget of the bureau during the bureaucrat's tenure... A bureaucrat's utility need not be strongly dependent on every one of the variables which increase with budget, but it must be positively and continuously associated with its size.

(Niskanen, 1973: 22–3)[4]

Likewise, in explanation of the behaviour of voters and politicians it is standardly assumed that voters act like consumers and political candidates like firms. Candidates aim to maximise votes and hence gain political office, voters to maximise the satisfaction of preferences for those goods the state can deliver.[5]

Once economic theory is applied to politics, the state no longer appears as a beneficent representative of the public good. Rather, it is argued that the self-interested behaviour of bureaucrat, politician and voter lead, if unchecked by institutional reform, to the constant expansion of government expenditure and provision, producing outcomes that are irrational and inefficient. 'Market failure' gives way to 'government failure' (Brennan and Buchanan, 1980; Buchanan 1975: ch. 9; Buchanan and Wagner, 1977; Niskanen, 1971; Wolf, 1987). The public choice theorist typically appeals to a free market economic policy, which attempts to rectify market failure, not by using the state to realise efficient outcomes by bureaucratic means, but by institutional changes within the market (Buchanan and Tullock, 1962: ch. 5). 'Government failure' is thereby avoided.

The public choice response to environmental problems that arise from 'market failure' – externalities, public goods and the absence of a market price on many environmental goods – has, then, been to find solutions within the market sphere itself. Direct government intervention is not required to solve problems of market failure. Rather, they can be resolved by a redefinition of property rights within the market. Thus, Coase's theorem (Coase, 1960) is invoked to resolve the problem of externalities: given perfect competition and the absence of transaction costs[6] solutions to negative externalities, for example pollution, are possible through a process of bargaining, if property rights are properly assigned either to the 'damaging' agent or the 'affected' agent. If the damaging agent has the rights, then the affected agent can compensate him not to continue the damaging activity; if the affected agent has property rights, the damaging agent can compensate her to bear the damage. Thus, for example, in the former case a pollution sufferer might compensate the polluter, in the latter, the polluter might compensate the sufferer.

Similarly, where unpriced public goods such as clean air and water exist, the optimal solution is not to place a shadow price on the goods, but to define property rights, if not directly over them, then over their use, for example, through pollution permits: thus tradeable pollution permits which allow markets in pollution are defended on the grounds that they address the interests of the actors directly, and hence do not make unrealistic demands on conscience or law; that they encourage pollution to diminish where it is cheapest for it do so; and that they even allow those with preferences for non-pollution to express those preferences directly within the market. (See Dales (1968) and Anderson and Leal (1991). For useful critical surveys of market solutions see Rose-Ackerman (1977) and Eckersley (1993).) The problems of environmental damage consequent on 'market failure' can be resolved not by treating environmental goods as *if* they had a price, but by directly bringing them within the realm of market contract. The problems have a solution within the sphere of voluntary market exchange and without recourse to government intervention that leads simply to 'government failure' worse than the failures it is supposed to cure.

What is dead and what is living in critiques of orthodox environmental economics?

How should the critic of orthodox market-based approaches to environmental problems react to this theoretically more robust and rigorous defence of the pricing of environmental goods? How much of the criticism aimed at cost–benefit analysis still hits the public choice alternative? An initial point to note is that if the public choice criticism of the benign view of the state assumed by cost–benefit analysis is correct, then it applies equally well to some of the major critics of cost–benefit analysis, most notably to Sagoff. Thus Sagoff, even more than the defender of cost–benefit analysis, assumes that when actors enter the political sphere they take on a quite different personality: that self-interested consumers become citizens concerned with the public good, that politicians express the values of citizens in public law, and that bureaucrats quite neutrally administer that legal expression of public values.

While, as will become evident, I have deep misgivings about the assumptions of public choice theory, it is difficult not to have sympathy with their scepticism about any theory that simply assumes that political actors are benign. Indeed, such scepticism need not be associated with free-market economics. Thus for example, the same scepticism is expressed in a very different political idiom in Marx's early critique of Hegel's benign view of bureaucracy: the bureaucracy does not stand above the egoistic domain of civil society, representing a universal interest; rather it is itself of civil society, the appeal to a universal interest disguising the pursuit of its own interests (Marx, 1843).[7] While it may be false that actors are necessarily and always motivated by narrow concerns with self-advancement, one cannot simply assume in advance that they are not.

However, while there is something right about the public choice critique of state benevolence, other environmental criticisms of cost–benefit analysis, if they are successful, do have purchase against the public choice perspective. For example the claim that markets cannot properly incorporate concern for the interests of future humans or of existing and future non-humans which necessarily cannot be directly expressed in market choices, still has power (O'Neill, 1993a: ch. 4). Of more general theoretical significance, there are important assumptions that public choice theory shares with cost–benefit analysis, especially concerning the criteria for what constitutes an 'optimal' outcome of either market transactions or government policy. In so far as both are founded in neo-classical theory, they both view as 'optimal' an outcome that most efficiently meets the given wants of the parties concerned: Pareto-optimal outcomes or potential Pareto-optimal outcomes, either in their pure economic forms or modified by some distributional constraint, are taken to be optimal as such. Furthermore, while Austrian economic theory departs from neo-classical standards of optimality, it shares the assumption that any principle of 'optimal' outcomes must itself be purely want-regarding: it takes as given the wants people happen to have and concerns itself with the satisfaction of those wants (Barry, 1990: 38).

The choice of want-regarding principles of optimality is standardly justified on one of three grounds:

1   Meta-ethical: A subjectivist account of the nature of ethical utterances, according to which they are merely expressions of preferences, entails that principles of public policy be want-regarding.
2   Welfare: Individual well-being consists in the satisfaction of the wants agents either have, or would have if fully informed, and hence public policy which is concerned with the optimal realisation of welfare must be want-regarding.
3   Liberal: Public institutions should be neutral between different conceptions of the good, and hence should not be concerned with the cultivation of 'desirable' wants, but only with the satisfaction of whatever wants individuals happen to have. The alternative classical perfectionist view, which conceives of institutions in terms of the pursuit of some particular conception of the good life is, at best, authoritarian, and at worst totalitarian.

At the centre of many critiques of mainstream environmental economics has been a rejection of the purely want-regarding principles of optimality it assumes and thus a rejection also of the defences that are offered of them (O'Neill, 1993a: chs 5–7; Sagoff, 1988). Public policy should be concerned not with the satisfaction of given wants, but with the promotion of those institutions that cultivate preferences for what *is* good. I will not rehearse here in detail the arguments for that position and against those for a purely want-regarding public policy. Very briefly, I believe one should respond to the arguments outlined above as follows:

1   Against the meta-ethical justification: A subjectivist account of ethical utterances, even if true, would itself be neutral between first-order principles of public policy, which themselves are on that view an expression of preferences; there is nothing in a subjectivist meta-ethics that rules out the 'preference' to cultivate certain wants (O'Neill, 1993a: 64–5).
2   Against the welfare justification: The view that preference satisfactionis, of itself, constitutive of well-being cannot be sustained, for desires answer to goods, not goods to desires. I want objects because I believe they are good; I do not believe they are good because I want them (*Aristotle Metaphysics*, 1072a: 2). Well-being is realised not by satisfying given wants, but by educating our capacities of judgement and our desires, such that we come to prefer what is good (O'Neill, 1993a: 65–82).

3   Against the liberal justification: There is no necessary relationship between an authoritarian or totalitarian politics and the defence of institutions in terms of their fostering a particular conception of the good. Any defensible account of the good life needs to recognise the internal plurality of the goods that are constitutive of it. Any defensible account of liberalism needs to engage with a defence of substantive values, in particular that of autonomy, and of an account of the institutions that foster them. The best defence of liberalism is one that returns it to its perfectionist roots, that holds with J.S. Mill that 'the first question in respect to any political institutions is, how far they tend to foster in members of the community the various desirable qualities moral and intellectual' (Mill, n.d.: 29).[8]

While I do not offer here a detailed elaboration of these responses, there is an assumption that underlies them which does need defence in the present context. The second and third responses depend on a particular view of the relationship between preferences and institutions that public choice theory explicitly denies. They assume that different institutions promote different preferences. The political problem given this assumption is to answer the question Mill asks: what institutions foster desirable preferences? With respect to environmental problems, what institutions nurture concerns for environmental goods? Public choice theory denies both the assumption utlined and the question that is consequent upon it. Preferences are taken to be prior to and explanatory of institutions. Individuals both in market and non-market settings act as rational self-interested agents. The question which, on the public choice account, needs to be answered is this: what institutions should we construct given that individuals are rational self-interested agents, who pursue their own ends both in the marketplace, and in 'nonmarket behavioral settings' (Buchanan, 1972: 22)? In the next section I defend the Millian assumption and argue against its modern public choice opponent.

Institutional economics: the old and the new

Public choice theory is often presented as a part of a revival of institutional economics. It represents a response, from within the neo-classical tradition, to the neglect of institutional questions in that tradition. Thus, problems concerning the institutional conditions in which markets operate – for example, concerning the definition of property rights against which market transactions take place; problems concerning the consequences of certain institutional forms, such as the unrestrained operation of existing political and bureaucratic institutions; and finally normative problems concerning the specification of optimal institutional arrangements – all become central from the public choice perspective. While this renewed focus on institutions is to be welcomed, the neo-classical approach to institutions is still liable to strike those of us educated outside this perspective as oddly skewed. There is a clear difference between this new institutional economics and the older institutional economics that traditionally opposed the neo-classicals' institutional myopia (Hodgson, 1988, 1993). I include within the category of old institutional economics not only the American tradition of institutionalism which included Veblen (Veblen, 1919), Commons (Commons, 1934) and others, but also that economics that took place within a broadly Aristotelian tradition, including the work of both Marx and Polanyi,[9] as well as much of the classical economic tradition.[10]

The central difference between the old institutionalism and the new neo-classical variant is that which I outlined at the end of the last section. The new institutionalism represents the extension of neo-classical theory into new domains and hence begins with the conventional axioms that define the rational agent within neo-classical theory. In doing so it starts with the assumption that preferences are given. The explanatory problem is to explain the emergence and nature of institutions given that assumption. Reference to institutions appears only in the *explanandum*, not in the *explanans*. The central normative problem becomes that of how to fashion institutions given that individuals are egoists.

Old institutionalism differs from the new in that it allows individuals' preferences to be explained by reference to the institutional context in which they operate: references to institutions appear in the *explanans*, not just in *explanandum*. Given those assumptions the normative problem becomes that of Mill outlined at the end of the last section: to determine what institutions should be sustained in order that individuals develop desirable preferences. That assumption underlies the classical political thought of Aristotle. The end of the polis is the good life (*Aristotle Politics*, 1280b: 38f.), where the good life is characterised in terms of the virtues: hence, the best political association is that which enables every person to act virtuously and live happily (*Aristotle Politics*, 1324a: 22). Hence also his influential criticism of the market in terms of its encouragement of the desire for the unlimited acquisition of goods and thus the vice of *pleonexia*, the desire to have more than is proper (*Aristotle Politics*, Book 1, chs 8–9) (for a discussion see Polandi (1957c), Meikle (1979) and O'Neill (1992)). The old institutional economics in the wide sense outlined above is the inheritor of this classical tradition.

Old and new institutional start from very different explanatory assumptions, and generate distinct normative questions. Which version of institutional is to be preferred? The question, in so far as it concerns explanation, is in the end one that has to be answered by reference to the canons of rational inquiry – adequacy to empirical evidence, explanatory power, consistency and so on. However, at present a strong presumption must be made for the old institutional. I say this, not only because of the absence of empirical support for many of the standard public choice positions (Dearlove, 1989), but because the new institutionalism has failed in any case to carry out its eliminative project of deleting references to institutions within its *explanans*. Reference to institutional contexts is smuggled in at the level of its assumptions about individuals' conceptions of their interests. Thus while public choice theorists claim to start from preferences that exist prior to institutions, their accounts of the nature of the self-interested preferences of individuals, of their 'utility function', changes according to the institutions they are describing. Within the market it is typically assumed to consist in the acquisition of consumer goods; within the political domain, in power through the acquisition of votes; within bureaucracy, promotion and advancement in status within the bureaucratic order.

Two points need to be made about these shifting assumptions about the actors' conceptions of self-interest. The first and more basic is that a simple and now familiar observation about the characterization of action entails that certain interests cannot even be specified outside a particular institutional context. Consider the politician's interest in the acquisition of votes. Individuals can only perform the actions of voting or acquiring votes when they are embedded in a particular position in an institutional context: it is *qua* citizen that an individual can felicitously vote, and only *qua* candidate that an individual can be elected. Moreover, the action of voting itself depends on a complex set of institutions which embody and are constituted by particular shared understandings. Only within certain institutional settings can the behaviours of marking crosses on papers, the raising of hands and so on be understood as 'voting'. In others, say, the raising of the hand in the auction room or the lecture hall, or the marking of crosses against persons' names in a classroom, they have different meanings. Hence, an interest in 'acquiring votes' or 'winning an election' is an interest that is only possible within a specific institutional setting. Similar points apply to the interest in 'promotion' and that of 'buying' or 'selling' 'consumer goods': such interests themselves presuppose an institutional context. (For a classic discussion of this familiar point, which is of particular relevance for the discussion here, see Taylor (1971). It is worth adding here that not only do assumptions about institutional context enter into the descriptions of interests, but they also arrive in the more substantive assumptions about the boundaries between different institutions in the modern world. It is, for example, simply assumed that votes and political office are not the sort of things that, in modern society, can be bought or sold. See, for example, Buchanan and Tullock (1962: ch. 9).)

The second point about public choice assumptions goes beyond the mere possibility of specifying interests to substantive explanatory problems: that is, in defining individual preferences differently in different contexts, public choice theory implicitly assumes, quite correctly, that different institutional settings foster different conceptions of self interest. Within the market setting, interests are defined in terms of the acquisition of property rights over objects; within the political domain, power is assumed to be the object of a person's interest; in the realm of bureaucracy, it is identified as the acquisition of status through promotion. The explanatory claims of the older institutionalism enter as unannounced, unnoticed and unwelcome guests into the new institutionalist's assumptions about the 'utility function' of the agent in different contexts. At the explanatory level existing public choice theories have not eliminated reference to institutions from their *explanans*. Substantive explanatory work has already been done at the level of claims about individuals' conceptions of their interests.

The implicit acknowledgement of the way in which different institutions foster different conceptions of an individual's interests has important implications for the public choice theorists' claim that they are simply extending the axioms of neo-classical theory concerning the rational self-interested agent into new domains. Two points need to be made here. First, given a full specification of the conceptions of individual self interest, it is simply not true that one can transfer assumptions about self-interested behaviour in the market to other domains. In other institutional contexts, quite different conceptions of interests are apparent, which can and do conflict with that fostered by the market.

Consider the old conflict between aristocratic and market institutions. In traditional aristocratic societies, honour is institutionally defined as the object of one's interest: to sacrifice one's honour for money would be a sign of vulgarity.[11] This conflict between the bourgeois world of markets and the aristocratic world of honour runs through nineteenth-century literature, and any adequate explanation of the cultural shifts in eighteenth and nineteenth century Britain would have to make reference to it. Or to take another example, consider the question of the commercialisation of science. It would be a mistake to see this either, in the fashion of public choice theory, as simply a way of taming 'professionals' who, under the guise of 'scientific values' conspire against the public in the pursuit of the same set of interests they have as 'market actors'; or, as opponents of public choice might have it, as an invasion of a purely 'altruistic' practice (science) by a sphere of egoistic behaviour (markets). It rather involves a shift in individuals' conceptions of their interests. In traditional scientific institutions one's interests were characterised in terms of recognition by peers of a significant contribution to one's discipline, recognition achieved through publication in a peer reviewed journal (Merton, 1968: 601; Ravetz, 1973). Commercialised science brings changes in the nature of intellectual property rights such that publication is redefined as an act in conflict with one's interests (O'Neill, 1990). Hence the spread of university instructions *not* to publish results, since to do so will be to miss the 'benefit in material terms from the intellectual property you have produced' (from a circular quoted in full in O'Neill (1992)). The assumptions about self-interested behaviour in the market cannot be transferred to other institutional contexts. In different roles in different institutions agents have quite distinct conceptions of their interests.

A second point, however, needs to be added to the first. It is far from clear just what assumptions about the economic agent in the market a public choice theorist is supposed to be taking over into non-market domains. The axioms that define the rational agent in neo-classical theory are a quite minimal attempt to characterise consistency in preferences, a point sometimes noted in its defence (Peacock, 1992). The rational economic agent is assumed to have preferences that are complete (i.e. agents can express preferences over any and all goods); reflexive (i.e. every good is as good as itself) and transitive (i.e. such that if x is preferred to y and y to z then x is preferred to z). The rational economic agent, thus defined, is then assumed to be concerned to maximise the satisfaction of a set of preferences, the 'utility function' in neo-classical jargon, under the constraint of a finite budget. Now, while I believe some of the neo-classical assumptions should be rejected, for example that concerning transitivity (O'Neill, 1993a: 111–15), I do not believe that they should be rejected because they assume an 'egoistic' individual. That individuals are 'self-interested' in the sense that they are concerned to satisfy a consistent set of preferences under budget constraints does not imply that agents are egoists in any strong sense of the term. It all depends what preferences they have: 'The postulate that an agent is characterized by preferences rules out neither the saint nor Genghis Khan' (Hahn and Hollis, 1979: 4).

The rhetorical power of public choice theory depends on its smuggling in through the 'utility function' a particular egoistic characterisation of individuals' preferences. Egoism, in the sense in which it is usually employed, either as a term of derogation, or as a term of political and ethical 'realism', depends on a particular account of the preferences individuals are taken to have. The egoist in the normal sense is an individual who desires only the possession of a narrow set of goods that can be possessed to the exclusion of others: 'the biggest share of money, honours and bodily pleasures' (*Aristotle Nicomachean Ethics*, 1168b: 16) to take Aristotle's list, to which one might add 'political power'. Public choice theory does assume such an egoist with preferences for this narrow range of goods. In doing so it inherits the late eighteenth-century shift in the language to describe the unlimited acquisitiveness, in which the classical terms *pleonexia*, greed, avarice and love of lucre were replaced by the term 'interest', and hence 'self-interest' was redefined in a narrow fashion (Hirschman, 1977: 31–42). However, in taking for granted this concept of self-interest, it goes beyond the basic formal axioms of neo-classical theory, and implicity introduces substantive claims about the content of agents' preferences. Moreover, in doing so its 'realism' becomes quite unrealistic.

To an egoist thus conceived the classical response, articulated by Aristotle, forms the proper reply: they have simply misidentified what the the goods of life are (*Aristotle Nicomachean Ethics*, Book ix, ch. 8). Thus, for example, those who are exclusively concerned with the unlimited acquisition of money are improperly called rational economic agents: they are neither 'rational' nor, in the classical sense of the term, 'economic'. The term 'rational economic agent' thus used is a technical euphemism for which the proper description is 'moneygrubber'.[12] Similar points apply to the professional politician driven simply by the desire for political power, the 'politico' or 'hack', or bureaucrat driven by the desire for promotion, the 'careerist'. The derogatory terms employed to describe those individuals express the proper attitude one should have towards them. They are individuals with a hopelessly narrow view of the goods that life has to offer. Moreover, contrary to the 'realism' of public choice, and despite the increasing colonisation of the non-market domains by the market, the recognition that this is so has not entirely disappeared.

It is false to assume that since individuals act as narrowly interested agents in the marketplace, 'the inference should be that they will also act similarly in other and nonmarket behavioral settings' (Buchanan, 1972: 22). Individuals are motivated by a variety of ends outside the marketplace: the scientist, by the desire to solve some problem; the ornithologist, by the desire to sustain a habitat in which a variety of birds can be found; the climber, by the desire to climb some new line on a rock face; the musician, by the desire to play a new and technically demanding work; the parent, by the desire to see her child happy and fulfilled; and so on along an endless list. None of this is to deny the existence of egoistic individuals. It is to deny that one can reduce individuals' interests to that narrow set of preferences exhibited in the marketplace and the centres of political power.

The weaknesses of public choice assumptions in this regard are most apparent in their treatment of associations. (The classic public choice treatment of associations is Olson (1965): see also Olson (1982).) The term 'association' can refer to a variety of formal and informal societies that are neither direct competitive actors within the market, nor direct competitors for political office, although they can and do have effects on both markets and political outcomes. They include voluntary associations that pursue some particular good – natural history societies, climbing clubs and the like; associations that exist within the economic sphere, but in which actors engage with one another in non-market ways – trade unions, professional associations and so on; organisations that serve some particular interest that is effected by state action – pressure groups and some charities; and finally public institutions that are often financed by the state, but are not of the state – universities, schools, hospitals, conservation councils and so on. Such associations form a mixed bag and it is problematic to treat all under the same heading – the last group of institutions in particular fits uneasily with others. Public choice is at its most vulnerable to empirical criticism in its treatment of voluntary associations. Their very existence is a problem given the assumption of a rational actor able to free-ride on the benefits they might bring. As Hirschman notes of Olson's influential *The Logic of Collective Action* (1965):

> Olson proclaimed the impossibility of collective action for large groups... at the precise moment when the Western world was about to be engulfed by an unprecedented wave of public movements, marches, protests, strikes and ideologies.
>
> (Hirschman, 1985: 79)[13]

That empirical weakness is a consequence of its assumptions about the nature of 'self-interest'. In public choice theory all associations are treated 'interest groups', where the term 'interest' is understood in the narrow sense in which it has come to be defined since the eighteenth century.[14] Given that narrow definition of interests pursued by associations, the problem becomes one of how an individual would incur the costs of joining an association rather than free-ride on others. The attempt to reduce all associations to interest groups in that sense is, however, a mistake. It fails to make proper distinctions between different kinds of associations. Some do exist simply to pursue some narrowly defined interest. However, others exist to pursue some good or 'interest' in the wider sense of the term: consider the wide variety of natural history, conservation and environmental associations. Still others aim both at particular interests and some good: professional associations, even where they are conspiracies against the public, are not *merely* conspiracies as the public choice theorist supposes – they also have an interest in the goods the profession serves, be it medicine, education, philosophy, economics, nature conservation or whatever. Finally, other associations might begin in 'self-interest' narrowly, but develop other interests whilst in their pursuit, for example in fellowship itself.

Not only do proponents of public choice theory fail to distinguish between different kinds of association, but they make a corresponding failure to distinguish between the different goods or interests an individual may have as a member of an association. A member of an association concerned with the pursuit of some practice, say science, can have two kinds of interests: first, in some achievement internal to the practice itself, in some particular empirical discovery or theoretical development; second, in some external good the association offers, in some form of recognition, in some institutional position, in an increased salary or whatever.[15] The public choice theorist, in implicitly defining interests in a narrow manner, has to treat the first kind of interest as 'really' simply instrumental for the second. However, that is quite implausible. Thus, in many settings, it is difficult to get individuals to fill administrative positions, even where it means promotion, because that would involve sacrificing time on the internal goals that really interest them. Moreover, some of the apparently narrower desires for possessing external goods an institution has to offer have their basis in interests internal to the practice it promotes: a scientist, for example, may desire promotion not out of mere careerism, but because it is a form of recognition of her achievements by competent peers.

The weakness of public choice theory when it is applied to associations is that it is precisely in associations that the wide variety of motivations and interests that move individuals is exhibited. In the market individuals do exhibit a preference for the acquisition of consumer goods; in politics, as it exists today, an interest in the achievement of power does predominate, and in bureaucratic organisations an interest in career advancement is a disposition that is fostered. However, in other associations a preference for a wide variety of goods is apparent. Moreover, as the old institutionalism asserts, such preferences are not givens that are brought to the associations. They are interests that are fostered by them. Indeed, just as interests in amassing votes is not possible outside a particular institutional context, so many of the interests fostered by associations could not exist without some such institional context. Thus, as Raz notes, it is only in the context of particular social forms that an interest in 'bird watching' is possible:

> some comprehensive goals require social institutions for their very possibility. One cannot pursue a legal career except in a society governed by law, one cannot practise medicine except in a society in which such a practice is recognised ... Activities which do not appear to acquire their character from social forms in fact do so. Bird watching seems to be what any sighted person in the vicinity of birds can do. And so he can, except that that would not make him into a bird watcher. He can be that only in a society where this, or at least some other animal tracking activities, are recognized as leisure activities, and which furthermore share certain attitudes to natural life generally.
>
> (Raz, 1986: 310–11)

Not only are such interests in a wider set of goods distinct from those exhibited in institutional contexts such as the market or politics, but a commitment to such goods is defined in terms of a refusal to make them commensurable with goods that satisfy the narrow set of interests that define those contexts. Hence, the now well-documented refusals of individuals to respond to willingness to pay surveys on environmental goods. Clearly, on one level, such refusals are not relevant to public choice theory which is not in the business of shadow pricing. However the refusals are of relevance at another level. They uncover widespread and proper convictions about the kinds of things that can be bought and sold. There are commitments that are central to the well-being of agents that are partially constituted by a refusal to put a price on goods. The person who could put a price on friendship, simply could not have friends. They simply do not understand the loyalties that are constitutive of friendship. Moreover they are thereby excluded from much of what is best in human life. Likewise with respect to other goods that individuals value, including significant places, environments and non-human beings (O'Neill, 1993a: 118–22; Raz, 1986: ch. 13). Thus, whatever the truth of Aristotle's comments about 'the many' of the classical Greek world – and one suspects aristocratic prejudices in this regard – the many of the modern world do not exhibit a concern only for that narrow set of goods that is characteristic of the egoist: money, status and power. Individuals engage in a large array of non-market and non-political social associations and practices, and have a correspondingly broader conception of their interests than that ascribed to them by the public choice theorist. The extent to which the behaviour of actors in the market and political world is at all civilised depends on those wider social engagements.

In its saner, more conciliatory and, in the proper sense of the term, 'realistic' moments, public choice theory grants that individuals are not always egoists in the uarrow sense, that they arc not solely motivated by the desire for money, power and status. The claim is restated in a normative way: that, while it may in fact be false that all persons are egoists, driven by avarice, we need to assume, in the design of good institutions, that they are.[16] This normative claim contains a partial truth. The problem of the vulnerability of institutions to the vicious, to the careerist, and to the lover of lucre and power, are problems that any plausible social and political theory has to take seriously.[17] It does not follow, however, that institutions must thereby be designed around the assumption that all persons are thus motivated. The institutions that one would arrive at by that principle are themselves likely to foster the very vices they are designed to check.

One important instance of this point is the familiar case against pure contractarian accounts of good institutions. The contractarian begins from the assumption that institutions are to be designed around egoists: the only defensible institutions are those which narrowly interested individuals would agree to enter through voluntary contract. The problem with that position is that 'a contract is not sufficient unto itself' (Durkheim, 1964: 215): contracts themselves are only possible against the background of non-contractual relations which both build and depend on trust, where trust is an attitude which it is irrational to take given the assumption of universal egoism. The point is one familiar to conservative political thought concerning the ethical presuppositions of the market. It is stated thus by Burke:

> If, as I suspect, modern letters owe more than they are always willing to own to ancient manners, so do other interests which we value full as much as they are worth. Even commerce, and trade, and manufacture, the gods of our oeconomical politicians, are themselves perhaps but creatures; are themselves but effects, which, as first causes, we chose to worship. They certainly grew under the same shade in which learning flourished. They too may decay without their natural protecting principles.
>
> (1826: 155)

Without a background of non-contractual relations, contract itself is impossible.

Universal egoism, in the derogatory sense of the term in which it refers to an interest in the acquisition of possessive goods, is neither a truth about individual behaviour in all institutional settings, nor a sound principle of institutional design. The new institutionalism needs to give way to the old.

Institutional economics and environmental goods: an agenda

Having attempted to bury public choice theory, as part of a proper funeral oration I return to two earlier points uttered in its praise. First, it is quite right to insist, against both cost–benefit analysis and many of its recent environmental critics, that one cannot simply assume a benign state inhabited by beneficent state actors, politicians and bureaucrats, who answer either to the preferences of consumers or to the judgements of morally upright voters. Second, the public choice theorist is right to insist that one consider questions about the institutional framework in which environmental decisions take place. However, those questions need to be widened beyond those the public choice theorist allows. The problem is not that of either explaining or designing institutions given universal avarice, but that of examining the ways in which institutions define and foster different conceptions of interests. Individuals' conceptions of their interests need to be the end point of analysis, not its starting point. Thus explanatory and normative questions posed by new institutionalism should be replaced by those posed by old institutionalism. The central questions to be asked of an institutional environmental economics are these: What institutional frameworks develop a concern for future generations and the non-human world? What frameworks encourage rational argument and debate about environmental matters?

Fortunately, to ask those questions is not to raise issues in a theoretical vacuum. Thus work already exists that starts from those questions in so far as they are concerned with future generations. For example, in a recent historical paper Duncan remarks that 'the institutional context in which agronomic decisions are taken should be the *first* thing to be characterized in any general agricultural history' (Duncan, 1992: 76 (emphasis in the original)). Whatever the truth or falsity of his account of the relationship between different forms of lease holding, property ownership, and sustainable agriculture, he is asking the right question. One of the first things that needs to be characterised in an environmental economics, quite generally, is the institutional conditions of sustainable economic practices: in particular, what institutions foster in individuals a wide conception of their interest that encourages sustainable practices? What institutions undermine such conceptions?[18] In raising those question Duncan is returning to explanatory and normative problems that were central to eighteenth century debates on commercial society: the civic humanist critics of commercial society were concerned in part precisely with the effects of the commercial mobilisation of property on links between generations (Pocock, 1975, 1985). Neither has that concern ever entirely disappeared. For example, the effects of the mobilisation of land and labour is a central theme in Polanyi's criticism of market society (Polanyi, 1957a: chs 14–15).

Where institutional economics is less developed is on the relationship between institutions and attitudes to the non-human world. Here more research is needed. Economics needs to move from concern either about shadow pricing or about real pricing, towards some appreciation of the institutional conditions in which individuals begin to appreciate the value of that environment.

Where would that emphasis on the institutional context for environmental goods lead? For reasons outlined in the last section, I believe that it will lead analysis away from both market-centred and state-centred approaches to environmental goods and towards an association-centred perspective.[19] The social dimension of environmentalism needs to focus on the question of what associations best develop a concern for environmental goods, and what conditions are required in order that such associations flourish. Even if it turns out that the market and state are institutions we are stuck with – and I retain the possibly utopian hope that they are not – it is the associational background against which they operate that makes the difference as to how far they can and will operate in an ecologically rational manner.[20]

Notes

1 For surveys see Mueller (1989) and Dunleavy (1991). The classic texts in the Virginian School of public choice theory are Buchanan and Tullock (1962) and Buchanan (1975). Typical of the Chicago School of public choice theory is Becker (1976). The Chicago version is much more closely tied to the extension of neo-classical theory to new domains than is the Virginian version, which has taken an increasingly Austrian turn: consider the influence of Hayek on Buchanan's later work – see, for example, Buchanan (1986a) *passim*.

2 This point was put to me by Mary Farmer just as 1 was finishing *Ecology, Policy and Politics: Human Well-Being and the Natural World*: this article is a belated response to that criticism. Sadly, the death of Mary has robbed her friends and colleagues not only of her companionship but also of her acute and scholarly criticisms.

3 Compare Mueller: 'Public choice can be defined as the economic study of non-market decision-making, or simply the application of economics to politics' (Mueller, 1979: 1).

4 See also Niskanen (1971). Downs (1967) defends a different version of a public choice account of bureaucracy, which includes altruistic motivations alongside narrower egoistic ones.

5 The major text defending this position is Downs (1957). An earlier classic attempt to apply economic models of behaviour to political actors, but with a more sceptical view of consumer sovereignty, is Schumpeter (1944).

6 Buchanan attempts to show that the theorem still has relevance in conditions of imperfect competition (Buchanan, 1969) and, under an Austrian re-interpretation, that transaction costs are not relevant to its truth (Buchanan, 1986b).

7 I develop a version of this criticism of Sagoff in a Marxian idiom in O'Neill (1993a: ch. 10).

8 For a powerful recent defence of perfectionist liberalism see Raz (1986). I defend the compatibility of perfectionism and pluralism in O'Neill (1995). It needs to be noted here that Mill's perspective on role of institutions on individuals' preferences sits uneasily with the psychologism he defends in Mill (1947: Book 6). However, it is the psychologism that needs to go, not the institutionalism.

9 See Polanyi (1957a,b). For a discussion of the influence of Aristotle on Marx and Polanyi see Meikle (1979, 1985) and O'Neill (1995).

10 I include here not only J.S. Mill, but also the work of Hume and Smith. Compare, for example, the views about the role habit plays in the formation of dispositions of character in Hume – see 'Of the Origin of Government', 'The Sceptic' and 'Of Interest' in Hume (1985) – and in Smith (Smith, 1981: V.i), with those developed by Veblen (Veblen, 1919).

11 Hence Hume's remarks about the incompatibility of absolute monarchy and commerce:

> Commerce, therefore, in my opinion, is apt to decay in absolute governments, not because it is there less *secure*, but because it is less *honourable*. A subordination of ranks is absolutely necessary to the support of monarchy. Birth, titles, and place, must be honoured above industry and riches. And while these notions prevail, all the considerable traders will be tempted to throw up their commerce, in order to purchase some of those employments, to which privileges and honours are annexed.
>
> (Hume, 1985: 93)

See also Aristotle's remarks on the effects of wealth on character in Aristotle's *Rhetoric* (BookII, ch. 16).

12 I owe this last point to Andrew Collier: 'If "rational economic agent" is defined to mean "person who pursues monetary gain in preference to all other aims" its corresponding term in ordinary English is not its homonym, but "moneygrubber"' (Collier, 1990: 118).

13 As Hirschman goes on to say, it is perhaps true that:

> the success of Olson's book *owes* something to Us having been contradicted by the subsequently evolving events. Once the latter had run their course, the many people who found them deeply upsetting could go back to *The Logic of Collective Action* and find in it good and reassuring reasons why those collective actions of the sixties should never have happened in the first place.
>
> (Hirschman, 1985: 79)

See also the problems that rational choice Marxism has with the explanation of collective class action.

14 In making *that* assumption they are the inheritors of the views of Smith: Smith was never an anti-socialist thinker – there was, when he wrote, no significant socialist movement to oppose. He was an anti-associationaiist thinker: professional associations, trade associations and guilds are conspiracies against the public, concerned with pursuit particular sectional interests (Smith, 1981: 1.x; *passim*).

15 I draw here on the distinction MacIntyre makes between practices and institutions in MacIntyre (1985: ch. 14). To employ the language MacIntyre uses would, however,

176   *John O'Neill*

be misleading here, since he uses the term 'institution' in a very particular and idiosyncratic sense.

16 The point is made in a variety of ways, and by appeals to a number of authorities. Sometimes it is made in economic terms: that ethical constraints are a scarce resource, the use of which should be minimised (Buchanan and Tullock, 1962: 27ff.). At others, in terms justice, that the 'immoral' or 'egoistic' should not be allowed to gain 'unfair' advantage from his or her fellows (Buchanan, 1962: 302–6). Often it is simply invoked as a principle of institutional design that represents an inherited wisdom (Buchanan, 1978: 17–18). In the final of these, Buchanan calls upon the authority of Mill's *Consideration on Representative Government* – 'the very principle of constitutional government requires it to be assumed that political power will be abused to promote the particular purposes of the holder' – conveniently forgetting the main thesis of that book concerning the educative and corrupting effects of institutions on the individual. Reference is also sometimes made to Hume:

> Political writers have established it as a maxim that, in contriving any system of government, and fixing the several checks and controls of the constitution, every man ought to be supposed to be *knave*, and to have no other end, in all his actions, than private interest.

(Hume, 1985: 42)

Hume goes onto say that 'it appears somewhat strange, that a maxim should be true in *politics*, which is false in fact' (Hume, 1985: 42–3). While Hume does believe that 'avarice, or the desire of gain, is a universal passion which operates at all times, in all places, and upon all persons' (Hume, 1985: 113), his point about knavery in politics is very different from its public choice counterpart. It is one that applies solely to the political and concerns the behaviour of men when they act in parties, such that the countervailing check of honour is absent.

17 Hence, there is this to be said for rule by lot: that unlike modem elective oligarchy, it selects these who do not have a desire to rule (see Burnheim (1985)).

18 I begain to address these questions in O'Neill, (1993b).

19 See also in this regard the welcome rediscovery ot associationai models of socialism (Hirst, 1989; Marteil, 1992; Yeo, 1987).

20 I have benefited in writing this chapter from the seminar series on Environmental Economics at the Centre for the Study of Environmental Change, Lancaster University. I would particularly like to thank Jonathan Aldred, John Foster, Geoff Hodgson, Michael Jacobs, Russell Keat, Mark Peacock, Geoff Smith and the journal's referees for their comments on earlier versions. I am also grateful to John Dearlove, Rob Eastwood, Mary Farmer, and Donald Winch for many conversations on the topics discussed here.

References

Anderson, T. and D. Leal (1991), *Free Market Environmentalism*, San Francisco, CA: Pacific Research Institute for Public Policy.

Barry, B. (1990), *Political Argument*, 2nd edn, New York: Harvester Wheatsheaf.

Becker, G. (1976), *The Economic Approach to Human Behaviour*, Chicago, IL: University of Chicago Press.

Brennan, G. and J. Buchanan (1980), *The Power to Tax*, Cambridge: Cambridge University Press.

Buchanan, J. (1969), 'External Diseconomies, Corrective Taxes and Market Structure', *American Economic Review*, Vol. 59, pp. 174–7.

Buchanan, J. (1972), 'Towards Analysis of Closed Behavioural Systems', in J. Buchanan and R. Tollison (eds), *Theory of Public Choice*, Ann Arbor, MI: University of Michigan Press, pp. 11–23.

Buchanan, J. (1975), *The Limits of Liberty*, Chicago, IL: University of Chicago Press.

Buchanan, J. (1978), 'From Private Preferences to Public Philosophy: The Development of Public Choice', in J. Buchanan (ed.) *The Economics of Politics*, London: IEA, pp. 1–20.

Buchanan, J. (1986a), *Liberty, Market and State*, Brighton: Wheatsheaf.

Buchanan, J. (1986b), 'Rights, Efficiency and Exchange: The Irrelevance of Transaction Costs', in Buchanan (ed.), *Liberty, Market and State*, Brighton: Wheatsheaf.

Buchanan, J. and G. Tullock (1962), *The Calculus of Consent*, Ann Arbor, MI: University of Michigan Press.

Buchanan J. and R. Wagner (1977), *Democracy in Deficit: The Political Legacy of Lord Keynes*, New York: Academic Press.

Burke, E. (1826), *Works V*, London: Rivington.

Burnheim, J. (1985), *Is Democracy Possible?* Cambridge: Polity Press.

Coase, R. (1960), 'The Problem of Social Cost', *The Journal of Law and Economics*, Vol. 3, pp. 1–22.

Collier, A, (1990), *Socialist Reasoning*, London: Pluto Press.

Commons, J. (1934), *Institutional Economics – Its Place in Political Economy*, New York: Macmillan.

Dales, J.H. (1968), *Pollution, Property and Prices*, Toronto: University of Toronto Press.

Dearlove, J. (1989), 'Neoclassical Politics; Public Choice and Political Understanding' *Review of Political Economy*, Vol. 1, pp. 208–37.

Downs, A. (1957), *An Economic Theory of Democracy*, New York: Harper & Row.

Downs, A. (1967), *Inside Bureaucracy*, Boston, MA: Little Brown.

Duncan, C. (1992), 'Legal Protection for the Soil of England: The Spurious Context of Nineteenth Century "Progress"', *Agricultural History*, Vol. LXVI, pp. 75–94.

Dunleavy, P. (1991), *Democracy, Bureaucracy and Public Choice*, New York: Harvester Wheatsheaf.

Durkheim, E. (1964), *The Division of Labor in Society* (trans. G. Simpson), New York: The Free Press.

Eckersley, R. (1993), 'Free Market Environmentalism: Friend or Foe?', *Environmental Politics*, Vol. 2, pp. 1–19.

Hahn, F. and M. Hollts (1979), 'Introduction in F. Hahn and M. Hollis (eds), *Philosophy and Economic Theory*, Oxford: Oxford University Press.

Hirschman, A. (1977), *The Passions and the Interests*, Princeton, NJ: Princeton University Press.

Hirschman, A. (1985), *Shifting Involvements: Private Interests and Public Affairs*, Oxford: Blackwell.

Hirst, P. (ed.) (1989), *The Pluralist Theory of the State*, London: Routledge.

Hodgson, G. (1988), *Economics and Institutions*, Cambridge: Polity Press.

Hodgson, G. (1993), 'Institutional Economics: Surveying the "Old" and the "New"', *Metroeconomica*, Vol. 44, pp. 1–28.

Hume, D. (1985), *Essays, Moral, Political and Literary*, Indianapolis, IN: Liberty Press.

Jacobs, M. (1991), *The Green Economy*, London: Pluto Press.

MacIntyre, A. (1985), *After Virtue*, 2nd edn, London: Duckworth.

Martell, L. (1992), 'New Ideas of Socialism', *Economy and Society*, Vol. 21, pp. 152–73.

Marx, K. (1843), 'Critique of Hegel's Doctrine of the State', in L. Colletti (ed.) (1974), *Early Writings*, Harmondsworth: Penguin.

Meikle, S. (1979), 'Aristotle and the Political Economy of the Polls', *Journal of Hellenic Studies*, Vol. 79, pp. 57–73.

Meikle, S. (1985), *Essentialism in the Thought of Karl Marx*, London: Duckworth.

Merton, R. (1968), *Social Theory and Social Structure*, New York: The Free Press.

Mill, J.S. (1947), *A System of Logic*, London: Longmans.

Mill, J.S. (n.d.), *Representative Government*, London: Routledge & Kegan Paul.

Mueller, D. (1989), *Public Choice II*, Cambridge: Cambridge University Press.

Niskanen, W. (1971), *Bureaucracy and Representative Government*, Chicago, IL: Aldine-Atherton.

Niskanen, W. (1973), *Bureaucracy: Servant or Master*, London: IEA.

Olson, M. (1965), *The Logic of Collective Action*, Cambridge, MA: Harvard University Press.

Olson, M. (1982), *The Rise and Decline of Nations*, New Haven, CT: Yale University Press.

O'Neill, J. (1990), 'Property in Science and the Market', *The Monist*, Vol. 73, pp. 601–20.

O'Neill, J. (1992), 'Egoism, Altruism and the Market', *The Philosophical Forum*, Vol. 23, pp. 278–88.

O'Neill, J. (1993a), *Ecology Policy and Politics: Human Well-Being and the Natural World*, London: Routledge.

O'Neill, J. (1993b), 'Future Generations: Present Harms', *Philosophy*, Vol. 68, pp. 35–51.

O'Neill, J. (1995), 'Polity, Economy, Neutrality', *Political Studies*, Vol. XLIII, pp. 414–31.

Peacock, M. (1992), 'A Critique of Critiques of Environmental Economics', Working Paper, Centre for the Study of Environmental Change, Lancaster University.

Pearce, D. and K. Turner (1990), *Economics of Natural Resources and the Environment*, New York: Harvester Wheatsheaf.

Pearce, D., A. Markandya and E. Barbier (1989), *Blueprint for a Green Economy*, London: Earthscan.

Pocock, J.G.A. (1975), *The Machiavellian Moment*, Princeton, NJ: Princeton University Press.

Pocock, J.G.A. (1985), 'The Mobility of Property and the Rise of Eighteenth-Century Sociology', in *Virtue, Commerce, and History*, Cambridge: Cambridge University Press.

Polanyi, K. (1957a), *The Great Transformation*, Boston, MA: Beacon Press.

Polanyi, K. (1957b), *Primitive, Archaic and Modern Economies*, Boston, MA: Beacon Press.

Polanyi, K. (1957c), 'Aristotle Discovers the Economy', in Polanyi (ed.), *Primitive, Archaic and Modern Economies*, Boston, MA: Beacon Press.

Ravetz, J. (1973), *Scientific Knowledge and its Social Problems*, Harmondsworth: Penguin.

Raz, J. (1986), *The Morality of Freedom*, Oxford: Clarendon Press.

Rose-Ackerman, S. (1977), 'Market Models for Pollution Control', *Public Policy*, Vol. 25, pp. 383–406.

Sagoff, M. (1988), *The Economy of the Earth*, Cambridge: Cambridge University Press.

Schumpeter, J. (1944), *Capitalism, Socialism and Democracy*, London; Allen & Unwin.

Smith A. (1981), *An Inquiry into the Nature and Causes of the Wealth of Nations*, Indianapolis, IN: Liberty Press.

Taylor, C. (1971), 'Interpretation and the Science of Man', *Review of Metaphysics*, Vol. 25, pp. 1–45.

Tullock, G. (1970), *Private Wants, Public Means*, New York: Basic Books.

Veblen, T. (1919), *The Place of Science in Modern Civilisation and Other Essays*, New York: Huebsch.

Wolf, C. (1987), 'Market and Non-market Failure: Comparison and Assessment', *Journal of Public Policy*, Vol. 7, pp. 43–70.

Yeo, S. (1987), 'The Socialisms: Statin, Collectivism, Associationalism', in W. Outhwaite and M. Mulkay (eds), *Social Theory and Social Criticism: Essays for Tom Bottomore*, Oxford: Blackwell.

11 Ecological modernisation, Ecological modernities

Peter Christoff

Ecological modernisation is emerging as a fashionable new term to describe recent changes in environmental policy and politics.[1] Its growing popularity derives in part from the suggestive power of its combined appeal to notions of development and modernity and to ecological critique. Yet competing definitions blur its usefulness as a concept. Does ecological modernisation refer to environmentally sensitive technological change? Does it more broadly define a style of policy discourse which serves either to foster better environmental management or to manage dissent and legitimate ongoing environmental destruction? Does it, instead, denote a new belief system or systemic change? Indeed, can it encompass all of these understandings? In this chapter, I want to examine current uses of the term in relation to the tensions between modernity and ecology which it evokes and suggest ways of diminishing its ambiguity.

It is widely acknowledged that since the late 1980s significant changes have occurred in the content and style of environmental policy in most industrialised (particularly OECD) countries. The nature and extent of these changes vary between nations,[2] reflecting their distinctive political, institutional and cultural features; the national economic importance of the sectors and industries targeted by new regulatory regimes and the extent and intensity of the environmental impact of those industries; the strength of popular environmental concern and of its political representation; the extent to which an implementation deficit (the failure to realise environmental standards and goals) exists and is recognised as a local problem, and the reasons for this deficit; and regionally distinct perceptions of the key international and global ecological problems which mobilised public concern during the 1980s.[3]

Nevertheless, despite local variations, these environmental policy changes have several generalisable features. They have aimed to shift industry beyond reactive 'end-of pipe' approaches towards anticipatory and precautionary solutions which minimise waste and pollution through increasingly efficient resource use (including through recycling). Problem displacement across media (air, water and land) and across space and time has tended to be challenged by a more integrated regulatory approach – as much to achieve greater administrative efficiency and to limit regulatory overload as to address the new environmental problems caused by such displacement. Prescriptive regulatory approaches and 'technological forcing' – applied in the 1970s as the sole or predominant strategy for achieving ongoing improvements in environmental conditions – are more often accompanied or displaced by co-operative and voluntary arrangements between government and industry: increasingly environment protection agencies seek to use industry's existing investment patterns and its capacity and need for technological innovation to facilitate improvement in environmental outcomes. A range of market-based environmental instruments have been deployed in response to the perceived exhaustion of the initial wave of regulatory intervention (Eckersley, 1995). In all, the new environmental policy discourse increasingly emphasises the mutually reinforcing environmental and economic benefits of increased resource efficiency and waste minimisation.

These developments reflect an evolving international discourse in response to commonly perceived environmental problems. However, they also reflect an increasingly sophisticated political response by governments and industry to popular mobilisation around issues such as nuclear power, acid rain, biodiversity preservation, ozone depletion and induced climate change. In other words, the new policy culture and its trends are not always simply or primarily intended to resolve environmental problems. They are also shaped by a contest over political control of the environmental agenda and, separately, over the legitimacy of state regulation (predominantly in the English-speaking OECD countries). In addition, they have been influenced by the growing pressures on nation-states generated by intensified economic globalisation and by changes in the structure and nature of production towards greater flexibility and international integration.

The strengthening of linkages between environmental and economic policies is especially observable in countries such as Germany and the Netherlands – in turn raising questions about the reasons for their exceptionally good environmental performance in contrast to countries such as the United Kingdom and the United States. For instance, in the 1980s and the early 1990s German environmental policy, under pressure from the Greens, has moved rapidly to address its failure to meet targets and standards adopted during the 1970s. The promotion of design criteria enabling comprehensive re-use of materials has been accompanied by regulations requiring that 72 per cent of glass and metals and 64 per cent of paperboard, laminates and plastics be recycled by 1995 (Moore, 1992). Regulations also encourage use of 'waste energy' for heating and power generation. The 1983 Large Combustion Plant Ordinance requires the retrofitting of all major power plants to cut pollutants contributing to acid rain by 90 per cent by 1995. Laws passed in 1989 ban CFC production and use by 1995. Germany has also committed itself to a unilateral reduction in carbon dioxide emissions of between 25 and 30 per cent by the year 2005 and, since 1990, has begun to articulate and implement a package of some sixty measures to enable it to meet this target (Hatch, 1995).

These changes have been supported by considerable government assistance. Weale (1992) reports that between 1979 and 1985, the German government subsidy for environmental research and development rose from $US 144.3 million to $US 236.4 million or from 2.1 percent of R&D to 3.1 per cent (the UK equivalent was 0.8 per cent to 1.1 per cent). This commitment is also institutionally defined: Germany has a separate Federal Ministry for Research and Technology which spends about 200 million DM per annum on research and development of environmental technologies (Angerer, 1992: 181). Since 1985, the level of German public subsidy for environmental research has exceeded that of the United States in absolute terms. Public investment also provides substantial support in the energy conservation fields, including research into energy conservation devices. As a result, within a decade German industry has become a global leader in the development and/or production of solar photo-voltaics, high-efficiency turbines, hydrogen-powered cars, energy-efficient household appliances and recyclable materials and products.

The economic advantages to countries and companies leading the field in environmental performance improvements have been recognised as considerable. It is estimated that by the year 2000, Japan will be producing some $US12 billion worth of waste incinerators, air-pollution equipment and water treatment devices, and MITI has proposed aid projects aimed at energy development in China, Indonesia and Malaysia, as a means of further tying and strengthening trade connections with these countries (Gross, 1992).

The extent of formal policy integration and of the diffusion of environmental principles into the practices of state, economy and society is also of particular interest. Governments in several countries – notably Australia, Canada, the Netherlands and the United Kingdom – have developed national plans for sustainable development, meta-policies aimed at the integration of national environmental and economic activity and at encouraging greater environmental awareness in civil society. In this, the Dutch National Environment Policy Plan (NEPP) has been significantly more successful than similar attempts elsewhere. This success is partly due to the highly corporatist nature of Dutch politics and planning, the Dutch state's acceptance of a significant role in facilitating and directing industrial development and environmental protection, and also the timing of the Plan's release in 1989, during a high point of international and national environmental concern. The NEPP has the explicit goal of achieving environmental sustainability in the Netherlands within one generation, by 2010, by recasting policies and practices in key economic sectors, including manufacturing, agriculture and transport, to limit waste production and environmental pollution (Carley and Christie, 1992; van der Straaten, 1992). Despite weaknesses both in its targets and ongoing implementation (Wintle and Reeve, 1994), the Plan nevertheless offers a programmatic approach to working towards measurable targets against which the public, government and industry can assess its progress and iteratively adjust the Plan.[4]

Over the past decade, Germany, the Netherlands, Japan and the Scandinavian block appear to have achieved above OECD average improvements across a range of industry-related national environmental indicators, including water quality and air pollutant emissions (OECD, 1995). In these countries there is now evidence of a decoupling of GNP growth from the growth of environmentally harmful effects, indicating increased economic output with decreased energy and materials consumption *per unit* of GNP. However, certain improvements in environmental conditions in the First World have been gained through displacement of high energy consuming and/or polluting industries (e.g. metal processing and primary manufacturing) to newly industrialising countries (NICs) and lesser developed countries (LDCs). Meanwhile, underlying increases in total material consumption in both industrialising countries and industrialised countries continue to enhance environmental pressures, suggesting both that the pace of reform is too slow and the root cause of the implementation deficit of the 1970s has not been overcome (WRI, 1994).

The uses of ecological modernisation

Positive aspects of these recent changes have been described by academic observers as evidence of a process of 'ecological modernisation' (EM), although their uses of the term vary considerably in scope and meaning. Specifically, leading exponents of the term in the German and English literature, such as Janicke, Hajer and Weale, use it in their policy analysis, sociological analysis or political theoretical discussion in ways which are occasionally problematic, partly because of a lack of clarity about whether the term is being used descriptively, analytically or normatively. Following discussion of these distinctive uses of EM, I want to propose a typology for ecological modernisation which emphasises the normative dimensions of the term.

Ecological modernisation as technological adjustment

EM has been used narrowly to describe technological developments with environmentally beneficial outcomes – such as chlorine-free bleaching of pulp for paper and more fuel-efficient cars. These are specifically aimed at reducing emissions at source and fostering greater resource efficiency (Janicke, 1988; Janicke *et al.*, 1992; Simonis, 1988; Zimmermann *et al.*, 1990).

Janicke, who perhaps first introduced 'ecological modernisation' into the language of policy analysis (1986/1990), for instance, refers to four broadly framed 'environmental political' strategies commonly found in industrial countries (Janicke, 1988). Two of these strategies are remedial (compensation and environmental restoration; technical pollution control) and two preventative or anticipatory (environmentally friendly technical innovation or 'ecological modernisation'; and structural change). For Janicke, EM is fundamentally a technical cost-minimisation strategy for industry and an alternative to labour-saving investment – a form of 'ecological rationalisation' which will lead simultaneously to greater 'ecological and economic efficiency' (1988: 23). It is primarily seen as a strategy intended to maintain or improve market competitiveness, in which the environmental benefits of such technological change are incidental rather than a core concern for innovation and implementation. In this sense, such a narrow version of EM does not necessarily reflect any significant and overwhelming changes in corporate, public or political values in relation to desired ecological outcomes. Rather, it is an outcome of capital's cost-minimising responses to new pressures – such as the adoption elsewhere of post-Fordist 'lean' production methods (Amin, 1994; Best, 1990; Wallace, 1995), resource price movements and scarcities (e.g. the oil crises of the 1970s); changes in consumer taste; and profit squeezes caused by taxes and regulatory strategies of the state – at a time when automation has reduced industry's capacity to increase labour's productivity. Innovation and implementation may be confined to those areas and types of technical improvements which ensure market competitiveness.[5] Consequently, such technological change may not contribute to lasting environmental improvements when viewed in the context of national or international ecological requirements.

For Janicke, moves towards sustainability depend on broader structural change, the second of his anticipatory strategies, which would lead to profound shifts in production and consumption patterns. These are not merely industrial responses to ecological symptoms (e.g. resource shortages) but incorporate precautionary analysis and associated restrictions on action and lead to constrained qualitative economic growth and a decrease in absolute resource use, pollution and environmental degradation (1988: 15–17, 1992). He sees the current period of multiple crises – unemployment, and accumulation, environmental and fiscal crises – which extends into the 1990s as also providing opportunities for the 'creative destruction' of old patterns and forms. The world market involves not only competition between enterprises producing new technologies but also competition between nations with stronger and weaker 'state steering capacity', a competition favouring those capable of breaking with the tendency to protect their old 'smoke-stack industries' and able to generate a framework for consensual transformation. Janicke's more recent empirical work documents the sites, conditions and (limited) signs of such industrial transformation (Janicke *et al.*, 1992).

Janicke and his colleagues fail to identify or address potential political economic contradictions in this narrow vision of an ecological modernisation embedded in larger processes of structural transformation. At what point are the currently developing patterns of unrestricted, globalised production and trade, and the cultural demands for increasingly specialised consumption, challenged? How will the corresponding growth in international markets for new 'lean' technologies and products be restrained to ensure regional and international ecological stability rather than ongoing expansion of total resource use and waste output? And, specifically given Janicke's views (1992) on state failure and the limits of state action, what institutions will participate in this enhanced process of regulation? What happens, within this larger scenario, to those countries – the technological laggards – unable to compete or perform economically and ecologically?

If these new clean technologies and products *are* truly ecologically sustainable – leading to a significant absolute decrease in resource use and to effective environmental preservation – what are their ramifications for trade, employment, accumulation and wealth distribution within and between nations, particularly if they are sought according to time frames which are dictated by urgent ecological demands (e.g. the potential need to cut Greenhouse gas emissions by up to 60 per cent within the next three decades)? Certainly, given its narrowly industrial focus, such EM would not necessarily serve to diminish total resource consumption or lead to the protection of 'unvalued', non-resource related ecological concerns.

Ecological modernisation as policy discourse

Others, such as Weale (1992, 1993) and Hajer (1995), have employed 'EM' more broadly to define changes in environmental policy discourse. For Hajer, the shift toward EM can be observed in at least six 'realms', namely in environmental policy-making, where anticipatory replace reactive regulatory formulae; in a new 'pro-active' and critical role for science in environmental policy-making; at the micro-economic level, in the shift from the notion that environmental protection increases cost, to the notion that 'pollution prevention pays'; at the macro-economic level, in the reconceptualisation of nature as a public good and resource rather than a free good; in the 'legislative discourse in environmental politics', where changing perceptions of the 'value' of nature mean that the burden of proof now rests with those accused as polluters rather than the damaged party; and the reconsideration of participation in policy-making practices, with the acknowledgement of new actors, 'in particular environmental organisations and to a lesser extent local residents', and the creation of 'new participatory practices' for their inclusion in a move to end the sharp antagonistic debate between the state and the environment movement' (Hajer, 1995: 28–9).

Hajer predominantly regards EM as a policy discourse which assumed prominence around the time of the European Community's Third Action Plan for the Environment and, more explicitly still, the 1984 OECD Conference on Environment and Economics. Such EM 'recognises the structural character of the environmental problematique but none the less assumes that existing political, economic and social institutions can internalise care for the environment' (1995: 31). Hajer sees this discourse as being largely economistic – framing environmental problems in monetary terms, portraying environmental protection as a 'positive sum' game and following a utilitarian logic. At the core of ecological modernisation is the idea that pollution prevention pays: it is 'essentially an efficiency-oriented approach to the environment' (1995: 101). In other words, economic growth and the resolution of environmental problems can, in principle, be reconciled (1995: 25–6).[6] 'Ecological modernisation uses the language of business and conceptualises environmental pollution as a matter of inefficiency while operating within the bounds of cost-effectiveness and bureaucratic efficiency' (1995: 31).

Hajer is most effective where he suggests that EM is a discursive strategy useful to governments seeking to manage ecological dissent and to relegitimise their social regulatory role. It permits a critical distancing from the interventionist remedies of the 1970s which, as Hajer believes, 'did not produce satisfactory results' and may serve to legitimate moves to roll back the state and reduce its regulatory capacities in the environmental domain. It also enables governments to promote environmental protection as being economically responsible, thereby resolving the tensions created by previous perceptions that the state was acting against the logic of capital and its own interests (of functional dependency on private economic activity). He suggests that such a strategy explicitly avoids addressing basic social contradictions that other discourses might have introduced:

> Ecological modernisation is basically a modernist and technocratic approach to the environment that suggests that there is a technoinstitutional fix for present problems. Indeed ecological modernisation is based on many of the some institutional principles that were already discussed in the early 1970s: efficiency, technological innovation, techno-scientific management, procedural integration and co-ordinated management. It is also obvious that ecological modernisation as described above does not address the systemic features of capitalism that make the system inherently wasteful and unmanageable.
>
> (1995: 32)

In other words, EM is not simply a technical answer to the problem of environmental degradation. It can also be seen as a strategy of political accommodation of the radical environmentalist critique of the 1970s, meshing with the deregulatory moves which typify the 1980s, with distinctive affinities with the neo-liberal ideas that dominated governments during this time, supporting their concern for structural industrial reform (1995: 32–3).

Hajer's own views here are unclear. He seems to approve of such political closure yet leaves open the question of whether or not EM might be, in the terms of the critics of Brundtland, a rhetorical ploy to take the wind out of the sails of 'real' environmentalists, one which displaces and marginalises the radical emancipatory aspects of environmental critique (1995: 34). He is even less clear about whether or not EM 'may not in fact have a more profound meaning as the first step on a bridge that leads to a new sort of sustainable society'. Hajer mainly sees EM as a counter to the 'anti-modern' sentiments he claims are part of the critical discourse of new social movements.

> It is a policy strategy that is based on a fundamental belief in progress and the problem-solving capacity of modern techniques and skills of social engineering. Contrary to the radical environment movement that put the issue on the agenda in the 1970s, environmental degradation is no longer an anomaly of modernity. There is a renewed belief in the possibility of mastery and control, drawing on modernist policy instruments such as expert systems and science.
>
> (1995: 33)

In this sense too, as it seeks to provide a soothing rhetoric promoting apparent remedial and anticipatory change, such a policy discourse may be profoundly anti-ecological in its outcomes, its narrow economism serving to devalue and work against recognition and protection of non-materialistic views of nature's 'worth'.

Ecological modernisation as belief system

Both Hajer and Weale also use the concept in more radical ways.[7] For Weale (1992), ecological modernisation represents a new belief system that explicitly articulates and organises ideas of ecological emancipation which may remain confused and contradictory in a less self-conscious discourse. It is an ideology based around, but extending beyond, the understanding that environmental protection is a precondition of long-term economic development. Weale's claims for EM as a belief system are important given the role of belief systems in organising and legitimising public policy.

Weale also sees EM as being focused on a reconceptualised relationship between environmental regulation and economic growth. It still includes an emphasis on achievement of highest possible environmental standards as a means for developing market advantage through the integration of anticipatory mechanisms into the production process, recognition of the actual and anticipated costs of environmental externalities in economic planning and the economic importance of strengthening consumer preferences for clean, green products (1992: ch.3, 1993: 206–9). However, 'once the conventional wisdom of the relationship between the environment and economy is challenged, other elements of the implicit belief system [which sees them in opposition] might also begin to unravel'. Regulation may 'no longer seem merely a mechanical matter'. EM thus prefigures systemic change and may, in its more radical forms, generate a broader transformation in social relations, one which leads to the ecologisation of markets and the state.

Under such circumstances, as Weale comments:

> the internalisation of externalities becomes a matter of attitude as well as finance, and a cleavage begins to open up not between business and environmentalists, but between progressive, environmentally-aware business on the one hand and short-term profit takers on the other. Moreover, the behaviour of consumers becomes important, so that the role of government policy is not simply to respond to the existing wants and preferences of their citizens, but also to provide support and encouragement for forms of environmentally aware behaviour and discouragement for behaviour that threatens or damages the environment. Once this view has taken root, the line from mechanical to moral reform has been crossed. The challenge of ecological modernisation extends therefore beyond the economic point that a sound environment is a necessary condition for long-term prosperity and it comes to embrace changes in the relationship between the state, its citizens and private corporations, as well as in the relationship between states.
>
> (1992: 31–2)

However, in *The New Politics of Pollution*, Weale does not develop his views on the transformations of both civil society and the state necessary to achieve ecological sustainability. What limits are posed by the state's dependent relationship to private sector economic activities and how can these be overcome given the increasing political and economic vulnerability of individual nation-states to global flows of capital? To what extent would transformations of civil society and in public spheres, rather than institutional changes to the state, drive the process of ecologisation?[8]

Ecological modernisation – some unresolved issues

It is possible to illuminate problems and issues left unaddressed or unresolved by the foregoing uses of EM by asking a series of interrelated questions. In different situations (different policy forums and different countries), quite different styles of EM may prevail – ones which can be judged normatively to tend towards either weak or strong outcomes on a range of issues, such as ecological protection and democratic participation. In this sense, these questions hint at the limitations of those forms of ecological modernisation which tend toward the first rather than the second of what might seem, initially, opposing poles.

EM – economistic or ecological?

In each of the uses of EM described earlier, the environment is reduced to a series of concerns about resource inputs, waste and pollutant emissions. As cultural needs and non-anthropocentric values (such as are reflected in the Western interest in the preservation of wilderness) cannot be reduced to monetary terms, they tend to be marginalised or excluded from consideration. This is clearly the case for EM narrowly defined as technical innovation. But it is equally true of those interpretations of EM which see the state shaping corporate activity and markets to (re)incorporate environmental externalities into the costs of production. As has been noted, such versions of EM may remain consistent with the traditional imperatives of capital.

Leading industries may welcome uniformly applied environmental regulatory regimes, as the redefinition of the boundaries of acceptable economic behaviour may represent a rationalisation of their markets which makes the rules of production and competition more certain or amenable to their entry or dominance. But ideologically and practically, such ecological modernisation may simply put a green gloss on industrial development in much the same way that the term 'sustainable development' has been co-opted – to suggest that industrial activity and resource use should be allowed as long as environmental side-effects are minimised.

Given this dominant emphasis on increasing the environmental efficiency of industrial development and resource exploitation, such EM remains only superficially or weakly *ecological*. Consideration of the integrity of ecosystems, and the cumulative impacts of industrialisation upon these, is limited and peripheral. In this sense, the entire literature is somewhat Eurocentric, deeply marked by the experience of local debates over the politics of acid rain and other outputs, rather than conflicts over biodiversity preservation. Although current uses of EM may be well-adapted to describing positive environmental outcomes in certain industrialised First World countries where a version of ecological sustainability may be created in the wasteland of a vastly depleted biological world, it may be positively dangerous if taken prescriptively by those nations where the conservation of biodiversity is a more fundamental concern or opportunity and/or which depend on primary resource exploitation to fund their traditional forms of economic growth, for example as in the case in Australia, Brazil and South Africa.

EM – national or international?

The uses of EM described earlier also remain narrowly focused on changes *within* industrialised nation-states. They are therefore unable to integrate an understanding of the transformative impact of economic globalisation on environmental relations. They offer only a diminished recognition of the increasingly internationalised flows of material resources, manufactured components and goods, information and waste; of the influence of multinational corporations on investment, national industrial development and the regulatory capacities of the nation-state; and of international deregulatory developments (such as GATT) and environmental treaties (such as the Montreal Protocol). Paradoxically, each of these facets of globalisation shapes yet distorts, provokes yet inhibits and undermines the emergence of strong forms of ecological modernisation at national and regional levels. Because of their nation-statist focus, these uses of EM – including those raising broader ideological and systemic concerns – still tend to remain focussed on localised end-of-cycle issues rather than encompassing the globally integrated nature of resource extraction and manufacturing in relation to domestic consumption, overvaluing local achievements and environmental impacts while undervaluing geographically distant factors.[9]

Consider, for instance, the internationally dispersed resources and environmental impacts associated with producing and running a nation's car fleet or with producing and using paper. Or the extent to which heavy transformative industries such as smelting, ship-building or car manufacturing have relocated to the NICs. In other words, although pollution levels and primary consumption of energy and other primary resources may have fallen in relation to GNP in certain European economies as these have become increasingly post-industrial, their *per capita* material consumption continues to grow – with environmental impacts now displaced 'overseas'.

Given this presently predominantly nation-statist view of EM, discussion of the emergent international institutions for environmental regulation and protection, and of environmental trends, remains under-developed where it occurs in the EM literature.[10] The literature fails to recognise that, because old forms of industrial activity with their associated environmental problems are being displaced to developing nations or regions and the transition to alternative technologies is occurring too slowly to prevent major global environmental problems (such as climate change), we may instead be moving towards what Everett (1992) has called the 'breakdown of technological escape routes' as the ecological pressure for change increases beyond the reasonable capacities for social and industrial reform.

EM – hegemonic progress or multiple possibilities?

In different ways, the types of EM described earlier are also presented as contributing to, or constituting, a unilinear path to ecological modernity. Consequently they seem to be offering a revival of mainstream development theory and of notions of uneven development and under-development, positing EM as the next necessary or even triumphant stage of an evolutionary process of industrial transformation – a stage dependent upon the hegemony of Western science, technology and consumer culture and propagated by leading Western(ised) countries. Such views of ecological modernisation may be validly subjected to the criticisms which were levelled against development theory two decades ago.

Theorists who implicitly or explicitly rely upon a simplistic division between traditional and modern societies ignore the potential for a multiplicity of paths to ecological sustainability which may rest in the diversity of non-Western cultures. They seem to suggest that all countries may undertake the great leap forward over the phase of 'dirty' industrialisation into the fully ecologically modern condition. But if ecologically modernising countries can not quite manage the great leap, then at least such nations will eventually be able to employ restorative technologies, salves and panaceas developed elsewhere to undo the ecological devastation resulting from the stage of aggressive industrialisation to which developing countries aspire or are now subject. In other words, when developing countries reach the levels of affluence which gives them the economic capacity to afford ecological modernisation, they will be able to turn to consider and repair the path of devastation which has bought them this luxury. In fact, such views of EM continue to offer a world divided by renewed or strengthened core–periphery relationships between industrialised and industrialising countries, with world markets and the motors of progress dominated by leading industrial state(s).

The problems here are most obvious when we consider the potentially disastrous local and global ecological (and social) costs of China, India, Indonesia or Brazil pursuing such a path to ecological modernity or the perpetual mendicant status of small nation-states such as the Solomons or Vanuatu, and also much of the African continent, which would continue to be trapped in a condition of ongoing cultural and technological dependency.

EM – technocratic or democratic?

There are also tensions between what different theorists describe as the preconditions for systemic or structural ecological modernisation. Some stress the transformative impact of environmental awareness on civil society and the public sphere and on the institutions and practices of government and industry. They emphasise the ways in which citizenship and democratic participation in planning may serve to socialise and ecologise the market and guide and limit industrial production. Others however favour a less emancipatory technocratic, neo-corporatist version of EM – one which may prove primarily a rhetorical device seeking to manage radical dissent and secure the legitimacy of existing policy while delivering limited, economically acceptable environmental improvements.

For example, Weale (1992), interpreting developments in Germany and the Netherlands, suggests that the systemic realisation of EM requires a pro-active, interventionist state supporting a well-developed culture of environmental policy innovation and offering significant public investment and subsidies as a means of achieving economic advantage and environmental outcomes. Such state activity would entail an integrated regulatory environment and strong structural and process cross-linkages between different parts of the state and the development of a synoptic and reflexive use of environmental information in policy formation and implementation. In addition, this transformation is enhanced by, or indeed *depends upon*, increased public participation in political decision making, including green political pressure through both the environment movement and parliamentary politics (including green parties); and increased public influence over industry behaviour through green consumer action and the activities of environmental pressure groups and organisations.

By contrast, Hajer (1995) and Andersen (1993) seem to believe that a more technocratic relationship between state and civil society will lead more effectively to systemic EM. Andersen (1993), who is specifically concerned to define preconditions for EM through comparative analysis of national environmental performance, describes a country's *capacity* for ecological modernisation as depending upon its 'achieved level of institutional and technological problem-solving capabilities, which are critical to achieving effective environmental protection and transformation to more sustainable structures of production'. He argues, in concert with Janicke and others, that there is also a close relationship between consensus-seeking policy styles and high levels of environmental protection in industrialised countries.

Andersen suggests that four basic variables govern the capacity for such ecological modernisation. First there is *economic performance*. This is the capacity of countries to pay for environmental protection – a factor which appears directly linked to the intensity of environmental pollution. Second, there is *consensus ability*, which Andersen believes is best developed in countries with neo-corporatist structures, which are seen as having consensus-seeking decision-making styles that are more amenable to dealing with new ideas and interests.[11] Third, there is *innovative capability*, which he describes as the capacity of both the state and the market institutions to remain open to new interests and innovations in the judicial and political system, the media and the economic system. Fourth, there is *strategic proficiency* – the capacity to institutionalise environmental policy across sectors. He identifies federal states, which face potential fragmentation and delay in implementation, and states evidencing strong compartmentalisation of the bureaucracy – concomitant with weak environment departments or agencies – as potentially suffering problems in this area (Andersen, 1993: 3). Andersen suggests that the presence of these variables or attributes seems to contribute to, or at least correlate with, the success of 'leading' European countries – such as Germany and the Scandinavian bloc – in achieving exceptional improvements in environmental conditions. But how do they apply to the NICs and LDCs? Again, what relationship between state and civil society and what forms of democratic participation are required, especially given the international dimensions of environmental problems, to enable the radical social and economic changes which ecological sustainability may require?

Insofar as EM focuses on the state and industry in terms which are narrowly technocratic and instrumental rather than on social processes in ways which are broadly integrative, communicative, and deliberative, it is less likely to lead to the sorts of embedded cultural transformation which could sustain substantial reductions in material consumption levels, significant and rapid structural transformations in industrialised countries and major international redistributions of wealth and technological capacity. In general, the extent and nature of institutional changes required to enable the full recognition of a discursive and participatory environmental politics (and to accommodate the transboundary and intertemporal nature of environmental risks and impacts) have not yet been explored in the EM literature.[12]

From weak to strong ecological modernisations

Given the range of uses to which the term has been put, can ecological modernisation be stabilised as a concept? One can differentiate between sometimes conflicting versions of ecological modernisation. These versions do not each merely describe some aspect of a more encompassing process of ecological modernisation but offer quite different real world outcomes. Some of these uses may be labelled narrow or broad, depending on the extent to which they are technological or systemic in scope or focus. More importantly, and reflecting the above discussion, it is possible to emphasise the normative dimensions of different versions of EM. I would suggest that different interpretations of what constitutes EM lie along a continuum from weak (one is tempted to write, false) to strong, according to their likely efficacy in promoting enduring ecologically sustainable transformations and outcomes across a range of issues and institutions (Table 11.1). The political contest between the environment movement on the one

Table 11.1 Types of ecological modernisation

Weak EM	Strong EM
Economistic	Ecological
Technological (narrow)	Institutional/systemic (broad)
Instrumental	Communicative
Technocratic/neo-corporatist/closed	Deliberative democratic/open
National	International
Unitary (hegemonic)	Diversifying

hand and governments and industry on the other is predominantly over which of these types of EM should predominate.

It is essential to note that weak and strong features of EM are not always mutually exclusive binary opposites. Some features of weak or narrow EM are necessary but not sufficient preconditions for an enduring ecologically sustainable outcome. Clearly, one does not abandon technological change, economic instruments or instrumental reason in favour of institutional and systemic change or communicative rationality. In many cases – although not all (for instance, technocratic or neo-corporatist versus deliberative and open democratic systems) – aspects of narrow or weak EM need to be subsumed into and guided by the normative dimensions of strong EM.

Ecological modernisation, ecological modernities

Finally, what of the tensions and contradictions embedded in the term at the point where ecological critique challenges the ways in which simple industrial modernisation defines its relationship to Nature?[13] Perhaps the most radical use of ecological modernisation would involve its deployment against industrial modernisation itself. To understand what this might mean, it is necessary to unpack the ecological and modernising components of ecological modernisation and look at their interaction more closely.[14]

Modernity has broken or swept aside traditional forms of order and certainty: as Marx put it, 'all that is solid melts into air'. Its dynamism may be attributed to the separation of time and space into a realm that is detached from immediate experience; the disembedding of social systems; and the reflexive ordering and reordering of social relations (Giddens, 1990: 16–17). By fostering relations with absent others, locationally distant from any given situation of face-to-face interaction, the process of modernisation increasingly overlays place (the immediate experience of location) with space (the abstract experience of location, into which the immediate experience of location is then fitted). It also replaces local time, based on an immediate experience of the rhythms of Nature and the requirements of one's immediate community, with abstract time – now most powerfully represented by the international acceptance of a standard differentiation of global time zones. The extreme dynamism of modernity, Giddens argues, also depends on the establishment of *disembedding* social institutions, ones which create or support the creation of abstract social relations and their associated organisations. The emergence of symbolic tokens (such as money), and expert systems, represents an essential feature of modernity and contributes centrally to this process of disembedding, which is then reflected, for instance, in increasingly global discourses as in science or law.

In addition, 'systems of technical accomplishment or professional expertise organise large areas of the material and social environments in which we live today' (Giddens, 1990: 27). Crucial among these systems are those of scientific understanding and technological performance. We live in and are dependent upon – that is to say, *trust* in – them for our survival and legitimate functioning.

These abstract expert systems constitute not only bodies of knowledge, but also lived forms of social relationship. We enter them whenever we turn on a light switch, fly in an aeroplane, go to the dentist or answer the telephone: their complexity and functioning are taken for granted in a socially learned, relatively unquestioned and automatic way.[15] Both types of disembedding mechanism (symbolic tokens and abstract expert systems) provide guarantees of expectations across time and space and stretch social systems as a result. They also promote a new awareness of risk, which is the product of the human-created technological and social characteristics of modernity. Risk and trust intertwine. Modernity is also notable for the development of new capacities for the reflexive appropriation of knowledge, in part born of the capacity to transmit and review which comes with the development of the book and other forms of recorded information. All knowledge and beliefs become available for scrutiny. Certainty is displaced.

These features together contribute to the emergence of the institutional dimensions of modernity. Giddens identifies four such dimensions, which are inter-related and interdependent: capital accumulation; industrialism; surveillance; and military power (1990: 59). Of particular interest in relation to ecological modernisation are the first three dimensions. Industrialism seeks the transformation of nature into created or recreated (managed) environments through processes of standardisation, rationalisation and reduction. The imperatives of capital accumulation are such that the hunt for markets and resources encourages the commodification of all aspects of individual cultures and nature which remain vulnerable. The capacity for surveillance – in the broadest sense, in terms of the apparatuses of consolidated administration, monitoring and registering of social and environmental facts – has a bearing on the development of modern forms of reflexive environmental management.

The last point to note here is the globalising tendency of modernity. Its global reach is partly a result of the imperial and colonising tendencies of capital accumulation. However, as modern technologies of transport, information-transfer and communication continue actively to redefine social relations, linking and integrating distant parts of the globe both as markets for commodities and abstract social networks, the notions of centre and periphery begin to blur. The flow of individuals, commodities, cultures and pollution across territorial borders also is leading to a practical redefinition of one of the other major institutions of modernity, the nation-state. Modernity brings with it the globalisation of risk by altering the scope, the type and the range of human-created environmental risks, which individuals now face, and also the globalisation of the perception of these risks.

How then can we characterise the relationship between 'modernisation' and 'the ecological'? Modernity is fraught with tensions and generates its own new contradictions: nowhere is this more evident than in relation to the environment. The emergent ecological critique of untrammelled industrialism – sharpened politically in recent years by perceptions of ecological crisis and of the need for precautionary consideration of the potential consequences of development – has a paradoxical relationship to the constitutive features of modernity described above. Itself a product of simple modernity, ecological critique both depends upon and resists the modern reorganisation of time and space. It makes radically problematic and contradictory the industrialising imperative which lies at the heart of modernisation by redefining the cultural and ecological limits to the instrumental domination of nature.

Ecologically re-embedding space and time

The birth of nature has been accompanied and shaped by the simultaneous creation of technological forces which lead to what McKibben (1990) has called 'the end of Nature' through human interference with previously autonomous natural systems worldwide (through induced climate change, the global transport of pollutants and so on). Driven by the imperatives of capital accumulation, industrialism – shaped by the alliance of science and technology – continues to transform nature in ways unimaginable to earlier generations. It does so deliberately, for instance, by introducing alien plant and animal species to new continents, by flooding valleys and levelling mountains and by creating new relations of physical and economic dependency between the country and the city and between the First and the Third Worlds. Colonial conquests have often also led to the unintended extermination of indigenous plants and animals through destruction of their native habitat or by introduced predators. Demand for export earnings and the development of industrialised monocultural agriculture and forestry have produced a wave of extinction that continues to roll across North and South America, Australia, Asia and Africa. Yet the ecological transformation threatened by the combined impacts of induced global warming and bio-technology is more comprehensive still.

The creation of a secular, scientific understanding of nature – indeed, the development of ecology as a scientific discipline – and the triumph of technological domination over natural cycles and ecological processes, depend upon and arise from the separation of time and space discussed earlier. The 'discovery' of 'remote' regions and exotic species enabled the scientific conceptualisation of natural systems, at the same time as it involved the commodification of those environments, and the imperial domination or appropriation, of non-Western knowledge of natural systems and species.

Yet the 'so-called economy of Nature, the interrelationship of all organisms' for which Haeckel (1870) coined the term 'ecology' in 1869, depends on cycles and time scales which are generally alien to those of the political and economic institutions of industrial society. An ecological critique that recognises and respects the importance of the cycles upon which the biological world depends, and which seeks to re-embed our relationship to nature in a local place and to redefine the relationship in ecological temporal terms, often stands in opposition to the transcendent, abstracting features of modernity (and its industrial manifestations) while still to some extent depending upon its conceptual frameworks. In other words, such ecological critique tries to undo the stretching of time and space, as it seeks to limit certain aspects of industrial modernisation in order to preserve the ecological integrity of natural systems, or to preserve cultural understandings and institutions, which are locally embedded and resistant to the resource-utilitarianism of all forms of industrial modernity.[16]

Let me give several examples of such critique, each relating to primary resource use. Harvesting temperate forests on an *ecologically* sustainable cycle which also respects the needs of dependent species may involve 300 or 400 year rotations and it is probably ecologically out of the question for complex, fragile rainforest systems. As such time spans may be commercially unviable, protection of non-resource species involves fundamentally rethinking how or whether one can use these forests. The international ban on whaling, based on moral considerations, defies the industrial/instrumental belief in the potential for whales to be harvested sustainably. For similar reasons, environmentalists now campaign to preserve wilderness areas and for animal rights in general. Consider also the conflicts between the environment movement and industry over the *representations* of place versus space, struggles with profound material consequences for particular rivers, forests and wetlands. One may recognise a fierce contest over images and counter-images of sites in the diametrically opposed terms used by developers and environmentalists to represent contested terrain through the Australian media as either significant places or exploitable spaces with few specifically valuable attributes – 'the last free river' versus 'a leech-ridden ditch' for the Franklin River in Tasmania; or 'magnificent Northern wilderness' and 'sacred ground' versus 'clapped-out buffalo country' for Coronation Hill, a proposed mine site in the Northern Territory. As Harvey (1993: 23) notes, in such cases 'the cultural politics of places, the political economy of their development, and the accumulation of a sense of social power in place frequently fuse in indistinguishable ways'.

Each of these examples stresses ways in which a non-economistic ecological critique is in tension with or begins to break away from industrial modernity even as it still uses the media, scientific information and political institutions which are products of late modernity as its tools. In other words, ecological critique is not (as Hajer would suggest) naively anti-modern, seeking to dismantle all abstract relations established through modernisation. Rather, as the product of modernity and something which continues to depend upon modernity's processes for its development,[17] it aims to discipline and restrain – to put bindings, brakes and shackles (Offe, 1992) – on the over-determining effects of globalised productive systems. Beck (1992: 23) writes of how the life of a blade of grass in the Bavarian forest ultimately comes to depend on the making and keeping of international agreements: ecological critique requires abstract systems and their institutions, and ecological considerations to coexist through the prioritisation of the latter.

The strongest or most radically *ecological* notion of ecological modernisation will often stand in opposition to industrial modernity's predominantly instrumental relationship to nature as exploitable resource. Recognition that over-production – the use of material resources beyond regional and global ecological capacities – must cease because of the threat of imminent ecological collapse, does not allow for the self-serving gradualism of the weak forms of ecological modernisation discussed earlier.

Reflexivity and risk, anxiety and mistrust

Giddens has noted that the forms of reflexivity involved in the continual generating of systematic self-knowledge do not stabilise the relation between expert knowledge and knowledge applied in lay actions. This is as true for scientific and technical systems as for sociology (to which Giddens was referring), for these systems also remain always at least one step away from the understanding which would control their impacts and are always on their way to creating new problems. Increased ecological awareness encourages recognition of the limits to our scientific comprehension of the physical world and therefore of the limits to our capacity to know and technically manipulate them. Our crude understanding of the interplay of biological systems and global climate is a good case in point.

However industrial modernisation has largely vanquished the traditional cultural forces which might control the abstract scientific appropriation of the environment or, more importantly, the impulse to transform nature (whether through biotechnology or *in vitro* fertilisation). At the same time, it has produced a new category of socio-technological failures – such as Chernobyl and the ozone hole – which is unprecedented in its spatial and temporal reach, respecting no territorial borders and potentially affecting future generations. The global extension of the catastrophic capacity of industrial modernisation is accompanied by the means to broadcast information about such disasters to populations which previously trusted expert systems and now become aware of these new risks, with their implications at the personal (cancer and death) and global (destruction of life on earth) levels of existence.

As Giddens, Beck and others point out, the resultant disenchantment with science and technological change, and the popular appreciation of the new risks they produce, has led to a transformation of public perceptions of progress. Optimistic notions of progress, based on uncritical belief in the benefits of the scientific and industrial appropriation of Nature, have now collapsed into anxiety and mistrust. Giddens argues that this new phase, which other theorists call postmodernity, is but an extension of modernity in process. 'We have not moved beyond modernity but are living precisely through a phase of its radicalisation', a period in which Progress is 'emptied out by continuous change' (Giddens, 1990: 51), However there is good reason to suggest that this underplays the discontinuities associated with cultural disenchantment with progress and particularly its handmaidens, science and technology. This disenchantment constitutes a radical departure from simple modernity and signals the establishment of a new, more anxious phase of reflexive modernisation (Beck *et al.*, 1994).

Those interpretations of ecological modernisation which are still embedded in notions of industrial progress, albeit more cautious but still bearing an evolutionary sense of technological adaptation through reflexivity, do not address the extent of this corrosion of trust in simple industrial modernity.[18] They accept that modernisation has become *more* reflexive, but only in the narrow and instrumental sense of improving environmental efficiency, rather than in the broad and *reflective* manner of ecological critique which fundamentally questions the trajectories of industrial modernity. By contrast, strong ecological modernisation therefore also points to the potential for developing a range of alternative ecological modernities, distinguished by their diversity of local cultural and environmental conditions although still linked through their common recognition of human and environmental rights and a critical or reflexive relationship to certain common technologies, institutional forms and communicative practices which support the realisation of ecological rationality and values ahead of narrower instrumental forms.

In conclusion, the concept of ecological modernisation has been deployed in a range of ways – as a description of narrow, technological reforms, as a term for policy analysis, in reference to a new ideological constellation and in reference to deeply embedded and ecologically self-conscious forms of cultural transformation – and bearing quite different values. As a result, there is a danger that the term may serve to legitimise the continuing instrumental domination and destruction of the environment, and the promotion of less democratic forms of government, foregrounding modernity's industrial and technocratic discourses over its more recent, resistant and critical ecological components. Consequently there is a need to identify the normative dimensions of these uses as either weak or strong, depending on whether or not such ecological modernisation is part of the problem or part of the solution for the ecological crisis.

Notes

1 For instance, see Simonis (1988), Janicke *et al.* (1992), Zimmermann *et al.* (1990), Weale (1992), Hajer (1995) and Andersen (1993).
2 For example, see Vogel (1986, 1990), Vogel and Kun (1987), Knoepful and Weidner (1990), Vig and Kraft (1990), Yaeger (1991), Weale (1992), Feigenbaum *et al.* (1993) and Wintle and Reeve (1994).
3 For instance, while transboundary problems such as acid rain and fallout from Chernobyl shaped environmental politics, policies and institutions in Western Europe, they were of little consequence in Japan and irrelevant to 'frontier states' such as Australia, where preservationist conflicts over the impacts of primary resource extraction – agriculture, forestry and mining – on relatively pristine environments predominated.
4 The NEPP has already undergone two four-yearly reviews, as required by legislation.
5 Consider the enormous gap between the technical capacities – which have been available for decades – to produce durable, safe, energy efficient and largely recyclable cars and the actuality to date.
6 Hajer's use of the term varies in its elasticity. As he extends his view of 'ecological modernisation' to the point that it seems all-embracing in its cultural inclusivity, it becomes hard to see what bounds EM as a discourse – a theoretical-methodological problems common to Foucauldian approaches to policy analysis. Perhaps it is therefore better to instead regard ecological modernisation as a meta-discourse or deep cultural tendency. It then becomes possible to read EM back into the nineteenth century movement for resource conservation and forward into the growing reflexivity of science and technology. That Hajer might want to add conservative and neo-liberal opposition to state regulation to his list of the signs of EM indicates some of the problems with his own ill-defined discursive approach to 'locating' EM.
7 Towards the end of *The Politics of Environmental Discourse*, Hajer briefly touches upon an ideal form of EM which he calls 'reflexive ecological modernisation'.

This represents a cultural tendency rather than merely a policy discourse and stands in opposition to 'techno-corporatist ecological modernisation' in its emphasis on democratic and discursive practices.

8 See Christoff (1996).

9 For instance, see Weale (1992: 78–9).

10 Both Weale and Hajer comment on the role which international forums, such as the OECD, have played in fostering EM as a policy discourse. For instance, Weale claims

> the main bodies responsible for developing the ideology of EM were international organisations, who sought to use the new policy discourse as a way to secure acceptance of common, or at least harmonised, environmental policies, the closest example being the EC.
>
> (Weale, 1993: 209)

He also discusses the evolution of new international environmental regimes as but does not integrate this discussion into his exploration of ecological modernisation (Weale, 1992: ch. 7).

11 Similarly, Jahn (1993: 30) notes that data seem to indicate that neo-corporatism has a positive impact on *environmental performance* and on *anti-productionist politics*. He comments that 'it seems reasonable to argue that the impacl of neo-corporatist arrangements on both dependent variables is dependent upon the influence of new social movements and associated green and left-libertarian parties on established politics'. However, importantly, he also notes Offe's observation that the cost of corporatist arrangements is the margmalisation of non-organised interests, which is antithetical to the democratic principles of new social movements and of Green politics.

12 Weale (1992: 31) and Hajer (1995: 280 ff.) suggest but do not explore such alternatives.

13 By 'ecological critique', I mean both the emergent scientific understanding of ecological needs, which has evolved out of the biological and physical sciences, and the nonnative and non-instrumental (re)valuation of Nature (including its spiritual and aesthetic aspects as these manifest in concern for preservation of species and ecosystems, wilderness and visual landscape values). Both are elements increasingly dominant, motivating features of the environment movement in the late twentieth century.

14 This section draws heavily upon Giddens' elegant long essay, *The Consequences of Modernity*.

15 Of course these newer forms of trust in abstract systems may be related to pre-modern forms of trust in cultural explanatory frameworks (religion, myth and so on). They coexist with, and interact in, the process of identity formation with more direct forms which are essential in face-to-face communities and intimate social relations (as in families).

16 This is not to argue for a return to essentialiscd and romantic, exclusionary and parochial notions of 'place', such as have been central to the campaigns of certain environmental communitarians. While arguing for the need to recognise and preserve the specific place-bounded nature of ecological relations, it is also important to note the ways in which cultural notions of identity and place have been irrevocably transformed by modernity as, globally, face-to-face communities are now infused by the informational attributes and other requirements of abstract exchange.

17 Its abstract knowledge of nature remains based on research and investigation, on the international transmission of new scientific information among scientists, environmental managers and environmentalists, as well as (potentially) upon the recovery and reauthorisation of aspects of local indigenous knowledge.

18 See Janicke (1988) and Hajer (1995: 33).

References

Amin, A. (1994), *Post-Fordism: A Reader*, Oxford: Blackwell.

Andersen, M.S. (1993), *Ecological Modernisation: Between Policy Styles and Policy Instruments – the Case of Water Pollution Control*, Paper delivered at 1993 ECPR Conference, Leiden. University of Aarhus, Denmark: Centre for Social Science Environmental Research.

Angerer, G. (1992), 'Innovative Technologies for a Sustainable Development', in Dietz, Simonis and van der Straaten (eds), *Sustainability and Environmental Policy*, Berlin: Bohn Verlag, pp. 181–90.

Beck, U. (1992), *Risk Society: Towards a New Modernity*, London, New York: Sage Publications.

Beck, U., A. Giddens and S. Lash (1994), *Reflexive Modernisation: Politics, Tradition and Aesthetics in the Modern Social Order*, Oxford: Polity Press.

Best, M.H. (1990), *The New Competition: Institutions of Industrial Restructuring*, Oxford: Polity Press.

Carley, M. and I. Christie (1992), *Managing Sustainable Development*, London: Earthscan.

Christoff, P. (1996), 'Ecological citizenship and Ecologically Guided Democracy', in B. Doherty and M. de Geus (eds), *Democracy and Green Political Thought*, London: Routledge, pp. 151–69.

Dietz, F.J., U.E. Simonis and J. van der Straaten (eds) (1992), *Sustainability and Environmental Policy*, Berlin: Bohn Verlag.

Eckersley, R. (ed.) (1995), *Markets, the State and the Environment: Towards Integration*, Basingstoke: Macmillan.

Everett, M. (1992), 'Environmental Movements and Sustainable Economic Systems', in Dietz, Simonis and van der Straaten (eds), *Sustainability and Environmental Policy*, Berlin: Bohn Verlag, pp. 114–28.

Feigenbaum, H., R. Samuels and R. Kent Weaver (1993), 'Innovation, Coordination an Implementation in Energy Policy', in R. Kent Weaver and B.A. Rockman (eds), *Do Institutions Matter? Government Capabilities in the United States and Abroad*, Washington, DC: Brookings Institute, pp. 42–109.

Giddens, A. (1990), *The Consequences of Modernity*, Oxford: Polity Press.

Gross, N. (1992), 'The Green Giant? It May Be Japan', *Business Week*, 24 Feb.

Haeckel, E. (1870), *Naturliche Schopfungsgeschichte*, Berlin: Reimer.

Hajer, M.A. (1995), *The Politics of Environmental Discourse: Ecological Modernisation and the Policy Process*, Oxford: Oxford University Press.

Harvey, D. (1993), 'From Space to Place and Back Again: Reflections on the Condition of Postmodernity', in J. Bird, B. Curtis, T. Putnam, G Robertson and L. Tickner (eds), *Mapping the Futures: Local Cultures, Global Changes*, London: Routledge, pp. 3–29.

Hatch, M.T. (1995), 'The politics of Global Warming in Germany', *Environmental Politics*, Vol. 4, No. 3, pp. 415–40.

Jahn, D. (1993), 'Environmentalism and the Impact of Green Parties in Advanced Capitalist Societies', Paper delivered at 1993 ECPR Conference, Leiden.

Janicke, M. (1986/1990), *State Failure: The Impotence of Politics in Industrial Society*, Oxford: Polity Press. (First published as *Staatsversagen: Die Ohnmacht der Politik in der Industriellgesellschaft*, Munchen: Piper GmbH.)

Janicke, M. (1988), 'Okologische Modernisierung: Optionen und Restriktionen praventiver Umweltpolitik', in Simonis (ed.), *Praventative Umweltpolitik*, Frankfurt, New York: Campus Verlag, pp. 13–26.

Janicke, M. (1990), 'Erfolgsbedingungen von Umweltpolitik im Internationalen Vergleich', *Zeitschrift für Umweltpolitik*, No. 3, pp. 213–311.

Janicke, M., H. Monch, T. Ranneberg and U. Simonis (1988), *Economic Structure and Environmental Impact: Empirical Evidence on Thirty-One Countries in East and West*, Berlin: Wissenschaftszentrum Berlin für Sozialforschung gGmbH (WZB).

Janicke, M., H. Monch, and M. Binder (eds) (1992), *Umweltentlastung durch industriell Struckturwandel?: Eine Explorative Studie uber 32 Industrielander (1970 bis 1990)*, Edition Sigma, Berlin: Rainer Bohn Verlag.

Knoepful, P. and H. Weidner (1990), 'Implementing Air Quality Programs in Europe', *Policy Studies Journal*, Vol. 11, pp. 103–15.

McKibben, B. (1990), *The End of Nature*, London: Penguin.

Moore, C.A. (1992), 'Down Germany's Road to Sustainability', *International Wildlife*, Sept.–Oct., pp. 24–8.

Offe, C. (1992), 'Bindings, Shackles and Brakes: On Self-Limitation Strategies', in A. Honneth, C. Offe and A. Wellmer (eds), *Cultural–Political Interventions in the Unfinished Project of the Enlightenment*, Cambridge, MA: The MIT Press, pp. 63–94.

Organisation for Economic Co-operation and Development (OECD) (1995), *OECD Environmental Data Compendium 1995*, Paris: OECD.

Simonis, U.E. (ed.) (1988), *Praventative Umweltpolitik*, Frankfurt, New York: Campus Verlag.

van der Straaten, J. (1992), 'The Dutch National Environmental Policy Plan: To Choose or to Lose', *Environmental Politics*, Vol. 1, No. 1, pp. 45–71.

Vig, N.J. and M.E. Kraft (eds) (1990), *Environmental Policy in the 1990s: Towards a New Agenda*, Washington, DC: Congressional Quarterly Press.

Vogel, D. (1986), *National Styles of Regulation: Environmental Policy in Great Britain and the United States*, Ithaca, NY: Cornell University Press.

Vogel, D. (1990), 'Environmental Policy in Europe and Japan', in Vig and Kraft (eds), *Environmental Policy in the 1990s: Towards a New Agenda*, Washington, DC: Congressional Quarterly Press.

Vogel, D. and V. Kun (1987), 'The Comparative Study of Environmental Policy', in D. Meinolf, H.N. Weiler and A.B. Antal (eds), *Comparative Policy Research: Learning from Experience*, New York: St Martin's Press.

Wallace, D. (1995), *Environmental Policy and Industrial Innovation*, London: Earthscan.

Weale, A. (1992), *The New Politics of Pollution*, Manchester: Manchester University Press.

Weale, A. (1993), 'Ecological modernisation and the Integration of European Environmental Policy', in J.D. Lieffernink, P.D. Lowe and A.P.J. Mol (eds), *European Integration and Environmental Policy*, London: Bellhaven, pp. 198–216.

Wintle, M. and R. Reeve (eds) (1994), *Rhetoric and Reality in Environmental Policy: The Case of the Netherlands in Comparison with Britain*, London: Avebury Studies in Green Research.

World Commission on Environment and Development (WCED) (1987), *Our Common Future*, Oxford: Oxford University Press.

World Resources Institute (WRI) (1994), *World Resources 1994–95 – A Guide to the Global Environment*, Oxford: Oxford University Press.

Yaeger, P. C. (1991), *The Limits of the Law*, Cambridge: Cambridge University Press.

Zimmermann, K., V.J. Hartje and A. Ryll (1990), *Okologische Modernisierung der Produktion: Struktur und Trends*, Edition Sigma, Berlin: Rainer Bohn Verlag.

Part IV
Policy

12 Power, politics and environmental inequality

A theoretical and empirical analysis of the process of 'peripheralisation'

Andrew Blowers and Pieter LeRoy

Introduction

> Les divisions territoriales sont donc de moins en moins fondées dans la nature des choses, et par conséquent perdent de leur signification. On peut presque dire qu'un peuple est d'autant plus avancé qu'elles y ont un caractère plus superficiel.
> (E. Durkheim, *De la division du travail social* (1893))

Since the 1970s, environmental problems have been prominent politically, in the developed countries of east and west as well as in the developing world. Environmental problems represent a new and specific challenge to existing political structures and processes. One of the major challenges arises from the relationship between environmental quality and social inequality. An equitable allocation of both environmental advantages (e.g. the accessibility and use of environmental resources) and disadvantages (e.g. the allocation of environmental risks) requires adequate political measures.

This chapter considers the sociological nature and political implications of the relationship between environmental quality and social inequality using examples of hazardous activities. Examples of such activities are *industrial plants*, especially chemical installations; *power stations*, especially nuclear power stations; significant *infrastructural works*, like highways, airports or high speed railway-lines and, last but not least, so-called *environmental infrastructure* such as waste disposal facilities and waste incineration plants. As both political awareness and environmental concern have risen, very few communities are prepared to accept the location of such activities on their territory. Therefore, these hazardous activities can be described as examples of 'locally unwanted land uses' (LULUs), (Popper, 1988). The resistance to these activities is partly based on self-interest and partly linked to a more general and altruistic environmental concern (Wolsink, 1993).

Since many of the examples of LULUs seem to be inherent in modern societies while others are essential to an effective environmental policy, they have to be located somewhere. The location of LULUs is, therefore, an 'inevitable' problem.

The way society deals with this locational problem is the starting point of this chapter. Among the questions that arise are: What roles do different social actors and factors play?; Under what circumstances is local resistance successful? Does successful resistance narrow the options? Where are the 'inevitable' LULUs eventually located? Is there any spatial as well as social and political pattern to be recognised in their eventual location? From these questions we derive our central thesis that *LULUs tend typically to be located in already backward areas and that, therefore, their location reproduces and reinforces processes of 'peripheralisation'.*

First, we will discuss briefly the pattern of social mobilisation that occurs in response to environmental threats posed by LULUs. We will stress the combination of traditional and modern elements within the mobilisation strategies of resistant communities. Second, we will establish the characteristics of peripheral areas and communities. As 'periphery' is not a static concept, we will have to define the process of 'peripheralisation', using both geographical and sociological perspectives. Although we will introduce some empirical evidence as well, this first part of the chapter mainly sets out a conceptual and analytical framework in the form of eleven propositions which are examined against the empirical evidence assembled in the second part of the chapter. These empirical data are drawn from detailed case studies in the United Kingdom and Belgium undertaken during the 1970s and 1980s. Finally, we shall formulate some theoretical, empirical and practical political questions which emerge from our analysis.

The social basis of environmental concern

Research on the social basis of environmental movements has been undertaken since they first emerged in the late 1960s and early 1970s (Buttel and Flinn, 1974; Harry *et al.*, 1969 and many others). One conclusion of these studies was that social concern over environmental quality and degradation, although widespread, was related to income and to socio-economic status in general. Those most concerned about environmental quality were the well educated and affluent members of the middle classes. Second, environmental consciousness was said to correlate with political attitudes such as 'liberalism' and 'cosmopolitanism'. The pattern of participation in environmental movements was shown to be very similar (for recent reviews of international research in this area (see Buttel (1987) and Lowe and Rüdig (1986); in the Netherlands both Ester (1980) and Nelissen *et al.* (1987) came to similar conclusions; for Belgium, see Leroy and De Geest (1985)). Repeatedly in different western countries, both environmental concern and participation in environmental groups have been shown to be higher among younger people, in the middle and upper social classes, and among politically liberal people. Enzensberger, back in 1974, therefore concluded that environmentalists were (and still are, as later research has proved) 'overwhelmingly members of the middle class and the new petty bourgeoisie'. Cotgrove and Duff (1980) suggested that the 'post-materialist' ideology of the environmental movement was a present form of 'middle-class radicalism'.

As Lowe and Rüdig (1986) and many others have argued, this kind of survey research on environmental opinions and participation produces a lot of unanswered questions. The first is to know what correlations between conventional sociological variables such as age, sex, income, education, socio-economic status and political opinion on the one hand, and environmental attitudes on the other, really do tell us about actual environmental behaviour. The discrepancy between attitude and behaviour is a long-known phenomenon in social sciences, as Ester (1980) has pointed out. A second problem with this kind of research is that opinions and attitudes are mostly regarded as independent variables, set apart from their social context. Situational variables, obviously, condition and determine variations in both public environmental consciousness and participation in environmental action groups. One of these situational variables is the actual environmental quality experienced, another is the degree of environmental threat caused by LULUs. Therefore, our first proposition is that *conclusions drawn from survey research may help to understand opinions and attitudes – what people say – in 'environmental peacetime', but do not help to understand people's behaviour and social processes – what people do – in times of environmental conflicts.* Understanding these processes requires deeper investigation of social processes through case studies.

The pattern of mobilisation over (spatially discrete) environmental threats

Case studies of environmental conflicts are available at both the national and local level. Although some of these studies are rather anecdotal, others establish an analytical framework exploring theoretical concepts such as (local or national) mobilisation processes, planning and decision-making processes, community power versus national state power and the rise and development of new political cleavages (Blowers, 1984a; Blowers and Lowry, 1987; Blowers *et al.*, 1991; Bridgeland and Sofranko, 1975; Castells, 1978; Gladwin, 1980; Hall, 1980; Lauwers and Van Lint, 1979; Leroy, 1979; Leroy, 1983). As they focus on the environmental conflict within its social and political context, these in-depth case studies, from some of which we will draw evidence later, reveal social and political processes that remain otherwise hidden.

One of these case studies, the Rupelstreek case (Lauwers and Van Lint, 1979), illustrates clearly both the differences between a survey approach and a case study approach and the inadequacy of the former under certain circumstances. Based on the literature on environmental consciousness and on participation in environmental groups, the Rupelstreek (in Belgium) was a community very unlikely to be particularly engaged in environmental matters. Although located between Antwerp and Brussels, the Rupelstreek had all the characteristics of a backward region, including an ageing population, a high rate of emigration, a region in economic decline and a low degree of political and cultural cosmopolitanism. In view of these characteristics, we would expect a low level of environmental concern and a low level of willingness for social action. But the size and intensity of the conflict, caused by the proposed location of an industrial waste disposal plant (1975–77), revealed exactly the opposite. Consequently, the question arises as to how to explain this high level of participation in environmental action and the relative success of this action.

Like other authors, Lauwers and Van Lint concluded that the participation in and the success of environmental action were above all dependent upon the capacity of a part of the local elite to mobilise the local community (or communities) involved. Throughout their campaigning, the efforts of the leaders aimed to create new (or renewed) feelings of local solidarity: *us*, against *them* – the national and regional authorities responsible for the location proposal. Therefore, the Rupelstreek case demonstrates that social mobilisation over particular, especially spatially discrete environmental threats cannot be understood in terms of age, socio-economic stratification and so on. As has been shown in many other case studies as well, mobilisation over LULUs actually cuts across the typical patterns of social integration of modern society, based on occupation and status, on political party membership and similar factors. Therefore, our second proposition is that *mobilisation over (local) environmental threats both activates and reveals traditional patterns of social integration that were supposed to be annihilated by modernisation – for example, patterns of integration based on kinship, on neighbourhood, on local or regional identification.*

We stress the phrase 'both activates and reveals' to distinguish our point of view from both the 'romantic' and the 'modernist' position. Of course, one must establish that leaders, through their actions and propaganda, partly appeal to an imagined community and try to idealise the local environment, in order to enhance people's identification with the local society concerned and, thereby, to widen the basis for societal mobilisation. But, localism cannot be appealed to, if there is no basic 'horizontal' integration pattern to be activated (we use the concept of 'horizontal' as it has been developed by Warren (1956, 1973) to describe changes in the structure and function of local communities). Local solidarity only temporarily overwhelms modern, 'sectoral' or 'vertical' patterns of solidarity and integration. Nevertheless, if these patterns of integration can be activated in times of 'threat to the local identity', or what is defined as such by some local elites, they would appear to be manifestations of basic, be it normally latent, social patterns. Although they differ in many respects, the ongoing social and political processes of renewed locality – and region – building throughout Europe once again falsify a central thesis of modernist rhetoric as if location and identification with localities and regions do not have any social meaning at all in modern society. The Durkheim quotation in the opening lines of the Chapter is of course a classical example of this rhetoric. Aside from the over-excitement about the local identity during an action campaign, environmental mobilisation and action groups, like some other voluntary associations, seem to play a role as 'adaptive mechanisms' in transitional situations of rapid social change within local communities (Leroy, 1983).

Peripheralisation: the characteristics of peripheral communities

As stated in the introduction, many questions arise from the scenario of local environmental conflicts, both from a sociological and political point of view. Sociologists may be interested in the strategies and the conditions under which social mobilisation is successful. Political scientists will be interested in the way the political system deals with this resistance, how it sets out its own strategies, reorganises planning and decision-making procedures and so on. At this point, however, we want to focus on the main issue of this chapter, the consequences of successful resistance in one place for the eventual location of LULUs. We there-fore restate our central thesis as: *successful resistance narrows the options; LULUs tend to be located in peripheral areas. Their location, consequently, reproduces processes of 'peripheralisation'.*

The idea of a peripheral community or area suggests that it is located on the edges of the mainstream. There is a geographical and spatial basis to the concept, the idea of communities that are physically remote or inaccessible (though not necessarily distant) from the central, dominant region which is the focus of com-munications and development. The concept also owes something to the notion of 'core and periphery' and the relationships of political, economic and cultural domination and exploitation that has been developed as an explanation for processes of uneven development in these areas (Castells, 1974; Claval, 1978). Hechter even used the concept of 'internal colonialism', thereby referring to the powerful core region exploiting those on the fringes (Hechter, 1975). Though there are problems with this 'internal colonialism' concept, his argument that the dominant 'diffusion model' of modernisation predicts a lessening of regional inequalities, whereas the 'internal colonial model' predicts that these will persist or even may be reinforced, seems to be analogous to our thesis of peripheralisa-tion. Finally, there is the social and cultural aspect of peripheral communities or regions, as they are mostly characterised by a homogeneous, traditional (i.e. working-class) social structure and related cultural pattern.

Basing a judgement on these connotations, the characteristics of peripheral com-munities may be summarised as geographically remote, economically marginal, politically powerless and socially homogeneous, though none of these variables in itself is sufficient for a community to be qualified as peripheral. Peripheral communities, in our definition, encompass each of these characteristics to a greater or lesser degree. For our purposes there is one further defining characteristic – the condition of environmental hazard or risk. As we indicated earlier, the communities with which we are concerned bear a disproportionate share of the burden of envi-ronmental degradation or risk resulting from modern industrial processes. We shall now briefly examine each of the characteristics of peripheral communities in turn.

Remoteness

Relative geographical isolation is a feature of peripheral communities. This does not necessarily imply that they are at the furthest distance from metropolitan centres, though this may be the case. Remoteness can also be a function of inaccessibility. Peripheral communities may be difficult to reach, not linked into national or regional motorways and railway networks. Therefore, our third proposition is that *peripheral communities are physically remote in terms of distance or accessibility from metropolitan centres*.

Economic marginality

Peripheral communities tend to be economically dependent either on a dominant employer or upon state welfare. The former may be termed *one-industry communities* or *monocultural communities*. The employment base is narrow with usually one major company and a range of dependent activities. Companies may be privately owned, state-controlled or a mixture of both. In the case of private companies, control is likely to be exercised from headquarters elsewhere responding to wider regional, national and international market processes. State-owned activities will take account of broader national interests. Both private and state-owned companies thereby reinforce the 'vertical' integration pattern (Warren, 1956, 1973). Therefore our fourth proposition is that *the economic fortunes of peripheral communities are determined by policy-makers operating in a wider world in which the needs of the local community play a significant, but not determining, part*. In some cases, economic restructuring through changes in technology or market forces has caused the progressive withdrawal of investment and employment or the total abandonment of peripheral communities (Bell and Newby, 1971; Miller and Form, 1963). The communities involved remain as distressed areas with very high rates of unemployment willing to accept job-creating investment almost regardless of the environmental risks that may be attached.

Powerlessness

The economic power of dominant companies is also reflected in the political sway they hold over peripheral communities. In the past, local companies exercised considerable power over local communities. Crenson (1971), in his masterly study of US Steel in Gary, Indiana, demonstrates how the company could exercise power without ostensible action through a process of non-decision-making, merely by a reputation for power. Non-decision-making is a key element of the neo-elitist critique of pluralist theories of power with their emphasis on participation by competing interests in an open and responsive political system (Bachrach and Baratz, 1970; Lukes, 1974). Other theorists emphasising the interests of capitalist companies would argue that the power of business resides in its ability to threaten investment withdrawal (Vogel, 1982).

Local power structures have changed over time (Warren, 1973). As companies have merged or restructured, there has been a tendency for the close identification of corporate power with local interest (the 'horizontal' pattern of Warren) to diminish. At the same time the power which local communities once exercised through their local councils has been progressively eroded as the central state has removed authority and increased its control over local spending and policy-making. This has intensified a condition of powerlessness reflected in our fifth proposition that *peripheral communities tend to lack effective political power and, consequently, the ability or willingness to influence or resist decisions taken elsewhere that affect their interests.* As Gaventa puts it, 'Power seems to create power. Powerlessness serves to reinforce powerlessness. Power relations, once established, are self sustaining' (1980: 256). Powerlessness may result from a perception that action would be fruitless or it may simply be brought about by indifference or acceptance. Or it could emanate from what Schattschneider (1960) once called the 'mobilisation of bias', a pervading set of values which predispose the community to inaction. But the vicious circle of powerlessness is also caused by the organisational characteristics of the community involved. Community power studies have clearly established the relationship between the economic, political and therefore organisational differentiation and the capacity of communities to mobilise political power (Bell and Newby, 1971; Cox *et al.*, 1974; Liebert and Imershein, 1977).

A culture of acceptance

A concomitant feature of political powerlessness and the lack of organisational differentiation is the absence of locally based social elites able to formulate opinion and mobilise support in defence of the community's wider and long-term interests. The local interest tends to be dominated by the need for employment on whatever terms it can be gained. Within the community there may develop a pervasive culture of support for the company from its dependent workers creating a defence against environmentalist opponents who are perceived to threaten their economic interests. The Tessenderlo case in Belgium, which will be discussed below, illustrates the mechanism (Leroy, 1981, 1983). At its most extreme there can develop what Loeb (1986), describing the nuclear complex at Hanford, US, has dubbed a 'nuclear culture', a culture of acceptance or cynicism about the morality of the project and the risks that are involved. Similarly Wynne *et al.* (1993), in a sociological study of Sellafield, noted an ambivalence combining complex feelings of defensiveness and acquiescence in the attitudes of a community commonly regarded as supportive of the nuclear industry. Opposition is mobilised by those living further away, who are not dependent on the industry and it is met by defensiveness and hostility. Therefore, our sixth proposition is that *peripheral communities develop a culture of acceptance, defensiveness and even hostility to external influence which reinforces their isolation and powerlessness.*

Environmental degradation

The characteristics of powerlessness, economic marginality and physical and social isolation render peripheral communities vulnerable to exploitation or neglect by the companies that dominate them. There is often a mutual protectiveness between company and community. In return for jobs and other forms of investment and patronage the company's workforce and their dependents will overlook the negative impacts of the company's activities; for, in truth, they have little choice, there is nowhere else for them to go. As a result, some peripheral communities offer sanctuary to activities which degrade and pollute the environment bringing risks to present and future generations. Therefore, a seventh proposition is that *peripheral communities are traditionally associated with polluting and risk-creating industrial activities.*

In the advanced industrial countries there are many examples of such peripheral communities. They include communities developed around hazardous activities such as petro-chemical complexes like Canvey Island or Ellesmere Port in the UK (Smith, 1988) and other 'pollution havens' such as oil refineries or waste disposal plants, including incinerators which present health risks to the local population (Gatrell and Lovett, 1991). Perhaps the most obvious cases are 'nuclear oases', communities clustered around unclear complexes Hanford in the US, Sellafield in the UK (McSorley, 1990) or Cherbourg in France (Zonabend, 1993). In certain cases environmental hazards have already caused severe pollution or accidents such as Love Canal, Niagara Falls, US, where seepage of toxic chemicals from a dump closed in the 1940s invaded the soil beneath the new homes of a neighbouring community causing it to be evacuated completely in the late 1970s. Perhaps the most extreme case of a peripheral community exposed to environmental hazards was Pripyat, the town belatedly evacuated after the Chernobyl disaster in April 1986.

The process of peripheralisation

Although we have established a number of characteristics of peripheral communities, this does not imply that the concept of peripherality is a static one. On the contrary, we want to stress the dynamic aspect of the concept, referring to the fact that these communities are the victims of *processes* of peripheralisation. These processes of peripheralisation are both push and pull. The pull factors are present in the characteristics of the communities we have already described. Given little choice, peripheral communities will opt for enterprises that provide a palpable benefit in terms of income whatever the longer term risks may be. The acceptance seems to be the greater as the new activities to be located are, technically or economically, linked with or similar to the industries they know. But, this situation is reinforced by the push factor, the refusal of other communities to accept risk-creating and polluting activities. Therefore, an eighth proposition is that *the process of peripheralisation reflects material self interest both on the part of those communities anxious to avoid the blight created by hazardous activities and those who have little option but to accept risks in return for economic benefits.*

Resistance to LULUs is often portrayed as evidence of 'not in my backyard' (NIMBY). At its simplest it represents an antagonism to any activity that threatens to depreciate the environmental (and therefore material) value of the locality. But, while there may be unanimity in defence of local interests, there may be division over the implications. For part of the population it will not matter where the

LULU is sited so long as it is anywhere but here (ABH). They do not challenge the activity itself and therefore will not see the consequences for other communities of their obdurate stance. Others may evince a wider, more disinterested, concern, challenging the need for the activity in anyone's backyard and urging alternative technologies and policies (Wolsink, 1993).

The increased resistance to LULUs is both a product of growing affluence in which environmental quality plays a part and of increasing political and environmental awareness of the damage and dangers of certain activities. But successful resistance to LULUs mostly depends on the capacity of the community or communities involved to mobilise against the threats 'to the local identity' and the local community. Throughout this mobilisation, campaign leaders try to reactivate particular patterns of social integration, especially so-called traditional patterns of 'horizontal' integration, based on neighbourhood, identification with the local community, the region and so on. These patterns, we argued earlier, cut across the modern patterns of integration based on occupation, income, political affiliation and similar factors. As mobilisation against LULUs creates cross-cutting coalitions, it temporarily overwhelms the socio-economic, political and ideological divisions which, in peacetime, characterise the community. Therefore, our ninth proposition is that *the success of resistance against a LULU depends on the capacity of local elites to forge a united front within the community, even though supporters may represent opposing positions and ideologies on other issues and differing views on the need for the activity itself.* Such mobilisation will tend to recur in communities newly threatened by the location of LULUs. Our contention is that in peripheral communities such mobilisation will not occur for two main reasons. One is that, as traditional patterns of social integration are predominant in peripheral communities, they by definition cannot be reactivated by modern elites. The other is that peripheral communities, as they are dependent on the threatening activity, will not succeed in mobilising a united front.

In certain circumstances the power to resist a LULU can be greatly enhanced by building a coalition among equally threatened communities. In the effort to stave off a perceived environmental threat, coalitions can be built which, like intra-community coalitions, cross socio-economic, political and geographical divides. Moreover, such inter-community coalitions may be able to draw in the support of nationally based environmental organisations and to develop counter-expertise to challenge the power of government and industry. Our tenth proposition, therefore, is that *where an unwanted activity is proposed in more than one location, coalitions cutting across social, political and geographical divides can be mobilised by the threatened communities, thereby increasing the power of local resistance.* Peripheral communities in general would be unlikely to participate in this kind of inter-community, regional or national coalition.

This deployment of power opposing LULUs, both on a community and an inter-community level, considerably narrows the locational options for these hazardous activities. The ability of the communities involved to mobilise and organise disparate interests in a united front greatly enhances the power to prevent the location of such activities, thereby making it increasingly difficult to find 'greenfield' sites for them. This leads us to our eleventh and final proposition, returning to our central thesis: *the power of mobilised coalitions to prevent the location of LULUs in some communities, combined with the powerlessness of peripheral communities to resist them, narrows the locational options, making the location of LULUs in peripheral communities politically almost inevitable.*

We shall now examine these propositions, using evidence from three in-depth case studies we have undertaken.

Air pollution: the case of London Brick, United Kingdom

The conflict

The first example is taken from a detailed study of a conflict between environmental and economic interests which took place in the Bedfordshire brickfields in south-east England during the late 1970s and early 1980s – see Figure 12.1. (A full version of this case is to be found in Blowers (1984a) and shorter versions appear in Blowers (1983, 1984b, 1985).) The London Brick Company, by a process of mergers and takeovers, had gained a monopoly of fletton brick-making, using the self-firing properties of the local Oxford Clay to manufacture bricks at low cost for a national market. Fletton brick-making at the time of the study producing around two-fifths of the national brick supply, is confined to the Oxford Clay Vale stretching from east of Oxford through Bedford and northwards to the Peterborough area in Cambridgeshire. It creates two environmental problems – a derelict landscape from the deep voids from which the clay is excavated, and air pollution from the sulphur dioxide, fluorides and mercaptans emitted from the stacks during the firing process. In the postwar decades there was a national need for bricks for reconstruction and brick companies were given extensive permissions for clay working. By the end of the 1970s London Brick was embarking on a major investment programme to replace ageing brickworks with two new 'superworks' in the Marston Vale in Bedfordshire. Quite unexpectedly it met strong opposition to its plans from the local community.

Up to this point the company had been secure from challenge. But local concerns about dereliction and pollution, latent till then, were suddenly unleashed when the company applied for planning permission for its new works. The company no longer had unchallenged power for several reasons: the national need for bricks had diminished, house-building had declined and alternative methods and markets were being exploited; with new works the workforce would probably shrink and brick-making was of declining significance in the local economy; and environmental concern was rising among certain groups in the local community. It was a community in transition, with traditional communities dependent on brick-making being submerged by an adventitious population working in a wide range of jobs in local towns and in London.

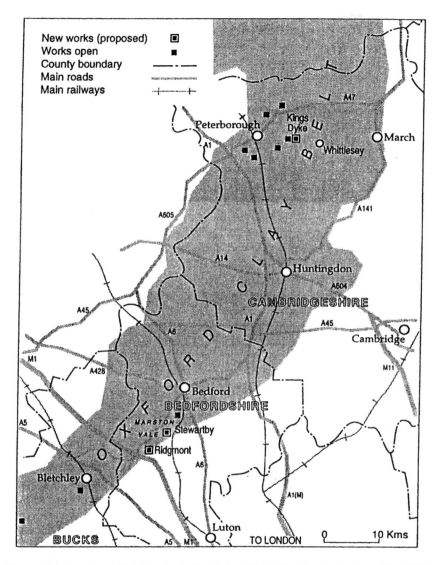

Figure 12.1 Location of brickworks in the Oxford Clay belt at the beginning of the 1980s.

The opposition to the company's plans came from local pressure groups and a group called Public Review of Brickmaking and the Environment (PROBE). Chaired by the local peer, the Marquis of Tavistock, the group included local MPs, farmers, Conservative and Labour county councillors and local business-men, and it was supported by medical and engineering experts. Pollution from fluorides became the central issue. Opponents claimed that fluorides from brick-making caused fluorosis (a wasting disease) in cattle and posed a threat to human health – though the evidence was inconclusive. It was easy to create anxiety about unknown dangers and very difficult for the company to defend itself against such charges.

The decision rested with the Bedfordshire County Council which was evenly divided. The dominant Conservative group was split between supporters of a capitalist company which provided jobs and investment in the local community and those reflecting farming, landed and amenity interests. The small Labour group was opposed to the company on environmental grounds, but in conflict with the trade unions who represented the interest in jobs in brick-making. The issue came before the full Council of 83 members on three occasions. The first time it was deferred and, on the second occasion, a combination of Conservative and Labour Councillors narrowly secured an amendment requiring pollution abatement measures to be applied to the new works – a condition the company claimed it could not meet. The company chose to interpret the condition to mean that abatement should be applied when the technology was available. The Council was unpersuaded and, on the third occasion, confirmed the condition passed at the second meeting.

Meanwhile external events were rapidly undermining the Council's position. In neighbouring Cambridgeshire there was already one new works and permission for a further new superworks was granted in early 1981 without the onerous pollution control condition applied in Bedfordshire. This provided the company with investment options. Shortly after this with a deepening recession hitting the construction industry and a five months' stockpile of bricks having accumulated, the company decided to shut down completely its Ridgmont works, the second largest in Bedfordshire, with the loss of 1100 jobs. Political fortunes had been reversed with trade unions, company spokespeople and their Conservative supporters seizing the initiative. With jobs overwhelming pollution as the key issue, the opponents of the company were in headlong retreat and a permission acceptable to the company was granted by the planning committee without further reference to the Council. By early 1994 the permissions had not been implemented.

Interpretation

In earlier days parts of the Bedfordshire brickfields may have possessed all the characteristics of a peripheral community (Cox, 1979; Hillier, 1981). With company villages like Stewartby and Brogborough built by the brick companies and dominated by brickworks there was the physical isolation, monocultural economy and social homogeneity of a workforce in thrall to the company. London Brick and its predecessors, with extensive planning permissions, were able to suppress or prevent the emergence of any challenge to their dominion. By the 1970s the brick-fields were clearly in transition. Brick-making was no longer the only significant activity. The waves of dependent immigrant labour from the new Commonwealth, eastern and southern Europe which had flocked to the brickfields ceased as brickmaking declined. Mobile, middle-class migrants began to infiltrate the villages around and in the Vale and moved into the burgeoning suburbs of Bedford, thereby bringing along modernisation in these parts of the region. As a result of this changing population, elites emerged concerned with environmental issues and ready to challenge the company when opportunity arose. Moreover the opposition displayed the characteristic cross-cutting coalition of traditional and modern interests which we have identified as a feature of environmental conflicts. Landed, farming and environmentalist interests spanning the political parties were combined in alliance against the company, its workforce and the trade unions. Both sides exerted pressure on the politicians. In the end economic pressures proved triumphant in the context of a recession.

The outcome depended on external factors prevailing at the time, in particular the situation in neighbouring Cambridgeshire. There the brick-fields were physically isolated, located in the flat, featureless Fenlands in towns like Whittlesey which were predominantly working-class. There was no comparable social change in this area, which still exhibited the characteristics of a peripheral community. Consequently there was no opposition to the company's plans; instead, the new investment with the promise of more jobs and less pollution from the taller stacks was welcomed. The tendency we suggested for hazardous industries to become concentrated in existing peripheral locations was confirmed.

Within the brickfields the coexistence of different communities, the one still peripheral, the other undergoing rapid change, provided the company with locational options. If it met resistance or intolerable demands in one area, it could relatively easily move to another. In a recession, with jobs at a premium, it could hope to secure permissions which it could cash in when the economy upturned. In the event, however, the company was taken over, the market never fully recovered and new works in Bedfordshire remain a distant, and probably forlorn, hope.

The location of hazardous industry: the Tessenderlo case, Belgium

The conflict

The community of Tessenderlo, located in western Limburg, in the north-east of Belgium, has been the scene of an environmental conflict over the location of a hazardous industrial plant – see Figure 12.2. The conflict (described in detail in Leroy (1981, 1983)) started in 1978 when Phillips Petroleum, an important American petrochemical company, applied for a permit for the production of mercaptans in a plant very near the centre of Tessenderlo. Mercaptans are a group of petro-sulphur compounds, most of them non-toxic, but causing a very penetrating, very unpleasant stench, even in concentrations of one part per billion (ppb) and below. Mercaptans are used, in the rubber industry among others, especially for the production of car tyres. Furthermore, mercaptans are used to give an odour to natural gas as it is distributed, thereby making it easily detectable.

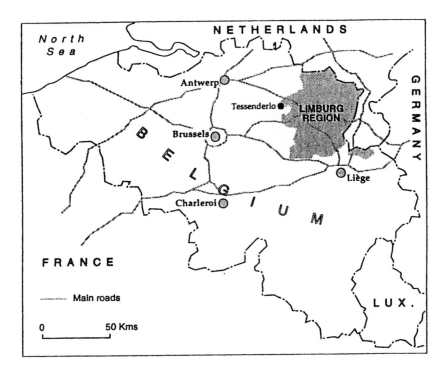

Figure 12.2 Location of Tessenderlo.

The most important locational factor for Phillips Petroleum was the availability of H_2S, produced by Tessenderlo Chemie (Tessenderlo Chemicals). Tessenderlo Chemie (TC) had been located in the very heart of the small town since the 1920s. More than half of Tessenderlo's 14,000 people lived within one mile of the plant. TC was responsible for a number of environmental problems, including high levels of emissions of SO_2, of mercury and other components in the air, and an enormous amount of radioactive plaster waste from phosphate ore processing, which caused radioactive surface water pollution. Over the years, these emissions have been causing a high level of soil pollution, and damaging houses and other buildings as well as vegetation.

These pollution problems had been known, though not in detail, for years to the authorities and to the citizens of Tessenderlo. The local people were fully aware of the risks from an industry so near to the city centre. In 1942, during the Second World War, a major explosion in the plant occurred, causing more than 180 deaths, hundreds of wounded and enormous devastation in the city centre. Although the causes of the explosion are still unclear – whether it was an accident or an act of sabotage – 'the disaster' is part of the collective memory of the city. Nevertheless, the Mayor's plan after the war to remove TC from the city centre to the periphery of the community was rejected by management, the workers and the local shopkeepers. The plant was rebuilt at the same location; the 'symbiosis' of plant and city continued.

This symbiosis tended to prevent the environmental problems caused by the industry from being discussed. Even the location, about a quarter of a mile from the same city centre, in 1972, of the Limburgse Vinyl Maatschappij (Limburg vinyl company; LVM) – an industrial daughter of TC producing monovinyl – hardly caused any environmental protest. The citizens of Tessenderlo were obviously used to chemical plants, even in their back yards. Only incidents (such as the 'green rain') that took place shortly after production started, caused some protests. Since LVM was prepared to compensate for any damage, the protest rapidly came to an end.

That was not the case when the Phillips Petroleum application for a permit was announced in the autumn of 1978. Within a few days, an environmental action group (BELT – better environment tessenderlo) was formed to protest against the location of this plant. The mobilisation by the action group was very successful and was backed by three of the five parties represented in the municipal council. BELT asked for a local referendum, supported also by the political parties opposed to the location of the chemical plant near the city centre. The referendum took place in March 1979 and underlined how successful the mobilisation had been. With about 70 per cent of the people participating, 93.4 per cent of the voters (i.e. about 64 per cent of the population) said 'no' to the location of the Phillips Petroleum plant.

Despite this result, the executive Board of Mayor and Aldermen, by four to two, decided to grant the building permit and to recommend the environmental permit which was the responsibility of the provincial or, in the event of an appeal, the national government. The environmental protest, although very successful in mobilising the local people on the referendum, did not succeed in its objective. In September 1979 Phillips Petroleum got all the necessary permits and the plant started production in February 1981. Within a few days, however, serious accidents occurred, whereby even citizens in Brussels (about 40 miles away) complained of a very penetrating and unpleasant odour, clearly caused by operating faults and accidents. These incidents gave rise to new actions by the environmental group but failed to mobilise the people a second time and attempts to widen the scope of protest also failed. Phillips was no longer the only subject of their environmental protest, which was directed against the overall environmental situation, including the environmental damage caused by TC. Although still active, since 1979 BELT has never been able to repeat its earlier mobilisation of substantial parts of the local population in favour of its environmental cause. Agalev, the Green party, closely linked to the environmental action group, obtained only one seat (out of 23) at the local elections in 1988. Another local political party, Volksbelangen (People's Interests), which rapidly grew in the 1970s and furiously opposed the Phillips location, lost a lot of its political weight. However the Christian Democrats and the Liberals (both traditional parties in Tessenderlo and both in favour of the Phillips location) regained political power, and the Social Democrats, who opposed the plant, kept the same number of seats. The Phillips story therefore seems to have been a short episode of higher environmental awareness in a peripheral community.

Interpretation

Tessenderlo was and still is an example of a peripheral community. It is located near the mining industry of Belgian Limburg, where pits have been successively closed down in the period 1966–92. At least until the 1950s, the lack of jobs, income and housing, combined with the attraction from the economically stronger regions of Antwerp and Brussels, made the western Limburg, including Tessenderlo, an area of out migration (Leroy, 1981). Tessenderlo itself remained a clear example of a one industry community. Since the 1920s, the Produits Chimiques de Tessenderloo – later on Tessenderlo Chemicals (TC) – has been by far the most important employer in the community. In 1960, TC accounted for as much as 95 per cent of all industrial employment and for 56 per cent of the overall employment in the area (Leroy, 1983). The symbiosis between the community and the industry, therefore, though obviously based upon this economic interdependence, had cultural, political and social dimensions as well. Tessenderlo therefore can be characterised as a peripheral, and in particular a one-industry community, within a situation of economic marginality and relative political powerlessness, with the typical homogeneous culture of acceptance we described earlier and, as we just have seen, a deplorable environmental situation.

This situation seemed to change in the early 1960s. From about 1959, the Tessenderlo area was one of the pilot regions for the regional economic policy of the Belgian government. This policy, designed and implemented at the same time in almost all Western European countries, tried to overcome the peripheral economic position of some regions by public investment in infrastructure (highways, canals, industrial parks and so on), in housing and other improvements in the regional economic climate, in order to attract private investors. In the Tessenderlo region this policy seemed very successful. From being an area of out-migration, western Limburg changed within a decade into an area of in-migration with an annual growth rate in Tessenderlo of about 10 per 1000 people per year from 1965 to 1974. The attractive investment conditions encouraged the location of many industrial plants and, in consequence, the local and regional economy in general grew very quickly, incomes increased rapidly, houses were built, and the community invested in public welfare and culture. In short, the regional economic policy seemed to stimulate a very quick process of modernisation within this somewhat backward region. This modernisation was not only evident in its economic dimensions. These changes in turn gave rise to changes in the political and cultural life of the community. A new political party, Volksbelangen (People's Interests), was set up. With the increasing number of industrial workers, the Social Democrats (a small party until then), rapidly gained support; with the high number of middle class in-migrants, many new socio-cultural organisations were set up while traditional organisations changed rapidly.

Within these changing conditions the economic importance of TC decreased as in 1974 only 24 per cent of industrial employment (instead of 95 per cent in 1960) and 17 per cent of overall employment depended upon TC. At the same time, the political influence of both Christian Democrats and Liberals seemed to decrease, as new and renewed political parties took over. In 1974 this political modernisation was clearly not developed sufficiently to cause any environmental protest against the location of LVM, which strengthened the dependence upon the traditional employer, TC, and brought further deterioration to the environment. But by 1979, economic, political and cultural modernisation was the main factor behind the eruption of environmental protest against the location of Phillips Petroleum. In-migrants played an important role in this protest (Leroy, 1983). Although they did not form a clearly defined social group, as a social category they had a different attitude towards the traditional local industry and especially towards the pollution it created. This attitude is easily comprehensible, first, as these in-migrants were not dependent upon the one industry for their jobs and incomes. Second, they were not familiar with the traditional symbiosis of industry and community (the 1942 disaster being no part of their collective memory). In their modernist view, this symbiosis was very unattractive, as it prevented the raising of legitimate environmental concern. In the third place, most of these in-migrants came to Tessenderlo to improve their quality of life, which was likely to be diminished by the environmental threats of this industry. It is quite understandable therefore that these in-migrants, with the modern parts of the local elites, took the leading role in the environmental protest in 1979.

How can we explain the eclipse of the environmental protest afterwards? The frustration of having lost the Phillips battle cannot be the only reason. The economic situation in the Tessenderlo region seems to be a more important factor. Owing to the oil crisis (1974) and the economic recession from about 1975, much of the industry that came to Tessenderlo in the 1960s had difficulties and some firms even closed down. From 24 per cent in 1974, TC and its daughter LVM in 1980 contributed some 40 per cent of the total industrial employment in Tessenderlo, and this reached over 50 per cent during the 1980s. Instead of economic modernisation and diversification, Tessenderlo became a one-industry community again, or at least a one-sector community. The economic activity in the region, very much as in the 1950s, is highly dependent upon the chemical industry. Not only economic development, but the social and political modernisation as a whole seem to have come to an end, leaving the area as backwards as it was in the 1950s. Environmental protest, obviously, played a role (as an adaptive mechanism) in the modernisation of this local society during the late 1970s. But as the economic crisis deepened in the 1980s environmental protests almost disappeared. Despite its location and its links to the economic centres of the country, Tessenderlo has once again become peripheral. The newly peripheralised community seems to have accepted both the traditional and the new environmental threats.

Radioactive waste: the battle of the Dumps, United Kingdom

The conflict

By the early 1980s the UK government and the nuclear industry were focusing on the problem of managing the burden of radioactive wastes which were produced in nuclear plants and accumulating as a result of the reprocessing activities at Sellafield and, to a lesser extent, Dounreay. In 1976 the Flowers Report had warned that the nuclear programme could not be continued unless a method was demonstrated 'to ensure the safe containment of long-lived, highly radioactive waste for the indefinite future' (HMSO, 1976, para. 27). For the next decade the government was embroiled in conflicts with local communities determined to prevent the development of radioactive waste disposal facilities. (These conflicts and their political implications are discussed in full in Blowers *et al*. (1991); summary versions will be found in Blowers (1988) and in Blowers and Lowry (1987, 1991)).

Accordingly the government initiated a search for potential disposal sites for the deep burial of high level wastes (HLW). A borehole drilling programme was started at a number of sites, mainly in the remote, sparsely populated upland areas of Scotland, Wales and northern England. As these areas were geographically remote but not peripheral in other respects there was immediate and determined opposition to the proposals. The campaigns were short and decisive, forcing the government to withdraw its programme in 1981. The conflict had demonstrated three aspects of the process of peripheralisation: first, the ability of communities to mobilise united local support against an external threat; second, the difficulty of establishing a hazardous facility in a greenfield location; and third, the possibility of drawing in expertise and support from other groups elsewhere including nationally based environmental campaign groups.

These national groups provide support for local groups as part of their broader campaigns to protect the environment. One of the earliest campaigns of the radical group Greenpeace was to oppose the dumping of intermediate and low-level nuclear wastes (ILW and LLW) in the Atlantic Ocean. It conducted spectacular media campaigns, exerted pressure on the London Dumping Convention to apply a moratorium on sea dumping and, when the transport unions refused to undertake the dumping operation in 1983, sea dumping by the UK was effectively ended. With its HLW and sea-dumping options blocked the government turned its attention to on-land disposal of ILW and LLW. In October 1983 the Secretary of State for the Environment announced that safe disposal was 'well within the scope of modern technology' (Hansard, 25 October: col. 156) and that two sites had been identified by Nirex (Nuclear Industry Radioactive Waste Executive, the body set up to manage ILW and LLW) as 'most worthy of detailed investigation' (Nirex, 1983: 1). The first was a disused anhydrite mined owned by Imperial Chemical Industries (ICI) at Billingham on Tees – a site designated for deep disposal of long-lived ILW (mainly fuel cladding, control rods). The second was a former wartime munitions dump owned by the Central Electricity Generating Board (and once destined for a possible nuclear power station) at Elstow near Bedford for the shallow disposal of short-lived ILW (resins, sludges, filters) and LLW (bulky large volume and lightly contaminated wastes) – see Figure 12.3. Opposition from both communities was immediate and sustained.

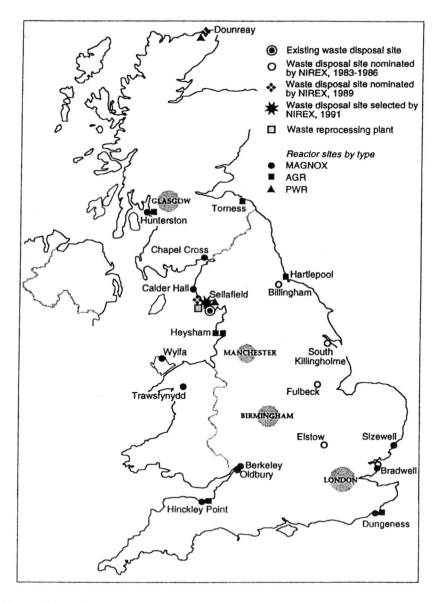

Figure 12.3 Radioactive waste sites in the United Kingdom.

In certain respects Billingham exemplifies a peripheral community. It is in north-east England, relatively remote from the metropolitan core, in an area of high unemployment dominated by steel-making and chemicals industries – a traditional working-class predominantly Labour area with a heavily polluted and degraded environment containing at the time 14.5 per cent of the country's registrable hazardous locations. None the less the campaign against the ILW repository spearheaded by Billingham Against Nuclear Dumping (BAND) was a model of its kind using media publicity, petitions, public protests and lobbying. The *coup de grâce* was administered when ICI, under intense pressure from the local community, including its workforce, declared its opposition to the project. This effectively denied Nirex access to the site and forced the government to abandon the project. Attention was now focused on Elstow, the last remaining option.

Elstow displayed none of the characteristics of a peripheral community. Only 50 miles from London, it was located within the core area of the country. It was relatively prosperous and had a heterogeneous population. The local environment, though scarred by brick-making, is predominantly a mixture of pleasant country towns and villages. Opposition here was led by the County Council which provided the counter-expertise and political lobbying and by Bedfordshire Against Nuclear Dumping (BAND) which mobilised the local community. Although there was disappointment when Elstow failed to gain a reprieve with Billingham, the campaign had persuaded the government that alternative sites for shallow dumping should also be investigated. Accordingly, in early 1986, three other sites in addition to Elstow, were announced – all in the clay belts of eastern England, in Conservative-held constituencies and all in public ownership. They were: South Killingholme near the industrial and port area of south Humberside; Fulbeck, deep in the farmlands of Lincolnshire; and Bradwell, on an estuary in Essex next to one of the first Magnox nuclear power stations – see Figure 12.3.

In the four communities protest groups were immediately established and, joined by Billingham, formed Britain Opposed to Nuclear Dumping (BOND) while three of the county councils (Essex excepted) formed the County Councils Coalition. Their first success came in the wake of the Chernobyl disaster, in May 1986, when the government withdrew proposals for shallow disposal of ILW. In order to avoid local opposition the government decided to grant permission for exploratory drilling at all four sites by way of a 'special development order' (SDO). This infuriated the local councils and protesters and solidified their opposition.

The campaign against shallow burial of LLW at any of the four sites reached its climax in the late summer of 1986 when the contractors employed to undertake exploratory drilling were met by blockades at each of the sites. Though dismissed by *The Times* as 'middle-class, middle-aged hooligans from middle-England' (19 August) the protesters gained national attention and sympathy for their cause. A report by the House of Commons Environment Committee concluded that the UK's radioactive waste policy was unclear and lacked public acceptability (HMSO, 1986). In May 1987, just before the announcement of the general election, the government withdrew its proposals for the shallow burial of nuclear waste, leaving it with no option but to begin its search for a solution over again.

In abandoning shallow disposal the government had established two principles: that the solution should be technically suitable and politically acceptable. The chosen method was co-disposal of both ILW and LLW in a deep-engineered repository; on-site storage was therefore not an option. In an effort to secure public acceptability Nirex sought open discussion of different deep disposal concepts and site selection. Predictably there was support for the concept of deep disposal provided it was somewhere else. Only in the areas around Sellafield and Caithness was there any support for a possible repository although in both areas there was also considerable opposition. Political expediency suggested, in the words of Secretary of State for the Environment Nicholas Ridley, that 'it would be best to explore first those sites where there is some measure of local support for civil nuclear activities' (Hansard, 21 March 1989, cols. 505–6). Consequently, selection of Sellafield and Dounreay for further investigation became a political inevitability.

Sellafield, where 60 per cent of the waste was produced and with its much bigger commitment to the nuclear industry in terms of employment, was the obvious choice. It would also reduce the distances over which radioactive materials have to be moved saving in the order of £1 billion in transport costs over the lifetime of the repository. After two years of evaluation, Sellafield was duly confirmed in July, 1991. Assuming that geological investigations confirm the potential of the site, Nirex intend to apply for permission to construct a repository which, given the certainty of an extensive public inquiry, is unlikely to be constructed ready to receive wastes before 2010. Opposition to the Nirex repository was overshadowed in the early 1990s by the conflict over the Thorp reprocessing plant at Sellafield. This brought conflict between economic interests in jobs and investment against environmental concerns voiced by opponents led by Greenpeace and Friends of the Earth. As that conflict subsides national and local attention will once again focus on the Nirex repository.

Interpretation

This case illustrates the spatial inequalities of power that result in hazardous activities becoming increasingly confined to peripheral communities. The apparent exception is Billingham, which appears to meet the criteria of peripherality, but which vigorously opposed the deep repository. But in this instance Billingham does not qualify as a peripheral community. It is in a large conurbation of over half a million people and its major industries are steel and chemicals, not the nuclear industry. Indeed, the intrusion of the nuclear industry right into the heart of the urban area was felt to be a threat which would blight existing economic activity and pose dangers for the population. Billingham may be a 'pollution haven' but it is not a 'nuclear oasis'; if the project had been related to existing hazardous activities it could have been a different matter.

In Billingham and each of the four communities selected for the shallow repository there quickly developed the united opposition from all parts of the community which, we have argued, typifies resistance to unwanted hazardous activities in greenfield locations. The Nirex proposals offered few, if any, economic benefits since few people would be employed and the proffered planning gains were regarded as bribes. On the contrary, Nirex was resisted because of the risks and blight it would bring to these communities. By developing a united front which extended the alliance of interests within the community to a coalition of interests *between* the communities it was possible to pool resources and expertise, to gather support from national anti-nuclear groups, to achieve national publicity and to mount a credible attack on the principles of government policy. Attention was diverted from site-specific proposals in an effort, ultimately successful, to defeat government policy.

The very success of the five communities made the selection of Sellafield all the more inevitable (Blowers, 1989). During the 1980s the management options for nuclear waste had been progressively narrowed as the HLW drilling programme was withdrawn, sea dumping was abandoned and the repository proposals were defeated. The government and Nirex, learning the lessons from defeat, adopted a more cautious and open approach, 'to promote public understanding of the issues involved and to stimulate comment which will assist Nirex in developing acceptable proposals' (Nirex, 1987: 4). Sellafield, with its heavy commitment to the nuclear industry, appeared to offer sanctuary to the beleaguered Nirex provided that, upon detailed investigation, the site met the safety criteria.

Sellafield is the archetype of a peripheral community. Situated in West Cumbria, it is far from any major UK conurbation and accessible only by a twisting road or a branch railway. It is in an area of high unemployment and around two-fifths of the local workforce is employed at the plant with most of the remaining activities indirectly dependent upon it. The nuclear industry can normally rely upon the support – enthusiastic or reluctant – of its dependents. But this support will not necessarily extend to the Nirex repository which provides few jobs and contains long-term hazards. Nirex may be seen 'as an outsider, unacceptable elsewhere in the country' (Wynne *et al.*, 1993: 3). Even if the site proves technically suitable it may not prove to be politically acceptable.

Some concluding questions and remarks

At the beginning of this paper we argued that research on attitudes does not provide understanding of behaviour (proposition 1). Detailed case studies conducted in specific areas for a substantial length of time are necessary to reveal the social and political processes at work during periods of environmental conflict. We have demonstrated that such studies can be a fertile source both for the generation of conceptual ideas and for the confirmation of theoretical assumptions.

Although different in many respects (country, period, kind of LULU involved) the three case studies discussed above have certain characteristics in common. First they illustrate the characteristics of peripheral communities (propositions 3–7) and identify the processes whereby these characteristics of peripherality are reproduced over space and time (central thesis and propositions 8 and 11). Second, in each of the three cases the opposition to the LULU is led by local elites forging a coalition representing groups of various socio-economic and political backgrounds and cutting across the typical divides of modern society (propositions 9 and 10). Third, these coalitions, in all three cases reactivate patterns of integration that were supposed to be rather traditional, as through, for example, the identification with a local community, be it a neighbourhood, a locality or a region, which is defined as threatened and the defending of which is necessary (proposition 2).

The brickfields case provides a striking contrast within one region of successful mobilisation in one area while there was little resistance in a more peripheral (and traditional) community. The Tessenderlo case illustrates the relative powerlessness of a one-industry peripheral community once economic diversification fails and the economic dependence on hazardous industries bars the way to both modernisation and effective environmental protest. The nuclear waste case, among other points, shows how it is possible to enhance the power of protest by building an inter-community coalition thereby making the location of hazardous activities in peripheral communities, which are unable to create such coalitions, almost inevitable.

Apart from the conclusions to be drawn from these case studies, both the analytical framework and the empirical evidence presented in this paper give rise to a number of conceptual, theoretical, empirical and practical questions. They also suggest some questions for further research.

Peripheralisation and democracy

The processes described above raise interesting questions about democratic participation and institutions. In the three case studies the intensity and effectiveness of local mobilisation, organisation and participation is revealed. In both the brickfields and the hazardous industry cases, and more especially in the case of nuclear waste, the power to decide rested ultimately with central government. In the case of the brickfields the government took a passive line preferring to see the decisions taken by the company and the local authorities. In the hazardous industry case the local protest, although representing a clear majority of the local people, did not succeed in preventing the location of a new hazardous plant. As the economic dependence upon the chemical industry increased, leaving the community peripheralised again, the action group was unable to mobilise sufficient power against the environmental threats. In the case of nuclear waste, local pressure enhanced by inter-community coalitions was sufficient to defeat government proposals even when the government had an impregnable majority and was not in any danger of political defeat in the constituencies proposed for nuclear waste dumps. The consequence was that Sellafield became the politically logical outcome, a nuclear oasis that would be favoured by every other area in the country relieved that the repository would go somewhere else.

This raises another question: what obligations are there to peripheral communities and how can they be discharged?

Peripheral communities and compensation

As we stated in the introduction, at least some LULUs are inherent to modern society, whereas others are essential to the environmental infrastructure. Since, therefore, they will have to be located somewhere, a theoretical and a practical question is how society deals with them. From a theoretical point of view, one can distinguish three main strategies – in short, coercion, compensation and persuasion (Etzioni, 1964). Both common sense and empirical evidence make it very unlikely that a persuasive strategy can be successful under these circumstances. But also coercion seems to be unworkable, indeed can be counter-productive by reinforcing the peripheral character of the community, as was the case at Tessenderlo. Coercion means centralisation, giving the central political level more options and power to intervene in the location process by directive, forcing thereby the local community to accept the hazardous activity. There are different examples of coercive strategies and measures in different European countries, their specific design depending on the basic political and legal structure of the state. Though not the most far-reaching, the recent proposal for a so-called NIMBY-law in the Netherlands, aiming to accelerate procedures for the location of different LULUs (waste disposal, power plants, maybe even asylums for political refugees), is a very typical example of the central government looking desperately for ways to overcome local resistance. The attempt by the UK government to subvert the local communities through the use of a special development order in the nuclear waste case is an excellent example of the counter-productive nature of the exercise of central power. Centralisation, in our view, will sharpen the locational conflicts rather than resolve them. Since it will increase the resistance of local communities able to mobilise opposition, leaving peripheral communities even more powerless, centralisation will reinforce the process of peripheralisation.

As it is becoming more difficult to secure sites for hazardous activities, peripheral communities hosting such sites will continue to bear a substantial burden of the national risk from such activities. Since there will be resistance to increased risk even in these communities, compensation is politically expedient and morally justified. Compensation can take various forms: economic (diversification of employment; provision of infrastructure); community benefits (welfare programmes and facilities; environmental enhancement); political (mediation, liaison and participation in decision-making). Empirical evidence on compensation being used under these circumstances is to be found in studies on the location of nuclear waste disposal in the US (Solomon and Cameron, 1985) and Canada (Department of Energy, Mines and Resources, 1986, 1990); and of household waste disposal in the Netherlands (Driessen and Leroy, 1992; Driessen *et al.*, 1990).

Nevertheless, resolving locational conflicts on hazardous activities is not only a matter of developing expedient procedures and taking appropriate measures of compensation. From a merely political point of view, complicated and long-lasting decision-making processes on the location of LULUs may be seen as inefficient. But from an environmental point of view these location processes require due caution, including political checks and balances to ensure careful decision-making. Otherwise, local resistance to the location of hazardous activities may be the only way in which environmental concern can be expressed.

A question for further research

The three cases explored here are concerned with spatially discrete hazardous activities. Similar examples of peripheral communities might be found in the nuclear oases in remote corners of the US such as Carlsbad in New Mexico, the site of a deep repository, or Yucca Mountain, Nevada, where it is proposed to locate a repository for high level wastes. But, further evidence is needed to show how far the process of peripheralisation can be applied to different types of conflict. For example, intuitively it seems probable that the protest against spatially linear intrusive developments such as motorways or high-speed train links also reveals similar processes of mobilisation, cross-cutting coalitions and a combination of modern and traditional patterns of integration that we have observed in our three cases.

Again, it may be possible to identify processes of peripheralisation at work on a much broader international scale. Heavily polluted areas occur various parts of the Third World where the need for economic development and dependence on major industries (often multinational companies) combine to reinforce a condition of powerlessness. It would be imprudent to push the parallels too far, but in general terms the process of dominance and dependence and of power and powerlessness which characterises the process of peripheralisation at sub-national levels can also be perceived at international level. A combination of empirical effort and theoretical insight is needed to identify the extent to which the processes we have described are capable of more general application.

Acronyms

ABH	anywhere but here
BAND	Billingham Against Nuclear Dumping
BELT	better environment Tessenderlo
BOND	Britain Opposed to Nuclear Dumping
HLW	high level waste
ILW	intermediate level waste
LLW	low level waste
LULU	locally unwanted land uses
NIMBY	not in my back yard
ppb	parts per billion
SDO	special development order.

References

Bachrach, P. and M.S. Baratz (1970), *Power and Poverty*, New York: Oxford University Press.

Bell, C. and H. Newby (1971), *Community studies*, London: Allen and Unwin.

Blowers, A. (1983), 'Master of Fate or Victim of Circumstance – the Exercise of Corporate Power in Environmental Policy-Making', *Policy and Politics*, Vol. 11, No. 4.

Blowers, A. (1984a), *Something in the Air: Corporate Power and the Environment*, London: Harper and Row.

Blowers, A. (1984b), 'The Triumph of Material Interests – Geography, Pollution and the Environment', *Political Geography Quarterly*, Vol. 3, No. 1.

Blowers, A. (1985), 'Environment and Politics in a Capitalist Society', unit 14 of *Changing Britain, Changing World: Geographical Perspectives*, Milton Keynes: Open University, pp. 1–26.

Blowers, A. (1988), 'No Place to Go: Nuclear Waste in the United Kingdom', *Alternatives* Vol. 15, No. 4.

Blowers, A. (1989), 'Radioactive Waste – Local Authorities and the Public Interest', *Radioactive Waste Management*, Vol. 2, No. 1.

Blowers, A. and D. Lowry (1987), 'Out of Sight, Out of Mind: the Politics of Nuclear Waste in the United Kingdom', in A. Blowers and D. Pepper (eds), *Nuclear Power in Crisis*, London: Croom Helm.

Blowers, A. and D. Lowry (1991), 'The Politics of Radioactive Waste Disposal', in J. Blunden and A. Reddish (eds), *Energy, Resources and Environment*, London: Hodder and Stoughton for the Open University.

Blowers, A., D. Lowry and B.D. Solomon (1991), *The International Politics of Nuclear Waste*, London: Macmillan.

Bridgeland, W.M. and A.J. Sofranko (1975), 'Community Structure and Issue-Specific Influences – Community Mobilization over Environmental Quality', *Urban Affairs Quarterly*, Vol. 11, No. 2.

Buttel, F.H. (1987), 'New Directions in Environmental Sociology', *Annual Review of Sociology*, Vol. 13.

Buttel, F.H. and W.L. Flinn (1974), 'The Structure of Support for the Environmental Movement', *Rural Sociology*, Vol. 39, No. 1.

Castells, M. (1974), *Monopolville – Analyse des Rapports entre l'Entreprise, l'Etat et l'Urbain à Partir d'une Enquête sur la Croissance Industrielle et Urbaine de la Region de Dunkerque*, Paris: Mouton.

Castells, M. (1978), *City, Class and Power*, London: Macmillan.

Claval, P. (1987), *Espace et Pouvoir*, Paris: PUF.

Cotgrove, S. and A. Duff (1980), 'Environmentalism, Middle-Class-Radicalism and Politics', *Sociological Review*, Vol. 28, No. 2.

County Councils Coalition (1987), *The Disposal of Radioactive Waste in Sweden, West Germany and France*, Norwich: Environmental Resources Ltd.

Cox, A. (1979), *Brickmaking: A History and Gazeteer*, London: Bedfordshire County Council and Royal Commission on Historical Monuments (England).

Cox, K.R., D.R. Reynolds and S. Rokkan (eds) (1974), *Locational Approaches to Power and Conflict*, New York: McGraw-Hill.

Crenson, M. (1971), *The Un-Politics of Air Pollution: A Study of Non-Decisionmaking in the Cities*, Baltimore, MD: The Johns Hopkins Press.

Department of Energy, Mines and Resources, Canada (1986) *Socially Responsive Impact Management: a Discussion Paper*; and (1990) *Opting for Co-operation*.

Reports to the Siting Process Task Force on Low-Level Radioactive Waste Disposal, Ottowa: DEMR.

Driessen, P. and P. Leroy (1992), 'Besluitvorming over Locaties voor Afvalstorplaatsen' (Decision-making on the location of waste disposals), in M. Herweyer and I. Pröpper (eds), *Effecten van plannen en convenanten* (The effects of plans and convenants), Deventer: Kluwer, pp. 177–97.

Driessen, P., J. van der Heijden and P. Leroy (1990), *Locatiekeuze van Afvalverwerkingsinrichtingen – een Beleidsevaluatief Onderzeok* (Location of waste disposals – a policy evaluation), Nijmegen: University of Nijmegen.

Enzensberger, H.M. (1974), A Critique of Political Ecology, *New Left Review*, No. 84.

Ester, P. (1980), 'Milieubesef in Nederland' (Environmental concern in the Netherlands), *Sociologische Gids*, Vol. 27, No. 2.

Etzioni, A. (1964), *Modern Organizations*, Englewood Cliffs, NJ: Prentice-Hall.

Gatrell, A.C. and A.A. Lovett (1991), 'Burning Questions: Incineration of Wastes and Implications for Human Health', in Clark, M., D. Smith and A. Blowers (eds), *Waste Location: Spatial Aspects of Waste Management and Disposal*, London: Routledge.

Gaventa, J. (1980), *Power and Powerlessness: Quiescence and Rebellion in an Appalachian Valley*, Urbana: University of Illinois Press.

Gladwin, T.N. (1980), 'Patterns of Environmental Conflict over Industrial Facilities in the United States, 1970–1978', *Natural Resources Journal*, Vol. 20, No. 2.

Hall, P. (1980), *Great Planning Disasters*, London: Weidenfeld and Nicholson.

Harry, J., R. Gale and J. Hendee (1969), 'Conservation: an Upper-middle Class Social Movement', *Journal of Leisure Research*. Vol. 3, No. 1.

Hechter, M. (1975), *Internal Colonialism: the Celtic Fringe in British National Development*, 1536–1966, London: Routledge and Kegan Paul.

Hillier, R. (1981), *Clay that Burns: A History of the Fletton Brick Industry*, London: Collier for the London Brick Company Ltd.

HMSO (1976), *Nuclear Power and the Environment*, Sixth Report of the Royal Commission of Environmental Pollution, Cmnd. 6618 (The Flowers Report).

HMSO (1986), *Radioactive Waste*, First Report from the House of Commons Environment Committee, Session 1985–86.

Lauwers, J. and J. Van Lint (1979), *Burgers in de Weer – de Mobilisatierond een Milieuproject* (Mobilisation over an environmental project), Antwerpen, Leuven: ACCO.

Leroy, P. (1979), *Kernenergie, Milieuconflict of Godsdienstoorlog?* (Nuclear energy: environmental conflict or war of religion?), Antwerpen, Leuven: ACCO.

Leroy, P. (1981), *Het milieuprobleem in Tessenderlo* (The environmental problem in Tessenderlo – Belgium), Antwerp: University of Antwerp.

Leroy, P. (1983), *Herrie om de Heimat – Milieuproblemen, Ruimtelijke Organisatie en Milieubeleid* (Environmental problems, the spatial organisation of society and environmental policy), Unpublished doctoral thesis, University of Antwerp.

Leroy, P. and A. De Geest (1985), Milieubeweging en milieubeleid (Environmental movement and environmental policy), Antwerp, Utrecht: Nederlandsche Boekhandel.

Liebert, R.J. and A.W. Imershein (1977), *Power, Paradigms and Community Research*, London.

Loeb, P. (1986), *Nuclear Culture: Living and Working in the World's Largest Nuclear Complex*, Philadelphia, PA: New Society Publishers.

Lowe, P.D. and W. Rüdig (1986), 'Political Ecology and the Social Sciences – The State of the Art', *British Journal of Political Science*, Vol. 16.

Lukes, S. (1974), *Power: A Radical View*, London: Macmillan.

McSorley, J. (1990), *Living in the Shadow: The Story of the People of Sellafield*, London: Pan Books.

Miller, D.C. and W.H. Form (1963), 'Industry Shapes the Community, and Industry–community Relations', in *The Sociology of Work and Organizations*. New York.

Nelissen, N., R. Perenboom, P. Peters en V. Peters (1987), *De Nederlanders en Hun Milieu* (The Dutch and their environment). Zeist: Kerkebosch.

Nirex (1983), *The Disposal of Low and Intermediate-Level Radioactive Wastes: The Elstow Storage Depot: A Preliminary Project Statement*, Harwell: Nirex

Nirex (1987), *The Way Forward: The Development of a Repository for the Disposal of Low and Intermediate-Level Radioactive Waste: A Discussion Document*, Harwell: Nirex

Popper, F.J. (1988), 'The Environmentalist and the LULU', in R.L. Lake (ed.), *Resolving Locational Conflicts*, New Jersey: Rutgers University Press.

Schattchneider, E.E. (1960), *The Semi-Sovereign People: A Realist's View of Democracy in America*, New York: Holt, Rinehart and Winston.

Smith, D. (1988), *Corporate Power, Risk Assessment and the Control of Major Hazards: A Comparison between Canvey Island and Ellesmere Port*, Unpublished PhD thesis, University of Manchester.

Solomon B.D. and D.M. Cameron (1985), 'Nuclear Waste Repository Siting: An Alternative Approach', *Energy Policy*, Vol. 13, No. 6.

Vogel, D. (1982), 'How Business Responds to Opposition: Corporate Political Strategies During the 1970s', Unpublished paper.

Warren, R.L. (1956), 'Toward a Reformulation of Community Theory', *Human Organization*, Vol. 15, No. 2.

Warren, R.L. (1973), *The Community in America*, Chicago, IL: Rand McNally.

Wolsink, M. (1993), 'Entanglement of Interests and Motives in Facility Sitting: the Not-in-my Backyard "Theory"'; Unpublished paper.

Wynne, B., C. Waterton and R. Grove-White (1993), *Public Perceptions and the Nuclear Industry in West Cumbria*, Lancaster: Centre for the Study of Environmental Change, Lancaster University.

Zonabend, F. (1993), *The Nuclear Peninsular*, Cambridge: Cambridge University Press.

13 The Global Environment Facility in its North–South context

Joyeeta Gupta

The Global Environment Facility (GEF) is engulfed in a cloud of international controversy. This chapter analyses the controversy in its context and provides some insights as to how the contentious issues can be resolved.

In 1987, the World Commission on Environment and Development (WCED, 1987) recommended that a mechanism be established to finance investments in conservation projects and national strategies to enhance the resource base for development in developing countries. Subsequently, France and Germany requested the World Bank to assess the potential for such a financial mechanism. In October 1991, the World Bank, the United Nations Development Programme (UNDP) and United Nations Environment Programme (UNEP) jointly launched the pilot phase of the GEF. This collaboration seeks to ensure an optimal combination of the skills of the three bodies. The GEF aims to provide funding to developing countries and countries in transition for investments and technical assistance, and to promote research in order to protect the global environment in the four areas of global warming, pollution of international waters, destruction of biological diversity and the depletion of the stratospheric ozone layer. The GEF had US\$1.3 thousand million over the first three years, and US\$2 thousand million have been pledged for the following three years. This is much less than anticipated, but it has the potential to raise higher funds in the future.

The GEF went through a pilot phase from July 1991 to June 1994. Following an independent evaluation (World Bank *et al.*, 1993) of the GEF in November 1993, agreement on the restructuring of the GEF was reached in March 1994 (World Bank *et al.*, 1994b). Developed countries wanted to establish the GEF in order to address global environmental problems. As developing countries have a role to play in these problems, the developed countries wished to assist them in addressing such problems. The GEF was established to provide a 'clearing house' where donors and recipients can achieve maximum efficiency, avoid competition, duplication or working at cross purposes and can ensure that there are no unnecessary gaps in the aid process. The developed countries have faith in the efficiency of the World Bank, and hence the World Bank was entrusted with a dominant role in the management of the GEF.

Despite the advantages outlined above, Southern negotiators and other actors have been critical of the pilot phase. Some of the criticism has been dealt with through the restructuring of the GEF, but nevertheless an analysis of the criticism is essential for an understanding of the way in which the GEF regime was formed. Developing countries are participating in all the different forums where the GEF is being discussed and they subscribe to the consensus view. This would in itself imply that they agree to all aspects of the GEF. However, interviews with negotiators and other actors within these countries indicate that, in general, they feel they have frequently *no alternative but to agree*. Hence, this chapter analyses their criticisms in the context of the negotiations to see if the contentious issues can be addressed.

The structure of the chapter

Theoretical structure

The chapter takes regime theory as its point of departure. This theory attempts to explain how co-operation leads to the formation and persistence of international regimes, defined as international principles, norms, rules and procedures (Krasner, 1982: 186). Realists argue that regimes are formed either by hegemons, or when the interests of all actors converge. This chapter studies primarily the consensus around the GEF in order to see if the consensus reflects a convergence of interests, hegemonic power or a combination of some other factors. Regime experts argue that fairer regimes are likely to last longer (Puchala *et al.*, 1982: 250). This chapter analyses the perception on fairness of the GEF regime to make inferences on its persistence and durability. Hence, it goes beyond the principles and norms to understand the role of the powers and interests in such regime development and its influence on the perception of fairness of the regime. In doing so, the argument builds upon the notion that power is not just reflected in the decisions taken but also in the non-decisions (i.e. the decisions not taken) (Bachrach *et al.*, 1970: 39–52) in the control over the agenda for discussion, and the way people's wants are shaped to eliminate their grievances (Lukes, 1974: 21–5).

Analytical framework

Additionally, a framework is presented for the analysis of the criticisms made of the role of the GEF. This framework consists of three levels, which can be viewed as 'walls within walls' (see Figure 13.1). At the lowest level problems with rules and norms, processes and projects within the GEF are encountered. At the middle level lie problems concerning the organisational setting and the process of decision-making, within which the rules, norms and processes are adopted and projects selected. Finally, at the highest level there are the problems with the powers and interests that influence the decisions on the organisational setting and, through the organisational setting, influence the rules norms, processes and projects. The arguments of the critics stretch all through the different levels, while the supporters try to confine themselves to the lowest level – that is, the level of agenda items.

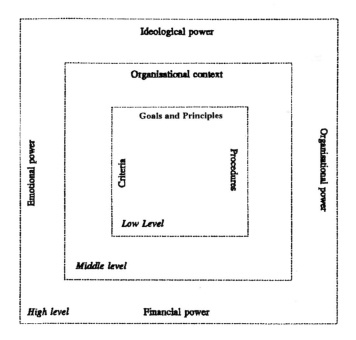

Figure 13.1 Walls within walls.

At this level the rest of the criticisms appear to be irrelevant, relevant criticisms being dealt with during the negotiations. At the middle level, the criticisms concern the organisational setting and forums and appear to be less negotiable. At the highest level, the inequality in power is visible and its link with the decisions taken at the other two levels becomes clear. This breeds distrust in the recipients, for which to be overcome the difference in the levels needs to be understood and perhaps should become the subject of North–South dialogue. This framework will also shed light on the reasons for international cooperation.

Before delving further, a few terms require definition. The word 'critic' refers to actors from the North and the South who have serious objections to the GEF. These actors include NGOs (Climate Action Network Africa, Kenya, Third World Network, Malaysia and so on) and researchers (such as B. Gosovic and V. Shiva). Interestingly, government officials provided the most severe criticisms during interviews with the author. The term 'supporters' refers primarily to the developed country governments, the GEF itself and some researchers.

Developed and developing countries pay into the GEF fund, but the largest proportion of the funds come from the developed countries, and hence they are defined as the 'major donors'.

There have been occasional references to the term 'South'. Some authors in the 1980s claimed that the concept of the 'Third World' both as a group and as an ideology was declining, by focusing on the vast differences between countries and the ability of some to climb out of the poverty trap. My research indicates a revival in the concept of the 'South'. Detailed research in four developing countries shows that with the end of the cold war they perceive that they are affected in at least four ways.

First, in the past developing countries could make requests for assistance either to the Eastern bloc or to the Western world. There was a choice and one of the two blocs would come to their assistance. This choice is no longer there. Second, in place of being a source of assistance, the Eastern bloc has become a favoured competitor for assistance from the West, putting developing countries in a weaker position. Third, developing countries enjoyed trade relations with the former Eastern European countries; and these trade relations are deteriorating with negative financial consequences for this region. Finally, the moral power enjoyed by developing countries who saw themselves as non-aligned in bloc politics no longer exists. A combination of these factors has led developing countries in general to feel less powerful than in the 1980s and to retreat behind the Group of 77 (G-77, a body established in the UN to represent developing countries) as their negotiating platform. There are clear differences between individual developing countries, but these are less important than those between them and the first world (Agarwal *et al.*, 1992: 11).

In a chapter that attempts to cover the views of the whole world, some cautionary remarks need to be made. First, although Southern actors are critical, they are also ambivalent. Their mandate is to tap whatever aid is available at whatever cost. This leads to dual positions that have affected both the negotiations and their feeling of dissatisfaction. These are dealt with in the section on power. Second, there are people in the South who actively support the GEF and those in the North who are critical. Hence the use of the words 'critic' and 'supporter'. Third, not all critics and supporters adhere to all views ascribed to them. Nevertheless, in general their views share a common basis. Finally, although it is logical that actors not involved in the negotiations should offer a critique, surely those who are negotiating should be able to display and make use of their opinion during the negotiations. But this has frequently failed to happen because of the speed of the discussions, the lack of preparations, and as a result of the diplomatic mandate (GEF South Centre, 1993: 1). Bachrach (1970: 47–51) advises that in such situations one should look at the grievances of those involved to understand their views.

Methodology

This chapter is based on a literature survey,[1] the results of the Independent Evaluation Committee and personal confidential interviews with delegates from developed and developing countries and other actors. In dealing with their perceptions, the justifiability of the views is less important than the perception itself since 'perceptions equal reality' in the context of politics and diplomacy (Carroll, 1988: 1). The chapter first examines the context of the debate and second, the criticisms within the three levels. Third, it draws conclusions on the factors that influence co-operation.

The discussion focuses on the reasons and grievances behind the formal consensus in meetings and especially in relation to the United Nations Framework Convention on Climate Change (FCCC). It does not focus on the projects undertaken by the GEF.

By virtue of its nature, the chapter tends to focus exclusively on criticisms. This is not meant to detract from what good the GEF has achieved. On the contrary; taking the advice of a senior European negotiator to the effect that 'in this phase we have to build confidence in the GEF and mutual understanding', the chapter is written in pursuit of mutual understanding.

The context of the controversy

The controversies surrounding the GEF have to be seen in the light of the discussions in the North and in the South. From these discussions it is evident that the context of the debate on the GEF is wider than the GEF itself.

First, interviews reveal that although none of the developing country governments doubted that the GEF had a role to play, they did not like the way in which the GEF was promoted from the status of *a* financial mechanism to *the* (interim) financial mechanism for the FCCC and the Convention on Biodiversity. Hence, parallel to the discussions on the GEF that take place within the negotiating forums of the GEF, discussions have also taken place in the negotiating forums of the FCCC and the Convention on Biodiversity.

Second, if the GEF had been promoted as a partial answer to four major environmental problems consistent with its modest financial resources, and if it had been presented as the environmental arm of the World Bank then, interviewees assert, that would be the relevant context. However, an official GEF brochure states that the GEF is 'closely linked' with the United Nations Conference on Environment and Development (UNCED). 'In the preparations for the United Nations Conference on Environment and Development, the GEF has emerged as a significant focus of international attention as an evolving instrument for multilateral co-operation in addressing global environmental concerns' (World Bank *et al.*, 1991: 10). The link with UNCED, however, has inevitable consequences as parties tend to associate this link differently. Thus, for critics, if UNCED was about global environmental problems, then why have only four problems been shortlisted for financing under the GEF (see the discussion on global versus local problems)? Supporters feel, however, that the GEF should finance those areas that are not covered by regular development assistance. Further, some negotiators feel that the conventions have assigned a task to GEF and that GEF should perform its own task. Others believe that in performing its own task, the GEF should continuously adhere to the main principles of the Conventions and UNCED. There are those who feel that the pragmatic, scientific, systematic approach is to de-link everything continuously in order be efficient. However, others prefer the social, ecological, systemic, comprehensive approach which asserts that it is the de-linking that has led to the current problem, and that the solutions should not be sought in cost-effectiveness in its traditional sense, but in a comprehensive approach taking socio-developmental-local aspects into account. These are fundamental differences in attitude.

Third, as the *only* (interim) operating entity of the major financial mechanisms of the post-UNCED era, the GEF has been discussed in many different forums such as follow-up meetings to UNCED and the Commission for Sustainable Development (CSD).

Finally, the actors involved in the debate are not just government officials and the representatives of the GEF, but NGOs, former politicians, captains of industry, academicians and scientists. The context is not just what is possible within the four walls of diplomatic discussions, but how that can be influenced through international discussions and exchange of information.

The lowest level

At the lowest level, the agenda items being debated within the GEF context are relevant. At this level, given the assumptions of the organisational structure of the GEF, negotiation on the controversial issues, in principle, is possible.

The GEF aims to provide funding for *incremental costs* of *global benefits* of *global issues* based on the principle of *cost-efficiency*. It is rational, first, that major donors should only want to fund measures to address global problems (i.e. problems that also affect them); second, that if there are any local benefits accruing from the project, the major donors would prefer to avoid paying for them; third, that major donors would like to pay only for the incremental costs of the necessary measures, and; finally, that major donors would like to pay only for projects that are cost-effective.

Critics feel that, despite its inherent logic, the world and its structures cannot be easily divided into different parts, in a manner amenable to such logical, systematic, deconstructive reasoning. Such reasoning is based on the economic and environmental fiction that the environment can be separated from development, that global benefits can be separated from local benefits, that cost-efficiency in the short run can lead to the best results in the long term.

Global versus local problems

In line with the view of the OECD governments, the GEF provides funding for four 'global environmental problems' – that is, global warming, pollution of international waters, destruction of biological diversity, destruction of the stratospheric ozone layer. However, an international team of authors (Agarwal *et al.*, 1992: 25–6) argues that the division of environmental problems into global and local has left the South 'holding exclusive responsibility for local problems' and that 'many in the South believe that this division is artificial; it denies and hides the international dimension of many so-called local problems'. They suggest criteria that should determine if a problem is global or not. These include problems geographically widespread in effect, problems whose causes may be local or national but whose effects are transboundary, and problems that are local or national in scale, but recur within many regions and problems which reflect international economic and political dynamics. Land degradation, including deforestation and desertification, has been added to the list of activities to be funded when it bears on the four focal areas, but Shiva (1992) states that this pays only lip service to the biggest environmental concern of the African continent and 'it is only when desertification has got global implications – that is, implications for the North – that the North is willing to give it consideration'. In response to the complaints, the restructured GEF will also fund Agenda twenty-one issues in so far as they relate to the four focal problems.

Global versus local benefits

The controversy around the separation of global and local benefits is another example. Doubtless, a politically satisfactory solution may be found to this problem. However, Colchester (1991) argues that measures taken to achieve global benefits which have no corresponding local benefits exacerbate conflicts between local interests and global concerns, divert attention to 'environmental projects' that are not priorities of the recipient country governments, draw expertise away from areas of crucial national concern and invest it in issues of global interest and emphasise *in situ* conservation rather than securing rural livelihoods. This is exemplified by the Tana river project, where the GEF intended to spend US\$6.2 million to help conserve ecological regions in the lower river basin and to protect two endangered sub-species of monkeys by the 'voluntary' resettlement of farmers and other residents. 'People need to understand that the Reserve is not merely a place "to protect the monkey", but to preserve an essential area for them, their children, Kenya and the world' (Bess, 1993: 13). This project has since been revised; but the controversy around the principle remains.

Cost-effectiveness

The GEF documents indicate that projects selected must be cost-effective. Cost-effectiveness implies that the goal – for example, reduction of greenhouse gases – should be achieved at the least (direct) cost possible. From the donors' point of view this will lead to an efficient disbursement of funds. However, critics (and economists) present arguments against this. First, cost-effectiveness can be achieved by minimising the middle persons involved per project and by optimising the economies of scale. Hence, large projects are preferred to small ones. Larger projects tend to have high social and cultural costs and an in-built inertia which makes them irreversible. Confidential internal memos in the World Bank reveal that almost 2 million people in the developing countries were forced to relocate as a consequence of World Bank projects in 1993, followed by 600,000 in 1994 (The Guardian, 1993). Some critics argue that cost–benefit analysis would be preferable to cost-effectiveness analysis (i.e. the project should lead to more benefit than harm), while others argue that where pure cost–benefit analysis is positive, but nevertheless leads to large social costs, these need to be taken into account in political decision-making.

Second, cost-effectiveness can be achieved more easily by focusing on short-term aspects as compared with long-term aspects. The education- and institution-building aspects tend to get neglected in the urgency built into efficiency to provide the relevant technology. Third, cost-effectiveness, by virtue of its definition, also leads to the 'project' approach. Critics argue that this approach leads to lop-sided growth in the community where they are based and that it cannot really lead to sustainable development (see also Parikh (1993); NGO statement (1993)). Fourth, cost-effectiveness, with its focus on minimising costs, implies that criteria such as information disclosure and public discussion of the projects concerned are given low priority (Gosovic, 1992: 239).

For these reasons, critics argue that cost-effectiveness has fundamental short-comings in decisions about large irreversible projects. In response, the basic pro-visions of the restructured GEF state that the GEF will ensure cost-effectiveness of its activities and will fund activities that are country-driven and based on national priorities (World Bank *et al.*, 1994c).

Incremental costs

The GEF will finance only the agreed incremental costs of projects – that is, the additional costs incurred if global environmental aspects are taken into account. According to independent evaluation (World Bank *et al.*, 1993: viii), the incremental costs principle has not been developed into a useful tool, it 'encourages a narrow project approach... that fails to encompass the broader considerations of national policies, program strategies, and institutional capacities that are funda-mental to achieving global benefits', 'encourages too sharp a distinction between global and national benefits' and 'weakens a sense of mutual responsibility for the protection of the global environment'. The restructured GEF will try to address these points.

Decision-making procedures

During the pilot phase, the G-77 argued that the negotiations should become more transparent, democratic and universal. NGOs demanded that all countries should be allowed membership into the GEF and to vote for the Governing Council; that the Governing Council should have balanced North–South representation, with unweighted voting powers; that the Governing Council should be given adequate powers in relation to the Secretariat on criteria for project selection, definition of environmental problems, approval of projects, allocation of funds; and that the chairperson of GEF should be elected.

Many of these complaints have been (partially) addressed. In the restructured GEF, an assembly of representatives from all participating countries will review

GEF policies. It will meet every three years. A Council of 32 constituencies, 16 from the developing countries, 14 from the developed and two from the countries in transition will be responsible for developing, adopting and evaluating the operational policies and programmes (World Bank *et al.*, 1994b). Decision-making in the GEF after the pilot phase is by consensus on issues when possible and qualified 'double majority' when consensus is not possible. Double majority requires a majority to be maintained both on the basis of 'one country one vote' as well as on the basis of financial contributions to the core fund. This is legitimised as the result of the marriage between fiduciary (World Bank) and political obligations (UNEP and UNDP). However, critics argue that weighted voting is undemocratic. As one ambassador interviewed said, it was

> somewhat ironic, but at the time that developing countries all the world over are told that you must hold free and fair elections, one person, one vote, we are also being told that in the international arena, one country, one vote is not the best way. Can you imagine what would happen if the government in your country or in mine was told to introduce a weighted voting system? We would be severely criticized and told that we are undemocratic.

One Asian diplomat expressed concern over whether weighted voting will be mostly on 'issues' whilst the bulk of the consensus decisions will be on 'non-issues'.

At this level, consensus between the parties can be reached on the agenda items. The consensus represents the highest, lowest common position of all parties (Sands, 1990). When the parties have differences of opinion – that is, no common position – then the consensus tends to reflect a compromise in which the weaker party gives in to the stronger party. Although consensus is achieved, the paradox is that 'mere concurrence as a formality is insufficient to ensure that effective co-operation will occur' (Caldwell, 1988). Hence the assumptions within which the consensus is reached need to be questioned.

The intermediate level

At the intermediate level the subject of debate is the assumptions within which negotiation takes place – that is, the related institutions and the way the agenda for discussions is set. The issues here are less negotiable. This section examines issues around the organisational framework of the GEF.

Initial decisions taken on project areas and the purpose of the GEF were decided first at a G7 meeting and then at a World Bank meeting where the recipients had no role. Only after the Bank had been given the major role in setting up the facility – with UNDP and UNEP as subsidiary partners – were seven Southern governments invited to discuss the GEF's framework (Tickell *et al.*, 1992). Once established, the GEF tried to create the link with UNCED and with the conventions. Most developing countries were opposed to a financial mechanism for the conventions located (partially) within the World Bank. Although there have been heated debates in different forums, the GEF won by default. Its supporters negotiated successfully within the FCCC and the biodiversity convention forums to ensure that the GEF was selected as (interim) operating entity for the funding mechanism.

Developing countries were opposed to the GEF for two reasons, the first being the control that the World Bank exercises on the financial policies of many of these countries and their desire to have an 'alternative window' for assistance, and the second being their concern about the ability of the World Bank to show the way to addressing the problem. The bottom line is that they clearly go to the World Bank for development assistance; but many of the negotiators feel strongly the need for a different body to deal with the environmental aspects. Critics feel that if all the available money for development and environment is concentrated in the hands of institutions closely connected with the World Bank, this gives developing countries a sense of losing their sovereignty and control over their own country. Researchers (Onimode, 1989) argue that World Bank projects have been implemented at the cost of increasing national debt, continuous debt servicing and stabilisation packages loaded against the poor majority, while benefitting the multinationals and the ruling groups. NGOs assert that past experiences in Bank loans for projects, structural adjustments and debt servicing are perceived as negative and the concern is that putting the Bank in charge of the 'green funds' would put developing countries further at the mercy of the Bretton Woods institutions (TWN No. 13, 1992: 2).

There are indications that the World Bank is reforming its policies, but past experiences have shaped the perceptions of these actors. Governmental actors from the North are sensitive to the views of the South, but feel that money should be efficiently spent, and the World Bank has experience and knowledge and will be the most appropriate body. They feel that the GEF will in some way help to 'green' the World Bank. Finally, they are opposed to the proliferation of multilateral financial instruments.

A major stated objective of GEF is to 'leverage' global benefits from regular Bank projects that might not otherwise take these global concerns into account. On the one hand the independent evaluation (World Bank *et al.*, 1993: xii) states that the GEF did not succeed in the pilot phase to mobilise environmental funding in associated World Bank projects because in some cases the GEF projects were added onto an already existing World Bank project, in some cases the World Bank financed project proceeded without the GEF component although they were developed jointly, and in several cases the link between the GEF project and the World Bank projects were weak, 'suggesting that it is unlikely that the GEF acted as a catalyst in mobilising the World Bank's resources'. On the other hand, some NGOs have concluded that GEF projects are being 'tacked on' to the front of up-coming bank loans in an attempt to mitigate or mask their environmental harm (Colchester, 1991):

> GEF grants may be associated to World Bank loans as a kind of 'window dressing' (Zimbabwe Photovoltaics project) as a 'bribe' to convince national governments to accept major policy changes (Nigeria Gas flaring project) or

as 'bait' to get governments to accept loans they would otherwise not take (Mali wood energy project).

> (Impact team (b), 7, 1992)

These perceptions may be less than fair, but they do exist.

As the secretariat is located within the World Bank and as the day-to-day functioning of the GEF occurs within Bank premises, the proximity has also meant that the GEF is affected by the procedures of the Bank, such as tight security, secretive information policies and rules of non-disclosure (Impact team (a), 7, 1992; Gosovic, 1992: 254–6). Bowles and Prickett, who have analysed the GEF pilot phase (1994: 10), conclude that the link with the Bank and the other agencies reduces the authority, flexibility and the objectivity of the GEF secretariat, and that the GEF secretariat should become operationally independent of the agencies and report directly to the participants. The relationship between the three implementing agencies has been the subject of much discussion in the NGO literature and the internal evaluation has also concluded that 'the synergy of the "comparative advantages" of the Implementing Agencies has not materialised' (World Bank *et al.*, 1993: xii).

In the restructured GEF the Secretariat will service and report to the other two bodies and will be functionally independent of the three implementing agencies. However, it will continue to be located in the World Bank premises.

Finally, the relationship between the GEF organisation and the conventions it serves is a source of controversy. The questions being raised by all parties is who controls GEF – the assembly of participants in the GEF (PA) or the relevant Conference of the Parties of the different conventions (COP)? The participants in the GEF may be different from those who ratify the relevant conventions leading to a conflict in interest and issue areas. In general, the developing countries would prefer the conventions to control the relevant parts of the GEF, from a legal perspective and also from the perspective that the conventions are negotiated on democratic principles which are preferable to the double majority system of the GEF. The major donors would, however, prefer to have some control over the contentious issues and would prefer the GEF to have more control. The independent evaluation concludes that the GEF global warming programme is not yet a coherent adjunct to the FCCC (World Bank *et al.*, 1993: x). The restructured GEF states that the use of GEF resources will be in conformity with the provisions of the conventions. Jacob Werksman, however, concludes that the GEF has been introducing concepts that depart from the commitments in the climate convention:

> If the GEF does not alter its approach, it is likely to find that it has developed for itself a series of policies that prove incompatible with the requirements of the Convention's financial mechanism and irreconcilable with the political priorities of the COP.
>
> (1993: 17)

To what extent the restructured GEF will indeed avoid pre-empting decisions that should be taken in other forums still remains to be seen. At this level, both supporters and critics are learning to live with the views of the other party in a constructive attempt at dealing with global environmental issues. This has led to formal consensus on many issues.

The highest level

Behind the 'consensus' on the organisational setting, one finds the highest – level of controversy – the level of power. Gosovic (1992: 238) argues that the GEF 'was entrusted despite the doubts about the Bank's ability to be the proper forum to handle the sensitive and politically explosive interface between the North and the South on environment and development'. Despite the views of the G-77, the OECD countries remained unshaken in their faith in the ability of the World Bank with its organisational mass to carry out this immensely challenging task. The GEF south centre in its advice to the G-77 stated that

> the GEF was pushed through prematurely, and before the outcomes for UNCED were known. It was inspired in part by a practical move to preempt alternative institutional solutions from emerging, and to place the mechanism firmly within the framework of the World Bank and thus under the control of the North.
>
> (1993, Annex II. 1)

This view is confirmed in Third World Network Papers. As Atiq Rahman, Coordinator of the Climate Action Network for South East Asia, Dhaka, said in an interview with the author, the decision to appoint the GEF as the interim financial mechanism for the climate convention was not a reflection of consensus, but a reflection of having no choice. The statement of the Malaysian representative at UNCED speaks volumes for the way in which negotiations are handled:

> We will accept the Global Environment Facility, and we will accept that it be administered by the OECD dominated World Bank. But can we not have a little say: can we not have more transparency in the administration of this fund? Surely, this does not amount to the South squeezing the North?
>
> (Statement of Malaysia, 1992)

The decision-making procedures in the pilot phase are experienced as examples of pre-emption – taking decisions that become non negotiable, and then allowing transparency and democracy over other minor decisions. These reflect the underlying power relations between the different countries.

Although power has several different definitions, I use power to imply the ability of a country and its negotiators to convince another country and its negotiators to accept a certain principle or decision, even though the other party may have serious doubts on the issue. Bachrach (1970: 24) argues that for a power relationship to exist (a) there should be conflict over values or a course of action between A and B, (b) B complies with A's wishes and (c) B does so because he is fearful that A will deprive him of a value or values which he regards more highly than those which would have been achieved by non-compliance. The interviews with the different actors reveal that there are differences between the Southern and Northern countries on the operating entity, that developing country delegates at the climate negotiations resisted on the GEF issue until it was clear that they had no choice. If the GEF was not to be the interim operating entity, then there was no other body going to be established. The choice between compliance and non-compliance was clear. If there was going to be no other fund, then there would be a case of deprivation. As one interviewee said:

> There is a line beyond which we cannot go... when a country gives us aid, the motivation is 30 per cent charity, 70 per cent control. One resists the control as best one can; but that's it. Diplomacy doesn't help to change the power relationship.

These features indicate that the power relationship has affected the negotiations.

On the basis of the interviews and the literature review four sources of power, although interrelated, can be identified: financial, organisational, ideological and emotional power. The sources in themselves imply power (reputed power), but is not actual power. But when these sources of power are exercised, actual power is witnessed.

Financial power of the major donors

The major donors have financial power; and those who pay more want to have a greater say in how the money is being spent, thus influencing negotiations. If developing countries were effectively to choose an alternative institution as the operating entity for a financial mechanism, industrialised countries might react by refusing to fund such an institution. Thus, financial power reduces the ability of developing countries to negotiate effectively on the middle level. It also influences decision-making structures leading, for example, to double majority systems. Furthermore, when donor countries wish to decide how their money is spent, this often leads to donor-driven projects, which tend to fail because of a lack of complementary interest and commitment at the recipient level. This affects the decisions taken at the lowest level. This can be contrasted with the national situation where there is a separation made between the way the taxes are collected and the way they are disbursed.

This is not just an exercise in theoretical speculation. During the 1993 December meeting on the restructuring of the GEF at Cartagena, the distribution of power between developed and developing countries within the GEF's Governing Council was an agenda item. The OECD proposal was that there should be 14 representatives of developed countries, 2 from countries in transition and 14 from developing countries, with the Chief Executive Officer of GEF (probably from the OECD) as chairman. Developing countries wished for more (17) seats to reflect their greater numbers. Although a compromise proposal was made by the OECD, France, followed by Germany, insisted that there should be a return to the original proposal or they would reduce their financial support to the GEF. Since then a compromise on this issue has been reached. Nevertheless, the nature of the financial mechanism regime has been heavily influenced by the hegemonic interests of the major donors.

Organisational power of the World Bank

When a body has a critical mass, because of its organisational and financial capacities, it can then steer decision-making procedures and attract new processes and mechanisms. This can be called the organisational power of a body. Clearly an existing body has this power over an as yet non-existing, body. Organisational power can on the one hand lend credibility and experience to the new process or mechanism, while on the other hand it can lead to the centralisation of activities. The organisational power of the World Bank has been instrumental in influencing the choice of the interim operating entity for the financial mechanism of the FCCC, as well as for the UNCED. Most developed countries have argued against the proliferation of funding mechanisms and in favour of the World Bank because of its reputation for efficiency. Gosovic concludes that, '[t]he two Bretton Woods institutions have become the centre of institutional power on the world development scene and the extension of the national policies and ideology of their major share-holders' (Gosovic, 1992: 256). The regime formation on the financial mechanism has been facilitated by the international organisations that have an institutionalised interest in the promotion of the regime.

Ideological power of the major donors and the World Bank

Ideological power works in two ways, first by dominating the context in which issues are discussed, and, second, as Lukes puts it, by shaping peoples' wants to eliminate their grievances. Theorists warn that the language of globalisation conceals dominant ideological structures (Carry, 1992: 43–60). When discussions take place within a society, the social values are implicit assumptions. When discussions take place between people of different societies, these assumptions are no longer valid. If one party assumes that they are valid, it faces the situation that it cannot follow the arguments of the other party and concludes that those arguments are irrational, because they do not logically follow from the implicit assumptions. This brings us to the dominant prevalent ideologies.

The current GEF regime is compatible with the dominant ideology. The ideology of the World Bank and most liberals centres around individualism, expressed in 'one person one vote' and 'one dollar one vote', and reductionism expressed in 'one problem one solution' (Gerlach, 1992: 71) and the generation of statistics. The South Centre Working Group (1993: 7) argues that:

> the quest for quantification is a trademark of international financial institutions and apparently the source of their strength. While necessary at certain

stages of programmes and project management, its apparent 'neutrality' cloaks the underlying political dimensions and subjective choices which can and do change completely the project calculation. Economistic efforts to quantify in order to facilitate financial disbursements and to reduce the real life complexity to a set of figures and formulae, should not substitute for visions and sensible and effective approaches to the problem on hand.

The ideologies of the Bretton Woods institutions has also had a great impact on developing countries. Gosovic argues that

> the Bretton Woods institutions, in particular, promote given development models, theories, and methodologies; they generate statistical data and choose how to present and interpret them; under the facade of technical impartiality, they play a profoundly political role in the national development of developing countries, devise fashions and fads of development thinking and foster their translation into practice, and influence, public opinion, decision-makers, and action world-wide. They also act to counter the South's own perception and analysis of its problems, armed with a well-established theory, methodology, and a few select indicators, plus a powerful institutional presence.
>
> (1992: 257)

The ideology, methodology and lifestyle come with the funds that are provided. Critics argue that this ideology is based on the presumption that the sum of all separate micro actions will take the society where it as a whole wishes to go. But this leads inevitably to the tragedy of the commons. The neo-liberal ideology and the need for efficiency in addressing problems, without thinking about what the consequences of the summation of all the individual actions will be, is the major problem. Thus as Tickell *et al.* put it:

> Although the demand for such funding has come from Southern governments, it is a demand that has fitted well with the agendas of many Northern interests since it effectively frames environmental problems in terms of 'solutions' which only the North can provide. Underpinning the call for new funds is the view that environmental and social problems are primarily the result of insufficient capital (solution: increase northern investment in the South); outdated technology (solution: open up the South to Northern technologies); a lack of expertise (solution: bring in northern educated managers and experts) and faltering economic growth (solution: push for an economic recovery in the North). Casting environmental problems in the language of development diverts attention from the policies, values, and knowledge system that have lead to the crisis – and the interest groups that have promoted them.
>
> (1992: 82)

Thus ideological power has had a role in shaping the wants of people in the South. However, this has to be contrasted with their indigenous ideologies.

In the post colonial period there might have been some common Southern ideology that would represent the South. Nationalism with strong state control was a dominant ideology, with import substitution and industrialisation playing a major role. With the post colonial generation, the spread of information systems and the rising power of NGOs and communities, with the rediscovering of their own identity, different processes have been set in motion in these countries. In the 1980s, the developing countries appeared to have broken up into small groups; but the 1990s have witnessed a revival in a Southern ideology (Agarwal *et al.*, 1992; Nyerere *et al.*, 1992), that although they have differences, these differences are less important than the difference between developing countries and the developed. One ideology that binds them together now is the notion that environmental problems are caused by the North, but the brunt of the consequent problems and the sacrifices will have to be borne by the South. The North thus has to compensate the South by funding the transfer of technology. But there is a growing realisation that

> a development strategy designed to imitate the life styles and consumption patterns of affluent industrial societies is clearly inconsistent with our vision for development of the South. It would accentuate inequalities, for it would be possible to secure such high consumption levels for only a small minority of the population in each country. Because it leads to a high level of imports and energy use, it would also cripple the growth process and intensify economic and environmental strains.
>
> (Nyerere *et al.*, 1990: 80)

'Another deeper struggle is between those who equate development with money, and those who equate it with empowering people' (Impact (a) 7, 1992: 1). The South Commission concludes that 'not only the growth of the national product but what is produced, how and at what social and environmental cost, by whom and for whom – all this relevant to people centred development' (Nyerere *et al.*, 1990: 13) should be considered. As Khor *et al.* sum up:

> The present environmental crisis (globally and nationally in the North and the South) and continuing poverty in the South are generated by the unsustainable economic model and consumption in the North, inappropriate development patterns in the South and an inequitable global economic system that links the Northern and Southern models.
>
> (1992)

When the causes of the problem are being discussed, one party sees 'rationally' the 'scientific' causes of the problem – that is, emission sources – whereas the other equally rationally sees the 'historic and systemic' causes of the problem – that is, the structural system of production, consumption and trade. If global environmental problems are to be addressed, their causes have to be identified. If the scientific causes are the only ones identified, then scientific and technological solutions appear appropriate. This would inevitably lead to the conclusion that advanced technology should be made available to developing countries. However, if historical and systemic causes are taken into account, then the technological solutions would appear to be of limited value. Furthermore, just discussing these historical and systemic causes would imply questioning the dominant ideological concern. If one accepts the statements of two groups of Southern experts that 'from a third world perspective, the development crisis and the environmental crisis in fact constitute a single social-ecological crisis – the most pressing challenge of our times' (Agarwal *et al.*, 1992: 18) and that

> in fact, the two phenomena – the global environmental crisis and socio-economic decline in the South – are the result of unsustainable systems of production and consumption in the North, inappropriate development models in the South, and a fundamentally inequitable world order; South–North relations are based on gross over-exploitation of, and under-payment for Southern resources and human labour.
>
> (Nyerere *et al.*, 1990: 17)

Then the attention shifts to the ideological basis of the problem – that is, the ideology that permits the development of this problem. Furthermore, if these two problems are related, then the climate change problem, with its century-long temporal dimension, its global spatial dimension, and its inter-sectoral dimension, cannot be left to the market system because this operates in the short term and externalises most of these dimensions (see also Gerlach (1992: 71–3)).

Critics argue that the dominant ideologies of individualism, liberalism, capitalism and perhaps also democracy, characterised by the prevalent approach of individual actions combining to achieve the collective goals of the society, may be inappropriate to deal with the systemic problem before us, as it is these ideologies and relevant methodologies that have caused the crisis.

Emotional power

Interviews reveal that the GEF has brought strong emotions to the surface – fear, anger and distrust being felt by actors of the South while most actors from the North are dispassionate or cynical. Since emotions colour perspectives, and perspectives equal reality in the context of politics and diplomacy, this also remains an outstanding issue.

Critics argue that history has given little reason to developing countries to trust their former colonial masters. Although it is all in the past, it is not forgotten and during discussions the historical aspects are brought up. The recent experiences with GATT, World Bank and the GEF have reconfirmed some of the anger. Anger is also the result of the perception that the World Bank is dictating terms and interfering in national policies, and that the governments of the North are dictating terms to the South. Evidence of that can be seen in the Report of the South Commission:

> The fate of the South is increasingly dictated by the perceptions and policies of governments in the North, of the multilateral institutions which a few of those governments control, and of the network of private institutions that are increasingly prominent. Domination has been reinforced where partnership was needed and hoped for by the South.
>
> (Nyerere *et al.*, 1990)

Fear of reprisal, rejection and isolation is another dominant emotion. 'Many developing countries were against the GEF but were afraid to speak up because of their dependency on the Bank' (TWN, 1992: 5) reports a magazine. The language used is not only about the conditionalities but also about the 'fears for conditionalities' (Khor *et al.*, 1992). 'If a country protests here against GEF, World Bank loans will kick it so hard that it won't know where to go', says Atiq Rahman.

In talking about the GEF, one African diplomat stated in an interview with the author: 'They don't seem to be transparent. There is a lot of scepticism about them. It probably reflects some fact and of course some history; there is anyway certainly not enough transparency to invoke trust'. Another diplomat from a small island state said that they were 'wary' of the GEF.

These emotions are not new, but the result of years of interaction between countries and, as one Southern diplomat explained, one should learn from history and history has not taught the 100-odd developing countries, who were colonies in the prewar period and experienced inferior trade terms in the postwar period, to trust the West or Japan. The past has a long shadow into the future, and future attitudes are predicated on past behaviour.

The difference between the South and the North is that the South is on the offensive in relation to the past; and the North is in the defensive in relation to the future. There is a certain amount of mutual distrust between the two communities. However, in order to deal effectively with global environmental problems, a working partnership is a must and mutual distrust needs to be replaced by good faith in each other.

Why co-operate?

Given the fundamental disagreements between the donor and recipient countries, it is difficult to envisage that co-operation was and is possible. How is it that when so many countries are opposed to the suitability of a certain institution for a particular task, that they are unable to negotiate successfully with the minority? Despite the difference in ideology and interests and the emotional undercurrents, one conclusion is that there is an acceptance by all countries that co-operation is necessary to address global environmental issues, demonstrating some kind of convergence of interest. On the other hand, the hegemonic power of major donors has a major role in shaping the outcomes of the negotiations. The institutionalised interest of powerful organisations also has a dominant influence. The dominant ideological power has shaped both the context of the negotiations and people's wants by reducing their grievances, although not eliminating them. The exercise of power in the negotiations leading up to the establishment of the GEF is seen as unfair by the developing countries. However, it is unlikely that this feeling of unfairness will lead to the breakdown of the negotiations. On the contrary, it reflects a deeper crises of different kinds of conflicting tensions in the major actors. Global environmental problems have forced a certain sense of *double reality* in people.

Southern government representatives face two kinds of tension. The first is the conflict between the temptation of the funding and the distrust in the ideology and the organisation. The fact that some money is available now, and more might be available in the future, attracts poor countries to the bargaining table. It also creates division among the poor countries, because there are not enough funds to go around. Coupled with the institutionalised use of diplomatic language and the desire to be 'socialised' into the process, countries are willing to negotiate. These factors result in posturing by developing country governments.

The second tension is the fatalism and belief in *Realpolitik* on the one hand, and their confidence in change on the other hand. The GEF South Centre (1992: 2) puts it like this: 'It is a tough world, dominated by the North and run on its terms, so let us at least get what we can on the terms offered'. In contrast, some of the negotiators interviewed felt confident that by being part of the negotiating process, they could effectively organise themselves, albeit slowly, to ensure changes in the future.

On the part of the World Bank, there is a different tension. This is the tension between the need to keep up with the times (as can be seen from their desire to set up the GEF) and the organisational inertia and rigidity in relation to ideologies and work patterns (Gosovic, 1992: 244) (as can be seen from the principles and procedures of the GEF).

On the part of industrialised countries, the tension is between the desire to maintain the *status quo* in a changing world of more than two hundred countries in which the minority status of the rich countries becomes more and more evident, and the desire to address global environmental problems in order to protect the security of future generations.

This double reality is further complicated by the notion of positional bargaining (Hurrell, 1991). The relative position of the country is central to international bargaining. States are positional rather than atomistic actors and are often hesitant about entering into co-operative arrangements if these imply negative implications for their relative power position. The solution is sometimes that all countries have to act together to keep their relative power position intact. Thus, there are at least two levels of reality in the negotiating countries. Reconciling these two levels of reality within the context of positional bargaining will be the major challenge for all those negotiating in relation to the GEF and in relation to other global environmental negotiations. At present, most negotiators both from the North and the South have used the symbolic value of politics, making a symbolic contribution to the future, while defending the present interests.

These conflicting tensions are further exacerbated by the power play in international politics that may lead at one extreme to a regime that 'may be an empty facade that rationalises the rule of the powerful by elevating their preferences to the status of norms. However, regime change is possible and linked with power and interest' (Puchala *et al.*, 1982). When the power becomes too skewed, countervailing powers may emerge. Potential countervailing powers can be identified in the 'shadow of the future', the spread of knowledge, the organisational strength and the demographic power of developing countries, the growth in the power of environmental NGOs and the neutralisation of the financial power in the GEF system.

One hypothesis of regime theory is that the 'shadow of the future' can counterbalance power asymmetries especially in relation to environmental questions (Hurrell, 1991). The future environmental consequence of actions in the South are cause for concern in the North, and hence, it has become important for the northern governments to involve the Southern governments in preparing for the future. The spread of knowledge through electronic mail systems (Econet and Greenet) and satellite television is instrumental in leading to convergent and/or divergent views in different countries. The growing power of the South as a unit in negotiations over the last six years, and its limited concern for future environmental problems in the face of the present pressing problems, is making poorer countries a force to be reckoned with. If they have a common stand on issues, they may change the shape of negotiations to come. The growing power of the NGOs in international negotiations coupled with their relatively non-bureaucratic operational methods and their research ensure that they are able to effectively influence people and governments worldwide. NGOs have also prepared insights as to how the South should negotiate in relation to the GEF. NGOs, with their link with the people at home as well as their link with the international forums, can ensure that governments do not commit themselves to actions that the people back home do not support. All these countervailing powers have to some extent helped in addressing some of the crucial controversies of the pilot phase through the restructuring of the GEF. But some crucial issues still remain.

Furthermore, NGOs can ensure that it is not just the GEF that gets blamed for its part in the problems but also developing country governments. The neutralisation of the financial power can be achieved by moving from the donor-recipient concept to the setting up of criteria on the basis of which individuals and companies pay towards a common fund on an absolute basis (i.e. people earning above a certain amount of dollars should contribute to the fund in national currency) and by setting up criteria on the basis of which individuals and companies receive the funds to use them. This will also address the rich people in developing countries, as well as focus on all the tax havens (banks) in the world. Money can be raised through special purpose levies, non-profit economic ventures including exploitation of the global commons, royalties on new products and technological processes derived from the global commons and biodiversity, taxes on pollution and energy intensity, taxes on multinationals, private initiatives and even global lotteries. This will help overcome the 'major donor syndrome' (Nyerere *et al.*, 1990). More research on the potential in this subject needs to be undertaken.

Conclusion

The North–South dialogue on GEF indicates that the critics have used the GEF as a forum and a subject to express the range of their grievances. Are their grievances relevant to the GEF issue? At the lowest level, their grievances are being taken gradually into account. The grievances at the middle and higher level are not. At the lowest level, 'global environmental problems' need to be dealt with. However, when these problems are prioritised over the local problems, the potential for consequent local problems is quite great. If 'global environmental problems' are to be addressed by local measures, this chapter would like to recommend that they should not be at the cost of the local people and their environment. The suggestion that measures should be taken 'within a framework condemning harm to the environment of other communities, empowering local people to control and manage their resources is generally the best guarantee of sustainable environmental management' (Nyerere *et al.*, 1990) should be given due consideration.

At the middle level, the organisational setting of the GEF is questioned. The recent leaks of the confidential memos within the World Bank have shown what the World Bank itself knows and acknowledges albeit privately. Although tempted by the reflection that the GEF should break completely free of the World Bank premises and control, this chapter recommends that donor countries should seriously reconsider in what manner they would like to see their money spent and deliberate on whether the need of developing countries to have an alternative source of funds can be given serious thought.

At the highest level, if power asymmetries have to be dealt with before global environmental problems are addressed, valuable time may be lost. This chapter does not advocate that power asymmetries should be dealt with. It merely indicates that when power becomes skewed in favour of a few countries, the possibility of a countervailing power becomes a reality. The restructuring of GEF is a first step towards introducing norms and ideas that represent the views of are South. The negotiating process has an in-built inertia in it and as the GEF becomes universal and a little bit more democratic and transparent, change becomes inevitable.

In the final long term analysis, from a socio-environmental perspective, it is not the aid and the technology that is really interesting, but the motivations and ideologies of society. The recommendation of the South Commission (Nyerere *et al.*, 1990) that it is not climate change, biodiversity and so on that are global problems, but the systemic causes and economic system that leads to them that needs to become the subject of international discourse.

Note

1 The author interviewed 19 delegates from 12 countries, 4 NGOs and the World Bank during the eighth round of the FCCC negotiations. The author also interviewed more than 120 actors, government officials, politicians, academics and non governmental

organisations in India, Indonesia, Kenya and Brazil (Brazilian interviews were conducted by a Brazilian lady for the author). The identity of the interviewees has been kept confidential at their request.

References

Agarwal, A., J. Carabias, M.K.K. Peng, A. Mascarenhas, T. Mkandawire, A. Soto and E. Witoelar (1992), *For Earth's Sake: A Report from the Commission on Developing Countries and Global Change*, Ottawa, Canada: International Development Research Centre.

Bachrach, Peter and Mortons, S. Baratz (1970), *Power and Poverty: Theory and Practice*, London: Oxford University Press.

Bess, Mike (1993), 'Memorandum dated 9 December 1992 on the Tana River primate National Reserve Action Plan Workshop: 13–14 November 1992: Community Action Plan Report and workplan', *IMPACT*, 9, Nairobi, Kenya: Climate Network Africa, p. 12.

Bowles, I.A. and G.T. Prickett (1994), *Reframing the Green Window: An Analysis of the GEF Pilot Phase Approach to Biodiversity and Global Warming and Recommendations for the Operational Phase*, Washington, DC: Conservation International and Natural Resources Defense Council.

Caldwell, L.K. (1988), 'Beyond Environmental Diplomacy', in J.E. Carroll (ed.), *International Environmental Diplomacy*, Cambridge: Cambridge University Press.

Carroll, J.E. (ed.) (1988), *International Environmental Diplomacy*, Cambridge: Cambridge University Press.

Carty, A. (1992), 'The Third World Claim to Economic Self Determination: Economic Rights of People: Theoretical Aspects', in S.R. Chowdhury, E.M.G. Denters and P.J.I.M. de Waart (eds), *The Right to Development in International Law*, Dordrecht, Netherlands: Martinus Nijhoff Publishers, pp. 43–60.

Colchester, Marcus (1991), 'The Global Environment Facility: Why the Bank should not be handling it', *press release*, Chadlington, UK: World Rainforest Movement (15 November).

El-Ashry (1993), 'Mechanisms for Funding,' *Environmental Policy and Law*, Vol. 23, No. 1, p. 48.

Gerlach, L.P. (1992), 'Problems and Prospects of Institutionalising Ecological Interdependence in a World of Local Independence', in G. Bryner (ed.), *Global Warming and the Challenge of International Cooperation: An interdisciplinary assessment*, Utah: Brigham Young University.

Ghai, Dharam (ed.) (1991), *The IMF and the South: The Social Impact of Crisis and Adjustment*, London: ZED Books.

Gosovic, B. (1992), *The Quest for World Environmental Cooperation; The Case of the UN Global Environment Monitoring System*, London: Routledge, pp. 223–71.

Gupta, J. (1993), *Interviews with Climate Change Negotiators*, Background Report 1, Amsterdam: Institute for Environmental Studies (confidential papers).

Hurrell, Andrew (1991), 'Regime Theory: A European Perspective (draft)', Paper prepared for the *Conference on the Study of Regimes in International Relations: The State of the Art and Perspectives*, Tubingen, Germany, 14–18 July 1991.

Impact team (a), 7 (1992), 'Financing Sustainability', *IMPACT*, Nairobi, Kenya: Climate Network Africa, December 1992, p. 1.

Impact team (b), 7 (1992), 'The Global Environment Facility', *IMPACT*, Nairobi, Kenya: Climate Network Africa, December 1992, p. 5.

Khor, Martin and Chee Yoke Ling, (1992), 'The Global Environment Facility: Democratisation, and transparency principles', *Earth Summit Briefings*, No. 15, Penang, Malaysia: Third World Network.

Krasner, Stephen, D. (1982), 'Structural Causes and Regime Consequences: Regimes as Intervening Variables', *International Organisation*, Vol. 36, No. 2, p. 186.

Lukes, Steven (1974), *Power: A Radical View*, London.: The Macmillan Press, pp. 7–59.

Macbean, A.I. and P.N. Snowden (1981), *The World Bank, IBRD, International Development Association (IDA) and the International Finance Corporation in International Institutions in Trade and Finance* (Second Impression 1987), London: George Allen and Unwin.

Newsreport from the Guardian, 1993: 'Miljoenen lijden onder projecten Wereldbank', *de Volkskrant*, Amsterdam: de perscombinatie, 6 November.

NGO statement, 1993, *Statement to the Fifth GEF Participants Assembly*, Beijing, China, 26–28 May 1993.

Nyerere *et al.* (1990), *The Challenge to the South: The Report of the South Commission*, Oxford: Oxford University Press.

Onimode, Bade (1989), *The IMF, The World Bank and The African Debt – The Social and Political Impact*, London: ZED Books.

Parikh, Jyoti (1993), *The GEF, Incremental Costs and the Paradigm of Partnership*, The Centre for Our Common Future, Geneva, Switzerland, March.

Puchala, Donald and Raymond, F. Hopkins (1982) 'International Regimes: Lessons from Inductive Analysis', *International Organisation*, Vol. 36, No. 2, Spring, Boston, MA: MIT.

Sands, Peter (1990), *Lesson Learned in Global Environmental Governance*, New York: World Resources Institute, p. 5.

Shiva, Vandana (1992), 'Why GEF is an Inadequate Institution for UNCED', *Earth Summit Briefings*, no. 19, Penang, Malaysia: Third World Network.

South Centre Working Group (1993), *Global Environment Facility and Sustainable development: Towards a Common Platform of the South, Revised Background Note Prepared for a Working Group on GEF South Centre* and *Aide memoire based on the Proceedings of the South Centre Working Group on GEF*, Geneva, Switzerland, 3–4 May 1993.

Statement of Malaysia, (1992), *Environmental Policy and Law*, UNEP, p. 232.

Third World Network (TWN) (1992), 'The Global Environment Facility', *Earth Summit Briefings*, No. 13, Penang, Malaysia: Third World Network.

Tickell, Oliver and Nicholas Hildyard (1992), 'Green Dollars, Green Menace', Editorial in *The Ecologist*, Vol. 22, No. 3 May–June, Cornwall, UK: Ecosystems.

WCED (1987), *Our Common Future*, World Commission on Environment and Development, Oxford: Oxford University Press.

Werksman, Jacob (1993), *Incremental Costs under the Climate Change Convention: The International Legal Context*, London.: Foundation for International Environmental Law and Development.

World Bank, UNDP and UNEP (1991), *GEF Brochure*, Washington, DC: GEF.

World Bank, UNDP and UNEP (1993), *Report of the Independent Evaluation of the Global Environment Facility, Pilot Phase*, Washington, DC: GEF.

World Bank, UNDP and UNEP (1994a), *The Restructured GEF: Questions and Answers*, Washington, DC: GEF.

World Bank, UNDP and UNEP (1994b), *GEF Bulletin and Quarterly Operational Summary*, May 1994, No. 11, Washington, DC: GEF.

World Bank, UNDP and UNEP (1994c), *GEF Draft Instrument for the Establishment of the Restructured Global Environment Facility*, March 1994, GEF/PA.93/6/Rev.5 Washington, DC: GEF.

14   Explaining national variations of air pollution levels

Political institutions and their impact on environmental policy-making

Markus M.L. Crepaz

Is there a systematic variation in air pollution levels across different countries? If so, how can this variation be explained? An empirical, comparative framework consisting of 18 industrialised democracies which are examined at two time periods (1980 and 1990) will be employed to explain country-specific variations of air pollution levels as a result of differences in the way in which various countries convert private desires into actual public policies. Data collected by the OECD on country-specific, man-made emissions[1] provide the empirical basis for systematic comparisons of similarities and differences in air pollution levels.

Aside from the institutional factors which are at the heart of this study, there are other factors which can explain environmental policies such as the vital necessity for action as a result of unbearable levels of pollution. For instance, if the pressure to act is extremely high as a result of high pollution levels it is most likely that efforts for environmental protection will be swifter and more sincere than if pollution levels are low (Jänicke and Mönch, 1988).[2]

The purpose of this study is to explain cross-national variation in air pollution levels as a function of institutional factors. The hypothesis put forward is that the type of interest representation systematically affects air pollution levels. 'Type of interest representation' refers to the mechanism by which private desires are turned into actual public policies. This study attempts to answer the following question: Can variations in air pollution levels be explained as a function of whether a country follows a corporatist or pluralist form of interest representation?

Corporatism and pluralism represent two quite different ways of how public desires are turned into actual public policies.[3] Corporatism refers to a system of interest representation in which a small number of strategic actors (usually representatives of capital and labour), organised in peak associations, represent large parts of the population in an encompassing fashion. Although the strategic actors are countervailing powers, their form of interaction is consensual, co-operative and goal oriented. Typical corporatist countries are Sweden, Austria, Norway, Germany and the Low Countries.

The pluralist form of interest representation is characterised by a large number of atomistic interest groups which are in a competitive struggle over access to the legislative process, using 'pressure politics' (Schattschneider, 1960). Pluralism follows an adversarial logic and is 'process oriented' (Bentley, 1908; Lowi, 1969; McConnell, 1966). Typical pluralist countries are the United States, Canada, Australia, New Zealand and Ireland.

Corporatism, on the other hand, is goal oriented. This form of interest representation deals with economic issues such as wages, prices, economic growth, unemployment and inflation. There is a tremendous literature on the effect of corporatism on macroeconomic variables and strike activity (Bruno and Sachs, 1985; Cameron, 1984; Crepaz, 1992; Crouch, 1985; Hicks and Patterson, 1989; Schmidt, 1982). Although not uncontested, (Jackman, 1987, 1989) the general tenor in the corporatist literature is that this type of interest representation tends to create lower unemployment and inflation rates, higher economic growth and less strike activity than the pluralist model.

Corporatist policies clearly deal with bread and butter issues. It is plausible that collective wage and price bargaining between employers' associations and unions, combined with a highly interventionist state, which in many cases complements stationary or low wage increases by 'social wages', domestic compensation and subsidies affect macroeconomic variables such as economic growth, inflation and unemployment. But what about environmental legislation? How can corporatism, if at all, influence environmental legislation?

This study argues that, *independently* of the policy field, it is the specific *institutional* arrangement of corporatism that explains the success of corporatist policy-making. Thus, the reasons that explain success of corporatist policy-making in the arena of macroeconomic policies should also explain success in the arena of environmental policy-making. The goal oriented character of corporatism, combined with its accommodative policy style and the encompassing manner in which interests are represented through peak associations is what explained the successes of corporatism in the macroeconomic field in the 1970s and 1980s. Why should that same institutional structure not be able to score similar successes in the field of environmental politics? Given the fact that environmental problems are ultimately economic problems, why should the tremendous expertise which corporatist countries have accumulated in guiding the economy, not also be applied for tackling environmental problems?

Quite fundamentally, this chapter argues that the success or failure of environmental policies is intimately connected to whether the system of interest representation is consensual and accommodative (corporatism) or whether it is adversarial and competitive (pluralism). David Vogel (1986: 195) made a similar argument when he claimed that 'the characteristics of a political regime are more important than the nature of the particular policy area itself in explaining policy processes'. According to Vogel,

> The most striking difference between the environmental policies of Great Britain and the United States has to do with the relationship between business and government. ... In Great Britain, the relations between the two sectors have been relatively co-operative ... In America, environmental

regulation has seriously exacerbated tension between business and government: each tends to accuse the other of acting in bad faith.

(1986: 21–2)

Unfortunately, Vogel (1986: 25) mistakenly describes the British system of interest representation as 'essentially corporatist', while he correctly identifies the US-system of interest representation as 'more pluralist' than Great Britain. It is true that Great Britain experienced phases of more deliberate planning such as the 'collectivist consensus' (1945–55) and the 'social contract' (1975–78) while the United States has no comparable experience since the Second World War. However, in a wider comparison with almost all industrialised countries, both Great Britain and the US can safely be categorised as belonging in the pluralist camp. Lijphart and Crepaz (1991: 239) created a composite measure of the degree of corporatism/pluralism for 18 countries based on the rankings of 12 'expert judgements'. If these 18 countries are rank ordered according to the Lijphart/Crepaz measure from most corporatist/least pluralist to least corporatist/most pluralist, Austria is ranked on top (most corporatist/least pluralist) and the United States of America (least corporatist/most pluralist) is ranked last (eighteenth). Great Britain ranks fourteenth using the Lijphart/Crepaz data, indicating that Great Britain is indeed more pluralist than corporatist.

Despite Vogel's (1986: 22) claim that the political regimes of Great Britain and the United States are quite different he arrives at the surprising conclusion that 'on balance, the two nations appear to have made comparable progress in controlling industrial emissions, safeguarding public health and balancing conservation values with industrial growth'.

This chapter attempts to go further than Vogel and to analyse in a systematic fashion the relationship between systems of interest representation and environmental outcomes (air pollution) based on a pooled time series/cross sectional analysis of 18 industrialised democracies at 2 different time periods (1980 and 1990–91). Vogel's results of similarities in the success of controlling industrial emissions in Great Britain and the US are not surprising if one admits that Great Britain and the United States are both rather pluralist countries. However, if the sample of industrialised democracies is extended from 2 to 18, ranging from the most corporatist countries such as Austria and Norway to the most pluralist countries such as the United States and Canada, decisive similarities and differences between the policy styles of various countries and their effects on air pollution levels should be revealed.

Contending hypotheses on the impact of corporatism on general air pollution levels

Two hypotheses on the effect of corporatism on pollution levels are introduced here. The first is called the 'pollution-promoting hypothesis', claiming that corporatism promotes pollution. The second hypothesis is called the 'pollution-retarding hypothesis' claiming that the inclusive institutional structure of corporatism allows the 'internalisation of externalities' which should manifest itself in lower pollution levels than in pluralist countries. Both hypotheses will be empirically tested in a pooled time series – cross national sample of 18 industrialised democracies at 2 time points, 1980 and 1990–91 (N = 18, t = 2), leading to a total of 36 observations.[4]

The pollution-promoting hypothesis claims that the 'material' concerns of corporatist policies are incompatible with 'post-material' interests such as environmentalism, participatory democracy, women's issues and so forth. One could plausibly argue that the more corporatist a country is, the higher the levels of air pollution, since the country is first and foremost concerned with high economic growth rates and reduction in unemployment and inflation. It is easier to defuse the distributive conflict by promoting economic growth than to attempt to reshape the size of the slices of a stagnant economic pie. This 'scramble for growth' provides the compelling logic of the pollution-promoting hypothesis. Although pollution levels do not necessarily have to be connected to economic growth, at the current stage of technological development increased economic growth is most likely connected to increased environmental pollution.

Most corporatist countries are characterised by strong socio-economic cleavage structures, which are the reasons why corporatist arrangements were instituted in the first place (Gourevitch, 1986; Katzenstein, 1985). Political stability is seen as a function of the ability of corporatism to 'deliver the goods' such as economic growth, low unemployment and inflation. The provision of these goods is the smallest common denominator which unites business and labour. 'The ultimate goal [of corporatism] is to maximize economic growth and productivity...The essence of corporatism, therefore, is a politics of representative efficiency' (Magagna, 1988: 429). The provision of these goods is the *raison d'être* of corporatist arrangements.

These goods however, are intrinsically material and do not leave any room for the representation of 'post-material' interests. Therefore, corporatism should actually increase general pollution levels rather than decrease them. The two camps, labour and business, are not countervailing powers when it comes to environmental legislation. Both should actively attempt to derail any legislation that might hamper either profits, wages or jobs. In addition, polluters have organisational advantages. They are smaller in number, command more resources and are more sophisticated with regard to political action than an unorganised public.

The second hypothesis is the 'pollution-retarding hypothesis'. The degree to which producer groups are encompassed is the crucial predictor with regard to air pollution levels. The more inclusive or corporatist the functional groups are, the higher the institutional capacity to deal with such a complex public good as environmental protection. An institutional structure based on a small number of encompassing, centralised groups, organised in peak association, has a strong incentive to 'internalise the externalities' (Olson, 1982, 1986) of their collective action and thus to lower the air pollution levels. The rationale behind Olson's argument is that the more encompassing organisations become, the more their interest and the general interest converge, and thus, the more dysfunctional it becomes to 'unload' the externalities of one party's action onto members of another party. Thus, as a result of their wider 'encompassment' these institutional systems have the capacity to internalise the externalities of their collective action. Therefore, they tend to behave more responsibly by minimising redistributive policies favouring particular groups and supporting policies which are more likely to approximate the general interest. Olson's argument of course dealt with distributive issues such as income levels to various group memberships. This logic, however, can also be applied to the field of environmental politics. Olson's pluralistic 'distributional coalitions' seek to be exempted from environmental regulations through lobbying and pressure politics, thus increasing income for their group membership. If distributional coalitions are successful in this endeavour, environmental policies, will be toothless, despite the fact that each group wishes to solve environmental problems. This of course represents the essence of Olson's 'logic of collective action' (Olson, 1965) which applies particularly if the good to be provided is public in character.[5]

Encompassing organisations on the other hand have a higher capacity to impose and enforce regulations on a larger part of society. Encompassing organisations are more 'goal oriented' than the myriad of small, atomistic interest groups in pluralism where outcomes are the result of pulling and hauling of social forces. In pluralism, outcomes are the function of process; in corporatism, outcomes are a function of deliberately guided action based on compromise, accommodation of countervailing interests and consensus.

Martin Jänicke claims that the 'consensus capacity' of a society is very important with regard to a society's ability to produce successful environmental legislation.

> The smallest common denominator, which also applies to environmental policies, is apparently the *style of politics*. Whether solutions in negotiations follow the rule that decisions should be made on a broad basis or whether one is responsive to the strongest singular interest is apparently very relevant for the result of policy... Where basic politico-economic decisions are made on a broad basis, not only are the costs of conflict smaller, but there is also a more balanced relationship between between new and old interests: new interests are responded to earlier and are not stalled as much as when there are established special interests who can achieve their goal on their own. Apparently, in industrial-political negotiation processes, environmental interests are taken into consideration earlier if the policy style is one of consensus... An active, cooperative policy-style is better for both the economy and the ecology than a *laissz-faire* philosophy.
>
> (1990: 223–4)

Cynthia Enloe, who pioneered comparative studies on environmental policies, comes to a similar conclusion:

> Among the countries here surveyed [United States, Japan, Great Britain, Soviet Union] the United States is perhaps the most severely underdeveloped

in terms of planning and coordinating capacity . . . The cultural preference for *laissez faire* relations [. . .] and the eschewance of ideological modes of debate enshrine pragmatism and *ad hoc* bargaining; while structural fragmentation in the form of federalism, local home rule, and 'sub-government' specialised policy clusters add further barriers to nationwide planning.

(1975: 326)

She points to Sweden's 'political culture [which] is remarkable for its positive evaluation on associational activities' (Enloe, 1975: 56) and she notes how Sweden's 'mode of politics encourages environmental policy-making through behind-the-scenes consultations between business executives and government officials' (Enloe, 1975: 57). Similarly, with regard to her case study of Japanese environmental policies she recognises the special style and scope of interaction between government and business, 'especially its consensual approach and the generally shared desire to advance Japan's national interests, both of which serve to overcome conflicts between government and business officials' (Enloe, 1975: 224).

What she isolates as central factors for successful environmental policies has an unmistaken affinity to the concept of corporatism as it is used in the comparative political economy literature. Lundqvist (1980: 191) in a comparative study of environmental policies entitled *The Hare and the Tortoise: Clean Air Policies in the United States and Sweden*, claims that it 'is not the physical-environmental, technological, or socioeconomic differences, but rather the political institutional ones, that account for the differences in clean air policy choice and change'. According to Lundqvist the US environmental policy style corresponded to that of the hare while the Swedish policy style corresponded to that of the tortoise:

Initially, policymaking [in the US] proceeded very swiftly and dramatically, with many policymakers trying to take the lead by outbidding each other . . . Later on, policymaking proceeded at a much lower pace and the total period of policymaking was very long and drawn out . . . The Swedish style closely resembled that of the tortoise. There were no dramatic jumps but rather, a slow and continuous movement . . . The key words were compromise and consensus rather than competition, continuity rather than popularity.

(1980: 183)

The Swedish corporatist structure imposed a particular policy-style of tackling environmental problems. The style is one which made it 'beneficial to opt for consensus rather than conflict, problem solving rather than profile-seeking' (Lundqvist, 1980: 184).

The concerns of Enloe, Jänicke and Lundqvist regarding the lack of institutional capacity in pluralist countries to shape environmental policies successfully are echoed in one of the most powerful critiques against pluralism. Although clearly not speaking about environmental policies in particular, Theodor Lowi's observation that interest group liberalism has lost the capacity to formulate and to debate policies meaningfully, could easily be applied to the realm of environmental policies: 'Interest group liberalism seeks pluralistic government, in which there is no formal specification of means or of ends. In a pluralistic government there is, therefore, no substance. Neither is there procedure. There is only process' (Lowi, 1969: 63). At the centre of Lowi's observation about 'empty' interest group liberalism lies his concerns over the lack of a core debate about policies in pluralism. Politics is no longer a debate about ends in political life – it is the 'detached' process which determines outcomes. The logic of pluralism impoverishes politics as it becomes devoid of content and substance.[6]

Corporatism and collective action problems

The 'problem of collective action' tends to occur particularly in large groups when the good to be provided is public in nature. In its most general form the problem of collective action refers to the observation that every individual in such a large group would like to have the public good provided but does not want to incur the costs of providing it (Axelrod, 1985; Hardin, 1982; Olson, 1965). Thus, individual rationality leads to collective irrationality. How can collective action problems be solved? The answer: by establishing institutions. One of the best-known institutions for solving the collective action problem of providing domestic order is the 'Leviathan, state' as Thomas Hobbes so powerfully stated more than 300 years ago. Since 'covenants, without the sword, are but words, and of no strength to secure a man at all' (Hobbes, 1968: 223) it is necessary to limit the freedom of the people and establish an intrusive and coercive state, the 'great Leviathan', to 'which we owe our peace and defence' (Hobbes, 1968: 227).[7]

How exactly should the institution of corporatism be better able to create lower levels of pollution than pluralism? To answer this question it is necessary to take a closer look at the origins and purpose of institutions. Enloe and Jänicke already pointed towards a higher institutional capacity of 'societal guidance' as a result of the institutional structure of corporatism. The purpose of institutions is, among others, to solve collective action problems, limit transaction costs and reduce uncertainty (Keohane, 1984; Knight, 1992; North, 1990). Corporatist institutions reduce the transaction costs in organising for collective action in order to tackle environmental problems because the number of participants is small, they are involved in an on-going relationship and interact with one another in different roles and positions.

Corporatism provides an institutional network which can be used to limit transaction costs of environmental policy-making, *if the conditions are right*.[8] Pollution abatement produces costs. Corporatism, because of its accommodative and co-operative character provides the ideal institutional bodies to institute efficient pollution abatement policies *once enough public pressure has been put upon them to take up this particular issue*. Its established networks between functional and officially political bodies reduce transaction costs of establishing, overseeing and executing environmental policies.

The main explanatory element which can explain variation in environmental successes is the varying institutional structures – that is, whether interest groups are atomistic, anarchistic and individualistic, or whether they are centralised, hierarchical and encompassing.[9] Since the role of institutions is 'to reduce uncertainty by establishing a stable (but not necessarily efficient) structure to human action' (North, 1990: 6) pluralism, which mimics markets, suffers from the typical symptoms of market failures, such as an inability to provide for public goods, externalities, adverse selection and moral hazard.[10] Corporatism provides not only the formal institutional framework (such as compulsory membership to functional bodies) to overcome market failure but provides also the informal constraints of a 'communitarian culture' which forces participants to behave in a co-operative manner. 'Organisations whose goals are supported by moral commitments, rather than merely by self-interest, are likely to be more assiduous in working toward their goal' (Hardin, 1982: 123).

The pluralist mode of interest representation is less able to produce environmental outcomes that are in the public interest. As Olson (1982) stated, the individually rational attempts of small, atomistic, narrowly interested distributional coalitions lead collectively to irrational outcomes; in Olson's terms, they lead to institutional sclerosis – the inability of the political system to institute growth-promoting policies since narrow distributional coalitions face 'uniquely perverse incentives' (Olson, 1986: 165). There is no reason why the pluralist process should not also suffer from producing sound environmental policies. Environmental regulation imposes costs on the private sector. In a pluralist setting, a myriad of distributional coalitions (lobbyists representing private economic interests) approach legislators in order to create legislation which is favourable for private economic interests but unfavourable for the public and the environment.

In Olson's terms

> the typical organization for collective action within a society will, at least if it represents only a narrow segment of the society, have little or no incentive to make any significant sacrifices in the interest of the society; it can best serve its members' interests by striving to seize a larger share of a society's production for them.
>
> (1982: 44)

If a given environmental bill imposed costs on a particular segment of society which is organised in special economic interest groups (such as lobbies for producers of spray-can products containing CFCs) it will attempt to reduce these costs by lobbying; thus, its activity tends to create externalities in the form of increased air pollution. Paradoxically, given the fact that the quality of the environment represents the ultimate public good, even those who produce CFCs would be affected by their own externality – that is, a reduced environmental quality. Still, the logic holds in so far as the costs the company incurs in complying with the environmental bill are direct, whereas the benefits are diffused. This is the fundamental problem of common pool resources – the common pool resource being clean air – a problem which many years ago Garrett Hardin (1968) termed 'the tragedy of the commons'.[11]

Corporatist systems of interest representation based on 'encompassing organisations' face different incentives. As opposed to pluralism, encompassing organisations have the capacity to internalise the externalities of collective action particularly if leadership of the encompassing organisation is exercised through peak associations. Olson, moving into the sphere of political parties in the American context provides an intriguing example. He argues that the US would profit from stronger parties which could discipline their representatives more. 'Individual members of Congress are overwhelmingly influenced by the parochial interests of their particular districts and by special-interest lobbies, and [that] incoherent national policies are often the result' (Olson, 1982: 50). If parties were stronger, more coherent and responsible policies would result. Returning to the sphere of interest representation, corporatism and the logic of encompassing organisation impose the necessary discipline to go beyond parochial, district-oriented policies.

Peak associations represent large sections of society; thus, they have to represent a more national perspective on policies. An example of an encompassing organisation is Sweden's LO (*Landsorganisationen*), the blue-collar union. The LO encompasses about 80 per cent of Sweden's workforce and is highly involved in every field of the policy-making process. Given this organisational feature, encompassing organisations must represent the interests of a larger part of society and thus cannot afford to be parochial.

Hypotheses, research design and data

The research design is a cross-national panel analysis consisting of 16 countries at two time periods: 1980 and 1991 (N = 18, t = 2) creating a pool of 36 observations. The countries used in this study are Australia, Austria, Belgium, Canada, Denmark, Finland, France, Germany, Ireland, Italy, Japan, Netherlands, New Zealand, Norway, Sweden, Switzerland, United Kingdom and the United States.

The dependent variables of this study are the country-specific, man-made emissions of air pollutants. Five of the most crucial air pollutants are analysed:

Sulphur oxides (SO_x): 'Sulphur oxides exert a pressure on human health; they contribute to acid deposition and thus have negative effects on aquatic ecosystems and buildings and may have negative effects on crops and forests' (OECD, 1993: 16).

Nitrogen oxides (NO_x): 'Nitrogen oxides play an important role in the production of photochemical oxidants and of smog, and contribute, together with SOx to acid precipitation' (OECD, 1993: 16).

Particulate matter: 'Particulate matter contributes significantly to visibility reduction and, as a carrier of toxic metals and other toxic substances, exerts pressures on human health' (OECD, 1993: 24).

Carbon monoxide (CO): 'Carbon monoxide can cause adverse health effects, in particular because it interferes with the absorption of oxygen by red blood cells' (OECD, 1993: 24).

Carbon dioxide (CO_2): 'Combustion emissions contribute to the increase of CO_2 atmospheric concentrations and thus to global air pollution problems: CO_2 is the gas that contributes the largest share to the greenhouse effect with its potential effects on climate, sea level and world agriculture' (OECD, 1993: 30).

The core theoretical independent variable of this study is the form of interest representation defined as a continuum between corporatism and pluralism. The political economy literature on corporatism is characterised by a bewildering variation in the operationalisation and meaning of this elusive concept. Therefore, rather than employing yet another 'new measure' of corporatism, this study uses the measures suggested by Lijphart and Crepaz (1991). The advantage of this measure is that is represents a composite index of twelve experts who have previously operationalised the concept of corporatism, creating a broad based average of this concept.[12] If the eighteen countries are ranked from the most corporatist to the most pluralist the following unsurprising rank order emerges: Austria, Norway, Sweden, Netherlands, Denmark, Switzerland, Germany, Finland, Belgium, Japan, Ireland, France, Italy, United Kingdom, Australia, New Zealand, Canada and the United States.[13]

The theoretical debate above has isolated the system of interest representation as a central predictor for successful environmental policies. 'System of interest representation' is defined as the mechanism by which latent private desires are turned into actual public policies. The two most prominent methods are pluralism and corporatism. From the discussion above flows the first and most important hypothesis: corporatism, because of its institutional structure produces environmental policies which result in lower air pollution levels than pluralist countries.

Obviously, the system of interest representation is only one among a number of other variables which might explain the variation in air pollution across time and space. Thus four control variables are introduced. First, environmental policy might be influenced by partisanship. However, an intact environment seems to be a goal almost every party is interested in achieving even though concern for the environment is not always driven by an inherent interest in this issue but rather by political considerations. This strategic behaviour is mirrored in the sudden 'greening' of both socialist and conservative parties since the late 1970s and early to mid-1980s when it became increasingly clear that in a number of European parliaments green parties were gaining representation, such as *Die Grünen* in Germany, the *Agalev* and *Ecolo* in Belgium, the *Lista Verde* in Italy, the *Vihreät/ de Gröna* in Finland, or the *Miljöpartiet de Gröna* in Sweden.

Although these green parties are extremely important in raising public consciousness in environmental issues, all these parties remained comparatively small and hardly influenced politics at the national level in the western European countries. As mentioned above, the real impact of the green parties has to be seen in how much they influence the established parties which have both a higher stake in power and the capacity to steer politics. As a result, the distribution of power on the traditional left–right continuum is used to hypothesise the impact of left or right parties on environmental policies.

Are right-wing or left-wing parties more interested in a sound environment? Which party is hit harder by steering an ecological course? There is no easy answer to this question; however, it is hypothesised here that left-wing parties have a stronger affinity to green parties than right wing parties. According to Hearl (1993) environmental policy agenda setting originates from left-of-centre parties. Left-wing as well as green parties are favourably disposed to interventionism by the the state. Right-wing parties tend to believe more strongly in employing market forces to solve environmental crises. Empirically, at the local and regional level in Germany for instance, the left and the green parties have indeed formed governing coalitions. Therefore, the hypothesis is put forward that the more socialist the government of a country is, the lower the air pollution levels will be.

As a second control variable, the per capita consumption of energy is introduced. The hypothesis is that the higher the per capita consumption of energy of a country, the higher its air pollution levels. The third control variable deals with the degree of affluence of various countries. Countries whose citizens enjoy a high level of income may create different levels of air pollution from countries whose citizens are comparatively poor. But in exactly which direction does the relationship hold? One might argue that the more affluent a country is, the higher the levels of pollution. This may be the case, but the converse relationship could also hold: the more affluent a country, the more it has the means for pollution abatement and consequently the lower the pollution levels. Studies have shown that the more prosperous a country is in comparative terms the lower are its levels of sulphur dioxide. 'If the level of affluence is lower, high or increasing emissions of sulphur dioxide are more accepted than if the level of prosperity is high' (Jänicke and Mönch, 1988: 392). Thus, the following relationship is hypothesised: the more affluent a country is, measured in terms of per capita income in US dollars, the lower the levels of air pollution.

The last control variable captures not just static levels of income but growth of GDP. The faster the growth of GDP, the more adversely the environment may be affected. Therefore, the hypothesis is that the higher the average of GDP growth from 1976 to 1980 and 1986 to 1990 the higher the levels of air pollution. Table 14.1 lists the data of man-made air pollution for eighteen countries in alphabetical order. These data represent the dependent variables.

It is assumed that the relationships hypothesised above are of linear and additive nature. Therefore, this econometric model employs an ordinary least squares estimation procedure with heteroscedasticity-consistent standard errors. The econometric model looks like this:

$$Y = C + \beta_1 \text{ Corp} + \beta_2 \text{Poldom} + \beta_3 \text{ Enercon} + \beta_4 \text{ GDPcap} + \beta_5 \text{ GDPgro} + e.$$

Y	=	dependent variables: SO_x, particulate matter (part.), NO_x, CO, CO_2
C	=	intercept
Corp	=	corporatism
Poldom	=	political dominance (average of the years from 1976 to 1980 and 1986 to 1990)
Enercon	=	energy consumption per capita (1980 and 1990)
GDPcap	=	GDP per capita in US Dollars (1980 and 1990)

Table 14.1 Country specific, per capita man-made emissions of traditional air pollutants (dependent variables) in 1980 and 1990–91 for eighteen industrialised democracies

	SO_x		*Part.*		NO_x		*CO*		CO_2	
	1980	*1990*	*1980*	*1990*	*1980*	*1990*	*1980*	*1990*	*1980*	*1991*
Australia	101.0	n.a.	18.0	n.a	62.0	n.a	252.0	n.a.	15.1	15.9
Austria	52.6	11.6	10.4	5.0	32.6	28.7	216.0	203.0	7.8	8.2
Belgium	84.0	42.1	27.0	n.a.	32.0	30.0	85.0	n.a	13.8	13.1
Canada	193.1	123.0	79.3	63.2	81.4	71.2	427.0	399.0	18.3	16.4
Denmark	87.6	35.2	9.0	n.a.	52.7	55.0	113.0	n.a.	12.8	12.8
Finland	122.1	52.2	20.0	n.a.	55.2	58.1	138.1	97.0	12.1	12.1
France	62.0	21.3	7.9	4.9	30.6	26.4	172.0	134.4	9.1	7.2
Germany	51.8	14.8	11.2	7.1	48.0	41.2	195.0	129.3	12.9	11.3
Ireland	64.0	53.4	27.6	29.9	21.5	36.5	146.0	129.6	8.0	9.0
Italy	58.0	34.7	7.8	8.7	28.0	34.6	98.5	107.5	6.8	7.3
Japan	11.0	7.1	1.0	n.a.	11.9	10.3	n.a.	n.a.	8.1	8.8
Netherlands	35.0	13.9	11.6	4.8	40.3	36.9	107.0	69.5	12.9	12.9
New Zealand	28.0	n.a.	7.0	n.a.	28.0	n.a.	180.0	n.a.	6.0	7.7
Norway	34.5	12.7	5.8	4.9	45.5	47.1	216.0	224.2	7.6	7.2
Sweden	60.0	15.0	20.0	n.a.	51.0	46.3	224.0	174.5	9.5	6.8
Switzerland	20.0	9.3	4.3	2.9	31.0	27.1	111.0	63.4	6.7	6.8
UK	86.0	65.8	23.5	16.4	41.9	48.4	89.0	116.7	10.5	10.5
USA	105.0	83.7	39.0	29.4	103.0	77.0	438.0	269.3	21.3	19.9

Source: Own calculations, based on OECD Environmental Data, Compendium 1989, table 2.1B; 19 and OECD Environmental Data, Compendium 1993, tables 2.1 A, 19; 2.1.B, 22; 2.1.C, 25; 2.1.D, 27; 2.2B, 33. The units for SO_x (sulphur oxide), particulate matter, NO_x (nitrogen oxide) and CO (carbon monoxide) indicate kilograms per capita while for CO_2 (carbon dioxide) the units indicate tonnes (1,000 kilograms) per capita. The CO_2 emissions represent totals of mobile sources, energy transformation, industry and others.

GDPgro = growth of GDP in percent (average of the years from 1976–80 and 1986–90)

e = error term.

Table 14.2 lists the various independent variables for 18 countries and 2 time points (1980 and 1990).

The results of Table 14.3 are not based on all observations since data were not available for all countries at both time periods (1980 and 1990), The sulphur oxide and nitrogen oxide model do not include Australia and New Zealand. Thus, 'N' for these two models is 32 rather than 36. Even more restricted is the particulate matter model as seven of the 18 countries did not report the latest data on particulate matter of the year 1990. These seven countries are Australia, Belgium, Denmark, Finland, Japan, New Zealand and Sweden. The number of observations for the particulate matter model is thus twenty-two. However, this does not create a systematic bias in either direction as these seven countries represent both instances of corporatist and pluralist interest representation.

The results reported in Table 14.3 of the multiple regression analysis generally confirm the hypothesised relationship between corporatism and the level of air pollution. In the sulphur oxide, nitrogen oxide and particulate matter model corporatism had a statistically significant effect in reducing these pollutants as

Table 14.2 Political dominance, energy consumption per capita, GDP per capita, growth of GDP per capita in per cent for eighteen countries in 1980 and 1990 (independent variables)

	Pol. dominance		Energy cons.		Income		Econ. growth	
	1980	1990	1980	1990	1980	1990	1980	1990
Australia	1.0	5.0	3.2	3.5	9580.0	17215.0	2.9	3.0
Austria	5.0	3.0	2.6	2.7	10250.0	20391.0	3.4	3.1
Belgium	2.4	2.2	3.6	3.5	11820.0	19303.0	3.2	2.9
Canada	1.0	1.0	6.4	6.0	10580.0	21418.0	4.0	1.5
Denmark	4.6	1.0	3.0	2.8	12950.0	25150.0	2.5	3.4
Finland	3.0	3.0	4.1	4.6	10440.0	27527.0	3.0	3.2
France	1.0	3.5	2.6	2.5	12140.0	21105.0	3.1	3.2
Germany	4.0	1.0	3.3	3.1	13310.0	23536.0	3.4	4.4
Ireland	1.4	1.2	1.9	2.3	5190.0	12131.0	3.1	3.0
Italy	1.2	2.0	1.9	2.1	6910.0	18921.0	4.8	4.5
Japan	1.0	1.0	2.1	2.4	8910.0	23801.0	5.0	2.8
Netherlands	1.8	1.7	3.7	3.5	11850.0	18676.0	2.6	0.3
New Zealand	1.0	5.0	2.2	3.0	7442.0	13020.0	−0.4	0.3
Norway	5.0	3.8	4.0	4.3	14020.0	24924.0	4.8	1.6
Sweden	1.6	5.0	4.1	3.8	14760.0	26652.0	1.3	2.3
Switzerland	2.0	2.0	2.8	2.9	15920.0	33085.0	1.8	2.8
United Kingdom	3.8	1.0	2.4	2.6	9340.0	16985.0	1.9	3.2
United States	1.0	1.0	5.8	5.4	11360.0	21449.0	3.4	2.6

Source: The measure of political dominance is from Manfred Schmidt (1992). They represent averages of the years 1976–80 and averages from 1986–90. The numbers tor the variable political dominance are interpreted as follows: 1 = bourgeois hegemony, 2 = bourgeois dominance, 3 = balance, 4 = social democratic dominance, 5 = social democratic hegemony. Data on energy consumption per capita are from *OECD Environmental Data*, Compendium 1989, Total Final Consumption of Energy, table 12.5 A , 235 and *OECD Environmental Data*, Compendium 1993, table 10.5 A, 205. The data represent the total final consumption of energy per 1 million population. The 'Income' column represents GDP per capita in US Dollars for the reference period of 1980 and 1990 and is published in the Basic Statistics: International Comparison section of *OECD, Economic Surveys* issues covering individual countries. The economic growth data represent averages of economic growth of the years from 1976 to 1980 and of averages of the years from 1986–90. The growth data are from *OECD Economic Outlook*, 1990, p. 175. The data for corporatism, not shown here, are from Arend Lijphart and Markus M.L. Crepaz (1991: 239). Their data represent units of standard deviations of corporatism.

compared to more pluralist countries. The results are statistically significant at the 0.05 level, the parameters have the expected direction and the results are robust.[14]

Partisan colouration of government does not affect the level of air pollution as indicated in Table 14.3. Similarly, economic growth, measured as averages from 1976 to 1980 and 1986 to 1990, has no statistically significant effect on these pollutants.

As hypothesised, the strongest predictor for levels of SOx, NOx and particulate matter is energy consumption per capita. As energy consumption increases, so do these three air pollutants. These parameters are highly significant ($p = <0.001$). In addition, income per capita affects the levels of sulphur oxides and particulate matter. As per capita income increases, SOx and particulate matter emissions decrease. However, this relationship does not hold with respect to NOx.

Table 14.3 Multiple regression estimates (ols with heteroskedasticity consistent standard errors) for pooled cross-sectional/time series panel analysis

	Sulphur oxide	Nitrogen oxide	Part. matter
Corporatism	−19.3 (5.2)*	−5.0 (2.5)*	−7.3 (3.1)*
Political dominance	4.6(3.4)	1.7(1.7)	−0.52(2.3)
Energy consumption	20.9 (3.4)**	13.63 (1.7)**	9.4 (1.9)**
Income	−0.003 (0.001)**	−1.4e−4(3.0e−4)	−0.001 (3.9e−4)*
Growth of GDP in %	−0.9 (3.9)	0.3 (1.9)	−0.4 (2.3)
Intercept	23.3	−5.2	1.6
R2	0.78	0.76	0.77
Adjusted R2	0.74	0.72	0.70
df	26	26	16

Notes
Standard errors are in parentheses.
* = significant at the 0.05 level.
** = significant at the 0.01 level. Two-tailed tests, 'df' = degrees of freedom.

Table 14.4 Multiple regression estimates (ols with heteroskedasticity consistent standard errors) for pooled cross-section/time series panel analysis

	Carbon monoxide	Carbon dioxide
Corporatism	−16.4(15.4)	−1.0 (0.49)**
Political dominance	7.0(11.2)	−0.2 (0.3)
Energy consumption	67.1 (9.9)***	2.5 (0.4)***
Income	−0.003 (0.002)*	5.7e−5 (6.8e−<5)
Growth of GDP (%)	13.0(11.7)	0.36 (0.34)
Intercept	−56.0	3.0
R2	0.73	0.67
Adjusted R2	0.66	0.61
df	25	35

Notes
Standard errors are in parentheses.
* = significant at the 1 level.
** = significant at the 0.05 level.
*** = Two-tailed tests, 'df' = degrees of freedom.

The adjusted coefficient of determination (R-squared) of the three models in Table 14.3 ranges between 0.70 and 0.72.[15]

The results in the CO model in Table 14.4 are based on 13 countries and 2 time periods creating 26 observations altogether. The countries that are not included in this analysis through lack of unavailable of data for the 1990 time period are Australia, Belgium, Denmark, Japan and New Zealand. Again, these countries balance each other in terms of degrees of corporatism and pluralism, creating an unbiased residual sample. Fortunately, for the CO_2 model all data are available for every country at every time point, strengthening the confidence in the results of those models for which not all data were available. The CO_2 model, thus, contains thirty six observations.

Inspection of the parameters of the CO model indicates that corporatism fails to reduce the level of CO emissions significantly. However, in the CO_2 model corporatism has the hypothesised effect of reducing these emissions. In both models, as in the others, energy consumption is the strongest predictor, indicating that as energy consumption per capita increases so do the emissions of these pollutants. Table 14.4 also contains evidence that more affluent countries are better able to suppress CO emissions than poorer countries as measured by the per capita income.[16]

The econometric model reveals a pattern: both energy consumption per capita and the system of interest representation are the strongest independent variables which can explain the variation of man-made, country-specific emissions of what the OECD considers to be 'traditional air pollutants'.

Conclusion

In this chapter it is argued that national variations in the patterns of how private interests are aggregated, funnelled and shaped into public policies matter with regard to the levels of air pollution in industrialised democracies. The goal-oriented, accommodative, co-operative and consensual style of corporatist policy-making results in lower emissions of traditional air pollutants than the process-oriented, competitive and disjointed form of pluralist interest representation.

Despite the intriguing results of the empirical analysis a warning is in order. Caution has to be exercised since the comparability of the air pollution data leaves much to be desired. In some countries the pollution levels are measured using different techniques, and in other countries pollution levels are estimated. In addition, definitions of 'total emissions' vary from country to country. Also, there are idiosyncratic factors at work, such as a particular industrial structure which leads to a particular pattern of air pollution in various countries. However, the data supplied by the OECD are still the most reliable and accurate to date.

Nevertheless, a rather provocative pattern emerged from this research. In four out of the five models corporatism significantly affected air pollution levels in the direction indicated by the hypothesis, indicating that the accommodative, goal-oriented, consensual policy style of corporatism is indeed more effective in reducing air pollutants than the atomistic and disjointed pluralist process.

The reason for this success is found in the institutional structure of corporatism. A clean environment is a public good. If the major societal actors are represented in an encompassing manner and through peak organisations, the 'strategic actors' have an incentive to internalise the externalities of collective action. The more encompassing the groups become, the more the group's interest and the general interest converge, and thus the more difficult it becomes to dump the externalities of one's action on to members of another group. This institutional logic of corporatism has a built-in incentive to represent 'public interest' in a more effective way than pluralism does.

In addition, corporatism is an elaborate institutional mechanism to equilibrate and accommodate conflicting interests. Environmental protection creates costs.

The already existing elaborate institutional structure can be used to tackle problems of economic adjustments which are bound to occur if the environment is to be protected. This lowers the transaction costs of organising, overseeing and enforcing collective action. While a sound environment is a good equally desired by everybody, institutions present different filters through which preferences are channeled. Thus, political outcomes are not only a function of individual preferences but also of how these preferences are structured, shaped and sculpted by different institutional frameworks. This study does not claim that environmental protection is less important in pluralist countries than in corporatist ones. Rather, the argument is about variations in institutional structures which can account for differences in outcomes. As Robert Grafstein (1991: 259) so eloquently stated, 'institutions help explain how the same set of preferences produces different outcomes when aggregated in different social settings'.

But the system of interest representation does not explain everything. Not surprisingly, energy consumption per capita proved to be the strongest predictor variable, providing empirical support for the intuitive hypothesis that energy consumption and air pollution are positively related. The political dominance variable was not significant in any of the five models, indicating that the traditional left–right dimension of politics cannot systematically explain variations in air pollution levels. As long as 'post-material' parties fail to gain access to executive power – and it does not appear as if they will achieve that goal soon – post-material partisan impact will be difficult to assess. The results of this analysis do not indicate that leftist parties are more permeated by green issues than rightist parties. Similarly, in none of the five models did economic growth affect air pollution in a systematic fashion.

The last control variable, per capita income, indicated that in three of the five models, it had the negative impact suggested by the hypothesis. As per capita incomes rise, sulphur oxide, particulate matter, and carbon monoxide emissions decrease significantly. Richer countries can afford to spend more on pollution abatement than poorer countries. In the larger context of the debate about post-materialism, these findings do indeed support Inglehart's scarcity hypothesis which argues that 'an individual's priorities reflect the socio-economic environment: one places the greatest subjective value on those things that are in relatively short supply' (Inglehart, 1990: 68). When 'people are safe and have enough to eat' (Inglehart, 1977: 22) their values shift from material (unemployment, income, inflation, economic growth) to post-material ones (clean air, the 'countryside', participatory democracy, minority's rights and so on).[17] As nations become more affluent they also have the means at their disposal to combat air pollution levels actively.

We are still left with puzzles, such as: Why is the corporatist system of interest representation more effective in reducing sulphur oxides than carbon monoxides? Goal-oriented environmental policy is more successful if the sources of pollution are centralised, as with nationalised, industrial plants for example. The more decentralised the sources of pollution the less successful is 'guided' corporatist policy-making. A glance at Table 14.1 indicates that all countries were quite successful in reducing SO_x between 1980 and 1990. However, more corporatist countries were even more successful than more pluralist countries. On the other hand, CO_2 emissions, which are the largest contributor to the greenhouse effect, are much harder to control with either goal-oriented or process-oriented policies. Little progress has been made within countries in reducing this kind of air pollutant between 1980 and 1991. This is partly the result of the decentralised character of the source of this particular pollution and its interactive effects with other human activities such a clear-cutting tropical rain forests.

Politics thrives on trade-offs. What makes corporatism so effective – its centralised, hierarchical, character – also makes it very susceptible to corruption, moral hazard and agency loss. There are reasons to believe that, while the corporatist system of interest representation may be effective, it may not very democratic. Ralf Dahrendorf warns that corporatism takes 'the political' out of the political process.

> Corporatism enters into an easy union with bureaucracy, and both tend to rob the constitution of liberty of its essence, the ability to bring about change without revolution... But fundamentally, corporatism takes life out of the democratic process. Arrangement replaces debate, consensus is substituted for conflict.
>
> (Dahrendorf, 1988: 111)

The dilemma is one of a negative trade-off between effectiveness of government and its ability to effectively deal with environmental degradation (or other policy fields) on the one hand, and the vitality of the democratic process on the other. I leave it up to the reader where she would like to place herself on that infelicitous line.

Notes

1 It is important to recognise the difference between 'emissions' and 'immissions'. Immissions measure the pollution levels from other countries 'immigrating' into a particular country. This is a crucial distinction because 'emissions' measure the country specific, idiosyncratic levels of pollution which are 'emitted' in one particular country. This allows for a meaningful cross-national comparison which is not contaminated by pollution which originated in other countries and which crossed national boundaries. If the data did not make this distinction not much could be said about the origins of country-specific pollution levels since polluted air does not obey national borders.

2 This is most clearly depicted in the cases of Great Britain and Japan. Both of these countries were forced to impose governmental regulation because environmental problems became intolerable. In Great Britain the passing of the Clean Air Bill in 1956 was dramatically accelerated after 5 December 1952 when a 'killer fog' descended over London for four days killing about 4,000 people (Vogel, 1986: 38). Similarly, Japan suffered from a number of horrible environmental catastrophes such as the *Minimata* disease as a result of mercury poisoning, the *Yokkaichi asthma* as a result of air pollution, and the *itai-itai* disease as a result of dumping cadmium waste into water that was used for rice paddy irrigation (Enloe, 1975: 231). To this list of 'learning it the hard way' can be added the horrible accident in Bhopal, the pollution of the Rhine river by

Sandoz, the poisoning of the people of Seveso by dioxin, Tchernobyl, and the Valdez oil tanker disaster.

3 In a corporatist arrangement, supposedly, there are no 'winners' or 'losers' only 'sharers'. For a most elaborate, ideal-typical definition of corporatism see Phillippe Schmitter (1974). Peter Katzenstein (1985: 32) defines democratic corporatism as

> an ideology of social partnership expressed at the national level; a relatively centralised and concentrated system of interest group; and voluntary and informal coordination of conflicting objectives through continuous bargaining between interest groups, state bureaucracies and political parties. These traits make for a low-voltage politics.

4 Since some air pollution data were not available for every country and every time period the total number of observations in this analysis ranges between 22 and 36.

5 A pure public good is defined by two elements: first, jointness of supply, meaning that the use of the public good by one person does not diminish the use of the good by somebody else; second, non-excludability obviously means that once the public good is provided, nobody can be excluded from its use.

6 These are precisely the concerns that motivated interwar corporatist thinkers such as Boivin and Bouvier-Ajam (1938: 50) who claimed that liberalism aimed 'to direct man towards the material world, to drain him of all notion of eternity, or social life, to make him a brute, wanting sentiments of charity, pity, altruism'. The development of corporatism was self-consciously anti-liberal. As Williamson (1985: 20) so powerfully states, 'Corporatism was, in effect, anti-liberal rather than anti-capitalist. Liberalism had broken down social bonds and turned society into a mass of atomistic, self-seeking individuals devoid of any higher moral purpose.'

7 For a differing viewpoint, see Michael Taylor (1987), *The Possibility of Co-operation*, Cambridge, MA: Cambridge University Press.

8 Austria represents a very good example of an extremely corporatist country where a 'Green' party has gained representation at the national level. In Austria, the 'social partners' (labour and capital) are involved in environmental policy. Most environmental policies economic costs. Dealing with these costs is a 'material' rather than 'postmaterial' issue. Therefore, corporatism represents a fitting institution to deal with these costs and adjustments. However, there is no indigenous impetus of the social partners to introduce, for instance, expensive filters in smokestacks. This creates costs and as a result reduces profits for the owners and endangers jobs for workers. Organisationally then, the social partnership is 'immune' to other than 'materialist' demands. If, however, as a result of an exogenous force (that is, governmental policies, pressured by environmental interests, are forcing the strategic actors to introduce environmentally sound policies) the expertise of the social partners can be instrumentalised to achieve these goals. The important point is that it takes exogenous pressure for the social partners to react to these new social demands. To aggregate and represent these new green issues is not in the natural domain of the social partners. However, when a particular project receives enough public attention, such as the referendum on the first and only nuclear powerplant in Austria in 1978, or when hundreds of young Austrians in 1984 blocked a site in a national park where a hydro-electric powerplant was planned, the political and economic infrastructure of the social partners can be used to work out compromises even in the field of environmental politics.

9 In political science, there is much interest currently in 'neo-institutionalism'. It focuses on the use of institutions, such as formal rules, compliance procedures and standard operating procedures to shape strategies and and goals of social actors. Different institutions can dramatically alter outcomes. Authors such as Arend Lijphart and Peter Katzenstein argue that differences in formal constitutional structures, such as whether a country employs a consensus model or the Westminster model of government, can have direct consequences on how this country is able to manage its societal cleavage

structure (Lijphart, 1977). Katzenstein (1985) also depends on institutions such as corporatism as explanatory factors which explain why small, open economies are able to cushion themselves against the ups and downs of the international business cycle. While Lijphart's and Katzenstein's use of institutions is of a functionalist character, the new institutionalism also comes in a rational-choice variant where institutions are seen as important in solving collective-action problems, agency problems, reducing trans-action costs when the number of participants is high, co-ordinating cases of multiple equilibria, and in limiting principal-agent problems by overseeing, and enforcing contracts (Alchian, 1950; Arrow, 1951; Bates, 1988; Powell and DiMaggio, 1991; Pratt and Zeckhauser, 1985; Shepsle, 1989; Zukin and DiMaggio, 1990).

10 It is important to note that while the authoritative style of corporatism may be suitable in solving collective action problems, its hierarchical, centralised and closed character invites agency loss as a result of moral hazard. As a general hypothesis, one might state that principal-agent problems should be larger in corporatist systems than in pluralist ones, since the effectiveness of corporatism lies precisely in the relatively unchecked nature of the power relations between the functional bodies and the state. For a more detailed debate about principal-agent problems in corporatist systems, see Crepaz (1995).

11 The difference between my application of Olson's logic and his original one is that he refers to distributional coalitions as 'overwhelmingly oriented to struggles over the distribution of income and wealth rather than to the production of additional output' (Olson, 1982: 44). I view the behaviour of pressure groups in the field of environmental politics as 'cost averting' rather than 'income increasing'.

12 For a lively debate over the vices and virtues of aggregating various measures of corporatism, see Keman and Pennings (1995) and Crepaz and Lijphart (1995).

13 The time period of corporatism covered by the various 'experts' ranges between the mid-1960s to the early 1980s. The end-point of the panel study includes the years 1990–91. However it is assumed that institutional structures such as corporatism do not vary dramatically over time. Thus, levels of corporatism/pluralism as assumed to be the same in these years as they were in the 1970s and 1980s.

14 All equations in all models were estimated using the 'robust' option in the statistical package called SST (Statistical Software Tools, version 2.0) by J.A. Dubin and R.D. Rivers (1985–90). The 'robust' option performs heteroskedasticity-consistent standard errors. Since the number of observations is between 22 and 36 the findings could be driven by a few outlying cases. Therefore, all models were tested for outliers by calculating the studentised residuals (residuals divided by their estimated standard deviations) and for leverage points by calculating the diagonal elements of the 'hat' matrix. Both of these sophisticated regression diagnostics are available in SST. For the studentised residuals, the values were conventionally set to 1.96. Large values – that is, bigger than 1.96 (positive or negative) of the studentised residuals – indicate outliers. In addition, the diagonal elements of the hat matrix were obtained. Belsley *et al.* (1980) suggest 2p/n as a 'rough' cutoff for values of the hat matrix. Values that exceed 2p/n may have a high leverage on the regression parameter estimate.

15 Inspection of the studentised residuals ('outliers') indicated that two observations (Finland and the US) crossed the conventional threshold of 1.96. Re-estimating the regression with these two cases omitted did not change direction or significance of the model. No other outliers were found in Table 14.3. Also, no observations passed the threshold for leverage points Table 14.3.

16 No observations crossed the threshold for outliers and leverage points in Table 14.4.

17 Inglehart's analyses are of course based on individual survey data, while this study uses aggregated national data. While taking care not to reify the state, I observe an affinity between Inglehart's findings based on individual survey data and the ones presented here based on aggregate data.

References

Alchian, Armen (1950), 'Uncertainty, Evolution, and Economic Theory', *Journal of Political Economy*, Vol. 58, pp. 211–21.

Arrow, Kenneth (1951), *Social Choice and Individual Values*, New Haven, CT: Yale University Press.

Axelrod, Robert (1985), *The Evolution of Cooperation*, New York: Basic Books.

Bates, Robert, H. (1988), 'Contra Contractarianism: Some Reflections on the New Institutionalism', *Politics & Society*, Vol. 16, pp. 387–401.

Belsley, David, A., Kuh, Eric and Richard, E. Welsch, (1980). *Regression Diagnostics: Identifying Influential Data and Sources of Collinearity*, New York: Wiley.

Bentley, Arthur F. (1908), *The Process of Government: A Study of Social Pressures*, Chicago, IL: University of Chicago Press.

Boivin, G. and M. Bouvier-Ajam (1938), *Vers une Economie Politique Morale*. Paris: Recueil Sirey.

Bruno, Michael and Jeffrey Sachs (1985), *Economics of Worldwide Stagflation*, Cambridge, MA: Cambridge University Press.

Cameron, David, R. (1984), 'Social Democracy, Corporatism, Labour Quiescence and the Representation of Economic Interests in Advanced Capitalist Society', in John H. Goldthorpe (ed.), *Order and Conflict in Contemporary Capitalism*, London: Oxford University Press, pp. 143–78.

Crepaz, Markus, M.L. (1992), 'Corporatism in Decline? An Empirical Analysis of the Impact of Corporatism on Macro-Economic Performance and Industrial Disputes in 18 Industrialized Democracies', *Comparative Political Studies*, Vol. 25, pp.139–68.

Crepaz, Markus, M.L. (1995), 'Of Principals, Agents, and the Decline of Austrian Corporatism. Anatomy of Legitimacy Crises in a Highly Corporatist System', in *Current Politics and Economics of Western Europe*, Vol. 5, pp. 187–203.

Crepaz, Markus M.L. and Arend Lijphart (1995), 'Linking and Integrating Corporatism and Consensus Democracy: Theory, Concepts, and Evidence', *British Journal of Political Science*, Vol. 25, pp. 281–9.

Crouch, Colin (1985), 'Conditions for Trade Union Wage Restraint', in Leon Lindberg and Charles S. Maier (eds), *The Politics of Inflation and Economic Stagnation: Theoretical Approaches and International Case Studies*, Washington, DC: The Brookings Institution, pp. 105–39.

Dahrendorf, Ralf (1988), *The Modern Social Conflict. An Essay on the Politics of Liberty*, Berkeley, CA: University of California Press.

Enloe, Cynthia (1975), *The Politics of Pollution in a Comparative Perspective. Ecology and Power in Four Nations*, New York: David McKay Co.

Gourevitch, Peter (1986), *Politics in Hard Times. Comparative Responses to International Economic Crises*, Ithaca, NY: Cornell University Press.

Grafstein, Robert (1991), 'Rational Choice: Theory and Institutions', in Kristen Renwick Monroe (ed.), *The Economic Approach to Politics, A Critical Reassessment of the Theory of Rational Action*. New York: Harper Collins, pp. 259–78.

Hardin, Garrett (1968), 'Tragedy of the Commons', *Science*. Vol. 162, pp. 1243–8.

Hardin, Russell (1982), *Collective Action*, Baltimore, MD: Johns Hopkins University Press.

Hearl, Derek (1993), 'Putting New Issues on the Agenda. The Role of Party "Families" and Party "Types"', Paper presented at the ECPR workshop in Leiden, Netherlands, 2–8 April 1993.

Hicks, Alexander and Dwight, W. Patterson (1989), 'On the Robustness of the Left Corporatist Model of Economic Growth', *Journal of Politics*, Vol. 51, pp. 662–75.

Hobbes, Thomas (1968), *Leviathan* (edited with an Introduction by C.B. McPherson), New York: Penguin Books.

Inglehart, Ronald (1977), *The Silent Revolution*, Princeton, NJ: Princeton University Press.

Inglehart, Ronald (1990), *Culture Shift*, Princeton, NJ: Princeton University Press.

Jackman, Robert, W. (1987), 'The Politics of Economic Growth in Industrialized Democracies, 1974–80: Leftist Strength or North Sea Oil?' *Journal of Politics*, Vol. 49, pp. 242–56.

Jackman, Robert, W. (1989), 'The Polities of Economic Growth, Once Again', *Journal of Politics*. Vol. 51, pp. 646–61.

Jänicke, Martin (1990), 'Erfolgsbedingungen von Umweltpolitik im Internationalen Vergleich', *Zeitschrift für Umweltpolitik und Umweltrecht*, Vol. 90, pp. 213–32.

Jänicke, Martin and Harald Mönch (1988), '... Ökologischer und wirtschaftlicher Wandel im Industrieländervergleich. Eine explorative Studie über Modernisierungskapazitäten', *Politische Vierteljahresschrift*, Vol. 19, pp. 389–404.

Katzenstein, Peter (1985), *Small States in World Markets*, Ithaca, NY: Cornell University Press.

Keman, Hans and Paul Pennings, (1995), 'Managing Political and Societal Conflict in Democracies: Do Consensus and Corporatism Matter', *British Journal of Political Science*, Vol. 25, pp. 268–80.

Keohane, Robert (1984), *After Hegemony. Cooperation and Discord in the World Political Economy*, Princeton, NJ: Princeton University Press.

Knight, Jack (1992), *Institutions and Social Conflict*, Cambridge, MA: Cambridge University Press.

Lijphart, Arend (1977), *Democracy in Plural Societies. A Comparative Exploration*. New Haven, CT: Yale University Press.

Lijphart, Arend and Markus, M.L. Crepaz (1991), 'Corporatism and Consensus Democracy in Eighteen Countries: Conceptual and Empirical Linkages', *British Journal of Political Science*. Vol. 21, pp. 235–46.

Lowi, Theodore (1969), *The End of Liberalism: Ideology, Policy, and the Crisis of Public Authority*, New York: Norton.

Lundqvist, Lennart, J. (1980), *The Hare and the Tortoise: Clean Air Policies in the United States and Sweden*, Ann Arbor, MI: University of Michigan Press.

McConnell, Grant (1966), *Private Power and American Democracy*, New York: Alfred A. Knopf.

Magagna, Victor, V. (1988), 'Representing Efficiency: Corporatism and Democratic Theory', *Review of Politics*, Vol. 50, pp. 420–44.

North, Douglas (1990), *Institutions, Insitutional Change and Economic Performance*. Cambridge, MA: Cambridge University Press. OECD *Economic Surveys* (various editions).

OECD *Economic Outlook* (various editions).

OECD (1989) *Environmental Data*, Compendium 1989.

OECD (1993) *Environmental Data*, Compendium 1993.

Olson, Mancur (1965), *The Logic of Collective Action. Public Goods and the Theory of Groups*, Cambridge, MA: Harvard University Press.

Olson, Mancur (1982), *The Rise and Decline of Nations*, New Haven, CT: Yale University Press.

Olson, Mancur (1986), 'A Theory of the Incentives Facing Political Organizations: Neo-Corporatism and the Hegemonic State', *International Political Science Review*. Vol. 7, pp. 165–89.

Powell, Walter, W. and Paul, J. DiMaggio (eds) (1991), *The New Institutionalism in Organizational Analysis*, Chicago, IL: University of Chicago Press.

Pratt, John and Richard Zeckhauser (1985), 'Principles and Agents: An Overview', in John Pratt and Richard Zeckhauser (eds), *Principals and Agents: The Structure of Business*, Boston, MA: Harvard Business School Press.

Schattschneider, Elmer, E. (1960), *The Semisovereign People: A Realist's View of Democracy in America*, New York: Holt, Rinehart & Winston.

Schmidt, Manfred, G. (1982), 'Does Corporatism Matter? Economic Crises, Politics and Rates of Unemployment in Capitalist Democracies in the 1970s', in Gerhard Lehmbruch and Phillippe Schmitter (eds), *Patterns of Corporatist Policy-making*. London: Sage Publications, pp. 237–58.

Schmidt, Manfred (ed.) (1992), *Politisches System und Politikfelder – Westliche Industrieländer*, Munich: Beck Verlag.

Schmitter, Phillippe (1974), 'Still the Century of Corporatism?', *Review of Politics*, Vol. 36, pp. 85–131.

Shepsle, Kenneth, A. (1989), 'Studying Institutions. Some Lessons from the Rational Choice Approach', *Journal of Theoretical Politics*, Vol. 1, pp. 131–47.

Taylor, Michael (1987), *The Governmental Process*, New York: Alfred A. Knopf.

Vogel, David (1986), *National Styles of Regulation. Environmental Policy in Great Britain and the United States*, Ithaca, NY: Cornell University Press.

Williamson, Peter J. (1985), *Varieties of Corporatism: A Conceptual Discussion*, London: Cambridge University Press.

Zukin, Sharon and Paul DiMaggio Paul (eds) (1990), *Structures of Capital. The Social Organization of the Economy*, Cambridge, MA: Cambridge University Press.

15 Citizens' juries and valuing the environment

A proposal

Hugh Ward

From the perspective of mainstream welfare economics, the environment should be preserved only if this improves human social welfare, allowing for costs in terms of consumption foregone. Cost–benefit analysis seeks to show whether or not this is the case by placing monetary values on the benefits from preservation and on the costs. Preservation is justified if the sum of monetary benefits across all members of society exceeds the sum of costs (e.g. Brent, 1996; Dixon *et al.*, 1994; Pearce, 1995).[1] Typically economists need to know individuals' willingness to pay (WTP) for different levels of provision of environmental quality in order to use this approach. For standard consumer goods market prices gives information on WTP. However, environmental quality usually is not traded in markets. Various other measures have been suggested. Hedonic methods use proxy measures such as that component of property values which cannot be explained by non-environmental determinants like nearness to employment. Travel cost methods estimate WTP by the travel costs people are willing to incur in order to enjoy desirable environments, for example, the travel costs people will incur to visit national parks. These methods are of restricted applicability. For one thing they cannot answer questions about how much people are willing to pay to address truly national, let alone global, problems.

In contingent valuation or constructed market methods the basic procedure is to ask a randomly chosen sample of individuals what it is worth to them individually in monetary terms to have environmental quality supplied at a certain level (Cummings *et al.*, 1986, ch.1). The sample average estimates how much that level of supply of the good is worth for the average member of society; and the value for the society as a whole is estimated by multiplying the sample average by the number of individuals in the society. This method provides a way of valuing things which cannot plausibly be captured using hedonic methods. A typical example is the existence value to individuals of knowing that some rare species has not died out.

Another approach would be to ask a group of individuals collectively to agree on an estimate of the monetary benefits to the society as a whole from providing the good at a particular level. Agreement might occur after a process of deliberation and debate in which the participants could absorb information and call for additional information from witnesses. If consensus could not be reached, voting over different proposed answers to the question would occur. If the participants were a socially representative sample of the relevant population, they would form a citizens' jury. The citizens' jury approach has distinct advantages over conventional contingent evaluation. These stem from the facts that: participants can be made better informed; the process is potentially more democratic and legitimate; it is less likely that measurement errors will occur; the social dimension of valuing, connected with collective identity formation, is more likely to be captured; and distributional issues can be addressed more directly. I also explore the possibility that the jury might allow for non-human interests.

The idea of citizens' juries was developed both in the US and in Germany in the early 1970s, partly out of concern for the low levels of participation in representative democracy and the passivity of relatively ill-informed citizens (Crosby *et al.*, 1986: 170; Stewart *et al.*, 1994: 2–5). The aim is to get a socially representative group of citizens to take a longer-term, better informed and more impartial view of significant social issues. Notice that the jury is representative in the sense that it is chosen so as to try to ensure that, before deliberation occurs, the distribution of opinions and perceived interests among the jurors reflects that among the citizenry as whole. Jurors are not seen as *representatives* or as agents of the people, responsible to them for policies that flow from their deliberations.

Researchers at the Thomas Jefferson Centre in the US have developed a methodology for implementing citizens'juries, and it has been put to a wide variety of uses, focusing both on national and local issues (Crosby *et al.*, 1986). The Institute for Public Policy Research (IPPR) introduced the idea to Britain in the 1990s and has run several citizens'juries. Typically these have been sponsored by local health care trusts or by local authorities and have involved allocating scarce monetary resources over different end uses. There are many similarities between the practices of the IPPR and the Jefferson Centre (Crosby *et al.*, 1997; Stewart *et al.*, 1994).[2] In both versions: jurors are paid; receive written and oral evidence; can cross-examine witnesses; discuss the issues among themselves; and are chaired by a trained moderator.

Citizens' juries often consider questions relating to the environment. German planning cells, closely related to the citizens' juries, have mainly been applied to issues concerning the local natural and built environment (Renn, 1984; Stewart *et al.*, 1994: 11–14) and related ideas such as Community advisory forums have been developed (Petts, 1997). Sometimes juries have considered questions which demand that environmental valuation is carried out, if only implicitly (e.g. Crosby *et al.*, 1986: 172–5). No-one has run a citizens'jury explicitly to carry out contingent evaluation, although this possibility was mentioned briefly by Jacobs (1996) as part of a general discussion of the role of deliberative democracy in environmental decision-making.

In the first section, I provide a regulative ideal for using citizens'juries in contingent evaluation. In the second, I detail the advantages of citizens' jury approach. Despite being called into question on a number of grounds (Cummings *et al.*, 1986; Foster, 1996: Part 1), environmental cost–benefit analysis is of increasing practical importance. Critics say that this is because it is consistent with the dominant rationalistic and economistic discourses which lead to the permeation of the political realm by the values of the market (e.g. Grove-White, 1996; Sagoff, 1988). In section III, I mount a limited defence of my approach against such criticisms.

Impartial judgement and citizens' juries

Cost–benefit analysis can be regarded as a form of utilitarianism with money values proxying utilities. The normative ideal that lies behind my proposal is Harsanyi's version of utilitarianism (e.g. Harsanyi, 1955). Individuals are asked to put themselves in others' shoes, using the method of extended sympathy to answer questions about others' interests. They embody these judgements in a utility function assigned to others. When arriving at a judgement about the benefits to society as a whole of some option, their personal summation weights the utilities of all individuals equally, for to use unequal weightings would be to fail to be impartial. Reasonable and impartial individuals may differ in the judgements they make about others' benefits. But many of these differences will be a function of factual questions that can be resolved using empirical evidence. So reasoned debate might lead to convergence of judgements.[3]

In reality this regulative ideal will only be approximated, but the jury could be set up in a way that makes for a closer fit with the ideal. The question posed should be 'what is a particular level of provision of environmental quality worth to the average citizen?'. Answering this question demands that jurors think through what it is worth to others to supply at this level. There are theoretical grounds for suggesting that when a citizens' jury debates about what the collective judgement should be it would be difficult for an individual to defend a partial position that placed undue weight on the benefits to himself or people with similar interests. There is considerable evidence that those who are open about their partiality are normatively sanctioned in democratic deliberation (e.g. Dryzek, 1987: ch. 15; Miller, 1992). Deliberation exposes people to others' points of view and creates a community within which it is much more difficult to ignore their interests (e.g. Jacobs, 1996: 220). It may, for instance, reduce purely NIMBY opposition to the location of socially needed facilities (Petts, 1995: 519–21). Normative pressures are certainly no guarantee against such partiality, but there is evidence from the US that participants in citizens' juries see the process as relatively bias-free (Crosby *et al.*, 1986: 176; Stewart *et al.*, 1994: 41). Second, the experience of running citizens' juries over other issues suggests that debate ought to lead to some convergence of judgements (e.g. Stewart *et al.*, 1994), albeit that voting can be used to resolve differences.

Many techniques exist to encourage deliberation in citizens' juries and to present information to jurors (Stewart *et al.*, 1994: 35–8). These are not particularly adapted to help jurors assign money values to things. However, conventional studies using contingent evaluation have used a whole battery of approaches to elicit valuations (e.g. Carson, 1991; Cummings *et al.*, 1986: ch. 4; Dixon *et al.*, 1994: ch. 5). For example, besides questions about WTP, experimenters may ask about individuals' willingness to accept (WTA) compensation. There is no reason why such procedures should not be used by moderators or witnesses in a citizens' jury context, although they would need to be adapted to help jurors put values on others' interests. The very process of debate within the jury ought to help in this regard, too.

Realistically jurists would need to think in terms of how the environmental good matters in monetary terms to token members of a number of social blocs, defined by similarity of interests, ignoring some of the variation across individuals within blocs. It seems inevitable that in the debate and questioning leading to the collective judgement that members would talk about how valuable the good was to them and to people like them. This is desirable from the standpoint adopted here. In a socially representative jury members act as surrogates for social blocs; and it is essential to answering the question that a collective sense develops of how much individuals belonging to different social blocs value the good.[4] Representing people like oneself in the debate would actually ease the difficulties of using the method of extended sympathy. It causes no problems so long as partiality is not exercised when making an overall judgement.

There is a range of ways in which deliberative forums could be used in environmental decision making (Jacobs, 1996). For instance, another potential approach is deliberative polling. In deliberative polling participants would be relatively well-informed and there would be debate (Fishkin, 1991) but ultimately participants would disclose an individual monetary value. These would then be averaged. So deliberative polling is a method lying between existing methodologies for contingent evaluation and the citizens' jury approach. My preference for the citizens' jury option stems from the fact that asking for a collective answer to the values placed by the average citizen seems more likely to engage norms of impartial debate. Moreover, the social dimensions of evaluation discussed below are more likely to be captured.

Jacobs rejects the idea that citizens' juries can be used in contingent evaluation, although he sees them as playing a potentially important general role in environmental decision making (1996: 222–3). He argues that jurors would not answer the question of how much environmental quality was worth to them as individuals in a way that would give satisfactory data for contingent valuation because they would inevitably concern themselves with the effects of their expressed views on others' payoffs, so that there would be an element of double-counting of utilities when the individual answers of jurors were added up (1996: 216–17, 223). My proposal avoids this problem. Jurors are not asked to express their personal evaluations but their judgements about what environmental quality is worth to society as a whole.

Discursive democracy operates according to the principle of communicative rationality:

> Communicative rationality clearly obtains to the degree social interaction is free from domination (the exercise of power), strategising by the actors involved, and (self-) deception. Further, all actors should be equally and fully

capable of making and questioning arguments (communicatively competent). There should be no restrictions on the participation of these competent actors. Under such conditions, the only remaining authority is that of a good argument, which can be advanced on behalf of the veracity of empirical description, and understanding and, equally important, the validity of normative judgements.

(Dryzek, 1990: 15)

This could be seen as another regulative ideal for citizens' juries and one likely to be violated in important respects. Convergence of viewpoints in citizens' juries may not be a matter of agreement on the facts: pathological processes of band-waggoning or stentorian opinion leadership by jurists or by moderators might occur. Sponsors might so tightly define the agenda that they foreclose choices (e.g. Petts, 1997: 369–70). The information given to jurors might be partial. Some jurors will be immune to information and to argument, fitting information into a pre-conceived framework. Proponents of citizens' juries are aware of some of these issues (e.g. Crosby *et al.*, 1986: 172; Stewart *et al.*, 1994). Different ways forward suggest themselves. One is to take the citizens' jury format more or less as it is, to articulate the problems and dilemmas clearly through field experience and incrementally to improve the method. This is the path that the Jefferson Centre and the IPPR have taken. Considerable attention has been paid to issues such as preventing articulate, well-educated people dominating proceedings. Acknowledging that some issues have been dealt with quite successfully, worries about the power of sponsors and the organisation running the jury persist. Another path would be to democratise the processes of jury commissioning, the bearing of witness, and jury deliberation. This would be part of a wider movement to democratise environmental decision making. Both paths are important. They are not mutually exclusive options.

The advantages of the citizens' jury approach compared to conventional forms of contingent evaluation

Informed evaluation

The literature on contingent evaluation stresses the need to explain to respondents the context of the problem and the difficulties of actually doing so within the time constraints (e.g. Carson, 1991: 132–40; Cummings *et al.*, 1986: 52–5; Dixon *et al.*, 1994: 80–1). Protocols for carrying out contingent evaluation differ in relation to the amount of contextual information they provide about the reason the cost–benefit analysis is being carried out and what considerations might be relevant to an informed judgement. However, typically little information is provided, there is little opportunity for respondents to ask questions, there is no opportunity for respondents to discuss the question among themselves, and there is no opportunity for respondents to get information from a diversity of sources. It is questionable whether evaluations represent informed judgements. With techniques analogous to opinion polling such as conventional contingent evaluation, it cannot be assumed that the quality of responses is high, because there is no deliberation (Fishkin, 1991). Critics of the conventional approach have already identified this as a significant practical problem. Knowing little about the situation, subjects 'anchor' their replies on the sort of menu offered to them in the question wording rather than thinking through the issues for themselves (Cummings *et al.*, 1986: 28–31, 41–3). Censoring what appear to be low quality responses is sometimes recommended (cf. Carson, 1991: 160), but this risks throwing out genuine but extreme evaluations.

In contrast, participants in a citizens' jury have much more time and information to make considered judgements. They are paid substantial amounts for participating, so it is much less likely that they will give random or poorly informed responses. Given the right sort of help, members of juries seem to be able to make good use of very large amounts of information, even when this is presented to them over relatively short periods of time (Crosby *et al.*, 1986; Stewart *et al.*, 1994), the deliberations of the group shaping their conceptions of experts and partially defining what forms of expertise are relevant (Petts, 1997).

Economists sometimes see the provision of extra information beyond the bare minimum necessary in contingent evaluation as problematic, because it may cause 'information biases' in which the very process of measurement changes individual preferences (Cummings *et al.*, 1986: 33–4; cf. Sagoff, 1988: 77). They attempt to judge the accuracy of contingent evaluation by whether it reveals the same preferences as those that would be revealed in a real market. This criterion is usually non-operational; there is no real market with which to make a comparison. In any case, why should the preferences revealed by an individual within a market, given constrained information obtained at a price, be normatively prioritised over preferences expressed in a non-market context, given fuller or lower-cost information? It is a standard argument in economics that if people get new information about risks or about costs they may change their behaviour, even though their utility function over the goods concerned does not shift (e.g. Becker and Stigler, 1977). Perhaps the real concern, then, is that the method of measurement changes the utility function. Yet unless information is biased, it does not seem to me to be a problem if new information modifies individuals' judgements about their interests, thus changing their utility function over actions or outcomes.

Democratising deliberation

In existing studies using contingent evaluation the information that is provided comes from one source. Often those sponsoring the study have an interest in the outcome. This could lead to suspicions about bias in the information provided. Many decisions about environmental public goods have very significant economic and political repercussions. To make them in a democratic way implies access to information from as wide a variety of sources as possible. There is certainly a greater variety of information available to the typical citizens' jury than to participants in a typical contingent evaluation survey. This reduces the probability that information will be biased.

At present the sponsoring body or the organisation running the jury typically determines the set of witnesses, although there has sometimes been an element of juror choice. There clearly are dangers in this (Stewart *et al.*, 1994: 31). Although there are practical limits on time and money, and although jurors may initially know little or nothing about which witnesses would be the most relevant, a citizens' jury should in principle be able to call on information from a wide range of witnesses. A still more radical alternative model, in line with the ideal of communicative rationality, would be to allow as many individuals or groups as wanted to bear witness to have access, rather than have the jury call witnesses. There is a danger that once a multiplicity of witnesses wish to give evidence, costs would escalate. Also proceedings might become quasi-judicial with witnesses hiring legal representatives. This would skew access to those who could afford good advocacy. These problems certainly need further thought, but a strong case can be made for opening up the jury process.

Greens often argue that their ethical values imply participatory, inclusive, community-based politics, both because this is inherently desirable and because it is necessary in order to achieve sustainability. Among other arguments for the second claim are: that participation in communal decision making may encourage citizens to see the point of view of those their actions harm, including future generations and even other species; that this style of democratic politics brings citizens' knowledge of local environmental conditions and local social needs to bear; that powerful decision makers should be challenged in a variety of local forums, increasing the chances that someone will articulate the Green perspective. Considerable controversy surrounds such claims (cf. Dobson, 1996; Eckersley, 1996; Goodin, 1992; Goodin, 1996; Saward, 1993, 1996) for they depend upon high participation rates among an informed citizenry. Yet rational individuals would have little incentive to participate or to be well informed when their voice or their vote is so unlikely to affect outcomes (Ward, 1996). These factors may help explain why political participation rates are low, even at local level, in countries like the UK (Parry *et al.*, 1992).

As the Green movement has come to exert some influence on the agenda and even on outcomes, its leaders have become more pragmatic about grass-roots democracy, seeing this more as a supplement to conventional political channels than as an end in itself (e.g. Doherty and de Geus, 1996, 2–3). Yet if major decisions that shape local possibilities and global outcomes continue significantly to exclude the environmental concerns citizens are willing to express in social attitude surveys, this pragmatic position cannot be regarded as satisfactory.[5] The dilemma is that informed participation is even more difficult to envisage once we go beyond the local level, even if the political will exists to go beyond conventional democratic forms: individual participation is even less likely to alter the outcome. The citizens' jury approach is of potential help here. Jurors are paid to participate. In a jury with as few as 12 members, the individual can expect to have a considerable influence on the outcome. Higher quality outcomes can be expected compared to other forms of direct participation such as referenda, where there is little or no incentive to be well informed.

Certain groups are better able to organise because they are numerically small, have a particularly intense interest, or have organisational structures able to deliver selective incentives (Olson, 1965). Part of the point of selection of socially representative citizens' juries is to avoid replicating the pattern in everyday politics whereby well-organised and resourced groups get a disproportionate say (e.g. Crosby *et al.*, 1986: 171; Stewart *et al.*, 1994: 9–10). Because of the collective action problems just discussed, these issues are difficult to address by using conventional forms of participation such as those envisaged by Greens. Citizens' juries form part of a possible response.

Legitimating decisions

Public suspicion of decisions in which cost–benefit analysis plays a part, such as where to build new airports or how to route new roads, is high. In part this is because the process is not open, but it may also be because important values are not properly weighed because they are difficult to quantify (e.g. Grove-White, 1996: 24–5). The suspicion is that by 'cooking' the values placed on things not bought and sold in markets the outcome can be made to correspond to what powerful interests within and without government want (e.g. Grove-White, 1996: 28–9). Citizens' juries could play a role in opening up part of the process to public scrutiny. Although this has not always been the practice so far, the activities of citizens' juries could be publicised and their deliberations carried out in the open. Bodies running juries generally come up with a public statement explaining the rationale for their collective viewpoint (Stewart *et al.*, 1994: 46). Such openness, together with the socially representative nature of the jury, should increase the legitimacy of the final decision taken.[6] There is a tension here, however: to the extent to which juries report back in this way, they might come to be regarded as responsible to citizens for outcomes. Participants in existing citizens' juries dealing with hard issues like health care are often unwilling to be held responsible, partly because the underlying problems they deal with are generated by others' choices. Given that the sorts of citizens' juries I envisage are dealing with only one aspect of a problem, they would need to be protected from the off-loading by others of responsibility.

I suggested earlier that divergences of evaluation will sometimes rest on disagreements about the facts, but they may go deeper than this. Judgements may be differ because participants have different conceptions of the good. Suppose that they sometimes do, and that differences in conceptions of the good cannot be reconciled by recourse to some foundational ethical argument, or even through a process of impartial debate (e.g. Barry, 1995). Even then the jury process, by exposing such differences, could perform a useful function. Conventional methods of contingent evaluation actually hide such differences by implicitly assuming that all individuals buy into a quasi-utilitarian ethic. Where this is not the case, it is important that this is recognised. If citizens' juries are adequately publicised and their proceedings reported, the failure to reach a consensual judgement, the existence of minority judgements and so on could signal broader social problems, in exactly the way in which divergent legal judgements do (Petts, 1997: 366). An implication of this argument is that less stress should be placed by moderators on reaching a consensual decision in citizens' juries than is commonly the case at present (Stewart *et al.*, 1994: 44–5). An important criticism of ideas about discursive democracy such as those of Habermas and Dryzek is that the drive towards consensus is coercive (e.g. Dobson, 1996: 136). Such coercion needs to be avoided in citizens' juries because the failure to achieve consensus is potentially a socially important fact.

From some perspectives it might be seen as a problem that citizens' juries could help legitimate environmental cost–benefit analysis. Because cost–benefit analysis is likely to end up striking compromises between conflicting values, some deep Greens who do not like such trade-offs might reject anything that legitimates them. Groups opposed to conventional methods of contingent evaluation could, however, use the citizens' jury method to see whether other conclusions can be arrived at. Such juries might provide alternative monetary measures of environmental values or might consider a different issue, such as whether it is right to proceed in some deontological sense. The relative openness of this method might lend weight to any critique that emerged – so long as the proceedings were not rigged. Citizens' juries could be used as a point of contestation from which to challenge the legitimacy of existing decisions.

The mis-measurement of value

One definitional feature of public goods is the non-excludability property that benefits can be enjoyed even by freeriders who make no contribution to supplying them. Environmental quality typically has this property. Economic theory suggests that it will be difficult to get a rational, self-interested individual truthfully to reveal his/her preferences for public goods when this may have negative consequences in terms, say, of the tax contribution he/she has to make (Samuelson, 1954). With respect to public goods there are often reasons for rational individuals to freeride on others' contributions; and declaring values lower than those actually held amounts to a form of freeriding if you believe that what you will finally pay is a function of your response. In conventional contingent evaluation, respondents may assume that the tax price they will actually be asked to pay is linked to their replies and declare a lower WTP. Replies to WTA questions may also evoke strategic responses. For one thing, people may artificially inflate their answers, believing that this may lead to higher compensation.

A number of studies suggest that biases such as these are unimportant, if they exist at all (Cummings *et al.*, 1986: 21–6). However, strategic behaviour provides a parsimonious explanation of one of the best-established regularities in contingent evaluation studies: respondents give lower answers to a WTP question than to WTA questions (e.g. Cummings *et al.*, 1986: 35–6). Economic theory suggests that even truthful answers should be different but it can be shown that the differences ought typically to be small (cf. Carson, 1991: 128–9). This is a controversial area and several approaches to the issues co-exist in the literature.[7] Whatever the truth of the matter, it seems best to design the procedure to discourage strategic behaviour of this sort. The citizens' jury approach may have advantages in this respect.

Members of a citizens' jury are asked to come up with a collective judgement about how much supplying the environmental public good is worth to the average individual. However imperfectly, we can expect norms of impartiality to operate when people make such a judgement. Both the question posed and pressures for an impartial answer would reduce the tendency to give a strategic answer calculated to serve self interest. When one individual contributes towards a public good, because of the non-excludability property, others benefit from spillover effects. In just the same way, if an individual strategically under-declares the value they place on a public good, this is likely to have harmful repercussions on others. The methodologies used to carry out contingent evaluation steer respondents' attention away from such spillovers. By asking about individuals' own evaluations and giving them few if any opportunities to interact with others who could be hurt, they steer attention away from the social and towards the personal. In a citizens' jury the fact that there are others, with different viewpoints and interests, with whom one is interacting on a face-to-face basis would, make it much more difficult to ignore spillover effects.

A second concern is that responses in conventional contingent evaluation may lack substance. Critics of this approach (Sagoff, 1988: 88) argue that this is partly because respondents have no time to deliberate, a problem which my approach explicitly seeks to address. Conventional contingent evaluation based on the WTP question may have advantages over attitudinal surveys that do not prompt individuals to think of the costs of environmental policies for which they are willing to express abstract support. On the other hand, some economists doubt whether hypothetical WTP correlates with actual behaviour (e.g. Cummings *et al.*, 1986: 50–2). The citizens' jury approach, too, may suffer from the problem that people could support policies knowing that any costs apparently implied for them were improbable if not entirely hypothetical. However, my approach does not seem any more likely to suffer from this problem than the conventional one. The way to address it is to make sponsors take the results of the citizens' jury seriously and to get the jury to debate the issue of the distribution of costs. This ought to bring home to jurors that their deliberations could have actual consequences for their pocket-books.

Valuation as a social process

Individuals' reasons for valuing the environment differ enormously, from the narrowly instrumental through the aesthetic to the biocentric. Nevertheless, for many people the value they derive from the environment and the price they are willing to put upon it arises as part of a process of collective identity formation.

Take Goodin's argument that people seek meaning and structure in their lives, that nature untouched by human hands provides this, so there is value in nature (Goodin, 1992: ch. 2). Although some seek the 'wilderness experience' alone, for most it is valued partly because it is experienced with friends. The experience sheds light upon and deepens the social relationships we have with those friends, often because of shared adversity not experienced in everyday life. The value placed on the environment goes beyond anything that we can conceive of as pertaining to individuals considered as isolated atoms with only extrinsic relations between them. Also, as Benton says (1993: 183–6), it is not just relations between individuals that are involved in identity formation but relations between people and places, people and nature, and people and the built environment.

To the extent to which it is interested in the question at all, economics tends to see valuing as an individual process. In line with this, conventional methods of contingent evaluation involve little or no meaningful social interaction. In contrast, the citizens' jury provides an interactive setting which would allow some of the social processes in which we value the environment to be mimicked. Social processes that occur in society as a whole could be simulated by social processes that occur in the jury. Suppose the question is how much should we pay to preserve a piece of heathland from development. One participant might relate how he as a child roamed the heath and how the children he knew made it their own domain. This might trigger the memories of others, perhaps reminding people of the shared sense of the importance of 'wild places' on the urban fringe to children, and the groundedness of local communities in their 'wild places'. The shared value of a sense of place might be measured using the individualising methodology of conventional approaches to contingent evaluation; but it is more likely to be captured using a citizens jury, because the interactions between members of the jury are more likely to lead to reflection on collective experience, identity and social value. There is a range of techniques described in the literature on participative planning for making the consequences of decisions more graphic, such as group drawing of maps of the perceived social space they inhabit and group enumeration of valued objects (e.g. Pretty *et al.*, 1995). These could help focus jurists' attention on questions of social value, too. Conventional methods may be more prone to undervalue the environment than the citizens' jury approach.

As Wynne argues (1989), the evaluation of risks is also a social process which is not captured by the 'objective' risks presented by science. People care about who is most subject to risk, whether they can choose to avoid it, who is responsible for it and so on. How much weight they give to these dimensions depends on the social context and is arrived at through collective deliberation that could be mimicked in citizens'juries and similar deliberative forums (Petts, 1997). The subjective probabilities that are allowed to enter the calculations of Harsanyi's utilitarians need not be seen as arrived at by individuals in isolation.[8] If Harsanyi's utilitarianism is an appropriate regulative ideal for my use of citizens'juries, there is no reason for them to stick to 'objective' probabilities either. Conventional approaches to contingent evaluation risk mis-measurement because they lack meaningful social interactions.

Distributional effects

Cost–benefit analysis suggests proceeding with a project when some will enjoy improved welfare and no one loses, if compensation is paid. In practice, compensation seldom if ever is paid. So it is an important part of project appraisal to identify the gainers and losers (Winpenny, 1991: 63–4). This leads some economists to suggest that explicit attention should be given to distributional issues by weighting costs and benefits, depending on whom they fall upon, or by placing side constraints on the degree to which inequality can be increased in the pursuit of greater overall social well-being (e.g. Brent, 1996: Part 4; Dixon *et al.*, 1994: 104–6). An egalitarian might give more weight to the benefits and costs of the poor, for instance. In effect this approach trades off maximisation of net social benefits for greater equality. Cost–benefit analyis also has to concern itself with when costs and benefits will be felt. Costs and benefits have lower weight in the overall calculation the further in the future they are felt, that is, they are time-discounted back to their current values. There are also distributional questions tied up with the rate of time discounting used when bringing flows of costs and benefits back to current values. For instance, if the costs of de-commissioning a nuclear power plant fall far into the future, their current discounted value will be low, which is to say that much of the costs of the project will be loaded on to future generations.

If distributional issues arise in cost–benefit analysis, the weightings should be democratically arrived at. They should not reflect the value judgements of the economists carrying out the analysis, or even their guesses about the judgements that a democratic procedure would give rise to. Citizens' juries can mimic the deliberation about distributional questions that could have occurred among an informed citizenry. At the same time that they consider what the environmental public good is worth to the average citizen, the members of the jury could consider the issue of how benefits ought to be distributed around that average, if they arrive at a consensus that the distribution implied by the unweighted utilitarian calculation is unfair. A long-standing puzzle in cost–benefit analysis is what rate of discount should be applied (e.g. Pearce, 1995). If the rate of discount is to reflect our ability as a society to feel empathy for future generations rather than the current views of that section of society which happens to deal in capital markets, setting key interest rates that govern Treasury views of the appropriate rate of social discount, there are various ways in which our feelings in this respect can be gauged as part of a political process, and the citizens' jury has the virtue that it allows informed deliberation among a socially representative sample of citizens. Moreover many conventional political forums suffer from built-in short-termism, because of competitive pressures. Deliberative forums like citizens' juries can escape such pressures. It may be that by ensuring that the jury has a representative spread of age groups, the chances of intergenerational sympathy being adequately expressed could be increased, too (Sandler, 1997: 69).

Some broader issues: nature's interests, the monetisation of values and the limited role of cost–benefit analysis

Nature's interests

It is easy to see how some Green concerns could be built into environmental cost–benefit analysis by treating sustainability as a constraint on the maximisation of human welfare. However, it is claimed by critics of cost–benefit analysis that it cannot capture the intrinsic value in nature that exists independent of human interests. This does not apply to my approach.

Goodin argues that interests arise out of objective value, and as nature has objective value, it has interests. To exclude the representation of these interests within a democracy is 'sheer human chauvinism' (Goodin, 1996: 837). Nature's interests cannot be directly enfranchised, but 'those entrusted with protecting nature's interest can often enough surmise those interests tolerably well and act on them politically with some confidence' (Goodin, 1996: 841). They can 'encapsulate' interests that cannot otherwise be feasibly represented. The chances of nature's interests being represented are maximised in a participatory democracy (Goodin, 1996: 845–7). For reasons already discussed, I am sceptical about increasing participation rates, but nature's interests could be represented within a citizens' jury.

The utility functions I rely on can be ascribed to natural entities that have interests in Goodin's sense. Harsanyi envisages individuals putting themselves in the place of another and constructing a Von-Neumann/Morgenstern utility function which they believe reflects how that individual would choose given her interests, *if* she was rational and *if* she could choose. There is no presupposition that the individual being empathised with is rational or is capable of acting in a strong sense; such utility functions could be ascribed to young babies or the severely mentally disabled. I assume with Greens that humans can empathise with nature, although whether they would do so in a citizens' jury context remains an open issue. So long as a natural entity has interests that can be empathised with, there is no reason why such a utility function should not be ascribed to it, even though it cannot feel pleasure or pain ('lower order' animals) or cannot act rationally (ecosystems). Such utility functions are not measures of pleasure and pain, as in classical utilitarianism. Normatively they reflect the idea that it best serves interests if expected utility is maximised – if things are likely to come out best on average, trading off interests and risks.[9] Harsanyi's approach implies balancing off interests and risks, not the balancing of pleasure and pain. Hodgson argues that cost–benefit analysis assumes a limited, subjectivist theory of value under which something is only of value if humans experience it as such (e.g. Hodgson, 1996). He fails to distinguish between sympathising with the position of other entities and taking their interests into account, on the one hand, and direct personal experience of the value in nature, on the other hand. My approach is not limited to things in nature that give rise to direct personal experience of value although it is limited to things that we can empathise with.

Many utilitarians have attempted to apply their position to all creatures that can feel pleasure and pain (e.g. Singer, 1990). This leads to the criticism that utilitarianism cannot generate an environmental ethic under which 'lower order' species, ecosystems and the physical environment are protected. However, once we ditch the idea that utilities reflect pleasure and pain, there is no reason to stop at the borders of sentience. Although to convincingly demonstrate this goes beyond what is possible in this chapter Harsanyi's approach allows a broad-gauged utilitarian environmental ethic to be developed.

Monetary measures of value

There is still the issue of monetising utilities. Technically this presents no problems. Using the Von-Neumann/Morgenstern procedure for measuring utility, money payoffs have a utility representation that gives a unique set of predictions about rational behaviour. Reversing the mapping, utilities can be translated into money. However, monetising may imply more than the construction of a yardstick for balancing interests and risks. It may carry other connotations and commitments. For some to make all the values involved in the environment commensurable through the medium of money is illegitimately to push economic rationality beyond its proper disciplinary boundaries into domains where this method will lead us astray (e.g. Foster, 1996: 6–7). Cost–benefit analysis often provokes opposition – not least among subjects in contingent valuation exercises – because it involves putting monetary values on things that people feel uncomfortable about treating in this way: human life; a medieval church; a unique ecosystem. It creates a a 'market for morals' (Sagoff, 1988: 88). Besides arguing that monetary evaluations of intangibles are likely to be ignored when push comes to shove in environmental decision making, Sagoff argues that it is a category mistake to put monetary values upon such things, because this is to treat judgements about what is right as if they are preferences:

> Private and public also belong to different categories. Public 'preferences' involve not desires or wants but opinions or views. They state what a person believes is best or right for the community or group as a whole. These opinions or beliefs may be true or false, and we may meaningfully ask that person for the reasons that he or she holds them. But an analyst who asks how much citizens would pay to satisfy opinions that they advocate through political association commits a category mistake.
>
> (1988: 92–5)

My approach involves public preferences generated through collective deliberation, judgement and justification. Participants are not asked to express what the environment is worth to them, as in the conventional approach, but to take part in deliberation about what it is worth for society or, even more broadly, for the community of the earth. This approach does not treat jurors as just a bundle of pre-given preferences, but actively encourages jurors to change their minds, if the evidence warrants this. It sets out to mimic social processes of valuing and does not purely involve the expression of a bundle of preferences held by an isolated individual 'social atom'. In contradiction to Sagoff's argument, it is perfectly possible to ask people to articulate and to justify on grounds of belief and under-lying values what their preferences are – to say why their preferences are right for them. This may not happen in the market or in conventional contingent evaluation (Keat, 1996: 38–9) but it should occur in a properly functioning citizens' jury: jurors would be forced to defend their personal evaluations because others would use these as evidence for making their own collective evaluations under extended sympathy.[10]

Rather than use a rationalistic method like cost–benefit analysis, Sagoff advocates making environmental decisions through the political and judicial process of the legislature, the courts, the electorate, and the politics of pressure and compromise that lie behind all these (1988: 95–7). Yet he fails to draw read-ers' attention to the patent failings of polyarchical political processes relative to his democratic ideals. Using a monetary yardstick is one way of clearly articulat-ing what the trade-offs are – and one that makes explicit value assumptions that are often hidden in polyarchical procedures.

The limits of cost–benefit analysis

Economists using cost–benefit analysis often reply to critics like Sagoff who do not wish to monetise values and to make trade-offs by saying that in reality deci-sion making compels us to do these things. From their perspective, absolutist eth-ical discourses of inviolable rights, such as those which ascribe rights to animals or other aspects of nature, are typically watered down and traded away in order that we can collectively respond to difficult issues (e.g. Pearce, 1995: 54). Putting money values on things, discounting, and (possibly) weighting payoffs are just ways of making more explicit the trade-offs which are endemic in political life.

Recognising this point, it could still be argued that an unnecessarily narrow role is ascribed to citizens' juries here, because the considerations that enter the decision making process are too restricted. As an alternative citizens' juries could ask whether it is right for a project to go ahead or not, with no attempt being made to steer the jury towards an answer purely based on interests/risks, whether in a monetised representation or not. The citizens' jury could simulate the process of consensus formation that might have gone on in society. Simulation might be advantageous because most people are not well informed and political processes of consent-formation in wider society are far from being carried out on the basis of equality of power.

Such a possibility might appeal to those who criticise the utilitarian basis of cost–benefit analysis yet advocate impartial debate Barry, for instance, is scathing about conventional forms of contingent evaluation; the reason why many people refuse to answer – indeed are scandalised by – WTA questions is that they do not wish to see environmental problems in utilitarian terms (1995: 156). Inflated answers to WTA questions might be a token of this rather than strategising to get compensation, as discussed above. Perhaps WTA questions transgress normative boundaries between what it is appropriate to marketise and what it is not, so that they provoke exaggerated answers (Peacock, 1996).

It is implausible that in getting to an informed, unforced consensus of the sort that Barry envisages (1995) people will ignore interests completely. Moreover, they will typically debate the social efficiency versus distributional equity question that, citizens' juries could confront. Not all conceptions of the good are directly want-regarding or interest-regarding. Yet the failure of some outcome to reflect such a conception will sometimes have consequences for individual interests. For example some may see the failure of a decision to respect what they regard as the rights of an animal as personal affront. I see no reason why this belongs in a different category to other aspects of their preference structure (cf. Keat, 1996: 40). Nevertheless, society will sometimes want to look beyond interests.

There are occasions when there is collective discomfort with apparently optimal cost–benefit trade-off There is no reason why this should change just because citizens' juries are involved. This does not mean that cost–benefit analysis is a pointless exercise or that the inclusion of citizens' juries as part of the process is beside the point. When its results seem implausible, cost–benefit analysis can still function to provoke us to think more clearly about the things that really are at issue, generating detailed reflection on what is left out. It can inform wider democratic debate even though it should seldom constitute the whole of it. In just the same way, the failure of a citizens' jury to come to a collective agreement could inform public debate.[11]

Conclusion

In what contexts would it be most appropriate to use citizens' juries to carry out contingent evaluation? Citizens' juries are not cheap to run compared with the forms of survey research necessary to carry out conventional contingent evaluation.[12] Opening up the jury process to all who wish to bear witness would make them even more expensive. This suggests that it would be more appropriate to use the citizens' jury approach when big issues are at stake, so that the potential costs of making the wrong decision are large. Typically the issues would be of at least regional significance. This practical argument is reinforced by the point that deliberative forums like citizens' juries seem particularly appropriate as a way of increasing citizens' participation once we move beyond the purely local level. An example of the type of decision at issue would be whether to build a major road over a nationally important, designated site, the jury method being used to value environmental harms that cannot be priced on the market.

It is particularly dangerous in a democracy to allow a government agency that is sponsoring a potentially damaging project, or has close links with developers or another sponsoring department, to design or to carry out a conventional contingent evaluation exercise. The reason is that it cannot be presumed that balanced and adequate information will be made available to respondents. In practical terms big, expensive cost–benefit analyses are likely to be funded and organised by the state. However, the citizens' jury approach would be an important check on the possibilities of bias – especially with a procedure open to more witnesses and driven more by the wishes of jurors. So the citizens' jury approach seems particularly appropriate where large government-sponsored projects are involved, such as green-belt industrial developments favoured by local or regional planners to encourage incoming investment and green-field sites sanctioned by national policies to increase the number of homes being built. If the citizens' jury approach is better at capturing the social dimension of valuing, it seems particularly relevant when major issues of collective identity, such as those surrounding the symbolic dimensions of major agricultural violation of Britain's 'green and pleasant land', are at issue.

The examples chosen to illustrate the most likely applications of the citizens jury approach are all ones in which cost–benefit analysis either is already in use or is strongly suggested. This chapter develops a proposal. It remains to be seen whether some of the benefits discussed would actually flow from the use of citizens' juries. Many practical problems not addressed here would, no doubt, loom large. Nevertheless, there is a potentially significant role for citizens' juries in contingent evaluation, because they could make it more pluralistic, open, informed, deliberative and accurate.

Notes

1 Social welfare is said to be improved if a policy makes at least one person better off and none worse off, allowing for possible compensation to be paid from the winners to any losers, that is, it is a potential Pareto improvement. As Samuelson pointed out (1954) it is a potential Pareto improvement to supply a public good such as environmental quality at a certain level so long as marginal social cost is less than the sum of marginal benefits across all the individuals in the public (Samuelson, 1954). The marginal social costs of private good consumption foregone can be measured by market prices, so long as the private goods are produced in competitive markets (Cummings *et al.*, 1986, 12–13). Individual benefits from preserving the environment are measured by willingness to pay for a particular level of environmental quality. This is the area under the individual's demand curve up to the level of provision concerned. If Samuelson's criterion is met, the sum of willingness to pay across the public must exceed total social costs, since the sum of marginal willingness to pay exceeds marginal social costs for all levels of provision below that in question.

2 There are also significant differences. IPPR juries differ because: the number of jurors is between 12 and 16, whereas it may be as high as 24 in the USA; jurors are not necessarily chosen by stratified random selection, as in the USA, but may be chosen in a number of other ways, including personal invitation; jurors are strongly encouraged to take decisions from a community-wide perspective, whereas no overt pressure to take this stance exists in the US; juries generally deliberate over a long weekend, but session may last as long as six days in the US; the jury is assisted by a Jurors' Friend or Advocate, a role yet to be developed in the US; sponsors may also be represented by an advocate, but this is not the practice in the US.

3 Harsanyi envisages utility values being imagined for others while I envisage monetary values being assigned. The monetisation of values can create problems.

4 With the limited numbers that usually participate in citizens juries in order to allow meaningful deliberation, it is unlikely that a pure random sample of jurors would result in a socially representative distribution of interests and opinions. In the USA sampling has sometimes been carried out on the basis of preliminary survey evidence on the incidence of attitudes towards the issue in the population, an attempt being made to get a jury that starts with the same mix of attitudes (Crosby *et al.*, 1986: 174). In the UK juries are often chosen so that they include members of the most obvious social blocs such as classes, ethnic groups and genders in rough proportion to those in the population.

5 Such attitudes arc expressed in many countries – even in poorer countries where the theory of post-material value change should not apply (Dunlap and Mertig, 1997). Some regard such attitudes as meaningless, because they are expressed knowing that the price for changing things will not have to be paid. I regard them as expressions of peoples' broader, long-term interests.

6 The closest approach to the one I am discussing in the existing literature is the Delphi method for contingent evaluation (e.g. Dixon *et al.*, 1994: 79–80). Here a group of experts is asked to place a value upon something. The first-round estimates are then circulated and a second round of estimates made. The process is continued until convergence is reached. Besides allowing no direct contact between participants, there could be suspicions that the conclusions arc deliberately biased by picking the 'right' experts.

7 Some argue that WTA questions are appropriate where people have the right not to be subject to the harm; whereas WTP is appropriate if someone has else has the right to go ahead and damage the environment (e.g. Dixon *et al.*, 1994: 75). This is linked with another explanation of the observed differences in answers: psychological differences in valuing linked to whether property rights are such that you should be compensated, on the one hand, or have to pay for a better environment, on the other hand (Dixon *et al.*, 1994: 75). Alternatively WTA questions may provoke people to think about what the good is worth to society, not just to themselves (Jacobs, 1996: 216).

8 Harsanyi's utilitarian calculate expected costs and benefits by multiplying utilities associated with various endstates to which an action might lead by the probabilities with which those endstates occur, then summing to get an average payoff associated with the action. Savage and others have extended this approach to circumstances where objective probabilities cannot be placed on endstates, using subjective probabilities instead (e.g. Jeffrey, 1983).

9 There is also a positive claim that humans act as if they maximise expected utility, but this is not logically entailed by the normative claim about what rationality entails. Whether people actually behave in the way that subjective expected utility maximisation theory suggests is controversial. This issue has been of some importance in the critical literature on contingent evaluation (e.g. Cummings *et al.*, 1986: 61–5).

10 In Keat's view the category mistake is in treating peoples' beliefs about rights, such as nature's rights, as if they are preferences that can be traded off against other want-regarding principles (Keat, 1996). I briefly address the issue of trade-offs of this sort below.

11 Most advocates of citizens' juries have seen their role as supplementary to other democratic institutions (e.g. Stewart *et al.*, 1994: 7; cf. Crosby *et al.*, 1986: 173). The thinking of Ned Crosby, the founder of the Jefferson Centre, seems to be moving in the direction of seeing citizens' juries as part of a multi-stage process of public deliberation involving deliberative polling and the use of juries at different stages both to define issues and, later, to choose between options (reported in Stewart *et al.* (1994: 48–9)).

12 Figures from tens of thousands of pounds up to a quarter of a million pounds are quoted for running a citizens' jury (Stewart *et al.*, 1994: 29), but arguably such costs are still low relative to the costs of getting a major decision wrong (Crosby *et al.*, 1986: 172).

References

Barry, B. (1995), *Justice as Impartiality*, Oxford: Oxford University Press.

Becker, G. and G. Stigler (1977), 'De Gustibus non est Disputandum', *American Economic Revue*, Vol. 67, pp. 76–90.

Benton, T. (1993), *Natural Relations: Ecology, Animal Rights and Social Justice*, London: Verso.

Brent, R.J. (1996), *Applied Cost–Benefit Analysis*, Cheltenham: Edward Elgar.

Carson, R.T. (1991), 'Constructed Markets', in J.B. Braden and C.D. Kolstad (eds), *Measuring the Demand for Environmental Quality*, Amsterdam: Elsevier.

Crosby, N., J.M. Kelly and P. Schaefer (1986), 'Citizens Panels: A New Approach to Citizen Participation', *Public Administration Review*, Vol. 46, pp. 170–8.

Crosby, N., J. Romslo, S. Malisone and B. Manning (1997), 'Citizen Juries: British Style', internet publication address http:/www.auburn.edu/tann/cp/features/juries.htm.

Cummings, R.G., D.S. Brookshire and W.D. Schulze (1986), *Valuing Environmental Goods: An Assessment of the Contingent Evaluation Method*, Totowa, NJ: Rowman & Allanheld.

Dixon, J.A., L. Fallon-Scura, R.A. Carpenter and P.B. Sherman (1994), *Economic Analysis of Environmental Impacts*, second edition, London: Earthsean.

Dobson, A. (1996), 'Democratising Green Theory: Preconditions and Principles', in Doherty and de Geus (eds), *Democracy and Green Political Thought: Sustainability, Rights and Citizenship*, London: Routledge.

Doherty, B. and M. de Geus (eds) (1996), *Democracy and Green Political Thought: Sustainability, Rights and Citizenship*, London: Routledge.

Dryzek, J. (1987), *Rational Ecology*, Oxford: Basil Blackwell.

Dryzek, J. (1990), *Discursive Democracy: Politics, Policy and Political Science*, Cambridge: Cambridge University Press.

Dunlap, R.E. and A.G. Mertig (1997), 'Global Environmental Concern: An Anomaly for Postmaterialism', *Social Science Quaterly*, Vol. 78, pp. 24–9.

Eckersley, R. (1996), 'Greening Liberal Democracy: The Rights Discourse Revisited', in Doherty and de Geus (eds), *Democracy and Green Political Thought: Sustainability, Rights and Citizenship*, London: Routledge.

Fishkin, J. (1991), *Democracy and Deliberation: New Directions for Democratic Reform*, New Haven, CT: Yale University Press.

Foster, J. (ed.) (1996), *Valuing Nature? Ethics, Economics and the Environment*, London: Routledge.

Goodin, R.E. (1992), *Green Political Theory*, Cambridge: Polity.

Goodin, R.E. (1996), 'Enfranchising the Earth, and its Alternatives', *Political Studies*, Vol. 44, pp. 835–49.

Grove-White, R. (1996), 'The Environmental "Valuation" Contoversy', in Foster (ed.), *Valuing Nature? Ethics, Economics and the Environment*, London: Routledge.

Harsanyi, J.C. (1955), 'Cardinal Welfare, Individualistic Ethics and Interpersonal Comparisons of Utility', *Journal of Political Economy*, Vol. 61, pp. 309–21.

Hodgson, G. (1996), 'Economics, Environmental Policy and Utilitarianism', in Foster (ed.), *Valuing Nature? Ethics, Economics and the Environment*, London: Routledge.

Jacobs, M. (1996), 'Valuation, Democracy and Decision Making', in Foster (ed.), *Valuing Nature? Ethics, Economics and the Environment*, London: Routledge.

Jeffrey, R.J. (1983), *The Logic of Decision*, second edition, Chicago IL: Chicago University Press.

Keat, R. (1996), 'Values and Preferences', in Foster (ed.), *Valuing Nature? Ethics, Economics and the Environment*, London: Routledge.

Miller, D. (1992), 'Deliberative Democracy and Social Choice', in D. Held (ed.), *Prospects for Democracy*, Oxford: Blackwell.

Olson, M. (1965), *The Logic of Collective Action*, Cambridge, MA: Harvard University Press.

Parry, G., G. Moyser, and N. Day (1992), *Political Participation and Democracy in Britain*, Cambridge: Cambridge University Press.

Peacock, M. (1996), 'Rationality and Social Norms', in Foster (ed.), *Valuing Nature? Ethics, Economics and the Environment*, London: Routledge.

Pearce, D. (1995), *Blueprint 4: Capturing Global Environmental Value*, London: Earthscan.

Petts, J. (1995), 'Waste Management Strategy Development: A Case Study of Community Involvement and Consensus Building in Hampshire', *Journal of Environmental Planning and Management*, Vol. 38, pp. 519–36.

Petts, J. (1997), 'The Public-Expert Interface in Local Waste Management Decisions: Expertise, Credibility and Process', *Public Understanding of Science*, Vol. 6, pp. 359–81.

Pretty, J.N., I. Guijit, I. Screams and J. Thompson (1995), *A Trainers' Guide to Participatory Learning and Interaction*, London: IIED.

Renn, O. (1984), 'An Empirical Investigation of Citizens', Preferences Among Four Energy Scenarios', *Technology Forecasting and Social Change*, Vol. 26, pp. 11–46.

Sagoff, M. (1988), *The Economy of the Earth*, Cambridge: Cambridge University Press.

Samuelson, P.A. (1954), 'Pure Theory of Public Expenditure', *Review of Economics and Statistics*, Vol. 36, pp. 387–9.

Sandler, T. (1997), *Global Challenges: An Approach to Environmental, Political and Economic Problems*, Cambridge: Cambridge University Press.

Saward, M. (1993), 'Green Democracy?', in A. Dobson and P. Lucardie (eds), *The Politics of Nature: Explorations in Green Political Theory*, London: Routledge.

Saward, M. (1996), 'Must Democrats be Environmentalists?', in Doherty and de Geus (eds), *Democracy and Green Political Thought: Sustainability, Rights and Citizenship*, London: Routledge.

Singer, P. (1990), *Animal Liberation*, second edition, New York: Harper Collins.

Stewart, J., E. Kendall and A. Cous (1994), *Citizens' Juries*, London: Institute for Public Policy Research.

Ward, H. (1996), 'Green Arguments for Local Democracy', in D. King and G. Stoker (eds), *Rethinking Local Democracy*, London: Macmillan.

Winpenny, J.T. (1991), *Values for the Environment: A Guide to Economic Appraisal*, London: HMSO.

Wynne, B. (1989), 'Building Public Concern into Risk Management', in J. Brown (ed.), *Environmental Threats: Perception, Analysis and Management*, London: Belhaven.

Index

Air pollution 254–70
Anarchism 3, 8
Animals 12
Aristotle 166, 169, 172

Barry, J. 39, 47–8, 139
Bio-rhetoric 60, 61
Biehl, J. 22–4, 26, 27, 28, 29
Bookchin, M. 3, 18–22, 26, 29

Citizens' juries 7, 276–92
Citizenship 28, 30
Civic virtue 34, 47
Climate change 13, 52, 97, 100
Contingent valuation 276, 279, 289
Convention on International Trade in
    Endangered Species (CITES) 104, 145
Corporatism 254, 255, 256–7, 260, 263,
    268, 270
Cost benefit analysis 160, 276, 277–8,
    287, 289, 290
Counter hegemony 134–7
Criminal Justice Act (UK) 117, 118, 122,
    128, 129, 137
Critical theory 21, 53–8

Daly, H. 153, 158
Deep ecology 29, 45
Democracy 4, 7, 8, 15, 20, 27, 28, 33, 54,
    55, 75, 117, 125, 153, 225, 242, 247,
    257, 269, 277, 279
Dobson, A. 53, 63, 64, 118, 135, 139,
    282, 284
Doherty, B. 125, 132, 139, 140, 282
Dryzek, J. 65, 278, 280, 284

Earth Day 12
Earth First! 121, 123, 124, 133, 139
Eckersley, R. 57–62, 78, 85, 153, 282
Ecofeminism 3, 18, 22–4, 27

Ecological modernisation 6, 32, 179–97
Economic growth 39, 78, 80, 118, 120,
    121, 127, 131, 133, 183, 184, 186, 188,
    255, 257, 266, 269
Environmental ethics 32, 53, 56
Environmentalism 94–114
European Union 184
Evolutionary ecology 58–9

Feminism 3, 8
Fox, W. 61
Free market environmentalism 5, 145–59
Friends of the Earth 101, 102, 125, 133

G-77 238, 242
Gandhi, M. 130
Giddens, A. 192–3, 196
Global Environment Facility (GEF) 231–51
Globalisation 94–96, 180, 244
Global warming *see* climate change
Goodin 284, 287, 288–9
Gramsci, A 134–135, 137
Green liberalism 32–51
Green Parties 263
Greenpeace 12, 13, 101, 102, 125, 126
Green political economy 5
Green political theory 3

Habermas, J. 2, 4, 52–72, 284
Hajer, M. 184–5, 190, 197

Institutional economics 16–74

James, W. 44
Janicke, M. 182–3, 190, 254, 258, 264
Juvenal 1

Liberalism 3, 32, 47, 95, 165, 204, 271
Libertarianism 148
Liberty 36, 150

Light, A. 63
Locally unwanted land uses (LULUs)
    203, 204–5, 206, 207, 210–12,
    224, 226
Locke, J. 35–8, 39–40, 43, 46, 115,
    138, 148
Lundqvist, L. 259

Marxism 18, 74, 75, 90, 95, 127, 134–5,
    136, 163, 166
Mill, J.S. 3, 35, 39–43, 49, 139, 165
Montreal Protocol 103, 188

Neutrality 34, 35, 37, 38
'new class' 74
'new politics' 75–6
new social movement 94, 96
New Zealand 73–94
Non-violent direct action 121
North American Free Trade Agreement
    (NAFTA) 105–6
North–South relations 99–100,
    233–4, 245–9

O'Riordan, T. 151

Pollok Park, Free State 114–42
Post materialism 74, 75, 205, 257, 269

Privatisation 150
Progress 39, 80, 82, 196
Public choice theory 160–1, 166, 172
Public goods 160, 162

risk society 2
Romantics 1

Sagoff, M. 160, 161
Shiva, V. 25, 27, 102, 237
Social ecology 18–31
Sustainability 5, 94, 183

Temporary autonomous zones 115–16
Torgerson, D. 56, 65

Utopianism 87–8, 98

Values Party 73, 79–81

Weale, A. 184, 186, 190
Wilderness 85, 86
Wissenburg, M. 32–5, 43–8
World Bank 231–51
World Commission on Environment and
    Development 231

Zero population growth 80